New Works in Accounting History

Richard P. Brief, *Series Editor*

Leonard N. Stern School of Business
New York University

A Garland Series

The Continuing Debate Over Depreciation, Capital and Income

Richard P. Brief

Garland Publishing, Inc.
New York and London 1993

Library of Congress Cataloging-in-Publication Data

Brief, Richard P.
The continuing debate over depreciation, capital and income /
Richard P. Brief.
p.cm.—(New works in accounting history)
Includes bibliograhical references.
ISBN 0-8153-1213-X
1. Depreciation. 2. Capital—Accounting. 3. Income accounting.
HF5681.D5B67 1993 93–9762

All volumes printed on acid-free, 250-year-life paper.
Manufactured in the United States of America.

Design by Marisel Tavarez

To Jean and Kristin

Brief, Richard P. *The Continuing Debate Over Depreciation, Capital and Income.*
ISBN 0-8153-1213-X

Corrigenda

The first sentence in the quotation on page 5 should read: "If we go back to the first principles, I think it must be admitted that an asset may be fairly defined as 'an expenditure on a remunerative object'; and, indeed, it may be taken as test of whether any particular expenditure is an asset or a loss to enquire whether, as a matter of fact, such expenditure was (looking back on it) worth the amount expended on it . . . ."

page 5, line 7 from bottom: "under went" should be one word.

page 7, line 5: "of profit determination" should appear in brackets, not parentheses.

page 7, line 6 from bottom: "balanced," not "balances."

page 7, line 4 from bottom: "summarised," not "summarize."

page 8, line 9: "and," not "an."

page 8, line 14: "and in any event," not "and event."

page 10, line 6: "accounting," not "account."

page 10, line 13: "Balance," not "Balanced."

page 12, line 2: "importance," not "important."

page 12, line 24: "reasonably," not "reasonable."

page 13, line 5 from bottom: "profession," not "procession."

page 13, line 2 from bottom: "increasing recognition," not "increase-recognition."

page 14. The fifth and sixth sentences in the third quotation should read: "It will give some idea as to the probability of the business being successful in the future, and it should enable us to determine whether the resources of the undertaking are sufficient to enable it to meet its debts as they fall due. We may, by looking at a Balance Sheet which has been prepared with reasonable honesty, satisfy ourselves . . . ."

page 15, line 14 from bottom: "companies should" should be in brackets, not parentheses.

pages 19 and 20: References should be to the *"Encyclopaedia of Accounting,"* not *"Encyclopedia of Accounting."*

page 23, line 24: "Bank," not "Banking."

page 23, line 4 from bottom: "Bank," not "Banking."

"Nineteenth Century Accounting Error," which is reprinted on pages 252–271, originally appeared in the *Journal of Accounting Research* (Spring 1965), not the *Journal of Accounting, Business and Financial History* (October 1990).

CONTENTS

A Solution to the Allocation Problem

Interest Rate Approximations

Financial Reporting and Analysis

Accounting Error

PREFACE

My career and research over the last 30 years has been significantly influenced by two teachers. I met Louis O. Foster when I was a senior at Dartmouth College and in the first year at The Amos Tuck School of Business Administration. Professor Foster was a legend at Tuck and, as I recall, "feared" by first-year accounting students. He was a stickler about terminology and wrote that

> One of the difficulties in the study of economics and accounting is that many of the terms employed are in everyday usage. Sometimes preconceived ideas must be abandoned, and a word in its new setting must be accepted as conveying a specific, possibly restricted, idea. . . .[1]

To drive home this need to pay attention to terminology a quiz was given early in the course and students were asked to define the meaning of the number associated with the fixed assets on a balance sheet. Most of us gave some kind of pseudo economic definition in terms of the value of future services, etc. In the first class after the quiz, Professor Foster acted horrified and wrote *VALUE* boldly across the full blackboard. Smiling, he cautioned us never to use any term in accounting unless it was defined clearly. My grade was an "F"—not a very auspicious beginning! The correct answer was simply that assets appear on the balance sheet at "book value" which is original cost less accumulated depreciation.

The lesson was clear. Accounting concepts have special definitions and loose language; ambiguity and wishful thinking about how closely accounting numbers correspond to "economic reality" had no place in accounting.

I also studied advanced accounting and accounting theory with

Professor Foster in 1957-1958 after a stint in the Air Force. The theory course was especially memorable. No numbers, only ideas. I couldn't believe this was *accounting*! We read journal articles and I remember one having to do with the periodicity concept. I can't recall the specific article (which I think was in *The Accounting Review*), but I was impressed with this paper because it used an analogy—the time line of a firm was the track of a railroad and a period was the (arbitrary?) space between the ties. My interest in questions of inseparability and jointness in accounting, which I am sure that Professor Foster encouraged, led me to write a term paper in the course arguing that working capital was as permanent a part of the asset structure of the firm as fixed capital.[2]

I am equally grateful to Professor Goran Ohlin who taught a course at Columbia University in European Economic History which I took in the spring term 1960. I also attended his seminar in the fall term 1960. Professor Ohlin triggered my interest in the question, "Does the choice of accounting methods influence behavior?", in a discussion of the Crédit Moblier, a nineteenth century French investment trust. I wrote a term paper on the subject and then expanded the idea in a paper written for the seminar. My interest in "accounting error" continued after Professor Ohlin left Columbia that spring and I wrote my Ph.D. thesis, *Nineteenth Century Capital Accounting and Business Investment*,[3] under Professor Harold Barger's supervision. I will be eternally grateful to Professor Barger for his willingness to supervise my thesis.

Thinking back on others who had an important influence on my career, I would like to recognize the important role played by the librarians of the American Institute of Certified Public Accountants. I began to use the Institute's library in the early 1960s and I am especially grateful to the Institute and to the librarians for their help. *The Accountant*, in particular, was a gold mine of information about the history of accounting and, in those days, the complete set, beginning in 1874-75, was immediately available. What a treasure!

Two colleagues at the Stern School also played an important role. Ernie Kurnow hired me in 1961 and was a most supportive mentor. It's hard to believe that the chairman of a statistics department encouraged a faculty member to write in the area of accounting history! My other close friend, Joel Owen, collaborated with me in work relating to the allocation problem and he taught me about the meaning and importance of the uncertainty concept. We had (and have) a lot of fun working together.

Finally, I would like to mention Basil Yamey and William Baxter whom I met in 1970 at the First International Symposium of Accounting Historians in Belgium. Basil and Will have been very supportive and they encouraged my interest in accounting history.

New York City
January 18, 1993

Richard P. Brief

NOTES

1. Louis O. Foster, *Introduction to Accounting* (Hanover, NH, 1953). Mimeographed.

2. "Working Capital," May 1958. Mimeographed. The question of the inseparability of working capital from other assets also was dealt with in my article with Joel Owen, "Present Value Models and the Multi-Asset Problem," that appeared in the October 1973 issue of *The Accounting Review.*

3. Published by Arno Press in 1976.

ACKNOWLEDGMENTS

"The Accountant's Responsibility in Historical Perspective," by R. P. Brief: *The Accounting Review*, April 1975, ©1975, American Accounting Association, is reprinted with permission.

"A Note on Rediscovery and the Rule of 69, " by R. P. Brief: *The Accounting Review*, October 1977, ©1977, American Accounting Association, is reprinted with permission.

"Cumulative Financial Statements," by R. P. Brief, B. D. Merino and I. Weiss: *The Accounting Review*, July 1980, ©1980, American Accounting Association, is reprinted with permission.

"The Role of the Accounting Rate of Return in Financial Statement Analysis," by R. P. Brief and R. Lawson: *The Accounting Review*, April 1992, ©1992, American Accounting Association, is reprinted with permission.

"The Origin and Evolution of Nineteenth-Century Asset Accounting, " by R. P. Brief: *Business History Review*, spring 1966, ©1966, President and Fellows of Harvard College, is reprinted with permission.

"Baily's Paradox", by R. P. Brief: *Accounting Historians Journal*, spring 1979 , ©1979, The Academy of Accounting Historians, is reprinted with permission.

"Hicks on Accounting, " by R. P. Brief: *Accounting Historians Journal*, spring 1982, ©1982, The Academy of Accounting Historians, is reprinted with permission.

"An Index of Growth Due to Depreciation, " by H. R. Anton and R. P. Brief: *Contemporary Accounting Research*, spring 1987, ©1987, The Canadian Academic Accounting Association, is reprinted with permission.

"Nineteenth Century Accounting Error, " by R. P. Brief: *Journal of Accounting Research*, Spring 1965, volume 3 #1, ©1965, Institute of Professional Accounting, is reprinted with permission.

"A Late Nineteenth Century Contribution to the Theory of Depreciation, " by R. P. Brief: *Journal of Accounting Research*, spring 1967, volume 5 #1, ©1967, Institute of Professional Accounting, is reprinted with permission.

"A Least Squares Allocation Model," by R. P. Brief and Joel Owen: *Journal of Accounting Research*, autumn 1968, volume 6 #2, ©1968, Institute of Professional Accounting, is reprinted with permission.

"The Estimation Problem in Financial Accounting," by R. P. Brief and J. Owen: *Journal of Accounting Research*, autumn 1970, volume 8 #2, ©1970, Institute of Professional Accounting, is reprinted with permission.

"A Reformulation of the Estimation Problem," by R. P. Brief and J. Owen: *Journal of Accounting Research*, spring 1973, volume 11 #1, ©1973, Institute of Professional Accounting, is reprinted with permission.

"Yield Approximations: A Historical Perspective: A Correction," by R. P. Brief: *Journal of Finance*, June 1983, ©1983, American Finance Association, is reprinted with permission.

"Corporate Financial Reporting at the Turn of the Century," by R. P. Brief: *Journal of Accountancy*, May 1987, ©1987, American Institute of Certified Public Accountants, is reprinted with permission.

"Approximate Error in Using Accounting Rates of Return to Estimate Economic Returns," by R. P. Brief and R. Lawson: *Journal of Business Finance & Accounting*, January 1991, ©1991, Basil Blackwell, is reprinted with permission.

"Approximate Error in Using Accounting Rates of Return to Estimate Economic Returns: A Correction," by R. P. Brief and R. Lawson: *Journal of Business Finance & Accounting*, November 1991, ©1991, Basil Blackwell, is reprinted with permission.

"Accounting Error as a Factor in Business History," by R. P. Brief: *Journal of Accounting, Business and Financial History*, October 1990, ©1990, Routledge, is reprinted with permission.

INTRODUCTION

This anthology of the author's selected work over nearly 30 years provides historical perspective and some current thinking on issues related to the continuing debate over depreciation, capital and income. Beginning with "first principles," and then discussing the origin and evolution of the debate over depreciation, capital and income, several related topics are addressed. These include the allocation problem, interest rate approximations, issues concerning financial reporting and analysis and the meaning and economic impact of "accounting error." The underlying themes concern the importance of history and the need for an appreciation of basic concepts and relationships in accounting.

The section on "first principles" begins with an introduction to an anthology of Dicksee's work and is followed by two other papers. Dicksee's place in accounting compares to Alfred Marshall's in economics and, therefore, a review of his writings seems like an appropriate place to start. In thinking about a particular problem, Dicksee often went "back to the first principles" and his early work used a venture or one-period model to introduce the problem of interim reporting where "it is absolutely impossible to draw a line at any particular date without it intersecting or cutting into a large number of transactions which at that moment remain uncompleted."[1]

Two other papers, "The Accountant's Responsibility in Historical Perspective" and "Valuation, Matching and Earnings: The Continuing Debate," pick up on the theme that at any particular point of time, the firm's uncompleted transactions are critical in evaluating performance. Thus, the question of uncertainty about the future is fundamental and needs to be addressed directly in the formulation of theory and in the choice of accounting methods.

The next section is concerned with the more traditional issues of depreciation, capital and income. As a body of literature dealing with the depreciation problem began to accumulate in the late nineteenth century, accountants became embroiled in debates over the nature of capital and income. The first anthology I edited for Arno Press in 1976, *The Late Nineteenth Century Debate Over Depreciation, Capital and Income* contained reprints of the classic articles on depreciation by Guthrie, Murray, Bogle, Ladelle and Turner as well as others by Best, Wade, Cooper and others which reflect the controversy. What was not recognized and is not now widely appreciated is that the debate about depreciation was really a debate about the nature of accrual accounting.

"The Origin and Evolution of Nineteenth Century Asset Accounting" surveys nineteenth century accounting practices dealing with fixed assets. The paper's "working hypothesis" is that accounting behavior will be driven by a firm's internal criteria unless external constraints restrict accounting choices. Whether or not progress in accounting has been retarded by regulatory agencies and the effect on economic development that this might have had are questions raised but not addressed.

Continuing in the area of the early history of depreciation, "Depreciation Theory in Historical Perspective" reviews some of the first articles on the subject. This paper was presented in 1970 at the First International Symposium of Accounting Historians and through the efforts of William Baxter, it was reprinted in *The Accountant* on December 6, 1970. At an early date, accountants seemed to agree on the idea of valuing fixed assets at original cost less depreciation and the related "going concern" principle.

Raw materials for the next article, as in several others, were collected while "browsing" in the library stacks. While I was looking at the 1948 volume of the *Economic Journal*, I noticed that J. R. Hicks had reviewed in the December issue a book by F. Sewell Bray, *Precision and Design in Accountancy.* My curiosity was aroused and I was quite startled to find Hicks writing that the justification for valuation at historical cost is "simply that the original purchase price is the one objective valuation of the asset. . . . Any other valuation must be a matter of judgment. . . ."

"Hicks on Accounting" is an analysis of Sir John Richard Hicks's views on accounting which, in spite of the popularity of of his theoretical writings on income and depreciation, were not well known. I was brought up on the view that, notwithstanding Hicks's comment that income and related concepts are bad tools which break in your hands" (p. 177), the chapter in *Value and Capital*[2] on income and depreciation provided the theoretical underpinning for the income concept in accounting. However, other work by Hicks gives more perspective on the subject.[3]

A number of books and articles have been concerned with depreciation in a dynamic framework.[4] Motivated by an article by Yuji Ijiri,[5] "An Index of Growth Due to Depreciation" deals with a point that both accountants and economists have discussed for more than a century. When "depreciation funds" are reinvested, the stock of capital grows. Most of the writings on this subject have been concerned with the growth of physical capital. In this article, the question of how financial capital grows when depreciation is revinvested is addressed.

"A Late Nineteenth Century Contribution to the Theory of Depreciation" reprints O.G. Ladelle's classic work, "The Calculation of Depreciation," adding historical perspective and some brief commentary about Ladelle. I stumbled on Ladelle's article while working on my Ph.D. thesis and skimmed it quickly to determine its relevance to nineteenth century asset accounting practices and business investment. The fact that the paper appeared in two installments and seemed a bit disjointed led me to skip it over. I returned to it later—perhaps as long as a year later—read it much more carefully and realized that it was an important work: "Ladelle made a great contribution to the theory of depreciation and. . . much commentary could have been avoided if his article had been given any recognition." The basic result was similar to what is now called "economic depreciation" and the standard reference to the subject is an article by Hotelling.[6] Hicks's chapter in *Value and Capital* and Anton's paper, "Depreciation, Cost Allocation and Investment Decisions," *Accounting Research* (April 1956), also are frequently cited in the literature.

Ladelle formulated the depreciation problem as one of dividing fairly a cost among joint "speculators" who each agree at the outset to "own" the asset for a specific year. His formulation had a "game theory flavor" and I discussed it with Joel Owen and this led to a decade or so of work related mainly to the allocation problem and three papers written with him during this period are reprinted here.

The first of these, "A Least Squares Allocation Model," generalizes the allocation problem in accounting in terms of three variables. Many, if not all, allocation methods in accounting can be derived from the model.[7] The allocation criterion has similarities to a quadratic loss function where, to make the notion of a loss in this context meaningful, one would have to, as Ladelle did, personify the "segments" of the firm to which the cost was being allocated.

The two other papers, "The Estimation Problem in Financial Accounting," and "A Reformulation of the Estimation Problem" reinterpret the allocation problem as an estimation problem. The idea here is simply that accounting methods can be viewed as part of a measurement process which has the objective of providing the user of financial statements with information about the future. The report of any interim period is, therefore, "sample" information about some longer time span. This general framework had been used to interpret interim reports of short periods such as a quarterly report, and it seemed reasonable to apply the same idea to other interim reports, such as an annual report, that cover a longer time span.

Arthur Thomas, in the second of two volumes on the allocation problem[8] devoted a chapter to estimation theory. While he recognized that estimation theory provides a way to analyze the allocation problem which avoids arbitrary allocations, he had two major criticisms. First, the theory applies only at the firm level. Second, since the allocations on which the estimates are based incorporate information about the future, it would be as useful simply to present that information directly rather than indirectly through the allocation process. The criticisms certainly have validity. Nevertheless, estimation theory adds substance to some important ideas that have been discussed in accounting and gives some direction for those interested in the information content of financial reports.

The section on interest approximations has some relationship to estimation. In both cases, the focus is on devising methods to provide information about parameters of interest. My first awareness of the work on approximating the rate of interest on an annuity was the result of reading Yuji Ijiri's article, "Approximations to Interest Formulas," appearing in the June 1972 issue of the *Journal of Business*. In that article, Professor Ijiri derived simple approximations to some common compound interest formulas. A student, John Petroff, working on an MBA thesis, used these formulas to simplify the problem of getting decision rules for choosing between alternative forms of a charitable remainder trust.[9]

I can't recall exactly why I continued research in the area of interest approximations or how I found out that work in this area had been in the domain of actuaries and mathematicians for several centuries. In any event, I learned that the libraries at the College of Insurance and Metropolitan Life Insurance Company had excellent collections of historical materials. Not surprisingly, without calculators and computers, a significant amount of attention was devoted to the subject and there was a very extensive literature in the area.

About this time I found out, as I was looking over a list of working papers from the Department of Finance at the Stern School, that Garbriel Hawawini had coauthored with Ashok Vora a paper on approximations to bond yields. I showed Garbriel copies of some of the older articles I had collected. Like myself, he found the work quite fascinating and he and Vora decided to edit an anthology of articles on interest approximations. They also wrote an article on the subject.[10]

Certain methods relating to interest calculations have a long history in accounting. One of the oldest approximation methods concerns "equating time of payments" which is discussed in Edward Hatton's 1696 text.[11] Equated time is the time that a series of payments with different maturity dates can be paid without "wrong on either Side" (p. 130) and is calculated as the weighted average of the time until each payment is made. The method assumes that simple interest can approximate compound interest. For more than two hundred years, every nuance of this problem has been discussed—in bookkeeping texts and in books on the theory of interest which were generally studied by actuaries.

The question that accountants should think about is the extent to which these interest approximation methods influenced accounting practices. Did straight-line and sum-of-years digits methods in accounting, for example, simply appear "out of the blue" or was the origin of these and other allocation methods related to interest approximation methods? For example, Todhunter pointed out in his article on the approximation of the yield of a bond bought at a premium or discount that the method is consistent with the straight-line method of allocating premium or discount.[12] Ladelle also discussed the conditions under which different depreciation methods approximate economic depreciation. And the "rule of 78" is certainly related to the sum-of-years digits method. Is there a closer link between interest approximation methods and accounting practices than is commonly realized?

The papers in this section give the reader only the flavor of this literature and the issues. The correction to Hawawini and Vora's article on the history of interest approximations points out that Augustus de Morgan,[13] who also wrote an article on the history of interest approximations (whom Hawawini and Vora cite) was making reference to Isaac Newton's early work on the approximation of the rate of interest on an ordinary annuity, not John Newton. This fact gives somewhat more credibility to the history of the subject although it is clear that for several centuries, some of the best scientific minds worked in the area.

The next paper is a note on the history of interest approximations. I was surprised to find that one of Ijiri's formulas appeared in the first volume (1851) of the *Journal of the Institute of Actuaries* and other recent work can be traced to the early literature on interest approximations. Following this piece is a very short note, called "Baily's Paradox," which reprints his calculation of the gold equivalent of an English penny compounded at 5% for 1810 years—357,000,000 spheres, each the size of the earth, filled with gold!

In 1974, Gould and Weil derived the "rule of 69" which is a simple approximation to determine how long it takes for a sum to double at a given interest rate. "A Note on 'Rediscovery' and the Rule of 69" documents that nineteenth century actuaries and accountants were familiar with the rule and suggests that scholars need to pay more attention to the past which can help to illuminate present-day problems. A good example of how the past can shed light on the present concerns accounting methods involving weighted averages. The use of weighted averages in accounting dates back hundreds of years and to understand, for example, why a weighted average earnings per share is calculated, one needs to recognize the relationship between this calculation and the problem of dividing income among partners with unequal amounts of capital invested. In each case, the accounting method can be viewed as an interest approximation. "Weighted Average Earnings Per Share" is an unpublished paper that addresses this issue.

The section on "Financial Reporting and Analysis" provides an historical perspective on the subject and deals with several related issues concerning the form of financial statements and how the information in financial statements can be used to estimate parameters of interest.

"Corporate Financial Reporting at the Turn of the Century" was commissioned by the American Institute of Certified Public Accountants for the Centennial issue of the *Journal of Accountancy.* There was no uniformity in the period—some companies disclosed little or no financial information and others reported very detailed statements. Questions about disclosure, classification and other modern issues began to be addressed and many features of modern financial reporting such as the disclosure of accounting policy, comparative reports and statements of sources and uses of funds are in evidence. The article concludes that while "most companies did not produce financial statements that would be termed satisfactory by today's standards, . . . the path that corporations would follow had already been marked by this time."

Following up on the thesis that the basic form of financial statements has not changed over this century, the next article, "Cumulative Financial Statements," argues that there may be new ways to present financial statements that might be more informative than the traditional format. The point is simply that a year's activities should not be viewed as an annual venture; therefore, more attention needs to be given to multi-year reports.

Two graphical forms of cumulative financial statements for Chrysler Corporation over the 1923–1975 period are devised to show what this kind of financial report might look like. Since a balance sheet is a cumulative statement of transactions at a point of time, the time series of cumulative statements will show how the balance sheet changes over time. In any event, more discussion of innovations in financial reporting is clearly needed.

While one of the cumulative graphs involved a multi-period accounting rate of return, questions about how accounting rates of return are used in accounting were not addressed. The next three items deal with this subject in greater detail.

The introduction to my book, *Estimating the Economic Rate of Return from Accounting Data,* provides a short history of the subject since 1965. In a sense, all of this research can be traced to the early efforts by actuaries to find a simple approximation for the yield on an annuity or a bond. The research also is related to work on economic depreciation where the internal rate of return plays an important role. When an asset (which could be the firm itself) is depreciated using economic depreciation, the accounting and economic returns are equal. Otherwise, the divergence between the accounting and economic rate of return depends on the economic value/book value ratios at the beginning and at the end of the multi-period time horizon. This relationship between the accounting and economic rates of return and the opening and closing market/book ratios is explored in the next article, "Approximate Error in Using the Accounting Rate of Return to Estimate Economic Returns." The note that follows corrects a mistake in the article.

The last paper in this section, "The Role of the Accounting Rate of Return in Financial Statement Analysis," is closely related to earlier work by Kay and Peasnell.[14] The article suggests that the *pseudo* internal rate of return, which is a multi-period accounting rate of return, should have a central role in financial statement analysis.

A key issue in this work concerns the critical importance of the comprehensive income concept. If a strict "clean surplus" doctrine is not adopted, the analytical integrity of the double entry system is destroyed and, unless specific adjustments are made to restore clean surplus, the fundamental identity between income and cash flows will not hold. This means that without "clean surplus," basic information cannot be extracted directly from financial statements. One can only suppose that the lack of concern about this problem, as is evidenced by some of the recent pronouncements of the Financial Accounting Standards Board which violate the comprehensive income concept, results from a failure to think about double entry as an analytical system.

The last two papers in this book deal with the subject of accounting error and its effect on behavior. The first of these, "Nineteenth Century Accounting Error," is concerned with accounting practices in the latter part of the nineteenth century and whether accounting policies had an impact on economic development. In the second paper, "Accounting Error as a Factor in Business History," the meaning of error in accounting is examined in more detail.

Hopwood spoke of "the diversity of influences that can impinge on accounting and its consequences, the often quite complex and shifting circumstances, issues, and practices with which accounting can be associated, and, of equal significance, the roles played by the unintentional and the unanticipated consequences of accounting change.[15] Historical perspective and clear thinking about accounting fundamentals are needed to help clarify the complex role that accounting plays.

Most of the papers in this anthology look to the past to try to understand the present-day "state of accounting" and I hope that some of this work helps to achieve this objective.

Notes

1. "The Nature and Limitations of Accounts, " *The Accountant*, February 16, 1903.

2. (Oxford: Clarendon Press, 1939).

3. A recent paper by Arjo Klamer gives explicit recognition to Hicks's interest in accounting details. See "An Accountant Among Economists: Conversations with Sir J. R. Hicks, " *Journal of Economic Perspectives* (Fall 1989). I commented on Klamer's article in the summer 1990 issue of *Journal of Economic Perspectives.*

4. Some of these are reprinted in my book, *Depreciation and Capital Maintenance* (New York: Garland Publishing, Inc., 1984).

5. "On the Convergence of Periodic Reinvestments by an Amount Equal to Depreciation, " *Management Science* (January 1967).

6. Harold Hotelling, "A General Mathematical Theory of Depreciation," *Journal of the American Statistical Association* (September 1925).

7. The original article contained two typographical errors in the main equations and these errors are corrected here.

8. *The Allocation Problem: Part Two* (Sarasota, FL: American Accounting Association, 1973).

9. The thesis was published by the Institute of Finance, at New York University's Graduate School of Business in *The Bulletin* (April 1974) under the title of " 'The Charitable Remainder Trust'- Is There a Better Way to Make a Large Donation?"

10. *The History of Interest Approximations* (New York: Arno Press, 1980 and "Yield Approximations: An Historical Perspective," *Journal of Finance* (March 1982).

11. *The Merchant's Magazine; or, Trades-man's Treasury* (New York and London: Garland Publishing, Inc., 1982).

12. Ralph Todhunter, "On an Approximation of the Rate of Interest Yielded by a Bond Bought at a Premium," *Journal of the Institute of Actuaries* (July 1897).

13. De Morgan was a well-known mathematician who included an appendix entitled "On the Main Principles of Book-keeping" in his book, *The Elements of Arithmetic* (London 1853).

14. J. A. Kay, "Accountants, Too, Could be Happy in a Golden Age: The Accountants Rate of Profit and the Internal Rate of Return," *Oxford Economic Papers* (November 1976) and K. V. Peasnell, "Some Formal Connections Between Economic Values and Yields and Accounting Numbers," *Journal of Business Finance & Accounting* (Autumn 1982).

15. Anthony G. Hopwood, ed., *Accounting from the Outside* (New York: Garland Publishing, Inc., 1988), p. xxxi.

First Principles

Dicksee's Contribution to Accounting Theory and Practice

A paper presented at the Third World Congress of Accounting Historians in London on August 18, 1980. The paper served as the introduction to an anthology of selected work of Dicksee, _Dicksee's Contribution to Accounting Theory and Practice_ (New York: Arno Press 1980).

Lawrence Robert Dicksee was born in 1864. In 1886 he was admitted to the Institute of Chartered Accountants in England and Wales and six years later, his best known work, Auditing, was published. His reputation earned him the appointment to a chair in accounting at the University of Birmingham in 1902. In that year he also began to teach at the London School of Economics where he taught for 25 years.[1] Dicksee died in 1932 and his achievements were described this way.

> The quality of Dicksee's achievement as a thinker and writer can hardly be realised by the present generation of students. By a stroke of original genius he created the modern science of auditing .... It was Dicksee's peculiar and remarkable contribution to professional history, not merely to grasp the importance and potentialities of the infant study but to set on a scientific basis the true relation between the functions of the accountant and those of the auditor ....[2]

Unquestionably, Auditing (1892) is Dicksee's best known book and has had the most influence on practice, both in Great Britain and the United States. This classic went into 19 English editions and an authorized American edition was edited by R. H. Montgomery in 1905. The second American edition appeared in 1909 and three years later the first edition of Montgomery's Auditing Theory and Practice (which is now in the 10th edition) was published. The influence of Dicksee on developments in the United States is indicated by Arthur Lowes Dickinson in the introduction to the American edition.

> The publication of an American edition of Mr. L. R. Dicksee's work on Auditing is further evidence of the growing importance to the community of a correct understanding of the principles of Accounting; and the fact that this edition has received the support of educational authorities throughout the country is full of promise for the future of the still young profession of the Public Accountant.

----

1. For further biographical data on Dicksee see Kitchen and Parker (1980), The Accountant, January 1, 1921 p. 3; September 18, 1926, p. 403; and February 27, 1932, p. 283

2. The Accountant, February 27, 1932, p. 283. The obituary was signed by "S.W.R." who was Stanley Rowland (Kitchen and Parker, 1980, p. 53).

Commenting further on Dicksee's contribution to accounting thought, Rowland noted that

> The immediate success of the first heir of his invention stimulated his activity and from that time onwards a constant stream of writing flowed from his pen. A complete list of his published books would occupy a very long column ....

The same point was made in a "Portrait Supplement" of Dicksee that appeared in the January 1, 1921 issue of The Accountant: "Other works [after Auditing] have followed in an almost continuous stream; indeed there can be no doubt that 'Dicksee' is the most prolific as well as the most widely read author of books on accountancy subjects."

A bibliography of Dicksee's work, which is given at the end of this paper, supports these views and shows the breadth of his work. Some of the most thought provoking ideas are found in articles published in The Accountant and The Accountants' Journal. Many of the articles were orginally presented as papers at meetings of the student societies throughout Great Britain or as lectures at the London School of Economics. Often, they also were reprinted in other journals and published as short monographs.

The publications are listed in chronological order and the publication history for each item is given.[3] Dicksee's contributions can be classified into roughly three phases which were not mutually exclusive. From 1892 to 1904 Dicksee devoted most of his efforts to traditional subjects in auditing and financial accounting. The second phase, 1905 to 1930, was devoted mainly to the area of information systems. In the third phase, 1920 to 1930, Dicksee reconsidered some critical issues in financial accounting. Shortly before his death, Dicksee also wrote a series of articles called "Popular Fallacies." They addressed a number of more philosophical issues which undoubtedly preoccupied him throughout his life.

----

3. The bibliography is based on Institute of Chartered Accountants in England and Wales (1912), American Institute of Accountants (1921, 1924, 1928, 1932) and British Museum (1959).

THE EARLY YEARS: 1892 - 1904

Following the publication of Auditing in 1892, Dicksee wrote 22 articles and books in the next 12 years. This work deals with aspects of auditing, bookkeeping, depreciation, goodwill, specialized accounting systems, foreign currency and accounting theory. Three articles written during this period stand out from the rest.

"Form of Accounts and Balance Sheets" (1893) is an expanded version of Chapter 5 in Auditing. This article is interesting because it is one of the first on the subject and because it illustrates the kind of imaginative logic that Dicksee would use in later years. Dicksee often attempted to begin exploring an issue by using what he called "first principles," and an early example of this technique can be found in his definition of an asset.

> If we go back to the first principles, I think it must be admitted that an asset may be fairly defined as "an expenditure on a remunerative object"; and, indeed, it may be taken as test of whether any particular expenditure is an asset or a loss to enquire whether, as a matter of fact, such expenditure was (looking back on it) worth the amount expended on it .... if (looking back on it) we think that if we had the opportunity of making the investment a second time we should have made it upon the same terms, we may fairly say that there is value for the original outlay; .... If, on the other hand, it appears that the value remaining for such expenditures is less than the original amount ..., it is obvious that ... depreciation has occurred.

Dicksee's view on the problem of asset valuation and the related problem of depreciation underwent significant changes in later years.[4]

Another outstanding work in this period is a lecture, "Profits Available for Dividends," delivered to the Institute of Chartered Accountants in England and Wales and published in 1895. Dicksee initially referred to an earlier debate between Ernest Cooper and Thomas Welton. It concerned the question whether

----

4. Kitchen (1976 and 1979) gives an interesting review of Dicksee's thoughts on depreciation and related problems.

profit is measured by subtracting revenue from expenses or by comparing the change in the value of net assets over two periods? In effect, Dicksee said this controversy was an "empty box" (p. 3).

> I must confess that, to my mind, a discussion conducted upon such lines as these could not be altogether profitable; for a very little consideration will suffice to show that if the Balance Sheet were indeed a "just" one, and the Profit and Loss Account indeed a "full" one, then by every law of double-entry it must necessarily follow that the result would in each case by the same ....

He then argued that

> The most convenient method of considering the question has always appeared to me to be to follow the order I have just indicated- to criticise each item in the Profit and Loss Account first, and then to see whether a Balance Sheet prepared from accounts so stated may fairly be said to fully and fairly disclose the true financial position of the company as at the date named.

Four sources of profits were analyzed and ordinary profits are divided into profit on transactions completed but not yet received in cash and profit on transactions not completed, whether received in cash or not. In analyzing expenses a distinction is made between those expenses that may properly be spread over a term of years and those that must be charged to the period in which they are incurred.

> It is only when we have adequate evidence that such expenditure was not incurred for the sole benefit of the period we are considering, and, moreover, that such expenditure may reasonably be expected to result in benefits accruing during future years, that we are justified in allowing any portion of it to be held in suspense ....

Advertising expense is used as an example to discuss deferred charges.

In the next several years Dicksee wrote Goodwill and Its Treatment in Accounts (1897) and a number of other articles and books. Advanced Accounting was published in 1903 and it begins by explaining the essential nature of the problems of asset valuation and profit determination. To deal with the subject along "systematic lines," the example of a single ship is used because "One of the most ancient (and therefore one of the simplest) modes of transacting business in through the agency of a ship" (p. 3).

Dicksee's "ship model" is a simple but effective device for explicating these basic issues.

> The problem [of profit determination] is ... quite simple, in that at the completion of each voyage it is possible to strike a balance of accounts, leaving practically no balances outstanding as represented uncompleted transactions .... this method of arriving at the profit depends for its accuracy upon the assumption that such payments have been made and charged up against Revenue as will make good any wastage that may have taken place in the original equipment of the undertaking .... consumption of specific stores which may be readily replaced by the purchases of others, and the indirect operations of war and tear and the lapse of time .... known as "Depreciation" (p. 4).

But any change in the value of asset due to causes outside ordinary operations, i.e., exogenous causes, should be ignored because the assets were not acquired

> with a view to there being eventually realised at a profit in the ordinary course of business, but with a view to their being <u>used</u> for the purpose of enabling trading profit to be made in other ways .... in any event it is quite an open question whether, pending realization (which is not contemplated), any more reliable basis of value could be adopted than the actual cost in the first instance (p. 5).

The basic idea embedded in the ship model is the distinction between a completed and uncompleted venture, i.e., between a single-period accounting model and multi-period model. This idea is a fundamental one and Dicksee made further use of it in a later section of <u>Advanced Accounting</u>, "Nature and Limitations of Accounts" (pp. 281-283). This section is a condensed version of a 1903 article having the same title and which begins by making reference to a pure venture model.

> If a particular venture has been undertaken and carried to a conclusion before the accounts in relation thereto are balanced, and the ultimate result then reduced to a cash basis, the most concise means of showing the transactions involved is, of course, a simple summarised Account of Receipts and Payments, and such a

> Statement will be a statement of <u>fact</u>, showing what sums have actually been received, what sums have been actually paid in respect of the venture, and what (if any) balance remains in the hands of the accounting party in cash.

However, in the case of most commercial concerns, the single-period model is of limited value for the following reason.

> It is manifestly inconvenient for a trader to wait until he has altogether retired from business, realised his assets, and paid off his liabilities, before attempting to form any idea of how he stands, and those who carry on their business upon such lines end, as experience shows, not infrequently in finding that their liabilities considerably exceed their assets. Consequently it is imperative that an attempt should be made at comparatively frequent intervals- and in any event not less often than once a year- to arrive as nearly as may be at the financial position; and for this purpose the books are regularly balanced, and the usual so-called "final" accounts (that is, the Balance Sheet and Profit and Loss Accounts) are compiled. In the nature of things, however, these so-called "final" accounts are not final, but are merely <u>interim</u> accounts.

Dicksee elaborates further on the problem of interim reporting.

> ... it is absolutely impossible to draw a line at any particular date without its intersecting or "cutting into" a large number of transactions which at that moment remain uncompleted. The precise effect and money value of these uncompleted transactions can only be estimated, and consequently a large number of the transactions that go to make up the Trading and Profit and Loss Accounts must also be, in a greater or less degree, dependent upon the estimates. In some businesses as, for example. that of a retail trader- the pending transactions will probably be relatively unimportant in amount, although doubtless extremely numerous. In other cases- as, for example, with a large firm of contractors- the number of pending transactions may be comparatively small, but their individual importance may be relatively enormous, and the manner in which they are treated very materially affect the financial result.

The 1903 article is Dicksee's last major effort in financial accounting theory. For the next quarter of a century, he focused most of his attention on the theoretical and practical implications of viewing accounting as a system of information processing. The foundation for this broader view of accounting can be traced to a paper, "The Importance of Accurate and Adequate Accounting" (1905).

THE SECOND PHASE: 1905 - 1930

The 1905 paper signals Dicksee's emerging interest in the subject of information systems. Having understood the basic problem of interim reporting, Dicksee began to think about the nature and use of accounting data. To do so, he again resorted to "first principles."

> The Science of accounting, in all its numerous ramifications, arises primarily out of the need that accounting parties should from time to time render those to whom they are responsible an account of their stewardship- that, at least, we may take to have been the original idea in the early days when capitalists were either quite illiterate, or at all events indisposed to concern themselves with so plebeian an occupation as commerce of any description.

However,

> Accounting is not a matter of arithmetic, or of mathematics of any kind .... Speaking generally, an account is ... a narrative of the doings of an accounting party; .... the method with which we are so familiar ... of reducing every transaction to a money equivalent, is not the <u>essence</u> of the account, but merely one of its numerous mechanisms.

This intriguing idea is elaborated on.

> ... an account ... is <u>not</u> merely a collection of figures and calculation, but essentially a narration, or history, of events, the ascertained (or estimated) money value of which is by no means only the essential point. In the absence of an adequate amount of "narration" it would be absolutely impossible for anyone- no matter how skilled in figures- to form any useful option as to their absolute, or even approximate accuracy .... Figures unsupported by explanatory narrative must be either accepted on trust or rejected incredulously; and therefore, in the absence of such

> explanatory narrative ... they must ... be regarded as entirely useless.[5]

Dicksee also reasoned that the objective of accounting is to provide timely information which would improve business efficiency and therefore the allocation of resources. He put it this way.

> Stated quite shortly, it may, I think be said that accurate accounting- and more particularly accounting arranged upon suitable lines, so as to give not merely a review of historical facts, but also summary of current results which may be likened to "news"- is of direct advantage to all undertakings as making for increased efficiency and economy .... In these days of competition business moves too quickly for anyone to rest content with a Balance Sheet and Trading and Profit Loss Accounts once every six or twelve months: he must be placed in possession of all detailed information which these accounts imply systematically, continuously .... the importance of providing not merely accurate, but also adequate systems of accounts will receive an increasing measure of attention at the hands of the profession ....

In "Modern Accountancy Methods in Relation to Business Efficiency" (1914), Dicksee goes deeper into the nature of financial information and comments on the multi-dimensional aspects of accounting data.

> The fallacy of the supposed perfection of the double-entry system, as handed down to us by the Lombardy merchants of the fifteenth century, is that, so to speak, it views everything in one plane. It is about as true to nature as a system of geometry which regards plane geometry as the only kind in existence, and ignores the fact that there is such a thing as solid geometry.

Dicksee then asks and responds to the question, how should a simple human action such as throwing a stone into a pond be recorded, an event which has many consequences?

----

5. J.R. Hicks made this point 40 years later [1948, p. 564]: "... there is hardly any situation which could be adequately depicted by a mere table of figures; every statistical table needs to be annotated, and in a similar way the full meaning of a accounting statement can only be expected to emerge in its accompanying report."

> The object in drawing ... attention to this very simple example of natural phenomena is to suggest ... that double-entry (as understood in the middle ages, and as to a large extent still practiced under modern conditions) is but an imperfect observation of all the consequences of those events which are conveniently called "business transactions."

In 1906 a book on office organization and management was published, followed by several articles on depreciation. Business Organization appeared in 1910 and a series of interesting lectures, "Business Methods and the War," came out in book form in 1915. The second decade in the twentieth century also produced interesting papers on fraud, inventory and office machinery.

The paper on fraud (1911) argued that

> No business can be conducted- profit can be earned- without incurring some risk, and the risk of loss by fraud is just as much one of these inevitable risks as in the risk of loss by way of bad debt. It would seem, therefore, that is not even desirable to attempt to obviate all risks of fraud; even if it were desirable, we may feel sure that it would be impracticable to do so on terms that left it possible to conduct a successful and profitable business.

The lecture on the auditor's responsibility for inventory valuation (1913), ahead of his time, lamented that

> On the principle that it is useless to strain at the gnat, if one must perforce swallow the camel, it is at least open to question whether the auditor is not just as entitled to accept the certificates of the clerical staff that the clerical work has be accurately performed, as he is to accept the certificate of (say) the general manager that the valuation of the various items has been conducted on proper principles.

And an early analysis of the use of office machinery (1916) predicted that

> there is a great and increasing field for the use of machinery in connection with offices in directions in which at present it is not by any means generally utilised.

Dicksee also considered social and economics problems of fatigue, monotony, unemployment and other effects of office automation. He was convinced that this new technology would have important implications for the accountant.

> Unless the Accountant is content to be pushed aside, and to be dispensed with, it behooves him earnestly to grapple with this problem of the application of machinery to office conditions; as rapidly as possible to make good use of his opportunities- the wasted opportunities of the past; and to approach the subject with an enlightened and open mind, thinking only of the best, the quickest, and the most economical means by which the most desirable result can be achieved. If what I have put to you this evening has awakened you to the importance of a serious consideration of the matter, my time and your time will not have been wasted tonight.

Four other major papers on business efficiency and information systems were written in the twenties. In "The True Basis of Efficiency" (1923), Dicksee stresses the human factor and mentions that he "was disposed to think that the matter of colour affected people very much." The paper, "Some Economic Aspects of Office Machinery" (1925), takes the position that economics and human behavior are inseparable.

> Of course this view of economics is an utterly different one from the view that is sometimes put forward that economics is an absolutely cold-blooded and non-human science. It recognises that we are here dealing with the actions and re-actions of human beings upon each other, and it will be just as well, I think, for us all to realise that it is not possible to divorce economics from the humanities.

This paper also argues that "the whole object of accounting, of course, is to build up information" and that

> the introduction of office machinery ... stimulates the demand for more information being compiled as an aid to management. It is in this way that we may reasonably assume that under all normal conditions there will be found enough work to be done to absorb all the workers already employed, so that the general effect of introducing office machinery- and the introduction, of course, will be gradually- is that the same number of workers are employed in producing the same quantity of information or records as before.

Dicksee then tried to answer some critics who felt, as some do today, that modern technology would dull the mind.

> It may be that the introduction of calculating machines, instead of calculation being a mental process, may deprive present and future generations of the opportunities of developing mentality that have been open to previous generations. If, however, there is anything in that argument, I think we must recognise that it might be applied equally well as an argument against the introduction of the metric system into this country.

In one of his final articles in the areas of information systems, Dicksee made the following prediction (December 21, 1929).

> ... future improvements in accounting methods must lie along the lines of employing perforated cards as full and detailed records of original transactions, subsequently handled by mechanical sorting, counting and tabulating machines, so that any described result may be reached at any desired moment with a minimum expenditure of time and trouble. It is clear that, so long as we retain the ability to build up our transactions in any desired form with any desired volume of detail, whenever we want information from any particular view-point, that is really all that is necessary. The laborious construction of ledger accounts merely for the sake of enabling them to be listed into a trial balance is surely but a relic of medieval superstition. Such an assertion may seem revolutionary to some. If so, it may be pointed out that not every form of revolution is undesirable. Many of the most important forms of movement are essentially revolutionary. In a mechanical age to veto revolution would be almost the same thing as vetoing motion itself![6]

----

6. Fifty years later, Burton (1980) described this revolution and its effects. "In the last quarter century, the accounting profession has experienced phenomenal growth, fueled primarily by a revolution in information processing technology, a dramatic expansion in the regulatory environment and an increasing recognition of the need for reliable financial information in the capital markets."

SECOND THOUGHTS ON FINANCIAL ACCOUNTING ISSUES: 1920-1930

Dicksee never lost interest in more traditional financial accounting problems and he wrote several papers and a series of articles in this area during the 1920s. Although his theoretical position had remained unaltered by time, he had several new and interesting ideas.

The 1920 paper, "Published Balance Sheets and Accounts," restates the view that a balance sheet is a list of "uncompleted transactions" and that if assets were revalued each year

> ... to produce a Balance Sheet which will get into close touch with actual facts, we found that we have entirely defeated our purpose and have got right away from the true facts of the position, the essential fact being that the business is a going concern which we are going to carry so far as we can anticipate, and which we have every reason to suppose that we shall be able to continue.

Thus, Dicksee's position on asset valuation did not change in 30 years.

> ... theoretically at least, we ought to ascertain what benefits will be received from this outlay in each accounting period during which it is any advantage to us whatsoever, and charge the corresponding portion of the cost against each accounting period. That is what is commonly done in practice, with such items as plant and machinery and the like ....

But Dicksee did formulate some new ideas about the purpose of a balance sheet.

> In ordinary practice Balance Sheets seem to be used, ... not merely as a means ... [to] test the degree of success with which a board of directors has conducted the affairs of the undertaking, but also as a means ... to determine what is the true value of the company's shares from time to time. It is very doubtful whether a Balance Sheet can be of much use for this latter purpose. The true value of the shares in a company depends, no doubt, to a certain extent upon what return would be likely to be made to shareholders in the event of the company being wound up, but it depends certainly to a greater extent upon the income derived from the possession of the shares and the degree of the probability of that income being maintained. The Balance Sheet as ordinarily prepared gives very little idea as to what shareholders may expect to receive if

> the company were wound up. It will give some idea as to the probability of the business being successful in the future, and it should enable us to determine whether the resources of the undertaking are sufficient to enable it to meet its debts as they fall due. We may, by looking at a Balance Sheet which has been prepared with reasonable honesty, satisfy ourselves that it is not likely that the company will be obliged to discontinue operations because it is unable to pay its debts, or may form the conclusion from looking at the Balance Sheet that there is a greater or lesser probability that it will be obligated to stop for want of money; but we can form no very useful idea from looking at any Balance Sheet as to whether the profits of the next few years will be as great as those of the last few years.

The final paper is in the area of financial accounting, "Auditor's Responsibility for Balance Sheet Values," was published in 1927, 41 years after becoming a chartered accountant. After a lifetime of writing, teaching and practicing accounting, Dicksee made seven recommendations for accounting practice.

> ... the very common practice of directors, when issuing accounts to the shareholders, of enclosing a stamped form of proxy in favor of some of their own number should be forbidden by law.

> ... companies should [not] be allowed to frame a provision in the articles of association as a result of which the holders of certain classes of shares are deprived of all voting power.

> ... when a company goes into compulsory liquidation ... every director of that company should submit to a public examination somewhat analogous to a public examination in bankruptcy, and , until he has obtained the Registrar's certificate that he has passed that examination, it should not be competent for him to sit as a director on the board of any other company.

> ... in a very large number of cases ... no real difficulty would be experienced in prescribing a statutory form of published accounts that would be a very great improvement upon the vast majority of published accounts that one gets under present conditions.

> ... in all cases, [companies should] publish something in the nature of a Revenue Account or a Trading and Profit and Loss Account, something which shows, however inadequately, how the profit has been arrived at,

> instead of merely giving us the bare figure and leaving us to guess as to its source.
>
> ... many companies might with advantages follow a practice of issuing accounts more frequently than once a year.
>
> ... if it be thought desirable to meet in some way what is undoubtedly a rather insistent public demand, even if it is not a very well informed demand, for balance sheets that are really statements of affairs- revaluations of assets from time to time- that might, I think, best be met by the publication, not necessarily every year, but, say, every five years, of something in the nature of valuation report like that which life assurance companies provide, quite independently of the annual balance sheet and not necessarily in any way linked up with it, but a quinquennial statement which would aim at showing the true position at the then current values as far as is reasonably practicable.

Dicksee ended his illustrious career with a series of 18 articles, "Popular Fallacies," published in The Accountants' Journal during 1930 and 1931. The topics range from the nature of goodwill to fatigue and unemployment. The issues raised are obviously those in which Dicksee had strong interest and personal conviction.

CONCLUDING COMMENT

Most students of accounting recognize Dicksee's contribution to auditing but few seem to know that he enriched other areas of accounting as well. His ideas were almost always original and many of them, especially in the area of financial accounting, have withstood the test of time. And the revolution in information processing predicted by Dicksee over 50 years ago already has occurred.

A large number of Dicksee's books and articles have been reprinted in recent years. Students, teachers and practitioners will enjoy Dicksee's style and find his ideas stimulating.

REFERENCES

American Institute of Accountants, Accountants' Index 1920 (New York: AIA, 1921).

________, Accountant's Index 1921-1923 (New York: AIA 1924).

________, Accountants' Index 1923-1927 (New York: AIA 1928).

________, Accountants' Index 1928-1931 (New York: AIA 1932).

Brief, R.P., ed., The Late Nineteenth Century Debate over Depreciation, Capital and Income (New York: Arno Press, 1976).

British Museum, General Catalogue of Printed Books (London: Trustees of the British Museum, 1956), Vol. 52.

Burton, J.C., "Where Are the Angry Young C.P.A.s?" The New York Times, April 13, 1980, C 16.

Hicks, J.R., Book Review of F. S. Bray, Precision and Design in Accountancy in Economic Journal (December 1948), pp. 562-564.

Institute of Chartered Accountants in England and Wales, Library Catalogue 1913 (London: ICAEW, 1913).

Kitchen J., "Lawrence Dicksee, Depreciation, and the Double-Account System," in Edey, H. and Yamey, B. S., eds., Debits, Credits, Finance and Profits (London: Sweet & Maxwell, 1974).

________, "Fixed Asset Values: Ideas on Depreciation 1892-1914," Accounting and Business Research (Autumn 1979), pp. 281-291.

________, and Parker, R. H., Accounting Thought and Education: Six English Pioneers (London: ICAEW, 1980).

BIBLIOGRAPHY: ROBERT LAWRENCE DICKSEE

o Auditing (London: Gee & Co., 1892). Nineteenth English edition, 1959. Authorized American Edition, 1905, edited by R. H. Montgomery. Second American edition, 1909. Reprinted by Arno Press, 1976.

o "Investigations: Their Object and Extent," The Accountant (March 11, 1893), pp. 228-234. Published in the Accountants' Journal (1892-93) and Leeds Chartered Accountant Students' Society Transactions (1892-93). Reprinted in M. Chatfield, ed., The English View of Accountant's Duties and Responsibilities: 1881-1902 (New York: Arno Press, 1978).

o "Forms of Accounts and Balance Sheets," The Accountant (November 11 and 18, 1893), pp. 954-959, 973-981. Published in The Accountant's Journal (1893-94) and London Chartered Accountants Students Society Transactions (1893). Reprinted by Arno Press, 1980.*

o Bookkeeping For Accountant Students (London: Gee & Co., 1893). Seventh English edition, 1913.

o "Profits Available for Dividends," in Four Lectures Delivered to the Institute of Chartered Accountants in England and Wales During the Years 1894 and 1895 (London: Gee & Co., 1895), pp. 33-59. Reprinted by Arno Press, 1980.*

o Comparative Depreciation Tables (London: Gee & Co., 1895). Third English edition, 1925.

o Goodwill and Its Treatment in Accounts (London: Gee & Co., 1897). Fourth English edition, 1920. Published in The Accountant (1897). Also published in The Accountants' Journal (1896-97) and Birmingham Chartered Accountants Students Society Transactions (1896-97). Third edition co-authored by F. Tillyard in 1906. Reprinted by Arno Press, 1976.

o "Bookkeeping with Special Reference to Joint Stock Companies," The Accountant (January 23, February 13, February 27, March 2 and April 10, 1897), pp. 116-119, 182-192, 210-214, 235-240, 339-334, 397-401. Published in the Accountants' Journal (1896-97, 1897-98) and Secretary's Journal (1897).

o Student's Guide to Accountancy (London: Gee & Co., 1897). Second English Edition, 1907.

o Bookkeeping For Company Secretaries (London: Gee & Co., 1897). Fifth English edition, 1914.

o The Liabilities of Auditors Under the Companies Acts," The Accountant (May 14, 1898), pp. 500-511. Published in The Accountants' Journal (1898-99) and London Chartered Accountants Students' Society Transactions (1898). Reprinted in M. Chatfield, ed., The English View of Accountant's Duties and Responsibilities: 1881-1902 (New York: Arno Press, 1978).

o Bookkeeping Exercises for Accountant Students (London: Gee & Co., 1899). Fourth English edition, 1925.

o Auctioneers' Accounts (London: Gee & Co., 1901). Published in George Lisle, ed., Encyclopaedia of Accounting (Edinburgh: William Greens & Sons,1903), v. 1, pp. 157-163.

o Solicitors' Accounts (London: Gee & Co., 1902). Third English edition, 1931.

o Advanced Accounting (London: Gee & Co., 1903). Seventh English edition, 1932. Reprinted by Arno Press, 1976.

o "The Nature and Limitations of Accounts," The Accountant (April 4, 1903), pp. 469-74. Published in The Accountants' Journal (1903-04) and Birmingham Chartered Accountants Students' Society Transactions (1902-03. Reprinted by Arno Press, 1980.*

o Depreciation, Reserves and Reserve Funds, (London: Gee & Co., 1903). Sixth English edition, 1934. Reprinted by Arno Press, 1976.

o "Cost Accounts Suitable to Jobbing Tradesmen," in George Lisle, ed., Encyclopaedia of Accounting (Edinburgh: William Green & Sons, 1903). v. 2, pp. 252-258.

o "Bookkeeping: Its Adaptability to the Requirements of Every Class of Undertaking," in George Lisle, ed., Encyclopaedia of Accounting (Edinburgh: William Green & Sons, 1903), v. 1, pp. 496-501.

o "Secretary," in George Lisle, ed., Encyclopaedia of Accounting (Edinburgh: William Green & Sons, 1903), v. 6, pp. 36-62.

o "Auditing," in George Lisle, ed., Encyclopaedia of Accounting (Edinburgh: William Green & Sons, 1903), pp. 163-193. Reprinted in R. Brief, ed., Selections from the Encyclopaedia of Accounting (New York: Arno Press, 1978).

o "Foreign Currencies and the Accounts of Foreign Branches, "The Accountant (February 4, 1904), pp. 281-291. Published in The Accountants' Journal (1903-04). Reprinted in R. Brief and B. Merino, "An Early Contribution to Accounting for Foreign Exchange," Accounting Journal (Autumn 1978).

o "Presidential Address: Annual Dinner, "The Accountant (November 19, 1904), pp. 626-631.

o Hotel Accounts (London: Gee & Co., 1905). Second English edition, 1912. Published in The Accountant (1912).

o "Importance of Accurate and Adequate Accounting," The Accountant (February 4, 1095), pp. 146-151. Published in The Accountants' Journal (1904-05) and Joint Transactions (1905). Reprinted by Arno Press, 1980.*

o Office Organization and Management, Including Secretarial Work (London: Sir Isaac Pitman & Son, 1906). Coauthored by Herbert Edwin Blain. Fifteenth English edition, 1951.

o "Depreciation; with Special Reference to the Account of Local Authorities," The Accountant (April 13, 1907 and July 1, 1907), pp. 482-492, 733-735. Published in The Accountants' Journal (1906-07), Joint Transactions (1907) and Secretary (1907).

o "Accountant on Depreciation," The American Gas Light Journal (May 20, 1907). Published in The Journal of Gas Lighting (1907).

o "Local Authorities and Depreciation," The Journal of Gas Lighting (April 16, 1907). Published in Electric Review (1907).

o "Depreciation," The Municipal Journal (April 19 and 26, 1907).

o Modern Commercial Text-Books for Use in Schools and Colleges and for Men for Business (London: McDonald and Evans, 1908).

o "Balance Sheets of Limited Liability Companies and Private Partnerships," Associated Accountants' Journal (1908).

o ABC of Bookkeeping (London: Longmans Green & Co., 1908).

o "Auditing, with Special Reference to the Accounts of Local Authorities," The Accountant (August 13, 1910), pp. 201-205.

o Business Organization (London: Longmans Green & Co., 1910). New edition, 1924. Reprinted by Arno Press 1980.

o Modern Methods of Accounting (London, 1911). See Book-Keeping Pamphlets, v. 4, n. 10.

o "Loose-Leaf Systems," The Accountant (November 11, 1911) pp. 652-656. Published in The Incorporated Accountants'Journal (1910-11) and The Accountants' Journal (1911-12).

o "Business Organization, with Special Reference to Fraud," The Accountant (December 2 and 9, 1911), pp. 761-767, 802-808. Published in The Incorporated Accountants' Journal (1910-11). Reprinted by Arno Press, 1980.*

o "Some Suggestions on Stock Accounts and Stockkeeping" The Accountant (May 3, 1913), pp. 668-73. Reprinted by Arno Press, 1980.*

o Mines Accounting and Management (London: Gee & Co., 1914).

o "Modern Accountancy Methods in Relation to Business Efficiency," The Accountant (November 14, 1914), pp. 581-586. Reprinted by Arno Press, 1980.*

o Business Methods and the War (Cambridge: University Press, 1915). Published in The Accountant (1915). Reprinted by Arno Press, 1980.

o Machinery as an Aid to Accountancy (London: Gee & Co., 1916). Published in The Accountant (1916) and South African Accountant and Auditor (1916). Reprinted by Arno Press, 1980.*

o Fundamentals of Manufacturing Costs (London: Gee & Co., 1917). Second English edition, 1928. Published in The Accountant (1917). Second edition reprinted by Arno Press, 1980.

o Office Machinery and Appliances (London: Gee & Co., 1917). Third English edition, 1928.

o "Efficient Administration: A Prime Essential to Britain's Economic Recovery," The Accountant (October 30,1920), pp. 479-481. Reprinted as Chapter I in L.R. Dicksee, The True Basis of Efficiency (London: Gee & Co., 1922). Reprinted by Arno Press, 1980.*

o "Published Balance Sheets and Accounts," The Accountant (November 20, 1920), pp. 561-564. Published in The Accountants' Journal (1921). Reprinted by Arno Press, 1980.*

o The Fundamentals of Accountancy (London: Gee & Co., 1921). Published in the Accountants' Journal (1920-1922).

o The True Basis of Efficiency (London: Gee & Co., 1922).

o "Goodwill and its Valuation in Accounts, The Accountants' Journal (August 1922), pp. 196-200. Published in Public Accountant (1923).

o "Costing," The Accountants' Journal (November 1922), pp. 388-97. Reprinted by Arno Press, 1980.*

o "Accountancy," Accountant's and Secretary's Yearbook (1912-25), pp. 1-4.

o "Fraudulent Accounting," The Accountants' Journal (May-December, 1924; January-April 1925), pp. 5-7, 85-89, 166-169, 241-244, 321-324, 404-407, 492-494, 566-569, 646-650, 721-725, 801-804, 885-889. Reprinted by Arno Press, 1980.

o *How to Install a Proper Accounting System* (London: Chapman & Hall, 1925).

o "Published Balance Sheets and Window Dressing," *The Accountant* (April 17, 1926), pp. 567-571. Published in the *The Canadian Chartered Accountant* (1926), *Indian Accountant* (1926), *Public Accountant* (1926, 1927), and *Incorporated Accountants' Journal* (1926).

o "Some Economic Aspects of Office Machinery," *The Accountants' Journal* (June, 1925), pp. 195-199. Reprinted by Arno Press, 1980.*

o *Published Balance Sheets and Window Dressing* (London: Gee & Co., 1927). Published in *The Accountants' Journal* (1925-1926). Reprinted by Arno Press, 1980.

o "Auditor's Responsibility for Balance Sheet Values," *The Accountants' Journal* (May 1927), pp. 57-66. Published in *Public Accountant* (1927) and *Canadian Chartered Accountant* (1928). Reprinted by Arno Press, 1980.*

o "Should an Auditor Resign?," *Australian Accountant and Secretary* (April 1928).

o "Staff Problems Arising Our of the Mechanisation of Bank Accounting," *The Account* (September 14 and 28, 1929), pp. 316-317, 375-376.

o "Accounting Methods - Yesterday, To-day and Tomorrow," *The Accountant* (December 7, 14 and 21, 1929; January 18 and 25, 1930), pp. 715-716, 756-757, 789-790, 75-76, 109-110. Reprinted by Arno Press, 1980.*

o "Mechanisation of Bank Accounting," *The Accountant* (February 2, 1929), pp. 133-135.

o *Garage Accounts* (London: Gee & Co., 1929). Published in *The Accountant* (1929).

o "Fifty Years of Chartered Accountancy; Origin and Growth of the Institute; Registration Hope." *Financial News* (May 14, 1930).

o *Securities and Their Transfer* (London: Gee & Co., 1930).

o "Audit of Share Registers," *The Accountant* (June 14, 1930), pp. 765-766. Published in *Commonwealth Journal of Accountancy* (1930).

o "Popular Fallacies," *The Accountants' Journal* (January-December 1930; January, March-July, 1931), pp. 641-644, 718-722, 803-806, 873-875, 8-10, 108-111, 157-159, 233-236, 297-299, 383-386, 458-460, 537-539, 600-602, 745-747, 817-819, 11-14, 92-94, 167-170. Reprinted by Arno Press, 1980.*

o *Gas Accounts* (London: Gee & Co., 1931).

*Richard P. Brief, ed., *Dicksee's Contribution To Accounting Theory and Practice* (New York: Arno Press, 1980).

The Accountant's Responsibility in Historical Perspective

Richard P. Brief

SEVERAL years ago it was reported (*The New York Times*, January 4, 1972) that many accountants, "like victims of an earthquake or the fist of Joe Frazier, . . . wander dazedly asking what happened; where did the force come from; why wasn't it foreseen; how could it have been avoided . . . ?" The article elaborated on the current state of the profession, indicating that "now, from within the profession itself, revolt is brewing . . . . And for more than 100,000 accountants themselves, the preservation of their professional credibility could not have higher significance. This credibility is under attack in the Congress, in the courts and within the profession itself." This revolt is not new. It has been brewing for nearly 100 years.

One way to gain insight into the vexing and unsettled questions connected with the responsibility of accountants is to approach the subject from an historical perspective. In the pages that follow we examine nineteenth and early twentieth century thought on various topics which have been, and continue to be, of concern to accountants. It will become evident that "history repeats itself" and that most of the basic problems considered by accountants now are also those which have perplexed the profession for nearly a century. Thus despite all the changes in the business environment, controversy within the accounting profession today has remarkable similarities to the discussion taking place decades ago. Why do certain accounting problems appear to be perennial and why has regulation and legislation apparently not solved many of the fundamental disputes in accounting?

The thesis of this study is that accounting controversy persists because profit calculations involve "uncertainty about the future." Legislation and regulation cannot reduce this controversy because they cannot eliminate the element of uncertainty from the problem of profit determination. Consequently, until the subject of uncer-

The original version of this paper was written while the author was a Visiting Professor of Finance, Dartmouth College. It was presented at the annual meeting of the American Accounting Association in August, 1974, during a session sponsored by the Academy of Accounting Historians. Comments and suggestions by the discussants, Professor David Green, Jr. and Mr. Leonard Spacek, and by Mr. Walter Oliphant, Professor Louis Goldberg, and the reviewers of THE ACCOUNTING REVIEW changed the manuscript in important ways. Their help is appreciated. In addition, some of the ideas expressed in this paper are a joint product of several years of discussion with my colleague, Professor Joel Owen. Research support was provided by the Tuck Associates Program, Dartmouth College, and it is gratefully acknowledged. Naturally, the author is solely responsible for this paper.

Richard P. Brief is Professor of Business Statistics and Accounting, Graduate School of Business Administration, New York University.

tainty is given a central position in accounting theory, the problems recognized in earlier times will continue to be deferred to later generations for resolution.

The paper is divided into three sections. The first surveys accounting thought on the subjects of disclosure and alternative techniques and questions concerning the scope of audit and audit certificate. Although there has been an enormous amount of legislation and regulation in these areas, many of today's problems are no different from those which preoccupied the profession during the last century. In the second section, the attitude toward the accountant's responsibility for forecasts and estimates is examined. Historically, an effort was made to minimize uncertainty-related problems by arguing that the accountant's main responsibilities was for "prosaic facts" and "dry realities." The third section concludes that this emphasis on the past rather than the future conflicts with the idea of profit as a return for risk bearing. However, the modern corporate concept of profit is a product of lawyers, not of accountants, and legislation governing the payment of dividends has had a significant impact on the development of accounting.

Legislation and Problems of the Accountant's Responsibility

This section considers two broad topics relating to the accountant's responsibility: full disclosure and alternative techniques and the scope of the audit and audit certificate. Nineteenth century accountants were concerned with the improvement of practice in these areas and many of them, like their twentieth century counterparts, advocated more effective regulation to reduce the degrees of freedom in accounting behavior. The profession was almost unanimous in its belief that accountants should take the lead in promulgating reform. However, there was a diversity of opinion on the specific changes in practice that were needed and some cautioned that certain kinds of regulation would have undesirable consequences.

Full Disclosure and Alternative Techniques

In the last quarter of the nineteenth century debate over the interpretation of the legal requirement that "dividends must not be paid out of capital" and the determination of "profits available for dividends" were inextricably connected to the depreciation problem and other familiar subjects (Brief, 1970). During this period accountants attempted for the first time to formulate theory, to codify methodology, and to clarify their responsibility. The development of accounting was marked by angry argument, caustic rhetoric, and more important, a very sophisticated and penetrating dialogue on a wide range of subjects.

Underlying much of the debate was the belief that reported profits had an effect on investor behavior. The nature of this relationship was boldly and sarcastically described in 1837 (*Railway Magazine*, p. 2): "Let it only be seen by six months working of that line [Grand Junction] that a profit will accrue to proprietors of 8 or 10 percent per annum and there is little hazard in predicting that other lines of great intercourse will be amply supported." Thus, when a railroad charged £14,625 to capital and paid a dividend by arguing that "the efficiency and the value of the engines have been materially increased" after the severe winter of 1838, the sufficiency of disclosure and capitalization policy were criticized by the *Railway Magazine*, which stated: "a more puny and meagre document we have never witnessed" (1838, p. 189). The subject of accounting error, its economic effect, and the accountant's responsibility for this error were a source of continuing argument throughout the period (Brief, 1965).

Many accountants advocated that the profession should take the lead in writing new legislation to improve business practices. One writer put it this way (*The Accountant*, December 12, 1885):

Is there a single word in the whole of the Acts restraining the payment of dividends out of capital? There is not; what is said seems to amount to this, that the payment of dividends out of capital can be made. . . . What are accountants doing towards drawing up formal suggestions on this and other equally important points on which the Companies Acts are notoriously at fault? Not going to sleep, let us hope.

In addition, a very competitive attitude towards others, notably lawyers, also is observed in the profession's formative years. This attitude is illustrated by the common complaint that "Existing law is deplorably defective, and . . . the Chartered Accountants acting through their Institute should be the first to move in the matter, and not allow the work to be done, and the honour to be appropriated by other and less capable hands" (*The Accountant*, December 19, 1885).

At an early date *The Accountant* (April 30, 1881) stated that "If a balance sheet be correct although condensed he [the auditor] is bound to sign it" because the auditor should not publicly disagree with management. But *The Accountant* also advocated full disclosure of the amounts charged to depreciation, the method of valuation, etc.:

A shareholder is entitled to know, not what is the true value of his shares, for that in most instances is a matter of opinion, but *how* the value of fixed assets has been estimated—whether at cost, at a valuation . . . , or otherwise, and what sums have been placed in reserve or written off for depreciation, running out of leases or other decreases in value . . .

However, although the editor argues that "Much of the information . . . might be given if the legislature made its publication compulsory upon all," he also believed that "it is difficult to enforce full information without committing an act of injustice towards companies, as opposed to private concerns, which need never print any balance-sheets" (June 4, 1881).

Although many accountants, in the nineteenth century as in the twentieth, argued that legislation which increases the amount of disclosure in financial statements and reduces the number of alternative methods is a desirable goal, others, like the editor of *The Accountant*, also considered some of the undesirable by-products of achieving these objectives. The extreme position was that "as I don't approve of too much grandmotherly legislation in a free country where a people should learn from their own experience how to take care of themselves, I don't approve of the State preventing undertakings being floated with an inducement of this sort" [returning interest on capital during construction] (*The Accountant*, December 4, 1886). In the same vein, when the editor of *The Accountant* discussed (October 8, 1881) the balance sheet of John Crossley and Son, Limited, which was criticized on the basis of inadequate disclosure by the *Citizen* newspaper, he reasoned, in effect, that inadequate disclosure would increase a firm's cost of capital:

Here, indeed, the entire assets are lumped together in one line, and we infer that no outsider is expected to take shares; in fact, none but a semiprivate concern would issue such a balance sheet. Any ordinary company would assuredly separate its freehold and plant, its stock-in-trade, its book-debts, and its cash, though it might include "minerals" perhaps with freeholds. The *et cetera* at the end of the liabilities means the reserves, no doubt, against discounts, bad debts and any other drawbacks. But the true answer of the public to such a balance sheet, however respectably audited, is to respectfully let the company's shares alone. *We therefore, consider that the "dissatisfied shareholder" must be deemed a goose.* (italics added)

Dicksee, doubtless the most influential nineteenth century accountant, also questioned the effect of legislating accounting practices (*The Accountant*, March 1, 1902):

> . . . even with regard to such important questions as the value of assets, provision for depreciation, the assessments of profits earned, and the distribution of unrealised profits, the Courts have shown a marvelous disinclination [to provide] principles for the safe guidance of the auditor. . . . No doubt it has acted wisely in adopting this course, however, because any attempt to state explicitly what the duties of auditors are in all cases would afford the best possible excuse in such cases for the insufficiency of the audit that has been performed.

And seventeen years earlier Matheson, responding to a criticism of failing to specify exact methods in his book on depreciation, had the same apprehensive attitude about fixed rules (*The Accountant*, January 3, 1885):

> . . . [regarding] the absence from my book of exact rates of depreciation for different classes of plant, I am more on my ground, and I venture to assert that any positive statements of rates would be more likely to mislead than inform . . . fixed rules are impossible, and examples, if offered for imitation, dangerous.

More recently, a strikingly similar view was expressed by the Chief Accountant of the Securities Exchange Commission, John C. Burton: "He was not happy with the old 18-man, part-time board. 'By writing precise rules,' he asserted, 'the board made it possible for people to observe the letter and avoid the spirit with the blessing—and often the assistance—of their auditors' " (*The New York Times*, June 25, 1972).

There were other arguments against regulation and they concerned the depreciation problem. For example, one writer said that legal requirements to charge depreciation before declaring dividends would be "injurious to companies and the public. . . . It would stop all enterprise because it would be absolutely impossible for companies to pay dividends in the early years of their existence" (*The Accountant*, December 14, 1889). Similarly, Lord Justice Lindley, in the landmark 1889 decision in *Lee* v. *Neuchatel* (41 LR Ch. 1, 19) went so far as to argue that the legal requirement to charge depreciation regularly and periodically would "paralyze the trade of the country."

Still another argument against legally requiring depreciation, which the business historian might usefully consider, was made by "an eminent accountant in the north of England." He argued (*The Accountant*, November 29, 1884) that the provision for depreciation ("money retained out of profits"):

> enables managers and directors to undertake continual new work without consulting their shareholders. It is only another way of providing fresh capital or avoiding a call, which might be resisted by those interested if it came in that form; and further in cases where you have several classes of shares upon which the capital is not equally paid up, or where you have debenture holders as well as ordinary shareholders, the rights of the respective parties are prejudicially affected by what can only be styled the misappropriation of funds intended for a specific object.

There were differences of opinion among accountants over basic questions and they were vigorously debated. However, judicial and statutory authority did not play a significant role in resolving these differences (Brief, 1966). Rather, the profession attempted to establish the limits of its own responsibility and the aims were, according to Dicksee (1915, p. xiv), somewhat Utopian:[1]

> If it should be thought that the standard I have throughout advocated is somewhat Utopian in character, and unattainable in practice, I can only reply that I maintain that, to me, an incomplete investigation seems worse than useless, and I am convinced that it is only by voluntarily accepting, and even increasing, the responsibilities of our position that we can hope to maintain and to increase the large measure of public confidence we at present enjoy.

Throughout the period, accountants

[1] The quote is taken from the preface to the first edition (1892) which was reprinted in subsequent editions.

fought to establish the profession as a permanent institution, but the battle still rages to determine whether "the honour [will be] appropriated by other and less capable hands."

It is now likely that unless accountants and their corporate clients take the initiative in reducing the number of acceptable accounting practices, financial disclosure will become much more a matter of law. There seems to be increasing pressure to limit the diversity of accounting methods by establishing an arbitrary set of rules. . . . If the accounting profession does not do so, "its position of eminence may be lost to those who seize the larger opportunity"[2] (Chatfield, 1974, p. 280).

Although the business setting has changed, nineteenth century debate on disclosure and alternative methods has a modern tone and many of the issues before the profession in the present day are those which concerned its original members. How can disclosure be improved? How much disclosure is desirable? How can the range of accounting alternatives be reduced? What are the effects of regulation? Then, as now, accountants were searching for satisfactory answers to these questions. Nineteenth century debate on the audit certificate is also relevant to today's problems.

Scope of Audit and Audit Certificate

The pure laissez-faire attitude in the last century towards the scope of the audit was illustrated in the early legal case of *Turquand* v. *Marshall* which was decided in 1869 (20 LT 766):

As to the publication of false balance sheets and including in them debts which were hopelessly bad, it was difficult to say where a debt was hopeless; and besides, if any shareholders were deceived into buying shares he might have his separate remedy, but each would have a different case, and the whole body could not sue.

The debtor in this case was the Confederacy! However, although the courts generally did not interfere in business affairs, accountants and other groups were more active in their advocacy of reform, and the audit and related problems quickly became a major issue which was actively discussed.

As early as 1883 there was an interesting controversy on the audit, sparked by a series of articles in a magazine called *Vanity Fair*. Significantly, *The Accountant* reprinted them in entirety, even though the comments were harshly critical of accounting practice.

Apparently, *Vanity Fair* thought that "auditors' certificates might be longer and better" and "legislation is needed" to achieve this objective. However, the editor of *The Accountant* argued that "In a simple matter such as an auditor's certificate we fail to see why any legal interference is called for. What the public and shareholders want is a readable assurance from the accountants, stating in plain English what they really have done" (October 27, 1883). With great sarcasm, the editor elaborated on this point (November 3, 1883):

We would suggest that in future the auditors' certificates should, in accordance with the defense now made for them, run thus:—We having been allowed to audit not from month to month, but only once a year; having had too little time to make an exhaustive report, because the documents are required for the printer; knowing that shareholders are generally impatient to get through the business; being paid a fee out of all proportion to the work required to be done; and being aware that the voting power is in the abso-

[2] Chatfield is quoting from Mautz and Sharaf (1961, p. 200). Similar comments can be found elsewhere. For example, Hawkins (1963, p. 168) commented, "Once more, the possibility of further government intervention in industrial reporting matters is imminent, principally because of the accounting profession's inability to narrow the areas of difference in accounting principles and management's resistance to its critics' demands for improved corporate disclosure." The same idea is echoed by *Business Week* (April 22, 1972). "Before such sweeping moves are widely demanded, the Wheat proposals give the accounting profession another chance to demonstrate that workable accounting and auditing procedures can be set in the private sector, with the broad-based cooperation of accountants, financial executives, security analysts, and educators."

lute control of the Board—certify that, so far as we, under these disabilities, can ascertain and dare disclose the facts, it is all right. This would at any rate let shareholders know from the certificate, as we know from the general chorus of certifiers, what the true meaning and value of the certificate really amounts to. Our complaint was and is that at present they do not know this, but that they are led and are meant to imagine that bladders are lanterns and auditors' certificates proofs of all excellences and complete solvency and security. . . .

We are not to be drawn off the scent by any invitation to discuss the powers of auditors or the technicalities of auditing. That is not the question. The question is—What is worth, and what, therefore, the use of an auditorial certificate in its various forms as it is now commonly given? We say it is worth next to nothing. Our critics say, not that it is worth much, but that it is very hard to make it worth anything. Very well. Then we and our critics are agreed. The certificate *is* worth next to nothing, and this being so, it is a delusion and a snare.

Then, in response to a letter, the editor of *The Accountant* argued that to remedy the audit's deficiencies, a direct approach was called for: "Cease making those damnable faces which are called Auditors' Certificates." Rather than paraphrase, these remarks are quoted in entirety in order to give the flavor of the lively debate which took place during the profession's first decade of development:

There is however one correspondent of *The Accountant* who signs himself "Anti-Twaddle," and who deserves special remark. He is very rude, but not more rude than illogical and ungrammatical. He too sets forth the difficulties of the poor auditor, and so feelingly that he has evidently suffered from them. The auditor gets no power, no time, and no money to talk of; he is not responsible except for the verification of figures put before him; he is the slave of the directors, who do not like to look at the worst side of affairs, and he has to satisfy also the shareholders, for we believe that if they have sometimes a strong objection to knowing the truth, they have at least as often as strong an objection to having lies told to them. And it is quite clear that, if this venerable Aunty were herself set to audit accounts and to frame thereon an auditorial certificate, she would unhesitatingly avoid any difference of opinion with directors, would carefully abstain from looking at the worst side of affairs, would very generously indulge the shareholders' strong objection to knowing the truth, and would, in spite of the insufficient time, power, and money, frame and publish a certificate that would make everything pleasant for everybody, and above all for Aunty. This is exactly what we complain of.

And yet, in spite of this injurious disclosure of the way in which certificates are moulded from the dirty mud of facts by the Sculptor-Director, and invested with artistic merit by the Ghost-Auditor, Aunty wants to have herself fastened on all concerns by an Act of Parliament which shall supersede directors and everybody else, and make Aunty a first charge on the concern, just as though she were an official liquidator or trustee. And she proposes that *we* should get her Act passed for her! No; we cannot do this. On the contrary, we say—Amend your certificates and not your Statutes; tell the truth if you know it, and shame the Director. If you don't know and can't find out—why say that; but in any case, cease making those merely damnable faces which are now called Auditors' Certificates. (November 3, 1883)

Some leading accountants took a constructive view of this criticism. Thomas Welton, President of the Institute of Chartered Accountants in England and Wales in 1891–2, believed that *The Accountant's* remarks on the auditors' certificate "would do great good even if they did no more than induce shareholders to more closely scan the wording of these documents . . . " (October 27, 1883). But the basic complaint was that accountants lacked authority to impose exacting standards. For example, the problem of requiring firms to charge "adequate" depreciation was of great concern in those days and Pixley (1887, p. 127) complained that "It is in the earlier years of a company's existence the auditor has the greatest difficulty in inducing Directors to charge an amount sufficient to provide for the past depreciation of the period." A similar comment appears in the preface to the second edition of the first book on depreciation (Matheson, 1910, p. ix–x): "Auditors, and especially those who have to deal with joint stock or other concerns, where the remuneration of the management is made wholly or partly dependent upon declared profits, know in what varied forms resistance to an adequate charge against profits for Depreciation is presented."

This conflict between the accountant and management, and its effect on the accountant's responsibility to shareholders, was recognized in the first years of the profession's existence, and questions relating to the auditor's independence were connected to the proxy system which permitted persons in fiduciary positions to vote on matters affecting their own interest. Once again, *The Accountant* (October 27, 1883) identified a critical problem:

> The audit of Public Companies' accounts was designed to control and check the action of directors in their administration of the affairs of Public Companies: and yet, as a rule, the auditors who are chosen for this purpose owe their employment to the very directors whom they are presumed so to control and check in the interests of the shareholders. This is one of the evils arising out of the proxy system, which I trust we may some day see abolished, as being utterly pernicious and vicious in root and branch. It should be laid down as an invariable rule that directors, trustees, or other persons in fiduciary positions should never be allowed the direct or indirect use of proxies in voting, or in fact to vote personally, on any subject affecting the performance of the duties imposed upon them by the trusts under which they act, or on the passing of the accounts as presented by them to their proprietary or *cestui que* trust.

This problem of the auditor's autonomy remains a topic of current interest, and recent suggestions for reform (Hawes, 1974) echo *The Accountant's* earlier argument:

> At a time when auditors are subject to a staggering number of lawsuits, intense pressures from managements to adopt accounting treatment that will put the best face on the financial statements and the difficult task of codifying accounting principles, legislation is needed to make stockholder approval of the appointment of auditors mandatory.
>
> Such legislation would underscore the fact that the auditor's client is the stockholders and thus would have an important therapeutic effect on the corporation.

This historical review of the audit certificate and scope of audit has demonstrated that many modern problems are not new. From the first, accountants recognized the limitations of the audit certificate and they raised questions concerning the auditor's independence. Many recommended more effective regulation but some took a more straightforward approach: "Amend your certificates and not your statutes." In summarizing this section, one conclusion is inescapable. After nearly a century of debate,

> . . . there is still no comprehensive, integrated statement of concepts on which accountants and statement readers can agree and rely. There is still no consensus as to the exact meaning of the standard audit opinion that financial statements present the results of operations "fairly" in accordance with generally accepted accounting principles. One result is that accounting methods have changed much more slowly than the accounting environment. And the profession has not solved its basic problems of disclosure, consistency and statement comparability (Chatfield, 1974, pp. 298–99).

The thesis of this paper is that accounting controversy persists because profit calculations involve "uncertainty about the future." The next section surveys the attitude toward the accountant's responsibility for estimates and forecasts.

Attitude Toward Accountant's Responsibility for Estimates and Forecasts

In the discussion that follows it should be borne in mind that a formal framework for studying decision problems under uncertainty has become generally available only in the last decade or so. Therefore, nineteenth century accountants quite naturally made an effort to avoid uncertainty-related problems. Nevertheless, these early theorists did begin to discuss topics related to the subject, and their attitude towards them had a significant influence on the progress in accounting.

Historical Attitude Toward Uncertainty

One of the earliest references to the problem of uncertainty in accounting can be found in a series of articles on audits which appeared in several 1881 issues of *The Accountant.* Referring to balance sheet audits, the editor asserted (April 23, 1881) "that the real object to be aimed at is such a verification that will be practically sufficient." The auditor's task is then compared to a judge and jury who are often obliged to be content with "little more than a reasonable probability." Thus, at the end of a period "some matters outstanding . . . must be introduced by estimation . . . to make the apparent profit a real measure of what has been accomplished in the period under review." However, the auditor should not "indulge in forecasts or in expressions of feeling, but rather adhere as coldly and impassively as he can to facts—hard, dry realities."

This logical contradiction between the necessity to make estimates and the adherence to dry realities is not resolved, but the writer does suggest a "trend analysis" for specific problems like estimating "probable losses" such as "bad and doubtful debts." Since the facts "keep changing almost hourly," the auditor should study past trends and advocate reserves in good years to be used in years when losses exceed the average. However, when a loss is certain, "no rule can be laid down," but "broad principles" which "favour moderation in the distribution of dividends, and . . . ample reserves is [sic] desirable. Yet he should likewise remember the possibility of excess in the latter direction" which might induce shareholders "to part with their shares at an insufficient valuation."

The principle of conservatism and the auditor's responsibility for estimates is discussed again (June 4, 1881):

> Generally he [the shareholder] should be enabled to see in the balance sheet which of the assets are matters of opinion, and which are matters of fact. When this part of the subject is clear, little doubt can rest upon the estimate of profit or loss, which may be deemed correct or otherwise according to the spirit in which matters of opinion are apparently handled.
>
> Estimates are often proper things to make use of, where they relate to subsidiary matters, and enables the balance sheet to be speedily prepared, but all estimates should be slightly to the disadvantage of the company, rather than tending the other way.

In the first paper on the ethics of accountancy in 1888 (*The Accountant,* December 12, 1888), John Mather flatly opposed any idea of chance or uncertainty in accounting However, once again, the views on this subject are not perfectly consistent:

> What is called the "glorious uncertainty of the Law"—illustrated not only in the varying interpretations of enactments, but often in the evidence of opposing experts in law suits—conveys an idea that rarely attaches to the figures, statements, or certificates of Chartered Accountants. And it is our hope and belief, that as we succeed in gradually raising the standard of the skill and the ethics of the profession, any such idea of chance or uncertainty will be still more foreign to its work in the future.

In other words, "There seems a general agreement that . . . the accountant may not prophecy 'unless he knows' . . . he must avoid the tempting region of fancy and stick to the prosaic facts." Stated differently, "in most cases an accountant is no better able than other people to forecast the business prospects of an undertaking which, however sound at the outset, may ultimately fail through mismanagement, change of fashion, invalidity of patents, or numberless unforeseen causes." Yet, according to Mather, the accountant, "in the opinion of many . . . is fully justified in dealing with those facts in their bearing upon the future . . . ." But how can the accountant do this if he must stick to the prosaic facts?

Further insight into the accountant's conflicting attitudes towards uncertainty is provided by Dickinson twenty-six years later. In concluding a discussion of the accountant's responsibility for earnings projections Dickinson (1914, pp. 226–27) said that:

It should be clear, therefore, from the above considerations that any estimate of future earnings must necessarily depend upon so many contingencies that it would hardly seem desirable that it should be put forth without calling specific attention to the assumptions involved; and an estimate with such qualification attached would hardly be of much service to the promoter and would not be incorporated in the prospectus.

However,

In as much as the community is being educated to consider that statements emanating from a public accountant deal only with facts, it may be said in conclusion that in such a case as that supposed, the accountant's duty should end with the submission on request of a carefully prepared estimate, accompanied by all necessary qualifications, without, however, any certificate there to . . . . (italics added)

Even though Dickinson rejects the inclusion of estimates in the prospectus, his proposal that all estimates should be accompanied by the assumptions on which they are based reflects modern thinking on the subject. Of greater significance, however, is his remark concerning the effort *to educate* the community that financial statements deal only with facts. It suggests that a conscious attempt was made by the profession to convince the public that the accountant is responsible only for "facts," and it also helps to explain why so many generations have come to regard accounting as an essentially historical discipline.

At the same time, accountants understood the tenuous nature of their argument. Even Dickinson (p. 236) recognized that "Every balance sheet is a matter of opinion." But he failed to make any explicit connection between the problems which require the accountant to exercise his "opinion" and the conditions which give rise to these problems—namely, uncertainty about the future.

These references to the uncertainty problem are generally in terms of estimating balances in asset and liability accounts at the end of each period. This perspective is consistent with a balance sheet approach to income determination. However, there were also discussions about another class of estimation and forecasting problems in accounting and they concerned the relationship between reported profits and future profits.

The first of these provides an amusing illustration of the "interim reporting problem." In 1883 The Hotels and City Properties Share Trust, Limited issued a four-month report and estimated the year's results by doubling the figures for the interim period. *The Accountant* (October 27, 1883) published a scathing criticism of this report:

Mr. Daniels has furnished the public with the result of working the Royal during the best four months of the year. But are we to understand that he pledges his professional reputation that *any* appreciable profit can be made during the remaining eight months, when Southend is little better than a howling wilderness, and when a stray Londoner at the Royal is looked upon with as much curiosity as if he were a friendly Zulu? During those dark and dreary months is there not an entire absence of excursionists, and as a rule are not the only occupants and best customers of that spacious bar which the prospectus says is a great source of profit, the neglected piermaster and the boatman?

In another reference to this general subject, Montgomery (1909, p. 324) seems to argue that the purpose of reporting the results of operations in past periods is to predict profits of future periods:

the certificate, therefore, should be a clear and unconditional certificate of accomplished facts, and not a mere estimate of possible—or even probable—future results, misnamed a "certificate." To the limited extent already mentioned it may be permissible, and even desirable, to modify the past results so that they may more usefully serve the purpose for which they are primarily intended—namely, provide a reliable index of future profits. But at the same time a certificate should relate not to the future, but to the past. . . .

Although Montgomery argues unequivocally that financial statements should reflect "accomplished facts," i.e., financial statements should be historical, he also points out that the primary purpose of reporting past results is to provide an index (estimate) of future profits. Clearly, the methods used to calculate past performance will influence this "index," but questions about this relationship were not raised.

Effect on Modern Accounting Thought

The early ideas on uncertainty and its relevance to accounting have not changed very much in the twentieth century. There are few extended discussions of the subject in modern texts and theoretical treatises and most references to the uncertainty problem are vague and ambiguous.

For example, van Pelt (1972, pp. 13–4) defines profitability as the "excess of revenues . . . over *known* costs . . . " (italics added), but also states that "estimates . . . will be required for the purpose of allocating costs." The *APB Accounting Principles* (1973, 1, p. 15) states that "Accountants have considered themselves primarily historians, not prophets . . . . However, *even* present accounting practices require estimates of the future" (italics added). How are estimates used in allocating costs? Which accounting practices require estimates of the future? What quantities must be estimated? What assumptions are the estimates based on? What estimating procedures are used? Questions such as these, and there are many others, have rarely been asked.

This historical review of the accountant's attitude towards uncertainty shows that the profession has always recognized that many of the numbers in financial statements are based on estimates of uncertain future events. At the same time, it also indicates that many accountants repeatedly stated that the accounts should reflect "prosaic facts" and "dry realities." This attitude toward uncertainty dominated thought; accountants, as well as the public, have been educated to believe that financial statements are essentially historical.

In the final section this attitude towards uncertainty is at least partly explained by the legal origin of the modern corporate concept of profit.

Uncertainty and the Corporate Concept of Profit

It is uncertainty about the future that makes profit a return for risk bearing (Edwards and Bell, 1961, p. 9). It is also uncertainty about the future that provides the *logical* motivation for calculating the "profit of a period," and the common procedure in accounting of assuming certainty about the future completely obscures the information content of period earnings reports (Brief and Owen, 1970, p. 167). Thus, by assuming that the future is known with certainty (or by deemphasizing and minimizing the importance of uncertainty), accountants have eliminated, or at least have obscured, that which they set out to measure.

However, as a practical matter, the origin of the modern corporate concept of profit is in dividend law, not accounting, and the purpose of this legislation was to protect the rights of creditors and different classes of shareholders. This legal origin of the profit concept had an important influence on accounting.

Kehl (1941, p. 14) indicates that "During the 1600's charters began including dividend regulations among their provisions. The most common limitation required that dividends be paid from profits. Such was the restriction used in 1620 in the charter of James I to the New River Company." And "By 1700, there had already been adopted in England two statutory standards, one or the other of which still controls dividend distributions under present day statutes in a great many American states" (Kehl, p. 4).

This legislation governing the payment of dividends produced the "capital impairment rule" and the "profits tests" which were the first statutory references to the modern corporate concept of profit. Dividends cannot be paid out of capital and/or dividends must be paid out of the *profit of a period.*

Historically, railroads, utilities, and other quasi-public enterprise used a cash receipts-less-disbursements method of calculating profit. This method implied that the value of assets was "permanent." And although it became evident that this assumption was not valid, the cameralistic origin of the method seems to have blocked accounting reform for this class of enterprise.

The profit calculations of other firms are more difficult to assess. At the beginning of the nineteenth century the "inventory method" was employed. This method was a balance sheet (direct valuation) approach to profit determination. Eventually, this method was replaced by the modern accounting concept of profit that assumes a going concern and computes profit by "matching" revenues and expenses. All of these approaches have been sanctioned by the courts at various times (Brief, 1966).

Leake (1912, p. 2) correctly observed that "when commerce was carried on by individuals, each on his own account, in a vast number of small undertakings, and there was no regular income tax, it was a matter of small moment . . . whether the surplus of receipts . . . was economic profits." On the other hand, the coming of modern corporation and the development of capital markets interacted with dividend law to make the concept of a year's profit one of the most important ideas in economics and, as May (1936, II, p. 307) put it, "the central question of modern accounting." Yet, Hatfield's comment (1927, p. 241) about the profit concept is as valid today as it was nearly fifty years ago:

> It is a peculiar fact that while all business is carried on for the purpose of securing profits, while the distribution of profits is continually the subject of controversy in the courts, while the ascertainment of profits enters largely into the discussion of every economist, the term is still vaguely and loosely used and without definition by either economist, man of affairs, jurist or accountant.

Thus, whereas dividend law conditioned businessmen, investors, and creditors to think in terms of the concept of "profit of a period," traditional accounting models that attempt to explain operationally the meaning of this concept in the context of the modern firm have been unsatisfactory. And as long as the term, "profit," is vaguely and loosely used and without definition, all areas of accounting responsibility that touch on questions concerning profit calculations must be a continuing source of controversy and dispute. This controversy will not subside until accountants become willing to acknowledge that in theory it is uncertainty about the future, not dividend law, that gives rise to the problem of determining the profit of a period.

Conclusion

Accounting thought in the nineteenth century is especially relevant to contemporary issues because the laissez-faire business environment produced a free and uninhibited exchange of views. The courts at this time were reluctant to interfere in business affairs and, unless fraud were an issue, business practices were determined by businessmen. Similarly, the statutes did not lay down specific rules governing accounting practices, and quasi-judicial administrative bodies such as the Securities Exchange Commission did not yet exist.

The last two decades of the nineteenth century were a "golden age" in accounting and most of the major issues connected with the subject of the accountant's responsibility were brought out in the period. Questions concerning full disclosure, alternative techniques, scope of audit and the meaning of the audit certificate were widely discussed in the first few years after the profession was formally established.

However, nineteenth century accountants did not "solve" most of the problems which they debated. One explanation for the perennial nature of controversy is the accountant's early attitude toward uncertainty. During the last century, the profession began to emphasize the historical nature of accounting calculations even though many theorists recognized that forecasts and estimates were inherent in most problems.

Thus one explanation for the persistence of accounting controversy is the failure to recognize that profit calculations involve uncertainty about the future. But given the legal origin of the profit concept, it is not surprising to find that accountants became more concerned with statutory and judicial references to profit than with the more abstruse questions associated with an uncertain future. What implications can be drawn from this historical study of the accountant's responsibility?

First, many modern proposals for reform can be traced directly to the nineteenth century. Indeed, the basic perspective of the accountant's responsibility has not changed very much, and recent suggestions for improving practice often repeat earlier ideas. Thus even though the economic environment was very different 100 years ago, the basic problems in accounting today closely resemble those which confronted the profession in the last century. Therefore, regulation and legislation do not seem to have produced many of the improvements in practice which were expected.

Second, there is recent evidence that the accounting profession's attitude toward uncertainty may be changing. The report of the Study Group on the Objectives of Financial Statements (1973) gives explicit attention to the problem of forecasting future cash flows. And the Forecasting Task Force of the MAS Development and Liaison Subcommittee of the AICPA (1974) considered questions concerning past profit as an "index" of future profit. This work could produce a radical change in the concept of profit.

If direct forecasts of cash flows and other information about the future are given in financial reports, the modern corporate concept of profit might become obsolete as a measure of either past performance or as an index of future performance. In the last analysis, a firm's performance depends on its cash flows, and if information about cash flows were provided by accountants, what purpose would be served by reporting profit figures that are based on conventional methods in accounting? And what purpose would be served by forecasting future profits, if direct estimates of future cash flows already were available? Questions like these will inevitably arise when more attention is devoted to the subject of uncertainty.[3]

Third, if the traditional opposition to forecasting and estimation overrides the current effort being made in some quarters to integrate forecasting and estimation problems within the mainstream of accounting theory, then the lesson of history will not have been learned. For most de-

[3] See, e.g., Thomas (1974).

bate in accounting inevitably must lead to a discussion of uncertainty about the future. This is the one area of thought which nineteenth century accountants were unable to deal with, and twentieth century accountants have not yet faced the problem squarely.

REFERENCES

Committee Reports:

American Institute of Certified Public Accountants, Study Group on the Objectives of Financial Statements, *Objectives of Financial Statements* (1973).

American Institute of Certified Public Accountants, Forecasting Task Force of the MAS Development and Liaison Subcommittee, March 28, 1974 Exposure Draft, *Standards for Systems for the Preparation of Financial Forecasts* (1974).

Journal Articles:

Brief, R. P., "Nineteenth Century Accounting Error," *Journal of Accounting Research* (Spring 1965), pp. 167–77.

———, "The Origin and Evolution of Nineteenth Century Asset Accounting," *Business History Review* (Spring 1966), pp. 1–23.

———, "Depreciation Theory in Historical Perspective," *The Accountant* (December 26, 1970), pp. 737–39.

——— and Owen, J., "The Estimation Problem in Financial Accounting," *Journal of Accounting Research* (Autumn 1970), pp. 167–78.

Hawes, D. W., "Towards a More Muscular Audit," New York *Times*, April 14, 1974.

Hawkins, D. F., "The Development of Modern Financial Reporting Practices Among American Manufacturing Corporations," *Business History Review* (Autumn 1963), pp. 135–168.

van Pelt III, J. V., "The Future of Accepted Accounting Principles," A Digest of the 1971–72 Gold Medal Award Winning Article, *Management Accounting* (August 1972), pp. 11–14.

Books:

Chatfield, M., *A History of Accounting Thought* (Dryden Press, 1974).

Dickinson, A. L., *Accounting Practice and Procedure* (Ronald Press, 1914).

Dicksee, L. R., *Auditing*, 10th ed., (Gee & Co., 1915).

Edwards, E. O. and Bell, P. W., *The Theory and Measurement of Business Income* (University of California Press, 1965).

Hatfield, H. R., *Modern Accounting—Its Principles and Some of Its Problems* (D. Appleton & Co., 1927).

Kehl, D., *Corporate Dividends—Legal and Accounting Problems Pertaining to Corporate Distributions* (Ronald Press, 1941).

Leake, P. D., *Depreciation and Wasting Assets* (Henry Good & Son, 1912).

Matheson, E., *Depreciation of Factories*, 4th ed., (E. & F. Spon, 1910).

Pixley, F. W., *Auditors: Their Duties and Responsibilities*, 4th ed., (Henry Good & Son, 1887).

Edited Books:

May, G. O., *Twenty-Five Years of Accounting Responsibility 1911–1936*, B. S. Hunt, ed. (American Institute Publishing Co., 1936).

Montgomery, R. H. ed., *Dicksee's Auditing*, 2nd ed. (New York, 1909).

Series:

APB Accounting Principles, Current Text as of June 30, 1973 (Commerce Clearing House, 1973).

Mautz, R. K. and Sharaf, H. A., *The Philosophy of Auditing*, American Accounting Association Monograph Number Six (American Accounting Association, 1961).

Thomas, A. L., *The Allocation Problem: Part II*, Studies in Accounting Research #9 (American Accounting Association, 1974).

RICHARD P. BRIEF

VALUATION, MATCHING, AND EARNINGS: THE CONTINUING DEBATE

In the history of accounting thought there is no other subject that has been more controversial than the determination of earnings (or income, profit, etc.) and the related problems of valuation and matching. The debate began over a century ago and since that time accountants, lawyers, government agencies, businessmen, the judiciary, educators and researchers have been asking what is income and how is it calculated?

The most recent effort to develop a conceptual framework for understanding the income concept was made by the Financial Accounting Standards Board (FASB, 1976). However, aside from a few references to the ideas of accountants writing in the nineteen thirties, almost all of the material cited in this study is of recent vintage. Thus, although the conceptual framework focuses on alternative approaches to income determination, it does not deal explicitly with historical evidence relating to these alternatives. Furthermore, while the study is concerned with the objectives of financial statements and the income concept, it does not examine either the factors which originally motivated the corporate concept of income or the events which led to the modern emphasis on current period income as a predictor of future earning power.

The purpose of this paper is to examine in a general historical perspective the alternative approaches to income determination, which the FASB discusses. They are the cost principle and matching versus the asset and liability view. Greater attention to the history of accounting and to the development of accounting thought should provide some additional insight into our present situation and, perhaps, an improved ability to predict future events in the field.

The first section of this paper highlights the transition from valuation to matching and summarizes several nineteenth century articles on the valuation problem to illustrate the continuing nature of the debate on the subject. The second section traces briefly the history of the income concept and shows that the original objective of income calculations was to determine the dividend fund; however, the phenomenon of reinvested earnings led to a reinterpretation of income in the twentieth century. Finally, we point out that there is still a need to develop a theoretical framework for understanding the income concept and several ideas which need further thought are mentioned.

The Transition from Valuation to Matching

In practice, the essential difference between the concepts of income as a change in a firm's value and as revenues less expenses is rather blurred. It can be argued that for valuation approaches, the definition of assets and liabilities determine income whereas for matching, income depends on the definition of revenues and expenses. However, it is obvious that the definition of revenues and expenses implicitly defines assets and liabilities.

Thus, the distinction between valuation and matching is really a matter of emphasis, although it is clear that the "inventory method," which was a balance sheet (valuation) approach, dominated in accounting until the nineteenth century.

Evidence to support this conclusion is found in the work of de Roover, Yamey, Littleton, Pollard and others.[1] Their research suggests that early manufacturers, trading companies, etc., defined profit as the change in the "value" of net assets in two successive periods. Quasi-public enterprises, like railroads and utilities, generally did not value assets; these firms used a form of replacement accounting, essentially a cash-based methodology for income determination.[2]

The fact that accounting practices for a large subset of firms required valuation of assets does not mean that an accounting concept of value was defined with precision. Assets might have been valued "at your discretion," with reference to "present value," as "cost or value," "as might be desired," or "at market value" (Brief, 1965, p. 22). Obviously, the word "value," even if preceded by a descriptive term, has a great many meanings, both in practice and in the law; and ambiguity in the meaning of the term always will be a problem connected with any accounting concept based on it.

The "modern" origin of the matching and cost principles can be traced to the last quarter of the nineteenth century. As one writer put it, "The simplest and broadest principle for regulating value and depreciation might be said to be its known capacity under normal circumstances to produce profit, subject, however, to its cost being used as the maximum value" (*The Accountant,* November 5, 1887). Others simply said that "it is not safe to take value as a basis" and Dicksee called the valuation approach "theoretically perfect but defective in practice" (Brief, 1966, p. 8). However, the matching of revenues and expenses to determine income evolved only slowly in business practice. As Edey and Panipakdi (1956) conclude, "There is, in fact, little doubt that this general idea of profit measurement as a comparison of valuations in successive periods was accepted from the beginning of our period" [1844-1900].

A series of articles by Ernest Cooper and Thomas Welton at the end of the nineteenth century illustrates the conflict over valuation problems in which accountants found themselves. Both Cooper and Welton were Past Presidents of the Institute of Chartered Accountants in England and Wales.

Cooper's first paper, "What is the Profit of a Company?," was reprinted in *The Accountant* (November 10, 1883).[3] His main argument was that "every accretion to the capital of a Companies Act Company is profit, and that profit is the surplus of assets over the liabilities, including with the liabilities the paid up capital, and that the amount of profit is arrived at by ascertaining that surplus after fairly estimating the value of all assets and liabilities." However Cooper rejected the idea of using replacement and exit values. As he put it, "Is a tramway or a Factory Company required . . . to consider for what the factory could be replaced, if destroyed, and then to value no higher than the cost of replacement?" The answer was negative for a "temporary" fall in value for permanent and nonmarketable assets. Exit values also were inappropriate: "Nor is it necessary to consider for what the property will sell, for a buyer of an unmarketable asset is not usually forthcoming . . . ."

Welton responded with a paper, "On the Profit of Companies Available for Distribution" (*The Accountant,* December 13, 1890). He argued the "public interest is not served by a continual revaluation of the permanent assets of a company" and that "No purpose is to be served by such revaluation, for it could not on any sound principle affect the distributions of dividends, nor would it prevent the market value from fluctuating daily, just as much as it does now." Therefore, "It follows...that in a Balance Sheet none of these items ought to be regarded as more than book figures."

For Welton, profit was measured as a change in value, but only "upon realisation." He justified this view by arguing that:

> To pretend 'to take into account' the value of all liabilities and assets in ascertaining profits...means, either to value the assets as I should do, or else (if the value means cash value) to do the very thing I have ventured to assume that no practical man would do, namely, to re-value not only tangible assets, but goodwill, at every balancing, and thus to show on the Balance Sheet a capital (including reserves) about equal to the market price of the stock.

Cooper's response was rather sarcastic (*The Accountant,* January 3, 1891).

> Whereas I sought to ascertain by what principles we are bound in ascertaining profit, whether by Statutes and judicial interpretation of them, or by custom and usage, Mr. Welton has taken far higher ground. To quote his words (p. 1), he weighs the question as one of "public policy," (p. 2), he seeks "what is best for the nation," and he points out "where (p. 4) the public interest is not served,"...
>
> Now some of these things may, or may not, have to do with what is available or distributable or divisible profit, but they have nothing whatever to do with the question, "What is Profit?"

In another paper, "Chartered Accountants and the Profit Question" (*The Accountant,* November 24, 1894), Cooper reviewed several judicial decisions to support his view that profit was the change in the net value of assets and liabilities, i.e., capital implies a measure of wealth, and the words Profit and Loss imply increase of wealth and diminution of wealth." Thus, whereas Welton accepted the fact that a balance sheet contained "book figures," Cooper believed that assets and liabilities are essentially wealth concepts. Therefore, he recommended the terms not be used because... "various items are found on both sides of Balance Sheets which are not strictly liabilities or assets."

C.R. Trevor, a discussant of Cooper's paper, rejected this argument and advocated a full disclosure of the fact that assets and liabilities are "book" values, not "real" values.

> ...in his judgment, lawyers and accountants went a good deal beyond their scope when they talked about making valuation. It certainly seemed to be the case that Chartered Accountants and auditors generally had got into the habit of allowing the public to believe that they were valuers when they were nothing of the sort. He thought they would find that as accountants they would get into very troubled waters unless they plainly stated, where they were asked to make an audit or to certify a Balance Sheet, that such Balance Sheet had been made without any responsibility being taken as regards the real value of the assets.

Of course, the waters are no calmer now. Terms like exit value, current value, replacement value and present value can be traced to the early literature, but we are not much closer to a resolution of the valuation problem than these nineteenth century accountants. Aside from demonstrating that "history repeats itself," are there any lessons that can be learned from this summary review?

First the cost principle and matching concept are not archaic relics of the past. In the development of accounting thought, valuation has been the dominant method of income determination; the cost principle is of comparatively recent origin. Thus, while experimentation with different concepts of value can provide data for evaluating current alternatives, there is data available in historical records that could have important implications for policy makers today.[4]

Second, there seems to be a general misconception about the evolution of the cost principle and matching. Ijiri, and no doubt many others, have said that historical cost valuation has been the "backbone of conventional accounting over many centuries" and that "only hardcore traditionalists seem to uphold historical cost" (Ijiri, p. 85). But historical cost and matching have been the backbone of accounting for less than a century. Therefore, the so-called traditionalists are really neoclassicists. This means that leading valuationists like Chambers, Sterling, and Edwards and Bell might be considered as advocates of a more classical doctrine.

Third, the matching and cost principles, which obviously have not produced ideal results, ought to be recognized as an ingenious solution to the "problem of value."[5] At the same time, it is difficult to understand, based on the historical evidence, why a valuation approach to income determination would "bring more rigor or discipline into accounting in the sense that some of the latitude presently permitted by the twin concepts of *proper matching* and *nondistortion of periodic net income* would be limited."

In any event, the controversy over different approaches to income determination is often confused with the questions, what is income and why is income calculated every year? In the next section, we investigate the evolution of the income concept in terms of the objectives of an interim reporting, e.g., annual reporting, apart from the methodology used to determine annua income.

The Earnings Concept in Historical Perspective

It may be instructive to begin this discussion of the income concept by referring to the accounting of the early adventurers in the Middle Ages, who, according to Ten Have (1976, p. 13), were "interested only in the value of the cargo at the time of homecoming." Interim income calculations were not made and the venture or voyage accounts were closed only when the entire venture was completed (p. 39).

Ten Have explains this behavior in terms of uncertainty about the future.

> One must not reproach the autocrats too strongly for not preparing balance sheets. What is the value on a given date, of cargo on its return voyage, considering that prices have already been falling with the news that a fleet was homebound? What is the value of the settlements, fortresses, ships and what not? Transmitting a message to the home country required about nine months; a storm on the ocean might cause an enormous profit to revert to a loss (p. 54).

Yamey (1964) also found that until 1800 firms generally did not calculate interim income numbers and that, if they did, it was likely that such calculations were made to check the accuracy of the books rather than to provide information useful for decision making. But Yamey explains that "This does not mean, however, that some businessmen may not from time to time review their overall business results and financial position." Adding, "...such periodic reviews, whatever satisfaction they may afford the businessman, are not likely to bear on the taking of particular decisions affecting the deployment of resources" (pp. 120-21).

Aside from "satisfaction," what created the need for periodic interim reports of income? Ten Have finds that as early as the fourteenth century, the associations of Italian merchants required an interim accounting for income to effect "dividend" distributions before a venture was terminated. And by the 1600s, corporate charters regularly began including dividend regulations among their provisions. The most common limitations required that dividends be paid from income (Kehl, 1941, p. 4).

Thus, although our conclusion is really a hypothesis, it seems reasonable to argue that secondary securities markets and regular dividend distributions institutionalized the need to make interim calculations of income. Of course, not all dividend distributions were accompanied by income statements, nor were all interim periods initially defined as one year. But when accountants first began to discuss the problem of income, they usually linked it to the question of dividends.

The great debate over what is income began in the late nineteenth century. The major issue usually concerned the amount of money that could legally be distributed to shareholders and this question, in turn, was related to the protection of creditors. But, as Yamey observes,

> Nowhere in the succession of Companies Act can any direct reference to the nature of the dividend fund be found. The legislature has thought it unnecessary or unwise to lay down definite rules or even general principles for the computation of the fund. It has been left to the judges to settle the questions which were bound to arise. The judges, however, could not or were not disposed to devise rules without attempting to justify them by reference to the supposed intentions of the legislature, on a matter on which it had never expressed its

opinion. It was believed that its view on dividends could be devined from the tenor and general provisions of the Acts. And history has shown that a reading of the Acts could suggest different intentions on the part of the legislature to different judges (1962, pp. 428-29).

This direct relationship between the income concept and dividends also was mentioned by Littleton, who wrote, "In the original joint stock companies the expectation was that the entire profit would be distributed at frequent intervals...When the idea fell into disuse through the development of corporate permanence, book value and par value fell apart" (1935, p. 114).

Littleton identified a critical event in the evolution of the income concept. As corporations began to reinvest income, the income constraint on dividends became less relevant to conduct and emphasis shifted to questions of reinvestment and the growth of income. This change in behavior helps to explain why the subject of dividend law was not as important in the United States at the start of the twentieth century as it was in Britain in the last few decades of the nineteenth century. Except for British dividend law, which was discussed by American writers like Hatfield (1909) and in a few books on the subject (Reiter, 1926; Kehl, 1941), the classic controversy over income and dividends no longer generated much interest. But the implications of reinvestment and growth were not immediately understood.

Preinreich (1932, 1935, 1936) was probably the first theorist to recognize formally the financial implications of corporate permanence and growth.

> *The yield of common stocks is not dependent upon dividend policy so long as that policy conforms to the principle of good management*...In the long run, this rule is subject only to the secondary qualifications in so far as

one kind of distribution may have a form-utility superior to another because it may create a smaller income tax liability, etc. (1936, p. 137).

However, Preinreich's work was not in the mainstream of accounting theory because it violated the entity theory.[6] Littleton (1935, p. 114), elaborated on this point in his review of Preinreich's book:

> ...[it will] bring about a condition which would practically merge the financial identity of the corporation and the investor...
>
> ... [the] corporation is more than an expanded proprietorship owing its debts to its bondholders.
>
> ... It is a mistake to create, however innocently, the impression that the correct measurement of investor income (a sort of interest-return at best is a more basic problem than the correct measurement of corporate income (the resultant of an interplay between cause and effect, expense and revenue).

Preinreich's contributions to the fields of accounting and finance were neglected. Nevertheless, emphasis in accounting literature also shifted to the subject of earnings; but these earlier discussions, unlike Preinreich's later work did not contain a formal model relating income and dividends. Instead, some writers discussed the relationship between reported income and future income, without considering reinvestment and dividend policy.

Montgomery was one of the first to mention this relationship. In the American edition of *Dicksee's Auditing* (1909), he states almost parenthetically that the primary purpose of calculating income is to predict future income.

> The certificate, therefore, should be a clear and unconditional certificate of accomplished facts, and not a mere estimate of possible—or even probable—future results, misnamed a "certificate." To the limited extent already mentioned it may be permissible, and even desirable, to modify the past results so that they may more usefully serve the purpose for which they are primarily intended — namely, provide a reliable index of future profits (p. 324).

This view is strikingly similar to the view of earnings stated in the conceptual framework developed by the FASB nearly seventy years later (1976, p. 20).

> The measurement of earnings is considered to be the central focus of financial accounting by those favoring the asset and liability view and by those favoring the revenue and expense view. Proponents of both views generally recognize and agree that:
> - Investors and creditors are interested principally in an enterprise's earning-power — its long-term average ability to produce earnings.
> - Reported earnings for a single accounting period such as a fiscal year cannot be equated with earning power.
> - Determining an enterprise's earning power is a function of financial analysis not financial accounting and reporting.
> - Providing information useful for determining an enterprise's earning power *is* a function of financial accounting and reporting.

However, this idea that period income provides an estimate of future earning power does not appear to be the major controversy in accounting today. Instead, it is the disagreement "over whether the investor's or creditor's ability to determine an enterprise's earning power is better served" by the matching concept, or by an asset and liability view, which is more of a valuation approach to the determination of earnings.

But this secondary issue has been debated for some time—and the debate is likely to continue until we recognize that if income reports are intended to provide information for predicting earning power, then any discussion of *how* to make income calculation should be directly and unambiguously related to this objective. However, until there is a formal investigation of the relationship between annual income numbers and future earning power under the matching and valuation approaches to income determination (Cf. Brief and Owen, 1973), it is difficult to understand how one can even begin to discuss which approach might best achieve the objective of financial reporting.

Without a model relating annual income and future earning power, all arguments are plausible, even Welton's apparent double talk about "secret reserves" (*The Accountant,* December 13, 1890).

> I entirely controvert the allegation that large secret contingency funds so operate, that retiring shareholders in banks or similar institutions are losers. Whilst such funds are being accumulated, the declared profits are lower than those actually made, and in that way market values are prevented from rising unreasonably high, as they otherwise would do, on the tacit assumption that adequate reserves must exist. No sooner is the required fund completed, than the profits assume their full dimensions, (including the benefit of interest from such

secret reserve), *and no one is then without information as to the earning power of the concern, and the consequent value of the shares* (italics added).

Conclusion

The debate over matching, valuation and earnings is a continuing one. The main problem in recent discussions of the subject is that by relating period performance to future earning power, accountants will be compelled to give more attention to the uncertain future when discussing alternative approaches to income determination. This is something they have been reluctant to do (Brief, 1975).

One way to make this problem more concrete is to imagine that the life of a firm is analogous to a ship voyage, like those of the early adventurers. As Dicksee said (1903, p. 3), this analogy provides a framework to discuss accounting problems "along systematic lines."

Every firm, like a ship voyage, has a beginning, a midstream and an end. The major issues in financial accounting involve questions about calculating measures of performance for the midstream or interim periods. Although accountants assist in writing the prospectus at the beginning of a voyage and participate in "winding up" at the end, these areas of the responsibility have never occupied a central place in the development of accounting thought.

Dicksee's simple ship model shows that there are two limiting choices on which to base a theory of interim reporting, i.e., a theory for determining income in a midstream period. First, if the objective of an interim report is to provide information useful to predict future earning power, a theory must be developed which directly connects the methodology on which the interim income calculation is based with the total income for the remainder of the voyage. Such a theory cannot be based solely on the transactions and events during a single interim period. Alternatively, and as the other limiting choice, if interim reports are prepared to reflect only the events in an interim period, without regard to expectations about the future, a cash receipts-less disbursements income concept would achieve this objective.[7]

Matching and valuation approaches to earnings determination are not, under existing theory, unambiguously related to either of these choices. The long debate over valuation, matching and earnings reflects this problem, and it can be expected to continue until this issue is addressed directly.

---

[1] For further discussion, see Brief (1965, 1966, 1970, 1976 a).

[2] This subject is examined in Brief (1966). Replacement accounting and the related double-account method assumes that the value of assets purchased with funds provided by owners and creditors is permanent. Therefore, technically, this form of accounting also is consistent with a revenues and expense approach to income determination.

[3] The papers by Cooper and Welton are reprinted in Brief (1976 b).

[4] An argument for the SEC's position on disclosing replacement values related to the need to experiment with different valuation methods.

[5] Even a valuationist like MacNeal (1970, pp. 44-47) recognized the ingenious reasoning on which the matching and cost principles were based.

[6] The breakdown between the correspondence of earnings and dividends resulted in the formulation of new theories in finance. These theories placed the investor in the center of the stage and directly considered reinvestment and growth variables. However, in accounting the entity theory views the corporation as separate and apart from its owners. Thus, it is common in accounting to speak of a firm's cash flows, even though a firm cannot consume and either must reinvest cash flows or pay them out in dividends. In this sense, one could argue that the concept of corporate earnings is inseparable from the investor. Issues like the proprietorship vs. entity controversy need to be reconsidered in a more modern context.

[7] Historical cash flows also would be a logical starting point for predicting future earning power. Existing methodology does not provide this basic data.

REFERENCES

Brief, R. P., "Nineteenth Century Accounting Error," *Journal of Accounting Research* (Spring 1965), pp. 12-31.

________, "The Origin and Evolution of Nineteenth Century Asset Accounting," *Business History Review* (Spring 1966), pp. 1-23.

________, "Depreciation Theory in Historical Perspective," *The Accountant* (December 6, 1970), pp. 737-739.

________, "The Accountant's Responsibility in Historical Perspective," *The Accounting Review* (April 1975), pp. 285-297.

________, *Nineteenth Century Capital Accounting and Business Investment* (Arno Press, 1976).

________, ed., *The Late Nineteenth Century Debate Over Depreciation, Capital and Income* (Arno Press, 1976).

________, and Owen, J., "A Reformulation of the Estimation Problem," *Journal of Accounting Research* (Spring 1973), pp. 1-15.

Dicksee, L. R., *Advanced Accounting* (Gee & Co., 1903).

Edey, H.C. and Panipakdi, P., "British Company Accounting and the Law 1844-1900," reprinted in Littleton, A. C. and Yamey, B. S. (eds.), *Studies in the History of Accounting* (Richard D. Irwin, 1956), pp. 356-379.

Financial Accounting Standards Board, *Conceptual Framework for Financial Accounting and Their Measurement* (FASB 1976).

Hatfield, H. R., *Modern Accounting* (D. Appleton & Co., 1909).

Ijiri, Y., *Theory of Accounting Measurement* (American Accounting Association, 1975).

Kehl, D., *Corporate Dividends: Legal and Accounting Problems Pertaining to Corporate Distributions* (Ronald Press, 1941).

Lev, B., *Financial Statement Analysis: A New Approach* (Prentice-Hall, 1974).

Littleton, A. C., book review: *The Nature of Dividends* by G. A. D. Preinreich, *The Accounting Review* (December 1935), p. 114.

MacNeal, K., *Truth in Accounting* (Scholar Book Co., 1970).

Montgomery, R. H., ed., *Dicksee's Auditing,* 2nd ed. (New York, 1909).

Preinreich, G. A. D., "Stock Yields, Stock Dividends and Inflation," *The Accounting Review* (December 1932), pp. 273-289.

________, *The Nature of Dividends* (Lancaster Press, 1935).

________, "Fair Value and the Yield of Common Stock," *The Accounting Review* (June 1936), pp. 130-140.

Reiter, P., Jr., *Profits, Dividends and the Law* (Ronald Press, 1926).

Ten Have, O., *The History of Accountancy* (Bay Books, 1976).

Yamey, B. S. "The Case Law Relating to Company Dividends," reprinted in Bater, W.T. and Davidson, S., *Studies in Accounting Theory* (Richard D. Irwin, 1962), pp. 428-442.

________, "Accounting and the Rise of Capitalism: Further Notes on a Theme by Sombart," *Journal of Accounting Research* (Autumn 1964), pp. 117-136.

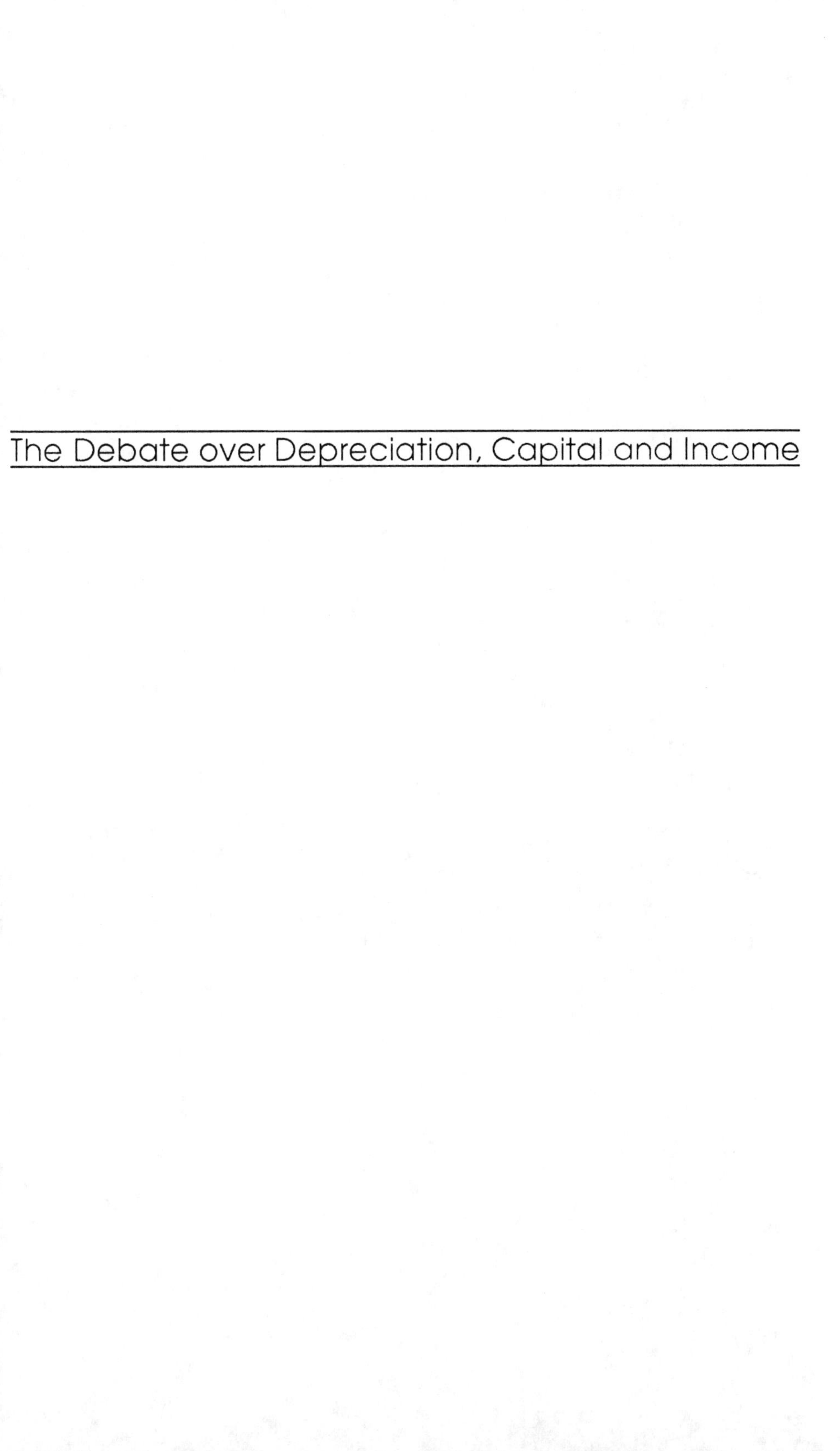

The Debate over Depreciation, Capital and Income

Reprinted from

THE BUSINESS HISTORY REVIEW

Volume XL, Number 1 Spring 1966

By Richard P. Brief
ASSISTANT PROFESSOR OF BUSINESS STATISTICS
NEW YORK UNIVERSITY

The Origin and Evolution of Nineteenth-Century Asset Accounting*

The methods used to account for business assets in Britain and the United States during the nineteenth century are here examined in a context of interplay between "internal economic criteria" and "external constraints."

Economists usually define profit as the change in the "value" of net assets in two successive fiscal periods. The application of this conceptual definition raises rather abstruse theoretical issues; consequently, during the last 100 years accountants have developed a set of pragmatic principles to deal with the problem of measuring asset "values" and profit.

Most modern asset accounting principles originated in the nineteenth century, but these principles together with consistent practices were accepted only slowly in business practice. An important reason for the sluggish acceptance of a *particular* set of accounting principles is that a firm would be expected to determine its business practices according to its own criterion of "usefulness" in the absence of any institutional compulsion toward a specific form of behavior. That is, the set of practices actually selected by a firm should be consistent with its goals; and given a choice, the one chosen would be that expected to yield maximum economic benefits. The nature of competition, the financial condition of the firm and its future capital requirements, the relationship between the decision-maker and other interested parties such as creditors, labor, investors, and a variety of other conditions would influence the selection of those practices that are to serve as the foundation for published financial data and for the determination of profits available for dividends.[1]

* This article is based on the author's unpublished study, "Nineteenth-Century Capital Accounting and Business Investment" (Ph.D. dissertation, Columbia University, 1964). I have profited from conversations with Professor Harold Barger, my dissertation sponsor, and Professor Carl Nelson. Research support from NYU is gratefully acknowledged.

[1] Veblen pointed out an additional factor which complicates the analysis when he

A more fundamental explanation for diversity concerns the element of strategic behavior among firms. As Morgenstern states, "there are degrees of freedom in behavior which are compatible with equally plausible descriptions of the system. . . . Consequently, a lie or falsification . . . is exceedingly hard to discover except by chance. Yet the chance factor itself is a necessary, constituent element of every social system. Without it 'bluffing,' a perfectly sound move in strategic behavior . . . would be impossible. But it is a daily occurrence. Bluffing is an essential feature of rational strategies." [2] Such "degrees of freedom in behavior" have produced diverse accounting methods. This is the chronic dilemma faced by the accounting profession and those that seek to impose uniform standards.

Since an arbitrary set of accounting rules is not likely to have the same value to all firms, either at a point of time or over time, it is only natural to find differences in accounting practices during the nineteenth century.[3] This is not to say that there is a unique, comprehensive, and authoritative set of generally accepted principles in the present day; but business firms, in general, are presently subject to more constraints. According to one source, competition in the nineteenth century meant that "companies should not publish detailed profit and loss" [4] and this point of view is not widely held today.

One way to gain insight into accounting principles is to analyze the historical change in their structure and the forces that influenced this change. In the pages that follow we examine the origin and evolution of methods used to account for assets in Britain and the United States during the nineteenth century.[5] Our "working hypothesis" is that accounting behavior will change only in response to internal economic criteria unless external constraints, such as an influential independent public accounting profession, judicial prec-

---

noted that "the interest of the managers of the modern corporation need not coincide with the permanent interest of the corporation as a going concern." Thorstein Veblen, *The Theory of Business Enterprise* (Mentor ed., New York, 1958), 78.

[2] Oskar Morgenstern, *On the Accuracy of Economic Observations* (2nd. ed., Princeton, 1962), 25.

[3] One would not *expect* to find diversity in accounting practices only if there were a set of accounting procedures that was actually optimal.

[4] *Accountant*, May 2, 1885, 5. Statement by the Chartered Mercantile Bank of India.

[5] The treatment of both British and American material may be justified on several grounds. First, there was a transfer of accounting knowledge and jurisprudence between the two countries. Many of the early British texts were sold in the United States and many of the early British accountants emigrated to this country. See, for example, James Don Edwards, *History of Public Accounting in the United States* (East Lansing, 1960). Second, as a practical matter, the amount of information available on accounting practices in the United States during the nineteenth century is very limited. For these reasons the two sources of evidence are dealt with more or less simultaneously.

edent, and/or statutory authority, effectively restrict the choice of accounting procedures.

The next section highlights the changing structure of nineteenth century asset accounting principles and practices. Then the role played by nineteenth-century legal and statutory authority in bringing about these developments is examined. Finally, some of the other factors that might have influenced the evolution of accounting are discussed and some of the broader implications of this change are mentioned.

Accounting Principles and Practices

To analyze nineteenth-century asset accounting, nineteenth-century business firms must be divided into two classes – permanent or quasi-public enterprise, such as railroads and utilities, and all other firms. In general, a different set of accounting practices was employed by each of these classes of enterprise although these sets were neither unique nor mutually exclusive.

Permanent Enterprise

Historically, permanent enterprise practiced some form of cash accounting and determined profit by matching cash receipts and disbursements. "Rational bookkeeping did not intrude into the management of public funds;" [6] and because of the quasi-public nature of these companies, their accounting practices seem to be an outgrowth of "cameralist" bookkeeping procedures. This is an important historical relationship. Dicksee, in discussing the double-account system, which is a formalized set of procedures based on what are essentially cash accounting methods, stated that "this idea, ingenious as it undoubtedly is, would appear to have emanated from a lawyer rather than an accountant. One seems to trace in it the well known affection of the Chancery for a cash statement, as well as its rooted distrust for accounts framed on any other basis." Kehl provides numerous references to legal cases in which the courts sanctioned a cash receipts less disbursements concept of profits.[7]

There was, of course, no accounting profession when these prac-

[6] Joseph Schumpeter, *Capitalism, Socialism, and Democracy* (Harper Torchbook ed., New York, 1962), 123n.

[7] L. R. Dicksee, *Advanced Accounting* (2nd ed., London, 1905), 130. Dicksee also stated that "the system [Double-Account] may be well applied, not merely to the accounts of Railway, Gas, Water, and Electric Light Companies, but also to Tramway, Canal, Shipping, Telephone, and Mining Companies, and to Companies owning property from the letting of which they derive regular income." *Ibid.*, 133; Donald Kehl, *Corporate Dividends* (New York, 1941), 58n, 63n.

tices were formulated. Yet, given the environment in which these procedures were adopted there is a certain logic to them and to the principles or assumptions implicit in their use. If fixed assets had been "permanently" maintained in working order and if all expenditures for assets had been made from funds provided only from stock and bond issues, then the method has some logical appeal.[8] However, such factors as obsolescence and physical deterioration, which necessitate replacement, cause cash accounting to become an inherently unstable method; but there was either less experience [9] and/or less concern [10] with these phenomena in the nineteenth century.

Whether or not one is able to rationalize the use of cash accounting, there are several practical deficiencies associated with this method. First, the recognition of depreciation is delayed until replacement. Second, since a firm may pay dividends out of profit, defined gross of depreciation, serious liquidity problems might arise when replacement was required. Third, the accounts kept under this method can be readily manipulated by "starving" a company or "overfeeding" it. These shortcomings became apparent at an early date and some railroads began periodically to record depreciation in the accounts.[11] However, the attempt to record regular provisions for depreciation did not persist over time, and most railroads began to practice replacement accounting, which is a modification of strict cash accounting.[12] The essential difference between cash accounting and replacement accounting is that the latter method calls for charging expenditures made on assets with

[8] Littleton believed that "there was a certain logic in the contention of railroad men that adequate renewal of parts would keep the equipment up to standard operating efficiency." *Accounting Evolution to 1900* (New York, 1933), 233.

[9] Hungerford supports this view. "In those days [1872] railroad accounting was a weird and uncertain thing. The great modern gods of accurate finance, obsolescence and depreciation, had hardly begun to show their heads." *The Story of the Baltimore and Ohio Railroad: 1827–1927* (New York, 1928), 165.

[10] Apparently, investors showed little concern over protecting their capital. According to Evans, "British investors were not so much interested in return of principal lent as in the receipt of interest." He pointed out that no provisions for default on mortgages were usually found in the Parliamentary Acts. *British Corporation Finance: 1775–1850* (Baltimore, 1936), 48.

[11] Harold Pollins, "Aspects of Railway Accounting before 1868," *Studies in the History of Accounting*, ed. by A. C. Littleton and B. S. Yamey (Homewood, 1956), 343–49. Perry Mason, "Illustrations of Early Depreciation Practices," *Accounting Review*, VIII (Sept., 1933).

[12] Replacement accounting is discussed by some nineteenth-century accountants. "No provision has been made in the Acts of Parliament for depreciation. The usual course is to see that everything is well kept up out of revenue and to charge all replacements as they occur against revenue." *Accountant*, May 17, 1885, 13. The "usual course adopted," however, was condemned in no uncertain terms. "It is not the practice of ordinary trading companies which is bad . . . but the practice of railway companies . . . a practice as vicious and full of temptation to managers and directors to manipulate accounts for their own ends and purposes as can well be imagined. It is, in fact, little short of an inducement to fraud." *Ibid.*, November 14, 1885, 30.

internal funds to capital. Otherwise, both methods produce similar results.[13]

The reasons for this apparent retrogression are not known, but one may speculate on the causes. The *Accountant* for June 27, 1885, reveals that a proposal was made in 1865 to introduce the principle of writing-off depreciation in railroad accounts, but the suggestion was rejected because "railway officials generally were opposed to the idea as impractical." According to Pollins, depreciation accounts were adopted during the 1840's in reaction to earlier scandals, but were abandoned when past provisions for depreciation were found to be inadequate.[14]

Accountants and others, past and present, have generally condemned the actual practices associated with replacement accounting; [15] but there is very little evidence in the nineteenth century to suggest that serious efforts were made to formulate a set of procedures that would remedy these deficiencies. Apparently, some accountants thought that the law actually prevented or at least impeded certain classes of enterprise from retaining "what appears to be profit," that is, depreciation reserves.[16] Dicksee also implies that the law might have affected accounting behavior:

> It has been thought by some that the method of stating the accounts [double-account system] absolved the company from making any provision to meet depreciation of its permanent assets . . . but what was really intended seems to have been that fluctuation rather than depreciation was to be disregarded; . . . it is not only possible but also perfectly easy for provision for depreciation to be made and stated in accounts kept upon the Double-Account System.

Nevertheless, "The Legislature," according to Dicksee, "does not require provision to be made to meet such Depreciation" although "it indirectly sanctions the provision of a prudent reserve;" and it is a "very generally accepted principle" for "those undertakings *not* specifically provided for by the Legislature to charge depreciation." In a later edition, Dicksee wrote that the double-account system assumes that rate of depreciation will not exceed the rate of replacement, and the single-account system assumes that the value assigned to assets is "actual." However, when it is difficult to assign "actual" value to assets and when assets are of "permanent" nature and represent the bulk of "working capital," the double-account system

[13] One might also distinguish between replacement accounting and retirement accounting. For the purpose of this discussion it is not necessary to make such a distinction.

[14] Pollins, "Aspects of Railway Accounting," 349.

[15] This subject is dealt with at greater length in my paper, "Nineteenth-Century Accounting Error," *Journal of Accounting Research*, III (Spring, 1965).

[16] Ewing Matheson, *Depreciation of Factories* (4th ed., London, 1910), 40.

might be employed.[17] This argument was used to justify the adoption of replacement accounting throughout the nineteenth century and later.

This discussion, together with Dicksee's severe criticism of replacement accounting in another text,[18] suggests that legal authority had a significant if not disturbing influence on the development of accounting theory for this class of enterprise.

There was no real change in the structure of accounting principles governing quasi-public enterprise in the nineteenth century. By the end of the period, a large number of these companies had gone into receivership; some went bankrupt and others were reorganized.[19] In the twentieth century many of these firms were nationalized in England and, in the United States, most of them became subject to some form of institutional control.

"All Other Firms"

The writings of Yamey, Littleton, and Pollard suggest that most early nineteenth-century firms in this classification, which includes manufacturers, trading companies, etc., defined profit as the change in the "value" of net assets in two successive periods.[20] This means that the principles and procedures that governed their asset accounting required some kind of valuation of assets to be made before profits were computed. This finding is meaningless, however, until the principles of asset valuation are defined; for in the absence of specific assumptions made about the nature of "value," the term has a great many meanings, both in practice and in the law.[21]

If an asset were properly "valued" at the end of each fiscal period there would be no need to isolate those elements that are usually considered in the process of asset valuation. That is, there would be no need to make any rules to distinguish between capital and revenue expenditures; and the problem of depreciation or appreciation would automatically be solved if assets were properly valued,

[17] *Auditing* (2nd ed., London, 1895), 229, 230 (italics added); (10th ed., London, 1915), 260.

[18] *Advanced Accounting*, 130–32. For similar criticisms, see E. Garcke and J. M. Fells, *Factory Accounts* (4th ed., London, 1893), 95.

[19] About 50 per cent of the track mileage constructed in the United States prior to 1900 was placed in receivership. *Poor's Manual of Railroads*, 1900, lxxii. In England over £100 million in the par value of the capital stock was written off in 1921. *Encyclopedia Britannica* (1946), XVIII, 930. The method of accounting for assets *could* have been *one* of the factors that contributed to this instability.

[20] Sidney Pollard, "Capital Accounting in the Industrial Revolution," *Yorkshire Bulletin of Economic and Social Research*, XV (November, 1963); B. S. Yamey, "Some Topics in the History of Financial Accounting in England, 1500–1900," *Studies in Accounting Theory*, ed. by W. T. Baxter and S. Davidson (Homewood, 1962); Littleton, *Accounting Evolution to 1900*.

[21] James C. Bonbright, *Valuation of Property* (New York, 1937); J. Commons, *Legal Foundations of Capitalism* (New York, 1924).

i.e., valued at "discounted future benefits." The difficulty, of course, is that a method to determine these "benefits" has never been achieved.

Historically, the process of valuing assets was analogous to taking an inventory; hence the "inventory method" has been associated with early asset accounting practices.[22] The inventory method is not unique but depends entirely on the principles governing the valuation of assets. The extent to which the valuation implies consideration of appreciation, depreciation, and a distinction between capital and revenue expenditures depends on the underlying assumptions made about the nature of "value." For example, if all outlays on an asset increase its value, all expenditures on the asset should be capitalized. If value equals original cost, all expenditures should be expensed. If value relates to earning capacity, an element of goodwill should be recognized. The early texts often mentioned or implied the possibility of recording appreciation and depreciation, but the principles governing entries in these categories were not elaborated.[23] This is not to say the more determinate procedures were unknown. Even before the Industrial Revolution certain "modern" accounting practices were employed; [24] but a variety of other methods was also adopted.

The early accounting literature contains discussions of procedure rather than theory or principle. The debate on accounting principles, which began in the nineteenth century, focused on the theory of asset valuation. One writer argued, "Market price or selling value should have nothing to do with it [valuation], but the original cost of the stock being assumed as a starting point, the only consideration is the amount of depreciation unrestored by repairs at the end of the period." [25] In 1876 this same principle is advocated

[22] Littleton, *Accounting Evolution to 1900*, 225; Mason, "Illustrations of Early Depreciation Accounting," 209 ff; Schumpeter, *Capitalism, Socialism and Democracy*, 123n.

[23] Perhaps the most authoritative reference to the indeterminacy of nineteenth-century accounting procedures is found in Alfred Marshall, *Principles of Economics* (8th ed., New York, 1948), 354–55n. For other evidence on this subject see: B. F. Foster, *The Merchants Manual: The Principles of Trade, Commerce and Banking* (Boston, 1838), 164; *The Book Keeper* (New York), September 14, 1880, 65; George Soulé, *Soulé's New Science and Practice of Accounts* (6th ed., New Orleans, 1901), 91; Victor S. Clark, *History of Manufactures in the United States, 1607–1860* (3 vols., New York, 1949), I, 373.

[24] Raymond de Roover, "Early Accounting Problems of Foreign Exchange," *Accounting Review*, XIX (October, 1944), 398.

[25] Pollins, "Aspects of Railway Accounting," 346, quoting from *Railway Times*, November 6, 1841, 1167. This statement implies that assets might be maintained *permanently* in working order; this contention was criticized later in the century. "We are continually faced with the argument that the property is kept fully up to the mark, and is, indeed, in a much better condition than ever, and the amounts expended upon repairs and renewals charged to the trading account is put forward as the proof." *Accountant*, December 10, 1894, 41. In the United States the same point was made. "If, in the case of plant, it is kept in perfect working order and all expenses connected therewith charged to revenue the question of setting aside a sum annually for depreciation must

in slightly revised form. "The simplest and broadest principle for regulating value and depreciation of plant might be said to be its known capacity under normal circumstance to produce profit, subject, however, to its cost being used as the maximum value." [26] There appears to be some agreement that original cost should serve as the maximum value; however, the method of computing depreciation is unspecified.

In 1880 a specific procedure to be used in computing depreciation was elaborated. "Every cautious trader writes off an annual percentage according to the average wear and tear or depreciation." [27] By 1883 the entire question of depreciation, according to one accountant, was open to "controversy" not as to the "fact of chargability" but only as to "volume and mode." As to principles of asset valuation, "matter and things fixed in permanent working position must not be treated as following the fluctuations of the market." [28] Neither market value nor present value are pertinent. Thus, assets should be valued "without reference to change in value from other causes than use" as it is "not safe to take value as a basis." [29]

Not all accountants, however, were in accord. One remarked that "it is what property would fetch, not what it cost, that settles its value." He continued, "We have a great deal of information as to how the depreciation is to be dealt with, but the contribution so far to the stock of information as to appreciation is by no means full or complete, the only suggestions being, perhaps, revaluation or suspension of the charge for depreciation." [30]

In 1887 the "inventory method" was explicitly linked to the modern concept of allocating depreciation on the basis of original cost. "In the case of buildings and machinery a deduction is made, but the effect is the same as taking the property and plant into stock at reduced amount, or at increased amount if additions during

---

depend upon the fact whether it has depreciated or not; . . . On this question it is impossible to lay down any fixed principles, although, as a rule, I believe the safest plan is to assume depreciation and make an allowance for it in the annual balance sheet." *Book Keeper*, July 5, 1881, 147.

[26] *Accountant*, January 6, 1876, 6. In addition, the auditor should insure that "no ordinary repairs had been charged to plant" and he also should receive explanations which would satisfy him "when the item of depreciation was omitted or seemed insufficient."

[27] *Accountant*, April 10, 1880, 5. Many of the references cited in this section include discussions of methods by which depreciation is to be calculated. See also, *Book Keeper*, January 2, 1883, 6. This article was based on a lecture made in England by Joseph Slocome of the Birmingham Accountants' Student Society on November 28, 1883. The communication between English and American accountants was evidently very rapid.

[28] *Accountant*, April 21, 1883, 6–7. It is also interesting to note that depreciation was defined for the purpose of replacement of capital. On this subject see: Yamey, "Some Topics in the History of Financial Accounting," 39–40.

[29] *Accountant*, November 5, 1887, 610–11. Similar views are expressed in *ibid.*, November 12, 1889, 692; Dicksee, *Auditing* (1895), 178.

[30] *Accountant*, September 1, 1883, 10. He argued, "I fail to see how the bringing in of such appreciation in land and goodwill can be escaped."

the period have been in excess of the deduction for wear and tear."[31]

The texts and journals in this period begin to confirm the principle that assets should be "valued" at original cost less depreciation due to wear and tear with all other fluctuations in value being ignored.[32] This value in modern accounting terminology is called "the value to the going concern;" and modern accountants regard the concept "as a point of view from which the value of fixed tangible assets can be regarded."[33] This does not mean, however, that all accountants accepted this definition of value and even some of those who advocated that all "fluctuations" be ignored accepted modifications to this principle. In practice, there is also evidence indicating that assets were often not valued at original cost less depreciation but were, in many cases, either not depreciated or appreciated. Furthermore, the specific bookkeeping practices connected with recording depreciation *and* appreciation were ambiguous; and the practices associated with distinguishing between capital and revenue expenditures were frequently criticized.[34]

As one critic of financial practices said in the *Accountant* of June 4, 1881:

> A shareholder is entitled to know, not what is the true value of his shares, for that in most instances is a matter of opinion, but how the value of fixed assets has been estimated — whether at cost, at a valuation . . . or otherwise, and what sums have been placed in reserve or written off for depreciation.

Conclusion

It is apparent that the asset accounting principles governing the practices of quasi-public enterprise did not change significantly during the nineteenth century. This set of principles was an outgrowth of cameralist bookkeeping methods and appears to have been institutionalized due to the public nature of these firms. Some

[31] *Accountant,* November 5, 1887, 610. Some economists also viewed depreciation as a change in the value of assets; others discussed depreciation in terms of original cost. G. S. L. Tucker, *Progress and Profits in British Economic Thought: 1650–1850* (Cambridge, 1960), 83–89. These early economists might not have seen any difference between the methods. In any event, the early economists probably did not have much influence on the business community. According to one accountant, economics was "a subject for the most part relegated to whitewashed rooms wherein the gas flickers, and to Public Houses on a Sunday evening. . . . The students of Economics are few and far between. . . . Economic science is practically in chaos." *Accountant,* December 15, 1888.

[32] Some writers said that the rate of depreciation should include a factor for obsolescence as well as wear and tear. *Accountant,* June 16, 1894, 547.

[33] *Accountants' Handbook,* ed. by Rufus Wixon (4th ed., New York, 1956), Ch. 19, p. 22. For an interesting historical reference to the meaning of "going concern value," see Dicksee, *Auditing* (1915), 184–87.

[34] Garcke and Fells, *Factory Accounts,* 103; Edwin Guthrie, "Depreciation," *Encyclopedia of Accounting* (London, 1903), II, 373; *Accountant,* November 12, 1887, 617. For references to accounting practices as distinguished from accounting theory see my "Nineteenth-Century Accounting Error."

contemporary accountants condemned these procedures; but even some of these critics seemed to accept the continued use of some form of cash accounting.

This is not to say that there were no logical reasons for the adoption of replacement accounting. These procedures are simple and extremely flexible in practice, thus permitting a wide range of accounting discretion. Further, the method avoids the complex problem of forecasting the useful lives of long-lived assets. Finally, replacement accounting permits higher "profits" to be earned in the formative years of a company that possesses long-lived assets since capital consumption charges are not recorded until replacement occurs. Nevertheless, replacement accounting, *unlike* many other nineteenth-century accounting procedures, is now considered an obsolete practice.[35] This suggests that its institutional origin checked the progress of accounting evolution.

Other firms began the century by inventorying the value of assets. The procedures associated with this method were indeterminate, and accountants developed the concept of "going-concern value" which slowly gained acceptance during the period. Yet, many accountants accepted certain modifications to this principle of asset valuation; and the practices of many firms during the nineteenth century were not consistent with this definition of value.

In a laissez-faire economy firms will choose the set of accounting principles and practices that has the highest utility, given the goals the organization is trying to achieve and the constraints under which it operates. This condition would necessarily lead to a diversity in accounting practices unless the diversity produced certain internal diseconomies or unless external constraints imposed on accounting practices insured conformity in practice. The question therefore arises as to whether there were other institutional forces that influenced the structure of accounting?

Influence of Legal Institutions

Nineteenth-century accountants were deeply concerned with legal decisions that related to accounting principles and practices. Indeed, nineteenth- and early twentieth-century accounting texts contained numerous references to the law and particularly to dividend law. Some of these cases shed interesting light on the nature of nineteenth-century asset accounting and the problems encountered by the accounting profession.

[35] Arthur Andersen and Co., *Accounting and Reporting Problems of the Accounting Profession* (2nd ed., 1962), 128.

Asset accounting becomes a matter for judicial consideration whenever asset valuation must be determined in the courts or by other legal authority. The purpose of the valuation, whether for rate-making, condemnation, or taxation, and the circumstances surrounding the litigation obviously have a profound effect on legal interpretation. Notwithstanding the difficulty of generalizing on the basis of a few legal decisions, it is possible to arrive at tentative conclusions regarding the influence of the judiciary on asset accounting principles and practices. In the pages that follow some important nineteenth-century dividend cases will be reviewed and, at the same time, the analysis will be supplemented by a discussion of other institutional forces that might have affected accounting behavior.

"By 1700 there had already been adopted in England two statutory standards, one or the other of which still controls dividend distributions under present day statutes in a great many American States." [36] Thus, the "profits test" and the "capital impairment rule" were the first legal references to asset accounting. Yet, the British courts did not define these rules with respect to fixed assets until the last decades of the nineteenth century and the United States Supreme Court never dealt squarely with these issues until the twentieth century.

"The courts in the period were reluctant to interfere in the internal affairs of a company," and, unless fraud were an issue, businessmen remained free to determine financial practices.[37] This was a laissez-faire environment in which the public accounting profession was just beginning to emerge; and in its formative years the accounting profession apparently was resented by the legal profession. As the *Accountant* of July 28, 1877, put it: "From the first, what we fear is that the bulk of the legal profession has looked upon accountants with ill-concealed dislike and jealousy." This theme prevails in many of the early issues of the *Accountant* and accountants appeared to be preoccupied with their status.

Depreciation

According to one source, every legal case in Britain in which the payment of a dividend out of capital had been an issue was decided

[36] Kehl, *Corporate Dividends*, 4.

[37] Evans, *British Corporation Finance*, 103. "As to the publication of false balance sheets and including in them debts which were hopelessly bad, it was difficult to say where a debt was hopeless; and besides, if any shareholders were deceived into buying shares he might have his separate remedy, but each would have a different case and the whole body could not sue." *Turquand* v. *Marshall*, 20 LT 766 (1869). The debtor in this case was the Confederacy.

with reference to the company's articles of association.[38] This meant that if the corporate charter omitted references to accounting practices, directors need not provide for capital consumption before declaring a dividend. Evidently some accountants engaged in some form of "wishful thinking" and/or failed to read the texts of certain decisions. "Now the Companies Act is undoubtedly not clear on the question of payment of dividends out of capital and it should be noted that on this point some of the text books are notoriously misleading inasmuch as they simply state the effect of a judgment, as that the Company A was restrained from paying a dividend before providing for depreciation; and so on, without pointing out that the decision was based on the company's articles of association." [39]

The case to which these references refer is *Davison* v. *Gillies.* M. R. Jessel, hearing the case which actually never went to trial, stated that "The word profits by itself is a word which is certainly susceptible of more than one meaning, and one must ascertain what it means in the articles." Since the articles required the directors to provide a reserve fund for maintenance, repairs, depreciation, and renewals, it was held that no dividend could be paid to the ordinary shareholder. By way of dicta, Jessel offered some interesting views on the subject of depreciation. "I should think no commercial man would doubt that that was the right course – that he must not calculate net profits until he had provided for all ordinary repairs and wear and tear occasioned by his business – in many businesses . . . there is a regular sum . . . set aside for this purpose." [40]

These remarks were made in 1879 and accountants of that period would have subscribed to this opinion. However, from a purely legal standpoint, the decision rested entirely on the articles of the company. Yamey and Reiter [41] confirmed this point, but Hatfield [42] seemed to recognize it only with some hesitation, and Littleton apparently misinterpreted the decision.[43]

[38] *Accountant*, January 16, 1886, 13. The exception was *MacDourgall* v. *Jersey Imperial Hotel Co.*, 2 Hem and M. 528 (1864), a case which did not involve fixed assets.

[39] *Accountant*, June 18, 1887, 356.

[40] 50 LJ (Ch) 192n, 193.

[41] Basil S. Yamey, "The Case Law Relating to Company Dividends," *Studies in Accounting History*, 431n; Prosper Reiter, *Profits, Dividends and the Law* (New York, 1926), 32.

[42] In one text, Hatfield states "at least so far as material wear and tear is concerned the early case of *Davison* v. *Gillies* . . . gives clear expression to the doctrine that depreciation must be reckoned." *Modern Accounting* (New York, 1922), 124. Later, he qualifies this remark in a footnote. "The oft-quoted decision in *Davison* v. *Gillies* was subsequently said to have rested entirely on special articles and not on general law," *ibid.*, 201n.

[43] In discussing nineteenth-century depreciation Littleton says that "allowance for depreciation in calculating profits available for dividends was also given support at this

In another case involving depreciation, it was held that where the articles did not require it, depreciation need not be recognized.[44] The court *agreed* with the Davison ruling! Reiter believed, however, that appreciation had counteracted depreciation and the decision therefore rested on the particular facts of the situation. He based that opinion on his interpretation of an earlier decision in which a company, according to the Act of 1877, reduced its capital in order to pay dividends. Reiter suggests that the act would never have been passed if a company were able to pay dividends out of capital.[45]

Prior to 1889 the statutory requirements relating to depreciation and profits available for dividends were either uncertain or non-existent. Nevertheless, the British income tax law of 1878 permitted a deduction for "wear and tear" and, as we have seen, British accountants had already begun speaking out on the subject. Their efforts focused on educating their own profession and the business community, attempting to secure the passage of full disclosure rules, and increasing the authority of the accounting profession.[46]

Although accountants had definite opinions on the treatment of depreciation, their responsibility and authority in financial matters were rather vague. The chief care of the auditor, "in some cases" was to "test the reality of the assets;" but the problem of distinguishing expenditures which should be capitalized was "not always in the auditor's province." However, the auditor should "see that the

---

time by the courts. . . ." *Accounting Evolution to 1900*, 220. He mentions *Davison* v. *Gillies* and *Dent* v. *London Tramway*, 50 LJ (Ch) 191, which grew out of the Davison case. The directors, based on the Davison ruling, passed the preference shareholders' dividend. However, in the Dent case profits were defined [with respect to preference shareholders] as "the surplus in receipts after paying expenses and restoring capital to the position it was in on the first of January of that year." Thus, by this rule, if depreciation is neglected in past years, it becomes a capital loss not affecting the dividend rights of preference shareholders. Although the decision is not unreasonable, the case hardly supports an allowance for depreciation. The case of *Knowles* v. *McAdam*, 3 Ex D 23 (1877), also mentioned by Littleton, does provide some support for depletion allowances. Here depletion was allowed for tax purposes. However, the case was held wrongly decided in *Coltness Iron* v. *Black*, 6 LR App (1881).

[44] Reiter, *Profits*, 33–34. The case was *Kehoe* v. *The Waterford and Limerick Railway Company*, 21 L.R. Ir. 221 (1881).

[45] Reiter, *Profits*, 28–29, 33. The decision referred to is *In re. Ebbw Vale Steel, Iron and Coal Co.*, 4 Ch D 827 (1877). Here depreciation was due to a fall in the value of iron and *not* wear and tear. However, the Ebbw Vale case is said to have arisen because the directors originally tried to reduce the company's capital before declaring a dividend; and after being unsuccessful they declared a dividend that was enjoined. Then the Act of 1877 was passed. The *Accountant* for June 18, 1887, states that the Companies Act of 1867 prevented directors only from "expressly" intimating that dividends are being paid out of capital. This statement apparently refers to the Ebbw Vale decision.

[46] "The Company Clauses Act, 1845, prohibits paying dividends out of capital but the Companies Act, 1862, contains no such prohibition. Such a prohibition is contained in Table A, but a company is not bound to adopt Table A, and if it does it can alter it by a special resolution." L. J. Cotton in *Guiness* v. *Land Corporation of Ireland*, 22 Ch D 366 (1882). The British tax law of 1878 permitted a deduction for "diminished value by wear and tear." Prior to 1878 the tax law permitted only a deduction for repairs and renewals, not to exceed "what is usually expended for such purposes during an average of three years preceding." Matheson, *Depreciation of Factories*, 26, 28.

actual provision made for depreciation is shown in the accounts" although his responsibility for bad debts was greater "than in the case of debatable provisions for depreciation." [47] Accountants complained that "if a balance sheet be correct although condensed he [the auditor] is bound to sign it," and the *Accountant* urged compulsory publication of the amounts charged to depreciation and the method of valuation.[48] In 1881 a bill was introduced into Parliament requiring the disclosure of past depreciation "in view of certain scandals in the over-valuation of private undertakings." The Bill of 1888, which was not enacted, provided for disclosure of the rate and amount of depreciation and the cost of additions to capital; [49] but it was not, according to one authority, "until 1908 that the first major step was taken on a path that was to lead to regulation far more detailed and effective than would have been dreamed of by the nineteenth century business man." [50]

When the capital maintenance rule and the requirement to record depreciation of fixed assets were finally tested in the courts, we find what amounts to a rule that unrealized capital losses on fixed assets are not charges against income. Thus, current income may be debited with an allocation for depreciation; however, failure to follow this procedure may preclude any charge for capital consumption. If there had been any uncertainty prior to 1889 it was dispelled by *Lee* v. *Neuchatel* and certain other subsequent decisions.

The facts of *Lee* v. *Neuchatel* are not clear from most law reports. Reiter, Bonbright, Hatfield, and Berle and Fischer consider the case in the category of depletion and wasting assets; but it would seem that this view is faulty.[51] The term of a lease is far more definite than the depletion on a mineral deposit.[52] While the cost of the lease is uncertain it appears that the company purchased it in 1873 for about £1,000,000. The concession was to expire in 1887 but

[47] *Accountant*, April 23, 1881, 6.

[48] *Accountant*, April 30, 1881, 6; June 4, 1881, 5.

[49] Matheson, *Depreciation of Factories*, 167; H. C. Edey and Prot Panitpakdi, "British Company Accounting and the Law," *Studies in the History of Accounting*, 375n.

[50] H. C. Edey, "Company Accounts in Britain: The Jenkins Report," *Accounting Review*, XXXVIII (April, 1963), 262. Prior to 1900 there were no compulsory audit provisions in Britain except for banks although it was not unusual for a company to provide for an audit. Dicksee noted, however, that the accounting certificate led to a misconception as to the "fact" of a balance sheet. *Auditing* (1915), 310–15. He also discussed "so-called auditors whose extreme ignorance is only equalled by their utter inability to appreciate the moral responsibility of their position." *Ibid.*, p. 360. There were a few legal cases involving the liability of auditors in England prior to 1900, but "so far as we are aware, no reported case in America has yet dealt with the liability of professional auditors." Dicksee, *Auditing*, ed. by R. H. Montgomery (New York, 1905), 326.

[51] 41 LR Ch. 1 (1889); Reiter, Profits, 38–42; Bonbright, *Valuation of Property*, 937; Hatfield, *Accounting* (New York, 1908), 264–65; A. Berle and F. Fischer, "Elements of the Law of Business Accounting," *Columbia Law Review*, XXXII (April, 1932), 619.

[52] Reiter indicates that "it would not be unreasonable for a court of law to include leases under this classification," *Profits*, 174. But assuming an inexhaustible mineral deposit the term of the lease would determine the *minimum* amortization of the cost of the lease.

was extended to 1907. This term would require about £30,000 to be written off annually; yet it appears that only £40,000 had been written off up to 1889.[53]

The defendant directors argued, among other things, that the assets had appreciated and that declaration of a dividend is a matter of internal management. The opinions of the Lord Justices are noteworthy. L. J. Cotton said that a company does not have to consider capital consumption and that the Davison and Dent cases rested on the articles. L. J. Lindley, aside from believing that the establishment of a legal principle requiring the recognition of capital consumption would "paralyze the trade of the country," asserted that a company may or may not have a "deterioration fund" but that the decision to do so is optional. L. J. Lopes defined profits, assuming that there was no qualification in the articles, as the excess of revenues over cash expenditures. Capital and revenue are separate.[54]

Three other decisions were decided with reference to the Lee case. In *Verner* v. *General and Commercial Investment Trust, Ltd.*, the company lost £75,000 on its investments. It was held that dividends could be paid without reference to the loss which was of *fixed* rather than *circulating* capital! Thus, losses of *fixed* capital need not be charged to profits.[55] *Wilmer* v. *McNamara* followed the line of thought established in the Lee and Verner decisions. Here it was ruled that depreciation of plant and goodwill need not enter into the calculation of profits available for dividends.[56] In *Bond* v. *Barrow Haematite Company* the directors were *allowed* to depreciate mining leases and blast furnaces because these assets were considered part of *circulating* capital. The preference shareholders had sued for payment of dividend.[57]

Dicksee summarized the legal requirement involving the recog-

[53] These facts are not certain but are consistent with the information found in *Acct. L. R.* (1889), 29; reprinted in Dicksee, *Auditing* (1915), 656–63. This information is not found in the law reports.

[54] *Ibid.*, 12. The significance of the Lee case was commented on in the accounting literature. The important fact is that "capital be represented by nominal assets, and that is sufficient unless there is fraud." *Accountant*, December 14, 1889, 677.

[55] 63 LJ Ch 246 (1894). This decision has been misinterpreted. One writer, commenting on this decision, said that the ruling meant "that price level decrease did not produce loss in a dividend sense." Littleton, *Essays on Accounting* (Urbana, 1961), 249. This was not the issue here. Moreover, few accountants would argue that an investment trust should disregard portfolio losses if the firm's capital included debt. One contemporary accountant commented on the Verner decision. "There is and often has been a wide distinction between the authorized interpretation of the statutes and the principles of sound accountancy, and, while respecting the former, we confess that we always regard the latter of more importance." *Accountant*, XX (1894), 176.

[56] 64 LJ Ch 516 (1895).

[57] 1 Ch D 353 (1902). Hatfield maintained that this case was "a clear expression of the same view" held in the Davison decision. This is not an accurate statement. *Accounting*, 135.

nition of depreciation. "It would appear 'doubtful' as to whether the law compels any company to make a provision for depreciation before declaring dividends out of its earnings. . . . The question of depreciation is rather one of prudence or of internal administration rather than legal compulsion."[58] Guthrie, putting the matter somewhat negatively, maintained that "false reckoning [of depreciation] has to be of the most flagrant character to be proved legal fraud;" but another accountant called it an "unwritten law to charge loss by wear and tear."[59] This "unwritten law" apparently had little effect on practice and Leake, an early authority on depreciation, maintained that the "present neglect to account systematically . . . [for depreciation] is a matter of long established custom rather than inevitable necessity . . . [and] continues in spite of, and not in consequence of, their [the accounting profession's] attitude."[60]

Since the development of the American economy lagged British industrial growth it is not surprising to find scant information on nineteenth-century asset accounting in the United States. The first reference to depreciation made by the United States Supreme Court was in 1876. The court said that "the public, when referring to the profits of the business of a merchant, rarely ever take into account the depreciation of the buildings in which the business is carried on, notwithstanding they may have been erected out of invested capital."[61] Two years later the Supreme Court ruled that only actual expenditures could be charged to profit. This attitude was also reflected in income tax laws and tax litigation.[62]

[58] Dicksee, *Auditing* (1915), 258. A similar statement was made in the 2nd ed. (1895). Even in a case where it was almost certain that bondholders were going to lose their principal, the payment of a dividend was approved. Yamey, "The Case Law Relating to Company Dividends," 437n.; reference is to *Lawrence* v. *West Somerset Mineral, Ry.*, 2 Ch. 250 (1918).

[59] Edwin Guthrie, "Depreciation," *Encyclopedia of Accounting*, II, 365; *Accountant*, August 8, 1903, 1014. There was a debate on the question of whether the "unwritten" law should be written. One of the debaters held that "if we were to apply such an amendment, you could stop all such enterprise, because it would be absolutely impossible for companies to pay dividends in the early years of their existence." *Accountant*, March 18, 1893, 254. Another said that "I have various addresses here from eminent men who regard the law as quite settled, that a provision for substantial depreciation is not necessary." *Ibid.*, 257. In this connection the following example is of interest. The Powayan Steam Tramway Company in its Prospectus of April 18, 1887, estimated profits and included depreciation; but when profits were less than estimated, no depreciation was charged. Certain legal opinion maintained that the dividend should not be paid but this "in no way shook the opinion of Lovelock and Lewis, the auditors" who put the question before the President of the Institute of Chartered Accountants. He said that "the dividend was permissible." *Accountant*, August 19, 1892, 393.

[60] P. D. Leake, *Depreciation and Wasting Assets* (London, 1911), 5.

[61] *Eyster* v. *Centennial Board of Finance*, 94 US 503; quoted in Reiter, *Profits*, 123. In an earlier case a state court refused to allow a charge for depreciation. *Tutt* v. *Land*, 50 Ga. 339 (1873).

[62] *U.S.* v. *Kansas Pacific Railroad*, 99 US 459 (1878); Floyd W. Windal, "Legal Background for the Accounting Concept of Realization," *Accounting Review*, XXXVIII (January, 1963), 29–31.

There is no evidence that the British accounting profession's agitation for reform had any counterpart in the United States during the nineteenth century. Montgomery and Hatfield were the pioneers in American accounting literature and their texts were not published until after the turn of the century. Some of the state courts in the United States did begin to recognize the necessity to provide for depreciation and in some cases dividends were enjoined. In fact, Reiter concluded that "the weight of authority since about 1897 has favored an allowance for depreciation." Bonbright, however, noted that "most of these decisions, to be sure, have been concerned with the calculation of profits for other purposes than for the determination of dividend, and their applicability to the problem of dividends might therefore be questioned." Furthermore, Montgomery believed that "it was doubtful if the law compelled any company to make a provision for depreciation before paying dividends out of its earnings."

Hatfield summarized American depreciation practices just after the turn of the century. "At that time any recognition of depreciation was relatively uncommon in the accounts of American corporations and the relatively few companies which showed depreciation in prosperous years grew faint-hearted when business was poor. . . . Corporations are still apt to look upon the charge for depreciation as being an act of grace rather than of necessity and the allowance is frequently less in the lean than in the prosperous years."[63]

Appreciation

In the nineteenth century depreciation was often viewed as a decline in "value."[64] We must therefore investigate the position of the law with respect to the unrealized appreciation of assets.

Littleton believes that the British courts clarified the statutory meaning of profits with respect to price-level increases in 1870. He argues that the case of *Salisbury* v. *Metropolitan* might be interpreted as signifying that price-level increases did not produce profits in a dividend sense. However, this decision had absolutely nothing to do with the recognition of an increase in the price level.

[63] Reiter, *Profits*, 126; Bonbright, *Valuation of Property*, 933. It is extremely interesting to note that the British courts permitted a deduction for depreciation in a rate case as early as 1838; and in a decision on a similar issue allowed a depreciation allowance even though the company did not set aside a "depreciation fund." *Accountant*, February 12, 1910, 232. This was 70 years prior to the Supreme Court's ruling on depreciation in *Knoxville* v. *Knoxville Water Company*, 212 US 1 (1909), a rate case which is often heralded as marking the legal recognition of depreciation. For Montgomery, see Dicksee, *Auditing* (American ed.), p. 207; Hatfield, *Accounting*, p. 140.

[64] There were several legal cases in which profits were defined as the change in the value of net assets without specifying the valuation procedure. *Birney* v. *Ince Hall*, 35 LJ 363 (1865); *Spanish Prospecting Case*, 1 Ch 92 (1911).

In fact, there was a considerable depreciation. The company had purchased land at a cost of £2,500,000 and the land depreciated to £1,200,000. The company tried to credit profit with £60,000 or the amount that *would* have been earned at 5 per cent if £1,200,000 had been invested. It is interesting to note that the accountants approved the procedures.[65]

There are few legal decisions in Britain which shed light on this subject. One of the Lord Justices in the Lee case said that depreciation need not be recognized since appreciation should be ignored; and in the Kehoe case it was argued that appreciation is an offset to depreciation. Most of the "modern" British accountants argued that all fluctuations in value except wear and tear should be ignored; but there is a great deal of discussion that suggests all "fluctuations" were not ignored. There is even some mention made of recognizing annual charges in goodwill that is based on fluctuations in earning capacity.[66]

The legal position on unrealized appreciation was just as ambiguous in the United States. Although the courts said that unrealized appreciation does not constitute *taxable* income, there were few dividend cases where this was an issue; and one can find some decisions in which the courts allowed the credit and others where it was disallowed.[67]

Bonbright, discussing dividend law in the twentieth century, concludes that "on the whole, the modern statute law, with few, but growing exceptions, leaves the law of dividends even more moot than ever before;" and as late as 1936, one authoritative source asserted that "present procedure is unsatisfactory in that it permits periodic revaluation of assets, up or down, in accordance with current price levels and expected business developments. Occasional uncoordinated 'appraisals' produce in the average financial statements a hodge-podge of unrelated values of no explicable significance to the ordinary investors." [68]

Montgomery also registers a strong complaint on the legal issue

[65] 22 LT 840 (1870); Littleton, *Essays*, 249.

[66] Dicksee, *Goodwill and Its Treatment in the Accounts* (2nd ed., London, 1900), 17.

[67] Bonbright cites the tax decision of *Gray* v. *Darlington*, 82 US 63 (1872), where unrealized appreciation was not considered income. *Valuation of Property*, 923. Windal cites the case of *U.S.* v. *Schillinger*, 27 Fed 973 (1876), in which a similar conclusion was arrived at. "Legal Background of Realization," 30. See also: Hatfield, *Accounting*, 283; Reiter, *Profits*, 70–73.

[68] Bonbright, *Valuation of Property*, 924. The following remark about present-day British Company law is strikingly similar. "It is a moot point (although some British accountants do not realise this) whether a British company can legally distribute a profit arising from the revaluation of unrealised fixed assets." Edey, "Company Accounts in Britain," 264; see also, American Accounting Association, "A Tentative Statement of Accounting Principles underlying Corporate Financial Statements," *Accounting and Reporting Standards for Corporate Financial Statements and Preceding Statements and Supplements* (1936), 61.

of recognizing unrealized appreciation. "The law on the subject of profits is not well settled and will not be, so long as the majority of lawyers retain their profound ignorance of the accounts, but it is quite likely that no legal obstacle would prevent a corporation from revaluing part of its assets and applying the excess so raised to surplus available for dividends." [69]

Capital vs. Revenue Expenditures

Few legal cases dealt with this subject. In *Bloxam* v. *Metropolitan*,[70] the company evidently charged items to capital that were considered working expenses by the courts. Thus, the courts "overruled" the auditors who approved the procedures. Another British legal decision that relates to this issue is *Cox* v. *Edinburgh and District Tramway Co.* In this case the obsolete plant of a tramway company was replaced with new equipment. The cost of the replacement was charged to capital and the old plant was *not* written off. The court approved this procedure, basing its decision on the theory that capital not represented by tangible assets is not necessarily lost. The court also said that "although it may be a prudent and proper thing to provide for the recurrence of such expenditures [replacements], and to set up a renewal fund, that is a question which the trader considers for himself, and one as to which, even in the case of limited companies, Courts of law are not accustomed to interfere." [71] Based on this decision it would seem that company directors in Britain had a great amount of freedom in accounting for fixed assets. Depreciation might or not be periodically charged to revenue and even in the absence of depreciation reserves, replacement expenditures might be capitalized. This meant that the capital consumption costs associated with obsolete plants might never be written off.

In two American cases the view was expressed that expenditures which enhance the value of property should be capitalized.[72] This meant that maintenance should be expensed and replacements should be charged to capital with the cost of the replaced asset being written off. Some railroads had adopted the policy of capitalizing only expenditures made with funds obtained through the issuance of securities; and, superficially, this practice might appear "conservative." [73] However, if these funds were used to maintain

[69] Robert H. Montgomery, *Auditing, Theory and Practice* (New York, 1912), 194.

[70] 3 Ch App. 377 (1868).

[71] 6 S.L.T. 63 (1898); *Glasgow Herald*, June 17, 1898, extracted in Dicksee, *Auditing* (1915), 719.

[72] *Hubbard* v. *Weare*, 44 NW 915 (1890); *Mackintosh* v. *Flint and Pere Marquette Ry.*, 34 Fed 609 (1888).

[73] *Union Pacific Railroad Co.* v. *US*, 99 US 402 (1878).

or restore existing property, this procedure could hardly be described as conservative.[74] A related consideration is that bond discount was normally capitalized in the construction account.[75]

Legal discussion fails to cast much light on the problem. However, some accountants did complain that the practices associated with distinguishing between capital and revenue expenditures often resulted in inflating the value of assets. That is, repairs, maintenance, and renewal expenditures were, in some cases, charged to capital.[76]

Summary

Perhaps the most obvious conclusion that can be drawn from this brief review is that nineteenth-century British and American business firms had a great deal of freedom in accounting for assets. The courts in the period were reluctant to interfere in financial matters, accountants had little authority to impose specific standards of accounting practices, and there were few, if any, effective statutory requirements relating to accounting behavior.

Thus, in Britain, we find that while the courts recognized depreciation as a cost in 1838 and acknowledged the importance of providing for capital consumption, they did not require depreciation in calculating profits available for dividends or for the purpose of maintaining capital intact. The English cases rested on the articles of incorporation and/or the decisions of the directors and not on any per se interpretation of the law. In the United States the courts did not permit depreciation in several of the early cases and authorities believed that there was no legal requirement to provide for depreciation before declaring a dividend. The case law on the treatment of unrealized appreciation and distinguishing between capital and revenue expenditures is not very illuminating. The very paucity of the cases suggests that the courts generally were not involved in the financial affairs of a business.

Conclusions

The purpose of this paper has been to determine the nature of nineteenth-century asset accounting principles and practices and the factors that influenced the change in the structure of these principles and practices. Did accounting behavior change only in

[74] For example, in 1869 the Erie Railroad appealed to the New York State Legislature for permission to issue bonds and stock for the purpose of *restoring* the roadway. Matthew Josephson, *The Robber Barons* (Harvest Book ed., New York, 1962), 136.

[75] Hatfield, *Accounting*, 70.

[76] Brief, "Nineteenth-Century Accounting Error."

response to the economic requirements of the firm during this period?

Historically, the accounting practices of quasi-public enterprise were profoundly influenced by legal arrangements that called for a cash receipts-less-disbursements concept of profit. This implies that the value of assets was assumed to be constant, an assumption that is valid only if assets are "permanent." Although it became evident that this postulate was invalid, the fact that these practices were institutional in origin seems to have blocked accounting reform. Notwithstanding certain arguments advanced to support the use of replacement accounting, we can only conclude that the accounting practices of this class of enterprise never responded to the economic requirements of these firms because of the legal and cameralistic origin of the method.

The methods used by other firms are more difficult to assess because of the differences in their practices. At the beginning of the century the "inventory" method was employed; but the procedures associated with this method are vague and ambiguous. The early texts stressed the importance of bookkeeping but failed to provide clear instructions.[77] Rational capital accounting was not composed of a unique set of procedures in this period; [78] and the Industrial Revolution was, apparently, "so strangely slow in making men aware of what it was doing to them." [79]

The growth of large-scale corporate enterprise possessing long-lived assets made the inventory method unworkable; or, put somewhat differently, more determinate solutions to the problem of accounting for fixed assets were needed. New principles were formulated and the accounting methods adopted did begin to deal directly with the problem of capital consumption. Given the complexity of the theoretical issues associated with accounting for fixed assets, it is interesting to note that a pragmatic method for dealing with the problem slowly evolved and crystalized due to the interplay of "free market" forces and the accounting profession. For example, it is in the economic interest of creditors to insure that capital is maintained intact. In addition, retaining part of cash-flow provides management with a "fund" for replacement, expansion, to meet emergencies, and so on. Furthermore, the confidence

[77] For example, one eighteenth-century text warns that "more gentlemen are lost by total negligence of the accounts than by vice." Done by a person of Honour, *The Gentleman Accomptant. . . .* (London, 1714), 85. Another text advises, "at proper times inspect your affairs; one design of keeping books is . . . that men may know the state of their affairs." John Ford, *A Serious Address to Men in Business Concerning the Right Ordering their Affairs; with Advice to those who have Unhappily Mis-Managed* (London, 1733), 22.

[78] See Pollard's conclusion in "Capital Accounting in the Industrial Revolution," 91.

[79] J. M. Clark, *The Economics of Overhead Costs* (Chicago, 1923), 7.

of the investing public is increased if the method of valuation is unambiguous; and increased confidence reduces subjective risk and influences the interest rate.

Judicial and statutory authority did not play a significant role in determining the course of accounting behavior. Indeed, many accountants were frequently disturbed by the law which did not enforce the "generally accepted" solution to the problem of accounting for assets. Various modifications to the "going-concern" concept were made and diversity in practice can be observed. Either this principle did not have equal utility in all cases, or, because accounting practice lagged theory, some firms might have adopted the "wrong" set of accounting practices due to ignorance or error.

The nineteenth-century experience is in sharp contrast with that of the twentieth century. The courts and other legal authority in the earlier period believed that businessmen should determine business practices; and the dynamic evolution of asset accounting principles occurred in this environment. In the twentieth century, statutory authority has played a dominant role in determining the course of accounting behavior; and, according to one authority, "Once more, the possibility of further government intervention in industrial reporting matters is imminent, principally because of the accounting profession's inability to narrow the areas of difference in accounting principles and management's resistance to its critics' demands for improved corporate financial disclosure." [80]

The accounting principles advocated in the nineteenth century were designed to protect the investor as well as the firm. Some said the legal requirement to charge depreciation would stop all enterprise. Others maintained that insufficient depreciation was an important cause of business failure.[81] These were economic arguments to support the use of *different* accounting methods. On the other hand, modern-day critics of financial reporting are concerned mainly with protecting the interests of investors [82] just as the lawyers who were responsible for the double-account system intended to "direct special attention to the importance of keeping a strict account of the expenditures of moneys received by the creation of Fixed Liabilities." [83] But the double-account system might have had certain effects which were the exact opposite of what was intended. For example, one could not possibly argue that replacement accounting

[80] David F. Hawkins, "The Development of Modern Financial Reporting Practices among Amercian Manufacturing Corporations," *Business History Review*, XXXVII (Autumn, 1963), 168.
[81] *Accountants' Magazine*, XII (June, 1908), 313.
[82] Hawkins, "The Development of Modern Financial Reporting," 166.
[83] Dicksee, *Advanced Accounting*, 130.

affords investors, and especially creditors, better protection than depreciation accounting. Similarly, basing depreciation on original cost does, in general, insure the maintenance of capital in a period of falling prices, and the last quarter of the nineteenth century was such a period. However, basing depreciation on original cost in a period of rising prices does *not* provide for the maintenance of real capital.

The regulations in the twentieth century were advocated in the public interest. Nevertheless, a leading modern accountant has recently stated that the public accounting profession "appears to regard a set of financial statements as a roulette wheel to the public investor — and it is his tough luck if he doesn't understand the risks that we inject into the accounting report." [84] And one student of British accounting reform has expressed dismay over the fact that a committee having a number of functions resembling that of the Securities Exchange Commission "had not, as a body, grasped properly one of the fundamental assumptions of economic life in the western world; that it is the directors' duty to make the best possible use of the equity entrusted to them." [85] On the other hand, "The principal reason given by modern management for its general noncompliance with critic's demands is the *old feeling* that such information would help competitors;" and perhaps there is *some* validity to this belief.[86]

In the absence of institutional constraint, accounting procedures would be expected to serve the economic interests of the firm. On that assumption we have traced the development of asset accounting and have seen how certain accounting principles slowly responded to the needs of business. Whether or not the progress of accounting has been retarded by institutional forces in the twentieth century and the effects that this might have had are questions that we cannot settle here.[87] A set of accounting principles may be "best" for a particular period in history, but changing economic conditions might call for different accounting practices and advancements in technology might make new methods available.

[84] New York *Times*, October 4, 1964. Statement made by Mr. Leonard Spacek, chairman of Arthur Andersen & Co. More recently, Mr. Spacek warned that "the profits reported for the year 1964 have a greater lack of comparability and are further removed from a reflection of the true facts than at any time in the last 30 years." *Ibid.*, February 21, 1965.

[85] Edey, "Company Accounts in Britain," 263.

[86] Hawkins, "Development of Modern Financial Reporting," 166 (italics added).

[87] In a study of the auditing provisions of the British Companies Acts, a similar question is raised. "The question further arises as to whether the control exercised by the statutes have had a stultifying effect upon the development of auditing theory and practice. These controls without a doubt set a lower level below which the practice cannot sink. Some have argued that this also sets a ceiling above which the practices cannot rise." Leonard W. Hein, "The Auditor and the British Companies Acts," *Accounting Review*, XXVII (July, 1963), 520. Hein goes on to say that the "ceilings" have been periodically raised.

COLLEGE NATIONAL DES EXPERTS COMPTABLES
DE BELGIQUE
A. S. B. L.
RUE DU CONGRES, 49 — 1000 BRUXELLES
TÉL. 18.29.86 - 18.20.93 — C.C.P. 605.68

L A C O M P T A B I L I T E A T R A V E R S L E S A G E S.

Exposition organisée à la
Bibliothèque Royale Albert Ier
du 2 octobre au 8 novembre 1970.

P R E M I E R S Y M P O S I U M
INTERNATIONAL DES HISTORIENS DE LA COMPTABILITE
DU 9 OCTOBRE AU 12 OCTOBRE 1970.

Etude présentée par :

Monsieur Richard P. BRIEF
Professor of Business Statistics and Accounting
New York University

==

Depreciation Theory in Historical Perspective.

It is a privilege to talk to you to-day. The subject I have selected to discuss is depreciation theory. As all of us know, depreciation theory is one of the most discussed and disputed topics in accounting. I think that we can improve our understanding of these controversies by first viewing them in an historical context.

A few introductory remarks. Although the history of thought has been essential to the progress in almost every discipline, accountants have traditionally neglected the subject. In what state of development would we find mathematics and economics, for example, if twentieth century scholars in those fields had ignored previous accomplishments ? Unfortunately, primary sources for the study of accounting history are not generally available to those who might otherwise make use of such materials. For example, one of the most comprehensive bibliographies on accounting history contains few, if any, references to primary data (1). Of course, copies of ancient bookkeeping texts have been discussed in the literature, but these references too frequently leave the reader with the impression that prior to the twentieth century, accounting was an underdeveloped discipline. This view is simply incorrect. Accounting thought reached a much higher level of sophistication by the end of the nineteenth century than most students of the subject realize; and these early discussions of accounting problems are relevant to, and do shed light on, contemporary issues.

Without a doubt, the best single source of historical information on accounting in The Accountant, a weekly periodical that was first published in England at the end of 1874 and which continues into the present. It is apparent, however, that few of those who have an interest in accounting history have had the opportunity to examine the early issues of this publication which contain a wealth of information in the form of articles, reprinted lectures, debates, editorials, and other materials on diverse topics in accounting, business and economics.

This paper is based primarily on the discussions relating to depreciation theory that appeared in The Accountant during the last quarter of the nineteenth century (2). We shall readily conclude that most of the issues that are debated in the present day were considered by accountants nearly 100 years ago.

John Mather's paper, "Depreciation in Relation to the Audit of Accounts" (January 8, 1876), is the first work on depreciation that is mentioned in The Accountant (3). It is probably the first paper by an accountant on the subject. The paper was delivered to the Manchester Institute of Accountants and was commented on but not reprinted (4).

Mather's talk was divided into three sections :

1) auditor's responsibility;

2) principles;

and

3) cases.

../..

The auditor, according to Mather, "did not feel his responsibility any the less because it was not legal or pecuniary, but moral, affecting his conscience and reputation, rather than his pocket".

With respect to principles, nothing charged to capital should be valued above cost, and ordinary repairs must not be capitalized. When depreciation was omitted or deemed insufficient, the auditor should call attention to this finding in his certificate : "The ommission or apparent undercharge should be specifically reported, if it was proposed to pay a dividend on the basis of the accounts in question".

In the last quarter of the century the interpretation of"paying dividends out of capital" and the problem of determining "profit available for dividends" were inextricably connected with depreciation. Accountants sought, first of all, to clarify theory, and second, to understand their responsibility in these matters. However, they were offered little assistance from legal and statutory authority which failed to specify rules of accounting behavior (5). This dissatisfaction with legal institutions is one of the dominant themes in the period.

The controversy is fascinating . In general, <u>The Accountant</u> was sharply critical of existing statutes :

> "Is there a single word in the whole of the Acts restraining"
> "the payment of dividends out of capital ? There is not; "
> "what is said seems to amount to this, that the payment of "
> "dividends out of capital can be made.... "
> "What are accountants doing towards drawing up formal sug- "
> "gestions on this and other equally important points on "
> "which the Companies Acts are notoriously at fault ? Not "
> "going to sleep, let us hope. "

Here, then, is the beginning of the great debate that lasted during the remainder of the century. Can dividends be paid out of capital ? What is the difference between capital and income ? Must a provision for depreciation be made before declaring a dividend ?

On the one hand, some accountants wanted stricter laws to define "proper" accounting behavior :

> "Existing law is deplorably defective, and.... the Charte- "
> "red Accountants acting through their Institute should be "
> "the first to move in the matter, and not allow the work to "
> "be done, and the honour to be appropriated by other and less"
> "capable hands (December 19, 1885). "

This view was expressed by accountants as early as 1881.

../..

> "A shareholder is entitled to know, not what is the true va-"
> "lue of this shares, for that in most instances is a matter "
> "of opinion, but how the value of fixed assets has been esti-"
> "mated...whether at cost, at a valuation.... or otherwise, "
> "and what sums have been placed in reserve or written off "
> "for depreciation, running out of leases or other decreases "
> "in value... "
> "Much of the information... might be given if the legisla- "
> "ture made its publication compulsory upon al (June 4, 1881)"

On the other hand, some believed, along with Dicksee, that legal requirements to charge depreciation before declaring dividends would be "injurious to companies and the public.... It would stop all enterprise because it would be absolutely impossible for companies to pay dividends in the early years of their existence." (6)

In the same spirit :

> "There is nothing improper in this (returning interest on "
> "capital during construction), and as I don't approve of too"
> "much grandmotherly legislation in a free country where "
> "people should learn from their own experience how to take "
> "care of themselves, I don't approve of the State preventing"
> "undertakings being floated with an inducement of this sort."

One of the most interesting characteristics of accounting literature in this period relates to the insights one obtains into the nineteenth century business environment. Conversely, the nineteenth century business environment permitted a free and uninhibited exchange of views and this is one of the major reasons why historical discussions of accounting problems are so interesting, useful and relevant to contemporary problems.

This early stage of the development of accounting ideas reflects the profound influence which legal institutions had on accounting thought. It is perfectly apparent that most of these early thoughts on capital and income were profoundly influenced by such institutions. These controversies frequently reflected the major judicial rulings and statutes (e.g., January 16, 1886 and December 14, 1889). Unlike the subject of economics, "a subject for the most part relegated to the whitewashed rooms wherein the gas flickers, and to Public Houses on a Sunday evening" (December 15, 1888), accounting was forced to deal practically with problems having abstruse theoretical dimensions.

The next major paper on depreciation appeared in 1883 : Edwin Guthrie, "Depreciation and Sinking Funds "(April 21, 1883)(8). Here we find the clearest exposition to date of a theory of depreciation.

Guthrie defined depreciation as a cost equal to the value of the asset that is "consumed" during the year. While not exactly measurable, it is based on the assumption of a certain term of useful existence of machinery or building. Declaring that the depreciation problem concerns the recoupment of capital outlay and not profit and loss, Guthrie also lists different methods and rates that might be used to calculate depreciation.

../..

In this lecture we also find the first reference to the present-day concept of "going-concern" and its corrolary the "cost principle", i.e., that "matter and things in permanent working position must not be treated as following the fluctuations of the market" (though the use of "valuation" to check depreciation was admissible).

As was the practice in those days, most papers were reviewed by members of the various accounting societies. William Haris commented on Guthrie's views. He argued that "it is what property would fetch, not what it costs, that settles value" and that the accounts therefore should reflect current values and "let tomorrow look after itself". The "cost vs. value" controversy continues to plague accountants to-day.

Harris urged further investigation of the appreciation problem and called for an empirical study of depreciation :

> "If we could only get a few examples of the actual figures"
> "showing the cost of the plant of a concern, the amount "
> "spent for repairs, the amount written off for depreciation"
> "and the amount realised by the sale of the materials.... "
> "we should perhaps have the most interesting and most reli-"
> "able paper on depreciation that has ever been written. "

Shortly after Guthrie's lecture, Ewing Matheson's articles appeared in a periodical called the Engineer. This series of papers on depreciation were not reprinted in The Accountant, but were published in book form (9). The Accountant, in editional comments, expressed pleasure upon hearing of the publication of Matheson's work (December 29, 1883). At the same time, it noted that

> "Since the (Matheson's articles) were published, numerous "
> "letters have appeared from manufacturers and others, many"
> "of whom take exception to the sound principles laid down,"
> "and endeavor to show that the depreciation of plant is often"
> "rendered difficult by lack of profit and that in such ca-"
> "ses it may be postponed. "

When the work appeared in book form however, The Accountant was very disappointed that Matheson did not actually show how to compute the rate of depreciation (November 15, 1884) (10). Matheson brilliantly responded to this criticism (January 3, 1885) :

> "Simple and rudimentary as some of my suggestions may ap- "
> "pear to you, and to your readers, my own experience tells"
> "me how often the simplest rules are neglected, and even "
> "apparently unknown to those whose capital is at stake. "
> "..... (regarding) the absence from my book of exact rates"
> "of depreciation for different classes of plant, I am more"
> "on my ground, and I venture to assert that any positive "
> "statements of rates would be more likely to mislead than "
> "inform... fixed rules are impossible, and examples, if "
> "offered for imitation, dangerous. "

../..

Matheson then provides an example to clarify this argument and shows that about ten variables are relevant to the determination of the proper rate of depreciation.

Most accountants would probably agree with Matheson's argument. One also might wonder, for example, how these issues would have been dealt with now in the United States if tax laws and other legislation had not prescribed depreciation rates; Indeed, the implication of Matheson's argument that the use of deterministic accounting procedures results in illusory and misleading accounting measurements is not given sufficient attention to-day.

At about the same time that this dialogue took place, there was a note (November 29, 1884) about the views of an "eminent accountant in the north of England". These ideas about the depreciation problem were unusual because they suggest certain fundamental economic consequences that might be associated with the advent of modern depreciation accounting. The economic historian might usefully consider them. "Speaking of "money retained out of profits" for depreciation", this eminent accountant said that

> "it enables managers and directors to undertake continual new" "work without consulting their shareholders. It is only a- " "nother way of providing fresh capital or avoiding a call, " "which might be resisted by those interested if it came in " "that form; and further in cases where you have several " "classes of shares upon which the capital is not equally paid " "up, or where you have debenture holders as well as ordinary " "share holders, the rights of the respective parties are pre-" "judicially affected by what can only be styled the misappro-" "priation of funds intented for a specific object. "

Nineteenth century accountants demonstrated an awareness of the economic implications of accounting practices. This relationship is frequently ignored in the present age.

Adam Murray's work on depreciation was the next major piece to appear (November 5, 1887). However, his treatment of the problem differed very little from Guthrie's earlier work. Murray advocated basing depreciation on replacement cost and this is probably the first reference to that concept.

The editorial comments on Murray's paper that appeared in The Accountant are in many ways more interesting than the paper itself (November 12, 1887). They were extremely critical, saying that the paper "does not exceed expectations". This language is rather strong, considering the fact that Murray was one of the leading accountants of the day.

Specifically, the paper was criticized on the following points :

1) The argument that charging less depreciation for an old machine if new machines are cheaper, i.e., if replacement cost is less than original cost, was considered erroneous;

2) the failure to comment on the proposal to compell limited companies to state in their Articles the rate of depreciation to be charged;

and

../..

3) the failure to criticize replacement accounting which is "notoriously practiced in his district".

It is this kind of lively discussion that makes The Accountant such an interesting and valuable source of information on the history of accounting.

Students of accounting on the continent also would find scattered materials having value for historical inquiry. John Mather, for example, delivered a paper on German balance sheets (February 11, 1888), and an excellent discussion of European company law may be found in the February 23, 1895 issue. There are numerous other discussions about accounting practices in other parts of the world during this period.

The most outstanding contribution to depreciation theory in the nineteenth century was O.G. Ladelle's brilliant essay, "The Calculation of Depreciation" (November 29 and December 6, 1890). Ladelle died of typhoid fever at the age of 28 before he was able to deliver the paper (11). One can only speculate about what his impact on accounting theory would have been, had he lived.

Ladelle saw the depreciation problem as one in which a group of speculators buy an asset, with each person being assigned the expected benefits for a particular year. For these uncertain benefits they must jointly agree on the proportion of the original cost each must pay. In his words,

> "....assume, for convenience of illustration, that a large number of persons, numbered from 1 upwards, purchase as a joint venture, an asset, which they do not propose to use simultaneously, but agree to use for a year apiece, in turn, and that we are asked to determine the method of apportioning the cost between them. For, if we can do this it is quite clear that the union of all these persons, into one firm can make no difference to our calculations, and that the same figures, will give the amounts which the firm ought to charge to each year in its accounts."

Although Wright (12), in evaluating Ladelle's theory criticized it on several counts, he did note that "the strength of Ladelle's position lies precisely in his recognition of the fact than an equitable allocation of intertemporal joint costs must rest upon a sound valuation of the bundle of residual services to be transferred from one period to the next". He also commented that "A striking feature of Ladelle's depreciation formula is its complete generality....". And Dewey (13), an economist, recently argued that Ladelle "proposed a revision of the accounting theory of profit that, if adopted, would have allayed most of the economist's misgivings about the (accountant's) treatment of capital gains and losses". Dewey continued :

> "Ladelle's proposal had the considerable merits of outlining an internally consistent way of treating capital gains and losses and underscoring the connection between profit and the divergence of *ex-post* results from *ex-ante* anticipations."

../..

The general depreciation method derived by Ladelle is almost identical to the so-called present value method of calculating depreciation. This method has been given other names such as the annuity method, compound interest method, economic depreciation, etc....and it has been discussed by numerous writers, especially in the last two decades. However, Ladelle's use of the problem of dividing cost among joint speculators as an analogy to structure the problem of allocating cost among joint time periods distinguishes his theory from all other work on the problem.

What conclusions may be drawn from this brief survey of nineteenth century depreciation theory ? First, most of the issues related to the problem of accounting for assets were extensively discussed and debated in the last century. The contemporary theorist could derive greater benefits from this material than is commonly realized.

Second, the laissez-faire environment in which the accounting thought developed provides the modern accountant with a new perspective to view his problems. Valuable new insights into current issues can be obtained from studying the literature from the earlier period. Third, these historical documents shed additional light on the problems of economic development in the nineteenth century, on the business environment, and on the development of the accounting profession. Much more work needs to be done in studying and synthesizing this early work.

FOOTNOTES.

(1) R.H. Parker : "Accounting History : A Select Bibliography", Abacus, 1 (September, 1965). No criticism of Parker's excellent bibliography is intented.

(2) The discussion that follows makes no attempt to summarize all the discussions on this subject during the period.

(3) Unless otherwise noted, all dates refer to a weekly issue of The Accountant.

(4) The Accountant reprinted many of the papers delivered to the numerous accounting societies in the last quarter of the century.

(5) See my "The Origin and Evolution of Nineteenth-Century Asset-Accounting", Business History Review, XL (Spring, 1966)
We shall not, in this paper, elaborate on the numerous and interesting discussions concerning the accountant's responsibility and the debates concerning the legislation of accounting behavior during the period. We would be remiss, however, by not noting that this material has current interest to the accounting profession. Adam Murray's paper, "On the Progress of Accountancy and the duties which come within the Scope of the Accountant's Practice" (December 24 and 31, 1881), is the first on the subject, although there were interesting articles on this topic earlier that year (January 23, June 6, September 24, October 1, 8, 15, 22, 29 and November 19). Some of these analyses of the problem are excellent.
For example, articles on why accounting practices can not be legislated are certainly relevant to contemporary problems. Stimulating discussions on the auditor's certificate may be found in 1883 and 1884, and Ernest Cooper's paper, "Chartered Accountants as Auditors of Companies" (November 13, 1886), contains a well-documented history of the subject. Another noteworthy treatment of this same subject apeared in 1902 : Arthur Lowes Dickinson, "The Duties and Responsibilities of the Public Accountant" (July 26, 1902).

It is also important to realize that not all of the information that would be of interest to a student of accounting thought may be found in formal articles. Consider, for example, the following remarks in a letter by L.R. Dicksee that appeared in the March 1, 1902 issue :

"....even with regard to such important questions as the value of as-"
"sets, provision for depreciation, the assessments of profits earned,"
"and the distribution of unrealised profits, the Courts have shown a "
"marvelous disinclination (to provide) principles for the safe gui- "
"dance of the auditor... "
"No doubt it has acted wisely in adopting this course, however, be- "
"cause any attempt to state explicitly what the duties of auditors are"
"in all cases would afford the best possible excuse in such cases for"
"the insufficiency of the audit that has been performed. "

(6) "Obligation of a Company to Provide for Depreciation of Wastings Assets Before Declaring Dividends", debate before the Glasgow Institute of Accounts Debating Society, December 14, 1889; March 18, 1893.

../..

(7) For example, Adam Murray commented in his paper, "Income Tax Practice" (January 12, 1884), "about the probability of persons returning their income Tax at a larger amount than it really was, and thus pay more than they ought to do, because they did not care to disclose the books to commissioners who happened to be in the same trade". In this business environment it is small wonder that accountants had a difficult job in imposing accounting rules on companies. But then, firms were concerned about the economic consequences of disclosing information. What are these consequences to-day ?

(8) Actually, two other papers were published before Guthrie's. The first, a paper by F.R. Goddard, "Treatment of Depreciation of Freehold and Leased Properties", was delivered to the Northern Institute of Chartered Accountants on November 8, 1882. However, it was not reprinted. The second paper was a lecture on auditing presented to the Birmingham Accountants Students'Society on November 28, 1882 and it was reprinted in the January 1, 1883 issue of the Bookkeeper, an American publication.

(9) Ewing Matheson, Depreciation of Factories (London : E. & F. Spon, 1884).

(10) See also the December 13, 1884 issue for a discussion of Matheson's work.

(11) The paper was reprinted and commented on in my "A Late Nineteenth Century Contribution to the Theory of Depreciation", Journal of Accounting Research, 3 (Spring, 1965).

(12) F.K. Wright, "An Evaluation of Ladelle's Theory of Depreciation", Journal of Research, 3 (Autumn, 1965).

(13) Donald Dewey, The Theory of Imperfect Competition - A Radical Reconstruction (New York : Columbia University Press, 1969), pp. 146-47.

3142/CV/VB.

The Accounting Historians Journal
Vol. 9, No. 1
Spring 1982

Richard P. Brief
NEW YORK UNIVERSITY

HICKS ON ACCOUNTING

Abstract: Whenever income and capital maintenance concepts are discussed at the conceptual level, a reference to Hicks is likely to be found. These references are misleading since Hicks himself believed that the proper basis of valuation in the financial statements of a firm is historical cost. He also argued that accountants should not make price-level adjustments. Hicks' views on accounting, which are scattered in his writings over a period of 35 years, are reviewed in this paper.

J. R. Hicks viewed accounting from a statistician's perspective and he emphasized the need for objective accounting data. Hicks also was concerned with the principles of account classification which he once called "the canons of orderliness."[1] The need for objectivity and order, together with a very strict interpretation of how accounts should be framed to monitor management, led this 1972 Nobel Prize economist to defend the practice of valuing assets at historical cost and to argue, as a corollary, that accountants should not make price-level adjustments.

This short description of Hicks on accounting differs sharply from the popular view. The misconception is due to the pervasive influence on accounting thought of Hicks' definition of a man's income as "the maximum value which he can consume during a week, and still expect to be as well off at the end of the week as he was at the beginning."[2] This income concept was introduced into accounting literature by Alexander in 1950 and, by the early 1960s, Zeff reported that the definition "recurs with remarkable frequency in economic and (especially) accounting writings."[3] Today, whenever the income concept is discussed at a conceptual level, a reference to Hicks is likely to be found.

Hicks himself warned that income and related concepts are "bad tools, which break in your hands."[4] However, with few exceptions, most theorists have not only ignored this admonition, but they also have overlooked other work by Hicks which is more directly related to accounting practice.

Hicks' interest in accounting was signalled in 1942 with the publication of *The Social Framework.* This book is a text on "Social

Accounting," which the author contends should be a first course in economics. Social Accounting is defined as "the accounting of the whole community or nation, just as Private Accounting is the accounting of the individual firm."[5] In the second edition (1952), Hicks commented that "when I wrote in 1942, I knew very little of the practice of accountants, and I am afraid professional accountants who read my book were often bothered by needless unorthodoxy in the use of terms." Among others, F. Sewell Bray is thanked for some "excellent coaching in accounting usages."[6]

Interesting ideas on accounting also are contained in *The Problem of Budgetary Reform* (1948) and noteworthy opinions are expressed in a review of a book by Bray that was published in the *Economic Journal,* also in 1948. Other works which have special significance for accountants include: "The Measurement of Capital" (1969), *Capital and Time* (1973) and "Capital Controversies: Ancient and Modern" (1974).

The purpose of this paper is to review Hicks' main thoughts on accounting practice. They concern the need for objectivity, the principles of account classification and the traditional questions of depreciation and asset valuation. These ideas, which are scattered in books and articles written over a period of 35 years, make it evident that Hicks' actual influence on accounting was the opposite of what he intended.

Objectivity of Accounting Measurements

In a 1948 review of a book by Bray, Hicks emphasized the need for objectivity and then defended the cost principle. He used the following argument to reach this conclusion.

The function of accounting, on the lowest level, is to make a record of business transactions. On a higher level, accountants devise a means to distill from the record of transactions summaries which "enable the meaning of the record to be grasped, as well as it can be grasped."[7] These summaries should be constructed using rules which do not introduce outside elements. But since no set of rules will produce summaries "which are equally meaningful on all occasions,"[8] the user of financial statements must exercise judgment in interpreting them.

Although the interpretation of financial statements is considered the highest part of the accountant's function, it should not get "mixed up" with the lower part because the accounts must be "as objective as possible."[9] "This demand is so exactly parallel to the demand that statisticians have had to make of their investigators . . . that its sense is readily acceptable, once we see it . . . ."[10]

The consequence of this position led to the conclusion that the justification for valuation at historical cost is "simply that the original purchase price is the one objective valuation of the asset . . . . Any other valuation must be a matter of judgment, and therefore belongs to the stage of interpretation, not to the stage of the compilation of the basic summaries."[11]

The need for objectivity is the central issue in accounting and it has two further implications. First,

> It reproves those economists who have demanded from the basic accounts information which those accounts cannot properly give. And it also reproves those accounting practices (such as the practice of valuing stocks at cost or market price, *whichever is the lower)* which edge a little interpretation into the work of summarising, and therefore diminish the objectivity of the basic tables.[12]

Second,

> Every statistical table needs to be annotated, and in a similar way the full meaning of an accounting statement can only be expected to emerge in the accompanying report. But the accountant's report goes to the directors, while his figures go to the shareholders; he has thus some public obligation to pack into his figures the maximum of information, even if he can only do this, within the limits prescribed, by some sacrifice of objectivity. How ought this difficulty to be got over? Should it be laid down that companies must publish an audited report as well as audited accounts? Or would this make the accountant, more than ever, master of the destinies of us all?[13]

Ordering of Accounts

In 1948 Hicks also wrote a short monograph, *The Problem of Budgetary Reform,* and it dealt with the classification problem. The importance he accorded this problem is evident in the initial discussion of the accounting and economic aspects of the definition of a budget surplus. The accounting aspect concerned maintaining order in government accounts and the economic dimension related to the relationship between government accounts and the rest of the economy. Although Hicks explicitly states that he writes as an economomist, he strongly contended that the accounting aspect is the most important consideration.

> If we can agree upon the principles by which the government's accounts should be ordered, the accounts of National Income and Expenditure could be adjusted to fit; but if we start from the other end, beginning from the economic requirements, we may easily be endeavoring to fit the government accounts into a framework with which it is difficult, and from their own point of view may be undesirable, for them to conform.[14]

For Hicks the principles of account classification had to do with problems like whether a distinction ought to be made between current and capital items. The main issue was not a matter of economics but rather a question of purpose. Different systems of account classification were needed for different purposes. Hicks repeatedly stressed the point of view that purpose is the critical determinant of accounting practice.

The possibility of putting government finances on a business accounting basis also was mentioned, but this "drastic" remedy was rejected even though

> It would provide a new and authoritative set of canons for orderliness; it would enlist the experience and influence of the accountancy profession in maintaining those standards; and it would facilitate the integration of the government's accounts with those of the rest of the economy in national income calculations, with all that implies for the smooth working of rational employment policy.[15]

A similar statement was made in the second edition of *The Social Framework* (1952) and it was repeated in the fourth edition (1971).

> The first thing that has to be done is to prepare the bricks out of which the structure is to be built, by constructing a standard set of accounts for the individual units out of which the national economy is composed. Much of this task has already been performed by professional accountants, and we can draw heavily upon their work at this stage of the argument.[16]

Hicks often referred to the accountant's positive contributions as well as his influential position. He even once discussed the influence of accounting practice on the history of economic thought.[17]

Depreciation Accounting

In 1939 Hicks and Hicks remarked that the calculation of depreciation presents "awkward problems."[18] This statement was often repeated. Hicks also called depreciation an "artificial" item that does not correspond to actual cash payments. It is "less solid" than other items in an income statement and there is "some room for judgment" about the precise sum to be put down, though accountants are generally guided by conventional rules about this "most uncertain" item.[19] Over a quarter of a century later similar comments are made.

> There are items, of which depreciation and stock accumulation are the most important, which do not reflect actual transactions but are estimates (by the accountant, not by the statistician) of changes in the value of assets which have not, or not yet, been sold.[20]

Exactly the same views were expressed in *Capital and Time* where the meaning of these estimates was elaborated on.

> These are estimates in a different sense from that previously mentioned. They are not statistician's estimates of a true figure, which happens to be unavailable; there is no sure figure to which they correspond. They are estimates that are relative to a purpose; for different purposes they may be made in different ways.[21]

Hicks never criticized the accountant's method of calculating depreciation. He simply observed that there was no firm economic solution to the depreciation problem and that the methods developed by accountants as soon as they were confronted with the problem "were probably what they had to do . . . . It is what they still do, even in this day."[22]

All English editions of *The Social Framework* (1942, 1952, 1960, and 1971) and the American editions (1945 and 1955) contained an Appendix on depreciation. The main point was that different people might estimate depreciation in different ways and the same person might have different estimates for different purposes. Again, the focus is on purpose.

Two particular estimates for the depreciation of a firms' fixed capital are discussed. The first is for the purpose of determining profits available for dividends and the second is made for the purpose of taxation. Conservative principles govern the calculation on which dividends are paid, whereas tax laws are based on a concept of fairness.

Hicks also pointed out that these depreciation estimates are not satisfactory for the purpose of determining national income when prices are unstable. Under inflationary conditions it is the task of the economists to work out methods to compute real depreciation. However, "although it is necessary, in the interest of fairness, to go back to the original purchase price (for that is firm ground, not somebody's guess), to do this is not economically satisfactory."[23] But Hicks never suggested that accountants ought to make this computation.

Asset Valuation

The idea that "the fixed capital used by a manufacturing firm may have half a dozen different values that can be plausibly put upon it"[24] often was repeated. Purpose was paramount.

> The measurement of capital is one of the nastiest jobs that economists have set to statisticians. Finding that it is so nasty, the working satistician very naturally asks for guidance. Will the economist please explain just what it is that he wants?[25]

The 1969 paper explicitly analyzes the accountant's practice of valuing assets at original cost and two reasons are given for making corrections to this valuation—price-level changes and technical progress.

It is significant that Hicks did not think that accountants should be the ones to make price-level adjustments. He concluded that the task of making price-level adjustments would be a formidable one and implied that on a cost-benefit basis, it would not be worthwhile to have accountants correct the accounts for inflation. Hicks put it this way.

> To correct balance-sheets of companies, one by one, so as to make them conform to the principle I have been outlining would obviously be a formidable undertaking. One could not expect that it should be done by the accountants, the purpose of whose calculations (as we have seen) is quite different.[26]

What was the purpose of the accountant's calculations? Hicks believed that "the first object of commercial accounting is to watch over the capital of the business . . . ."[27] Thus, accountants could not be expected to make price-level adjustments because

> If one asks why the company needs a balance-sheet the answer must surely be given in terms of its obligation to its shareholders and to other creditors. It has to show, periodically, what it has done with their money.[28]

This emphasis on stewardship led to the conclusion that

> The balance-sheet of the company, as explained, is designed to show shareholders what has been done with their money. If it is this which has to be shown, the original cost of the actual assets held is the magnitude that is relevant.[29]

The other reason for adjusting original cost is technical progress. However, from an accounting viewpoint, technical progress is part of obsolescence and is taken into account in choosing the method of depreciation. But from an economic viewpoint, Hicks argues the accountant is too pessimistic because "he does not allow (and from his own point of view is quite right not to allow) for the increase in the productivity of new investments that come from technical progress."[30] Therefore, the accountant's measure of depreciation normally overstates the gross investment needed to maintain capital since real capital increases faster than it appears to do on financial statements since the reinvestment of depreciation allowances is made on continually more favorable terms.

There is no ambiguity about Hicks thoughts on the accountant's responsibility for asset valuation. Financial statements should be based on historical costs and adjustments for price-level changes should be made by the user, not the accountant.

Concluding Comment

At the 1969 meeting of the International Statistical Institute where Hicks presented the paper, "The Measurement of Capital," another paper on the same subject was given. The opening remarks are jocular, but the message captures Hicks' attitude towards the valuation problem which accountants face.

> Without the threat of thumbscrew, and indeed with no urging at all, an economist may often be found to declare that his idea of a measure for a stock of capital is to equate it to the present discounted value of the future stream of

> earnings that the stock of capital will generate. This is so inherently unmeasurable that it will amuse a statistician until he perceives that the suggestion is offered somewhat more than half-seriously.[31]

When it came to practical problems of measurement, Hicks sought to avoid the kind of definitions that are more "at home in those simplified models beloved of economic theorists" than in a world of "flesh and blood."[32]

Hicks' emphasis on the need for objectivity and his conception of the meaning of stewardship led him to defend the traditional practice of valuing assets at original cost less depreciation and to argue that accountants should not make price-level adjustments. These views will surprise those (and there are many) who have used the Hicksian income concept to develop a conceptual framework in accounting.

POSTSCRIPT

After this article went into production the author received a letter from Sir John Hicks. Although Hicks indicated that he did not have time to do more than glance at a copy of the article, he commented that "I had no idea when I wrote that chapter in *Value and Capital* that it would be taken up by accountants; and The Social Accounts as I first envisaged them, were a pure economist's construction. By the time of the later editions of that book [1952, 1960, and 1971] I had this further experience, and the same applies to all my later writings." The experience Hicks is making reference to is a 1949 meeting (which was referred to in the 2nd edition of *The Social Framework*) with, among others, Richard Stone and F. Sewell Bray. This meeting led to the publication of *Some Accounting Terms and Concepts* (Cambridge: Cambridge University Press, 1951). I have not seen this book. Hicks then went on to say that "it is perhaps in the IIPF paper ["The Concept of Income in Relation to Taxation and to Business Management," Proceedings of the 35th Congress of the International Institute of Public Finance, Taormina, 10-14 September, 1979, Detroit, Michigan 1981] which I sent to you that this becomes clearest."

The 1979 paper compares the accountant's depreciation with "true" depreciation. Its basic conclusions are consistent with his earlier work. Hicks once again stressed that "The accountant's conventional way of measuring income, though (as we have seen) it has elements in it that are arbitrary, is largely based upon actual transactions . . . . It would not be an improvement to replace this relatively firm assessment by one that in practice must be even more, even much more arbitrary." He also emphasized that "when it is proposed to make corrections to the conventional allowances, to adjust to inflation, the question of whether the conventional allowances were appropriate, even in absence of inflation, is bound to be raised. So one comes back to the subjective assessments—how much can be *safely* taken out of the business—from which the accountant's procedure had been thought to be an escape."

Both the 1974 paper delivered at the annual meetings of the American Economic Association and the paper given at the IIPF meeting in 1979 should interest the accounting historian for another reason. In these papers, Hicks directly addresses questions involving the history of accounting. In addition, in his letter Hicks also remarked that "I see that the journal in which you are publishing is on the history of accounting. I wonder if it is known to your friends that one of the most remarkable contributions of accounting to civilization is the beginning of the year on the first of January. The Florentine merchants in the fifteenth century found this sense of orderliness (as you rightly call it) vexed by the practice then and in other places long after common of beginning on March 25. They wanted to have their yearly accounts made up of a tidy number of monthly accounts, so they looked for a feast of the Church which fell on the first day of the month, and found it on the first of January." The reference Hicks provides is to a French economic historian, Yves Renouard, who in 1969 published a book of essays which I have not yet seen.

I am grateful to Sir John Hicks for his thoughtful comments. I also thank Professor Edward Stamp for suggesting that I communicate with Hicks.

FOOTNOTES

[1]*The Problem of Budgetary Reform,* p. 14.
[2]*Value and Capital,* p. 172.
[3]Zeff, p. 620.
[4]*Value and Capital,* p. 177.
[5]*The Social Framework* (1942), p. vi.
[6]*The Social Framework* (1952), p. vii.
[7]Review, p. 562.
[8]Review, p. 563.
[9]Review, p. 563.
[10]Review, p. 563.
[11]Review, p. 563.
[12]Review, pp. 563-564.

[13]Review, p. 564.

[14]*The Problem of Budgetary Reform,* p. 6.

[15]*The Problem of Budgetary Reform,* p. 14.

[16]*The Social Framework* (1952), p. 224; (1971), p. 260.

[17]"Capital Controversies: Ancient and Modern," p. 310.

[18]"Public Finance in National Income," p. 147.

[19]*The Social Framework* (1942), p. 225.

[20]"The Measurement of Capital," p. 254.

[21]Capital and Time, p. 155.

[22]"Capital Controversies: Ancient and Modern," p. 312.

[23]*The Social Framework* (1942), p. 275. A similar statement is made in the fourth edition (1971), pp. 301-302.

[24]*The Social Framework* (1942), p. 102.

[25]"The Measurement of Capital," p. 254.

[26]"The Measurement of Capital," p. 259.

[27]*The Problem of Budgetary Reform,* p. 15.

[28]"The Measurement of Capital," p. 253.

[29]"The Measurement of Capital," p. 258.

[30]"The Measurement of Capital," p. 261.

[31]Evans, "Some Comments on Measures of Changes in Capital Stock Aggregates," p. 265.

[32]"Maintaining Capital Intact: A Further Suggestion," pp. 132-133.

BIBLIOGRAPHY

Alexander, Sydney S. "Income Measurement in a Dynamic Economy." *Five Monographs on Business Income.* American Institute of Accountants, 1950; reprinted, Lawrence, Kansas: Scholars Book Co., 1973, pp. 1-96.

Evans, W. Duane. "Some Comments on Measures of Changes in Capital Stock Aggregates." *Proceedings of the 37th Session.* International Statistical Institute (London 1969). Vol. XLIII, Book 1, pp. 265-275.

Hicks, J. R. *Value and Capital.* Oxford: Clarendon Press, 1939.

_______________ and Hicks, U. K. "Public Finance in National Income." *Review of Economic Studies* (February 1939), pp. 147-155.

_______________. *The Social Framework.* Oxford: Clarendon Press, 1942.

_______________. "Maintaining Capital Intact: A Further Suggestion." *Economica* (May 1942), pp. 174-179 in Parker, R. H. and Harcourt, G. C., eds. *Readings in the Concept and Measurement of Income.* Cambridge, University Press, 1969, pp. 132-138.

_______________ and Hart, A. G. *The Social Framework of the American Economy.* New York: Oxford University Press, 1945.

_______________. Review of *Precision and Design in Accountancy* (London: Gee, 1947), by F. Sewell Bray. *Economic Journal* (December 1948), pp. 562-564.

_______________. *The Problem of Budgetary Reform.* Oxford: Clarendon Press, 1948.

_______________. *The Social Framework.* 2nd ed. Oxford: Clarendon Press, 1952.

_______________. Hart, A. G. and Ford, J. W. *The Social Framework of the American Economy.* 2nd ed. New York: Oxford University Press, 1955.

_______________. *The Social Framework.* 3rd ed. Oxford: Clarendon Press, 1960.

_______________. "The Measurement of Capital." *Proceedings of the 37th Session,* International Statistical Institute (London, 1969), Vol. XLIII, Book 1, pp. 253-263.

________________. *The Social Framework*. 4th ed. Oxford: Clarendon Press, 1971.

________________. *Capital and Time*. Oxford: Clarendon Press, 1973.

________________. "Capital Controversies: Ancient and Modern." *American Economic Review* (May 1974), pp. 307-319.

Zeff, Stephen A. "Replacement Cost: Member of the Family, Welcome Guest, or Intruder?" *The Accounting Review* (October 1962), pp. 611-625.

An index of growth due to depreciation*

RICHARD P. BRIEF *New York University*
HECTOR R. ANTON *New York University*

Abstract. While factors such as inflation, technological change and growth often have been discussed in connection with the adequacy of provisions for depreciation under a historical cost model, there is another dimension to the capital maintenance problem and it concerns the multiplier effect of depreciation. When an amount equal to depreciation is reinvested, a firm's productive capacity tends to increase. Reinvestment of depreciation also increases a firm's financial capital if book depreciation is more accelerated than economic depreciation. Based on a model developed by Ijiri (1967), this paper derives an index of this growth due to depreciation. The index estimates a bias in conventional depreciation methods that has been overlooked in the literature on the subject. This bias has implications for inflation accounting because if conventional depreciation methods have a built-in growth bias, adjustments for inflation may be a type of double counting. A second implication mentioned concerns the bias in accounting rates of return.

Résumé. Bien que des facteurs tels l'inflation, les changements technologiques et la croissance ont souvent été examinés à propos de la pertinence des provisions pour dépréciation dans le cadre du modèle au coût historique, un autre aspect du problème de préservation du capital subsiste et il concerne l'effet multiplicateur de l'amortissement. Lorsqu'un montant égal à l'amortissement est réinvesti, la capacité d'exploitation de la firme a tendance à s'accroître. Le réinvestissement de l'amortissement fait aussi augmenter le capital de la firme si l'amortissement comptable est plus accéléré que la dépréciation économique. En se basant sur un modèle élaboré par Ijiri (1967), cet article dérive un indice de cette croissance attribuable à l'amortissement. L'indice estime un biais des méthodes traditionnelles, qui a été négligé dans les recherches consacrées au sujet. Ce biais a des implications en comptabilité des effets de l'inflation, car si les méthodes d'amortissement traditionnelles comportent implicitement ce biais de croissance, les redressements relatifs à l'inflation peuvent être assimilés à un double comptage. Une deuxième conséquence est signalée, soit le biais relatif aux taux de rendement comptable.

Introduction

Although it is generally believed that historic cost depreciation provides "insufficient" depreciation allowances, there have been contrary views. During the 1930s some economists argued that because of falling prices and technological

* The authors would like to thank the reviewers for their helpful comments.

Contemporary Accounting Research Vol. 3 No. 2 pp 394–407

improvement, "Re-investment of part of the present depreciation allowances will maintain productive capacity. Business can invest all of its depreciation allowances only by expanding its productive capacity" (Altman (1939, p. 426)).[1] A decade or so later under very changed economic conditions, Eisner (1952) showed that when a firm's gross investment grows at a constant rate, depreciation exceeds replacement requirements, even if prices rise modestly.[2] More recently, Hicks (1979, p. 84) reasoned that, "If, with economic progress, the prices of 'machines' are falling, relatively to the prices of finished products, more will be deducted, on the accountant's method, than is necessary to keep the business in working order as a going concern."[3]

There is another dimension to questions relating to the adequacy of depreciation that does not depend directly on factors such as inflation, technological change and growth. It concerns the phenomenon that when an amount equal to the depreciation of a period is reinvested, the firm's productive capacity increases.[4] This tendency for depreciation to expand physical capacity has been called the "Lohmann-Ruchti Effect" after West German economists of the early 1950s (Takatera (1960, p. 50)) and the Depreciation Multiplier (Horvat (1958); de Wolff (1966)).[5]

One criticism of the literature on the multiplier effect of depreciation is that even if a firm's physical capital increases due to the reinvestment of depreciation under certain assumed conditions, reinvestment of depreciation does not necessarily increase financial capital (Gordon (1953), Edwards (1961), Gynther (1968) and Fabricant (1971)). These writers define financial capital as the present discounted value of the firm's future cash flows. Therefore, the argument is simply that if book depreciation equals economic depreciation (Hotelling (1925)), the reinvestment of an amount equal to depreciation would keep financial capital constant. To increase financial capital, book depreciation must be greater than economic depreciation, i.e., reinvestment must be more than is needed to maintain financial capital so as to make the firm "better off" in the sense that the present value of the firm has increased.

Of course, it is not likely that regular or book depreciation methods equal economic depreciation. The lack of equivalence has been discussed by Fisher

1 See also Hansen (1939, p. 359). Chase (1940, p. 234) blamed depreciation practices for providing excessive allowances but quipped that the situation will not be corrected by putting The American Institute of Accountants in the "dog-house". Carey (1940) wrote an editorial on this subject and, a few months later, May (1940, p. 347) disputed the evidence and argued that depreciation provisions are "inadequate to provide either for the amortization of capital invested therein or for the replacement thereof when replacement becomes necessary."

2 The literature on this thesis, both pro and con, is extensive: Domar (1953); Eisner (1953a, 1953b, 1954); Kane (1952); Kaufman and Gleason (1953); Mason (1935); Mautz (1954); May (1954); Schiff (1954).

3 Similar comments were made in Hicks (1969, p. 261).

4 The idea can be traced to Karl Marx (Horvat (1958)). An early reference to the expansionary effect of depreciation in accounting literature is James (1916).

5 Takatera (1960) supplies an extensive bibliography on the subject including some of the references previously cited.

and McGowan (1983, p. 83), Kay (1976, p. 449) and many others in connection with the measurement error in using accounting rates of return to estimate economic returns. In contrast to the research on the bias in accounting rates of return, the emphasis in this study is on the effect of depreciation policy on financial capital. If depreciation is more (less) than is needed to maintain financial capital, i.e., more (less) than economic depreciation, the reinvestment of an amount equal to depreciation will have a tendency to increase (decrease) financial capital. The increase (decrease) will not, of course, be reflected in the financial statements because when an amount equal to book depreciation is reinvested, net book value remains constant under the rules of double entry bookkeeping. Therefore, the question which needs to be addressed is how to estimate the bias caused by the choice of a depreciation method other than economic depreciation.

The derivation of the bias given here is based on work by Ijiri (1967) who showed that when a firm reinvests an amount equal to depreciation in fully depreciable assets, and applies the same depreciation method to all investments, the periodic reinvestments converge to the *P*eriodic *R*einvestment based on *D*epreciation (PRD) constant.[6] After a short discussion of the PRD constant in terms of physical capital, a numerical example is used to explain how a PRD policy can affect financial capital. Then an index of the growth in financial capital due to depreciation is derived analytically. The index shows the bias in using book value as an estimate of financial capital when there is a divergence between book depreciation and economic depreciation.

The PRD constant

Assume that a firm initially invests one dollar in a depreciable project that has a life of four years. At the end of the first and subsequent years, the firm reinvests in identical, perfectly divisible projects an amount equal to depreciation. If straight line depreciation is used to depreciate the original investment and all later projects, the reinvestment in each year converges to a limiting value. This value is called the PRD constant.

Table 1 shows the arithmetic of a PRD constant. The column totals give the amount of reinvestment in a year, beginning with an initial investment of one dollar. The rows corresponding to each column total indicate the depreciation on each amount reinvested. Thus, one dollar is invested in year 0 and depreciation on this investment is $.25 in each of the next four years. Reinvestment in year

6 While it is, of course, more usual to assume that there is no direct causal relationship between depreciation, reinvestment and cash flows, it is, as Ijiri (1967, p. 32) pointed out, "... a near-sighted argument to say that depreciation has nothing to do with the funds flow of a firm". In a similar vein, Dorfman (1981, p. 1019) commented, in connection with a model that also assumes the reinvestment of depreciation, that although some theorists would deride the model as far-fetched, "Farfetchedness is the characteristic of all economic theories which are simple enough to yield intelligible insights, which is why none of them ought to be taken literally". Furthermore, it is, in fact, more realistic to assume that depreciation is reinvested as opposed to the more usual, unstated assumption in accounting that depreciation funds are left idle until replacement takes place at the end of an asset's life.

TABLE 1
The PRD constant

Reinvestment in year	Depreciation in year 0	1	2	3	4	5	6	7	8	9	10	11	12
0	(1)	.2500	.2500	.2500	.2500								
1		(.25)	.0625	.0625	.0625	.0625							
2			(.3125)	.0781	.0781	.0781	.0781						
3				(.3906)	.0977	.0977	.0977	.0977					
4					(.4883)	.1221	.1221	.1221	.1221				
5						(.3604)	.0901	.0901	.0901	.0901			
6							(.3880)	.0970	.0970	.0970	.0970		
7								(.4069)	.1017	.1017	.1017	.1017	
8									(.4109)	.1027	.1027	.1027	.1027
9										(.3915)	.0979	.0979	.0979
10											(.3993)	.0998	.0998
11												(.4021)	.1005
12													(.4009)

one is \$.25 and depreciation on this reinvestment is \$.0625 in each of the next four years, i.e., in years two, three, four and five. Reinvestment in year two is \$.3125 and equals total depreciation in the year. Depreciation on the reinvestment of \$.3125 is \$.0781 in the next four years. The depreciation-reinvestment process continues until the amount of reinvestment converges to \$.40 per year in the long run. The PRD constant is, therefore, 0.4. By year 12, the difference between the actual reinvestment of \$.4009 and the long-run figure of \$.40 is small. The project has a four-year life; therefore as long as there are no early retirements, gross book value in the steady state equals the amount of reinvestment in four successive years, or \$1.60. Of course, since the new investments are always offset by depreciation, the firm's net book value (original cost plus additions less depreciation) always equals \$1.00.

In order to interpret the PRD constant in terms of physical capital, an assumption must be made about the manner in which the physical capacity of the project deteriorates. Suppose the initial project is a machine of the "one-hoss shay" variety that has a constant annual capacity of 10 units of product (total four-year capacity of 40 units) until the end of its four-year life when its capacity falls to zero. In this situation, the firm will have 16 units of annual capacity in the steady state, with four units of annual capacity contributed by the machine purchased in the current year, 4 units from the machine purchased one year ago, etc. Total capacity at any moment remains unchanged at 40 units because 16 units of total capacity are contributed by the machines purchased in the current year, 12 units from the machines purchased one year ago, etc.

The formula Ijiri (1967) derived for the PRD constant, a, is expressed as a fraction of the initial investment:

$$a = 1 / \sum_{t=1}^{n} t p_t \tag{1}$$

where n is the *assumed* life of the project and p_t is depreciation in year t, stated as a fraction of the project's original cost. Since no salvage value is assumed,

$$\sum_{t=1}^{n} p_t = 1.$$

That is, a project is fully depreciated at the end of its assumed life. The restrictions on the p_t are $p_t \geqq 0$ and $p_n > 0$, and all conventional depreciation methods have these properties.

Equation (1) can be evaluated for traditional depreciation methods. For example, with straight line depreciation, it can be shown that $a = 2/(n + 1)$. If $n = 4$ and $a = .4$, the firm's physical capacity will be 1.6 times its initial annual capacity in the steady state. For sum-of-years digits depreciation $a = 3/(n + 2)$. If $n = 4$ and $a = .5$, the annual physical capacity will increase by a factor of 2 in the steady state. Thus, the depreciation multiplier equals na.

Unlike de Wolff (1966), whose results were derived for different assumptions about an asset's pattern of physical deterioration assuming straight line depreciation, Ijiri's formula is more general and applicable to any depreciation method. However, when the PRD constant in equation (1) is used to analyze the effect on physical capital of reinvesting an amount equal to depreciation, it is necessary to assume that all assets are "one-hoss shays" in order to add up the physical units of annual capacity for each vintage of machine. That is, it must be assumed that a machine has a constant annual capacity over its lifetime. Significantly, this restrictive assumption is not needed to analyze the effect of a PRD policy on a firm's financial capital, because specific assumptions about the physical properties of an investment project are not relevant to the problem of aggregating cash flows from investments made in different time periods.

Effect of PRD policy on financial capital

Assume that a firm begins operations by investing in a project that costs $15,000 and has cash flows of $6,000 per year over a four-year period. Cash flows are received at the end of each year and are stated before the reinvestment of an amount equal to depreciation. The project's internal rate of return is .21862.

The calculations that follow are based on straight line depreciation with a four-year life and assume that an amount equal to the depreciation in each year is reinvested in projects which have the same internal rate of return and cash flow profile as the initial project. Therefore, the net cash flows in a period are identical with book income. Net cash flows also equal dividends to owners. Taxes and other expenses are assumed to be factored in the analysis.

Table 2 presents the firm's cash flows and asset values over a 12-year period and in the steady state. The first column in Table 2 shows the amount of reinvestment in each year, expressed as a percentage of the initial investment. These numbers were derived in Table 1 and are given on the diagonal of that table. Column (2) in Table 2 gives gross cash flows. The gross cash flows in year one are $6,000. Gross cash flows in year two consist of cash flows from the initial investment of $6,000 plus the cash flows from the $3,750 reinvestment at the end of year one. This reinvestment represents 25 percent of the initial project; therefore, cash flows in year two are $6,000 plus $1,500, or $7,500. Alternatively, total cash flows in year two can be derived by multiplying $6,000 by the total of the investments made at the beginning of years one and two, stated in terms of fractional projects, i.e., $1 + .25 = 1.25 \times \$6{,}000 = \$7{,}500$. Similarly, cash flows in year three can be obtained by multiplying $6,000 by the fractional projects started at the beginning of years one, two and three, i.e., $1 + .25 + .3125 = 1.5625 \times \$6{,}000 = \$9{,}375$. In subsequent years, cash flows are found by multiplying $6,000 by the fractional projects started in the previous four years. In this example, four years is both the actual life of the project and the assumed life on which the book depreciation method is based.

Column (3) in Table 2, depreciation, is the product of the reinvestment in each year (equal to depreciation), stated as a percentage of the original cost of the initial project, and $15,000, the cost of the initial project. Column (4), book

TABLE 2
Cash flows and asset values

Year	(1) Reinvestment percent	(2) Gross cash flows	(3) Depreciation (1) × $15,000	(4) Income/ dividends (2)–(3)	(5) Present discounted* value of dividends at beginning of yr.
1	25	$6,000	$3,750	$2,250	$15,000
2	31.25	7,500	4,688	2,812	16,029
3	39.06	9,375	5,859	3,516	16,721
4	48.83	11,719	7,325	4,394	16,861
5	36.04	8,649	5,406	3,243	16,153
6	38.80	9,311	5,820	3,491	16,441
7	40.69	9,764	6,104	3,660	16,544
8	41.09	9,861	6,163	3,698	16,501
9	39.15	9,396	5,873	3,523	16,410
10	39.93	9,583	5,990	3,593	16,475
11	40.21	9,651	6,032	3,619	16,484
12	40.09	9,563	6,014	3,549	16,469
	.	.	.	.	.
	.	.	.	.	.
	.	.	.	.	.
Long run	40.00	9,600	6,000	3,600	16,467

* Discount rate based on internal rate of return of 0.21862.

income, is the gross cash flows in column (2) minus book depreciation (reinvestment) in column (3). Income equals dividends, or net cash flows.

There is no information in Table 2 on net book value. Since net book value equals the initial investment plus cumulative amounts reinvested minus cumulative depreciation, net book value always equals $15,000.

The present discounted values at the beginning of years 2 to 12 and in the steady state in column (5) are the present values of the future dividends which are given in column (4). For example, the present discounted value at the beginning of year two of $16,029 is obtained by discounting $2,812 (dividends in year two), $3,516 (dividends in year three), etc. The present discounted value in the steady state, $16,467, is the present value of the $9,600 perpetuity, i.e., 9600/.21862.

The ratio of the firm's present value in the steady state of $16,467 to the initial value of $15,000 is an index of growth due to depreciation. In the next section, this index is derived analytically and is shown to equal the ratio of the PRD constant in equation (1) for the book depreciation used by the firm, to the PRD constant for the economic depreciation method implied by an individual project's cash flow profile and internal rate of return.

Index of growth due to depreciation

Assume again that an amount equal to depreciation is reinvested in projects which are, except for scale, identical in all respects. Under a PRD policy, the cash flows from a single project must be distinguished from the firm's cash flows (column (4) in Table 2) which are defined after the reinvestment of an amount equal to depreciation.

Let a be the PRD constant for book depreciation which is the depreciation method actually used by the firm, and X_t, $t = 1, 2, \ldots, N$, the cash flows at the end of period t for the initial investment, before reinvestment of an amount equal to depreciation. Note that N is the actual life of a project and it may be different than n, the life assumed for book depreciation. Also, let V_1 be the cost of the initial investment project and r be the internal rate of return.[7]

Annual cash flows from projects in any year i in the steady state equal

$$X_i = aX_1 + aX_2 + \ldots + aX_N = a \sum_{t=1}^{N} X_t. \tag{2}$$

That is, in the steady state, cash flows from existing projects at the end of year i equal the cash flows from the reinvestment at the beginning of period i (one period earlier), aX_1, plus the cash flows from the reinvestment at the beginning of period $i - 1$ (two periods earlier), aX_2, ... plus cash flows from the reinvestment at the beginning of period $i - N + 1$ (N periods earlier), aX_N. In the steady state, book depreciation in year i, D_i, equals the PRD constant multiplied by the project's initial cost, V_1, which also is the initial present value of the firm, i.e.,

$$D_i = aV_1. \tag{3}$$

Therefore, the firm's cash flows after reinvestment in the steady state equal

$$X_i - D_i = a\left(\sum_{t=1}^{N} X_t - V_1\right). \tag{4}$$

and in the steady state the firm's present discounted value, W_i, is the capitalized value of the firm's cash flows (a perpetuity),

$$W_i = \frac{a\left(\sum_{t=1}^{N} X_t - V_1\right)}{r}. \tag{5}$$

The index of growth due to depreciation, g, is the ratio of the steady state value, W_i, to the initial value, V_1. That is,

$$g = \frac{W_i}{V_1} = \frac{a\left(\sum_{t=1}^{N} X_t - V_1\right)}{rV_1}. \tag{6}$$

From the results in the Appendix which derives the PRD constant, a^*, for

7 To avoid mathematical complexities and questions about the convergence of the PRD constant, it is assumed that r, the internal rate of return, is constant and unique. This will always occur when the initial cash outflow is negative, all others are positive, and the sum of the cash flows is positive.

economic depreciation,[8] the index of growth due to depreciation simplifies to

$$g = a/a^*. \tag{7}$$

The growth in a firm's financial capital is caused by the divergence between book depreciation and economic depreciation. When book depreciation is more accelerated than economic depreciation (and a is greater than a^*), the firm reinvests more than is needed to maintain capital in the early years. In the long run this speedup in the timing of reinvestment increases the firm's cash flows and, therefore, its present value.[9]

Note that since net book value is constant under a PRD policy (and equals V_1), and since the firm's cash flows in equation (4) equal accounting income, the accounting rate of return, k, in the steady state is

$$k = \frac{a\left(\sum_{t=1}^{N} X_t - V_1\right)}{V_1}. \tag{8}$$

Therefore, from equation (6),

$$g = \frac{k}{r}. \tag{9}$$

and the bias in accounting rates of return relative to r is directly related to g.[10]

8 Another derivation of the PRD constant for economic depreciation was given by R.P. Brief and J. Owen in an unpublished paper, "The Long-Run Investment to Maintain Income and Wealth", written in the late 1960s. The derivation here is more direct. It should also be pointed out that Ijiri's derivation of the PRD constant assumes that $p_t \geqq 0$ and $p_n > 0$. Therefore, the project's cash flow profile is assumed to be consistent with this requirement. See Anton (1956) and Beaver and Dukes (1974) for discussions of the relationship between the project's cash flow profile and economic depreciation.

It has also been pointed out to us that a^* can be derived directly from equation (5) by simply noting that when book depreciation equals economic depreciation, the firm's present value must be constant. Consequently, W_t must equal V_1. Therefore, substituting a^* for a, the derivation of the PRD constant for economic depreciation in equation (A4) can be obtained from equation (5).

9 Sussman (1962) questioned whether depreciation caused this result, arguing that investment opportunities rather than depreciation explains why a firm grows. In this paper investment opportunities are, in effect, held constant and depreciation is viewed as a source of funds.

10 Equations (8) and (9) also can be derived from a model developed by Solomon (1966) to analyze the relationship between the accounting rate of return and the internal rate of return. Solomon assumes that the firm invests in an identical project at the beginning of each period for the first N periods of its life. The source of funds for these investments is unspecified as are the details about the reinvestment of cash flows. In period N and thereafter, the firm reaches a steady state by reinvesting in each period an amount equal to depreciation which is equal to the original cost of a project, V_1. In Solomon's study the firm's steady state income is

$$\sum_{t=1}^{n} X_t - V_1$$

and its book value is $(1/a)V_1$, i.e., cash flows are invariant to depreciation policy, but the firm's book value is not. In this study, the reverse is true. The firm's income (cash flows) in the steady state is

$$a\left(\sum_{t=1}^{n} X_t - V_1\right)$$

and book value V_1. Thus, even though the ratio of income to book value in the steady state is the same in both models, the models have very different interpretations.

To illustrate, suppose that book depreciation, p_t, is sum-of-years digits depreciation and economic depreciation, p_t^*, is the annuity method which can be approximated by "reverse" sum-of-years digits depreciation.[11] Also, based on Skinner's (1982) study, let the assumed life, n, of a project equal one-half of the actual life, N. Therefore,

$$p_t = \frac{2(n - t + 1)}{n(n + 1)} \frac{2(.5N - t + 1)}{.5N(.5N + 1)}, \quad t = 1, 2, \ldots, .5N$$

$$p_t^* = \frac{2t}{N(N + 1)}, \quad t = 1, 2, \ldots, N.$$

Evaluating the PRD constants for book and economic depreciation, a and a^*, we get

$$a = 6/(N + 4)$$

$$a^* = 3/(2N + 1).$$

Thus, the index of growth due to depreciation is

$$g = a/a^* = (4N + 2)/(N + 4).$$

If $N = 10$, $g = 3$. As an example, if the initial project costs $10,000 and earns an economic return of .20, the firm's cash flows in the steady state are $6,000 as compared to the $2,000 that would have been reported for economic depreciation. The firm's present value also increases by a factor of three, from $10,000 to $30,000. The $10,000 figure is the reported net book value, which is constant over time. This means that the accounting rate of return of 0.6 overstates the internal rate of return.

Conclusion

While the implications of assuming reinvestment of an amount equal to depreciation has not been completely overlooked in accounting, most of the writing on the subject has dealt with a very specific issue in inflation accounting. When depreciation is reinvested in noncash assets whose prices rise, a number of writers have said that this appreciation should be a factor in assessing the adequacy of depreciation (see, e.g., Solomons (1948), Trumbull (1958), Edwards (1954) and Gynther (1966, pp. 120–134)). However, except for the references already given and a few others like Mason (1961, pp. 34–37), accountants seem to have ignored the more basic idea that the reinvestment of an amount equal to depreciation has a multiplier effect even when prices are constant.

Depreciation will have an expansionary effect on financial capital, i.e., the index of growth due to depreciation, g, is greater than unity, if the PRD constant for book depreciation, a, is greater than a^*, the PRD constant calculated for economic depreciation. This will occur whenever book depreciation is more

11 Anton (1956) gives the conditions under which economic depreciation would be equal to straight line, sum-of-years digits and other depreciation methods. See also Beaver and Dukes (1974).

accelerated than the economic depreciation method. While it is difficult to generalize, three factors will tend to make book depreciation more accelerated than economic depreciation. First, book depreciation is based on the assumed life of a project, which has been estimated at about one-half of the actual life (Skinner (1982)). Second, the reaction to inflation in the U.S. since the 1950s has been to make depreciation methods more accelerated. Third, inflation increases nominal cash flows which, other things being equal, decelerates the economic depreciation method.[12]

The growth due to depreciation has several implications. First, the analysis suggests that there is a tendency for the firm to expand, both in terms of physical capital and in terms of nominal financial capital, due to the reinvestment of depreciation. This possibility has obvious implications for inflation accounting. If conventional depreciation methods have a built-in growth bias, adjustments for inflation may be a type of double counting.[13]

A second implication of the growth due to depreciation concerns the bias in accounting rates of return. When g is greater than unity, reinvestment of depreciation will produce an upward bias in accounting rates of return as equation (8) shows. This bias may be a factor in explaining why accounting rates of return are generally higher than market based rates of return (Barlev & Levy (1979)).

Finally, while the subject of depreciation and capital maintenance is, perhaps, one of the more controversial topics in accounting, these economic aspects of depreciation have received almost no attention in accounting literature. In the depression, some notable economists argued that depreciation led to excessive savings. During the 1950s, other economists suggested that in growing firms, depreciation exceeded replacement requirements. Nevertheless, only a few accountants entered this debate and those who did flatly rejected the idea that conventional depreciation allowances might be "excessive". Clearly, these conflicting ideas merit further study.

Appendix

Derivation of PRD constant for economic depreciation

Let X_t be the project's cash flows at the end of period t, N the actual life of a project and r the project's unique and positive internal rate of return. Define V_t as

12 For example, assume that without inflation a project with cash flows at the end of years 1, 2 and 3 of \$130, \$120 and \$110, respectively, costs \$300. Economic depreciation would be $p_1^* = 0.33$, $p_2^* = 0.33$ and $p_3^* = 0.33$. Now assume that the annual rate of inflation is 0.40 and that cash flows increase by the rate of inflation. Therefore, cash flows become \$182, \$235.20 and \$301.84, and economic depreciation based on the new cash flows and rate of return will be $p_1^* = 0.07$, $p_2^* = 0.28$ and $p_3^* = 0.65$. As a consequence, the PRD constant for economic depreciation, a^*, will decrease from 0.5 to 0.39 and, for a given book depreciation method, g, would increase by 28 percent.

13 Hicks (1979, p. 84) seems to be making this point in a related context: "Yet it seems inevitable that when it is proposed to make adjustments to the conventional [depreciation] allowances, to adjust for inflation, the question of whether the conventional allowances were appropriate, even in the absence of inflation, is bound to be raised".

the present value of the project's future cash flows at the beginning of period t, where

$$V_t = \sum_{j=t}^{N} \frac{X_j}{(1 + r)^{j-t+1}}.$$

Now let p_t^* be the economic depreciation method, expressed as a fraction of the initial project's original cost which also equals V_1. That is,

$$p_t^* = \frac{V_t - V_{t+1}}{V_1} \tag{A1}$$

Since $V_{N+1} = 0$, substituting p_t^* for p_t in equation (1) gives

$$\sum_{t=1}^{N} tp_t^* = \sum_{t=1}^{N} \frac{t(V_t - V_{t+1})}{V_1} = \frac{\sum_{t=1}^{N} V_t}{V_1}. \tag{A2}$$

The numerator of equation (A2) can be simplified.

$$\begin{aligned}\sum_{t=1}^{N} V_t = X_1(1 + r)^{-1} &+ X_2(1 + r)^{-2} + \ldots + X_N(1 + r)^{-N} \\ &+ X_2(1 + r)^{-1} + \ldots + X_N(1 + r)^{-N+1} \\ &\qquad\qquad + X_N(1 + r)^{-1}.\end{aligned} \tag{A3}$$

The "columns" on the right hand side of equation (A3) are regular annuities. Therefore,

$$\begin{aligned}\sum_{t=1}^{N} V_t &= \frac{X_1(1 - (1 + r)^{-1})}{r} + \frac{X_2(1 - (1 + r)^{-2})}{r} + \ldots + \frac{X_N(1 - (1 + r)^{-N})}{r} \\ &= \frac{\sum_{t=1}^{N} X_t - \sum_{t=1}^{N} X_t(1 + r)^{-t}}{r} \\ &= \frac{\Sigma X_t - V_1}{r}.\end{aligned} \tag{A4}$$

Substituting this result into equation (A2) and then into equation (1), the PRD constant for economic depreciation is

$$a^* = \frac{rV_1}{\sum_{t=1}^{N} X_t - V_1}. \tag{A4}$$

This result is used to derive the index of growth due to depreciation in equation (7).

References

Altman, O.L., *Verbatim Record of the Proceedings of the Temporary National Economic Committee* (The Bureau of National Affairs, Inc., 1939) Volume 3, pp. 422–435.

Anton, H.R., "Depreciation, Cost Allocation and Investment Decisions," *Accounting Research* (April 1956) pp. 117–131.

Barlev, B. and H. Levy, "On the Variability of Accounting Income Numbers," *Journal of Accounting Research* (Autumn 1979) pp. 305–315.

Beaver, W. and R. Dukes, "Delta-Depreciation Methods: Some Analytical Results," *Journal of Accounting Research* (Autumn 1974) pp. 205–215.

Carey, J.L., Editorial, *The Journal of Accountancy* (March 1940) pp. 161–162.

Chase, S, "Capital Not Wanted," *Harper's* (February 1940) pp. 225–234.

de Wolff, P., "The Depreciation Multiplier," *Review of Economics and Statistics* (November 1966) pp. 412–418.

Domar, E.D., "Depreciation, Replacement and Growth," *The Economic Journal* (March 1953) pp. 1–32.

Dorfman, R., "The Meaning of Internal Rates of Return," *Journal of Finance* (December 1981) pp. 1010–1022.

Edwards, E.O., "Depreciation Policy Under Changing Price Levels," *The Accounting Review* (April 1954) pp. 267–280.

———, "Depreciation and the Maintenance of Real Capital," in: J.L. Meij, ed., *Depreciation and Replacement Policy* (Quadrangle Books, 1961) pp. 46–140.

Eisner, R., "Depreciation Allowances, Replacement Requirements and Growth," *American Economic Review* (December 1952) pp. 820–831.

———, "Depreciation Allowances, Replacement Requirements and Growth: Rejoinder," *American Economic Review* (September 1953a) pp. 614–621.

———, "Conventional Depreciation Allowances versus Replacement Cost," *The Controller* (November 1953b), reprinted in: S. Davidson *et al.*, *An Income Approach to Accounting Theory: Readings and Questions* (Prentice-Hall, Inc., 1964) pp. 266–272.

———, "Depreciation Allowances and Replacements Restated," *The Controller* (May 1954) pp. 228, 248.

Fabricant, S., "Inflation and the Lag in Accounting Practice," in: R.R. Sterling and W.F. Bentz, eds., *Accounting Perspective* (The South Western Publishing Co., 1971) pp. 115–152.

Fisher, F.M. and J.J. McGowan, "On the Misuse of Accounting Rates of Return to Infer Monopoly Profits," *American Economic Review* (March 1983) pp. 82–97.

Gordon, M.J., "Depreciation Allowances, Replacement Requirements and Growth: A Comment," *American Economic Review* (September 1953) pp. 609–614.

Gynther, R.S., *Accounting for Price-Level Changes: Theory and Procedures* (Pergamon Press, 1966).

Gynther, M.M., "Future Growth Aspects of the Cash Flow Computation," *The Accounting Review* (October 1968) pp. 706–718.

Hansen, A.H., *Verbatim Record of the Proceedings of the Temporary National Economic Committee* (The Bureau of National Affairs, Inc., 1939) Volume 3, pp. 338–347.

Hicks, J.R., "The Measurement of Capital," *Bulletin of the International Statistical Institute*, Proceedings of the 37th Session (London, 1969), reprinted in: J. Hicks, *Wealth and Welfare* (Harvard University Press, 1981) pp. 204–217.

———, "The Concept of Income in Relation to Taxation and to Business Management," *Proceedings of the 35th Congress of the International Institute of Public Finance*, Taormina, 10–14 September, 1979, in: J. Hicks, *Classics and Moderns* (Harvard University Press, 1983) pp. 189–206.

Horvat, B., "The Depreciation Multiplier and a Generalized Theory of Fixed Capital Costs," *The Manchester School* (May 1958) pp. 136–159.

Hotelling, H., "A General Mathematical Theory of Depreciation," *Journal of the American Statistical Association* (September 1925) pp. 340–353.
Ijiri, Y., "On the Convergence of Periodic Reinvestments by an Amount Equal to Depreciation," *Management Science* (January 1967) pp. 321–335.
James, C.C., "Depreciation and the Value of Public Utilities," *The Journal of Accountancy* (December 1916) pp. 409–416.
Kane, J.E., "Relationship Between Depreciation Allowance and Maintenance of Capital During Inflation," *The Journal of Accountancy* (December 1952) pp. 697–701.
Kaufman, F. and A. Gleason, "The Effect of Growth on the Adequacy of Depreciation Allowances," *The Accounting Review* (October 1953) pp. 539–544.
Kay, J.A., "Accountants, Too, Could be Happy in a Golden Age: The Accountant's Rate of Profit and the Internal Rate of Return," *Oxford Economic Papers* (November 1976) pp. 447–458.
Mason, P., "Depreciation and the Financing of Replacements," *The Accounting Review* (December 1935), in: S.A. Zeff and T.F. Keller (eds.), *Financial Accounting Theory: Issues and Controversies* (McGraw-Hill, Inc., 1964) pp. 155–166.
———, *Cash Flow Analysis and the Funds Statement*, Accounting Research Study No. 2 (AICPA, 1961).
Mautz, R.K., "Another Look at Depreciation Allowances," *The Controller* (January 1954), reprinted in: S. Davidson *et al.* (eds.), *An Income Approach to Accounting Theory: Readings and Questions* (Prentice-Hall, Inc., 1964) pp. 272–276.
May, G.O., "The Relation of Depreciation Provisions to Replacement," *The Journal of Accountancy* (May 1940) pp. 341–347.
———, "Concepts of Business Income and their Implementation," *The Quarterly Journal of Economics* (February 1954) pp. 1–18.
Schiff, E., "A Note on Depreciation, Replacement and Growth," *Review of Economics and Statistics* (February 1954) pp. 47–56.
Skinner, R.C., "Fixed Asset Lives and Replacement Cost Accounting," *Journal of Accounting Research* (Spring 1982) pp. 210–226.
Solomon, E., "Return on Investment: The Relation of Book-Yield to True Yield," pp. 232–244; in: R.K. Jaedicke, Y. Ijiri and O. Nielsen, eds., *Research in Accounting Measurement* (American Accounting Association, 1966).
Solomons, D., "Income – True and False," *The Accountants Journal* (October 1948) pp. 363–370.
Sussman, M.R., "A Note on the Implications of Periodic 'Cash Flow'," *Journal of Finance* (December 1962) pp. 658–663.
Takatera, S., "Economics of Depreciation Financing," *Kyoto University Economic Review* (April 1960) pp. 49–63.
Trumbull, W.P., "Price-Level Depreciation and Replacement Cost," *The Accounting Review* (January 1958) pp. 26–34.

A Late Nineteenth Century Contribution to the Theory of Depreciation

RICHARD P. BRIEF*

The unrecognized dispute in the theory of depreciation is whether too much or too little has been written on the subject. In 1957, Davidson began an article, "Depreciation is probably the most discussed and most disputatious topic in all accounting." [1] In the first (1912) edition of his *Depreciation and Wasting Assets*, P. D. Leake began, "Because it closely concerns Profit and Loss, the subject of Depreciation and Wasting Assets is of universal importance, and yet it has hitherto received little or no systematic attention." [2] One might suppose, then, that during the 45 years between these observations most of the discussion appeared. But this supposition is wrong. In 1890, a remarkable paper by O. G. Ladelle appeared in which the first two sentences were, "Depreciation is a subject on which we have of late heard much. Much has been written, and said, upon the necessity of taking account of it, and also upon the different ways in which this may be done." [3]

To my knowledge, no attention has been paid to this article by Ladelle; I can find no references to it.[4] I contend that Ladelle made a great contribution to the theory of depreciation and that much commentary could

* Assistant Professor of Business Statistics, New York University. I am indebted to the Schools of Business, New York University, for a grant to support this research. I also thank the librarians of the American Institute of Certified Public Accountants, New York, New York for their invaluable assistance.

[1] Sidney Davidson, "Depreciation, Income Taxes and Growth," *Accounting Research*, July, 1957, p. 191.

[2] P. D. Leake, *Depreciation and Wasting Assets* (London: Henry Good & Son, 1912).

[3] O. G. Ladelle, "The Calculation of Depreciation," *The Accountant* (November 29, 1890), p. 659.

[4] That Leake was apparently unaware of Ladelle's important work is characteristic of accountants' traditional lack of concern with the professional literature.

have been avoided if his article had been given any recognition. The primary purpose of this paper is to accord recognition to Ladelle's work. Two ways to proceed suggest themselves: (1) to quote and paraphrase extensively, intertwining my own comments, or (2) to present Ladelle's paper in its entirety thereby minimizing commentary by me. I choose the latter on the assumption that the 1890 volume of *The Accountant* is not readily available to those who would be interested in examining it. Two subsidiary purposes are (1) to present a few biographical notes about Ladelle, and (2) to attempt to place Ladelle's work in historical perspective.

THE CALCULATION OF DEPRECIATION

By Mr. O. G. Ladelle, A.C.A.

Depreciation is a subject on which we have of late heard much. Much has been written, and said, upon the necessity of taking account of it, and also upon the different ways in which this may be done.

We have heard, that to obtain the true measure of Depreciation of an asset we should take various courses, as *e.g.*:

(1) Take the actual decrease in its market value.

(2) Divide the cost (less residue) by the number of years that it is expected to last, and write off each year the quotient thus obtained.

(3) Write off each year a constant proportion of the balance then standing.

(4) Set aside each year such a constant sum, as, with its interest, will accumulate during the life of the asset to an amount sufficient to replace it.

(5) And yet sundry other ideas are adopted.

but there is, I think, a field still untouched, for these rules are all defective, either from inaccuracy or from being applicable to special cases only; and though theoretical discussions are sometimes apt to be dry, yet I venture to submit, that to us accountants, having to take account of almost every sort and kind of asset, rules for special cases, however practical and useful, are insufficient; and that to be ready in every variety of cases that may come before us, not merely to propose a scheme of our own, but to review the particular system that has been already adopted, to see exactly how far it is true and how far fallacious, and to point out its particular defects and their consequences, it is important to have distinctly formulated in our minds, the abstract theory upon which calculations of depreciation in general should rest, and this in a form so general, as to be universally applicable.

It is therefore, to a discussion of this general theory that I now venture to ask this society to honour me with its attention. It is, of course, seldom convenient to work out this theory in its full detail, but my meaning in saying at the close of my paper that we must revert to the general principle, is, that it is this theory which should form the base of our considerations, and guide our general ideas, in propounding or assenting to, the scheme of depreciation for use in any case that may come before us.

I shall, for simplicity, assume the rate of interest to be constant, and this, I think, will generally suffice; but if it should be desired to deal with varying rates we may do so, by adopting symbols yet more general (*a*)

(*a*) for writing i_n for the interest of 1 for n

$$f_n \text{ for } (1 + i_n)$$

$$\text{and } | f_n \text{ for } (f_1 \cdot f_2 \cdot f_3 \cdots f_n)$$

our expression in notes (*d*) and (*g*) becomes $b_n - i_n \, (P - \Sigma v_n) \, | \, f_{n-1}$.

Allow me, in opening this discussion, to assume, for convenience of illustration, that a large number of persons, numbered from 1 upwards, purchase as a joint venture, an asset, which they do not propose to use simultaneously, but agree to use for a year apiece, in turn, and that we are asked to determine the method of apportioning the cost between them (*b*).

(*b*) for, if we can do this, it is quite clear that the union of all these persons into one firm can make no difference to our calculations, and that the same figures, will give the amounts which that firm ought to charge to each year in its accounts.

Now here it is clear that we must not re-value the asset each year, but must entirely disregard market fluctuations, for each speculator is as much entitled to the benefit of any rise, and liable to the loss of any fall, in the market value of their joint asset, as is any of his fellows; and even though after No. 1 has used it for his year, the market should be so risen that the asset is fairly worth its original cost, yet No. 1 cannot call upon the remaining joint speculators to share that value and that cost amongst them, but must pay his just proportion with the others.

To ascertain what this proportion is, it may be stated that as the purchase price is the present value of the total future enjoyment of the asset, so, it is equivalent to the sum of the present values of its enjoyment during each successive year of its duration—so that if we write

b_n for the value of the enjoyment of the asset during its nth year, and
v_n for the present value of this b_n

then if No. 1 pay v_1, No. 2, v_2 and so on, in each case No. n paying v_n the vendor will receive in the aggregate the exact purchase price, and each speculator will pay exactly his fair share for the use of the asset during his year—and if then we can determine the values of v_n our apportionment is complete. (*c*)

(*c*) Let P = Purchase price.
$\therefore P = \Sigma v \infty$ where the symbol Σ is used to denote that we are to sum the series stated, giving to the variable (∞) every integral value from unity to the limit indicated (infinity.)

But it may be that those speculators who are to enjoy the asset in future years, will not care to pay for it now, and they may, therefore, agree that No. 1 shall pay at once the whole cost, and that the others shall recoup him at the end of his year the proportions thus paid on their accounts, together with interest thereon for the interval—these payments to be actually made, however, by No. 2, who will in turn recover from No. 3 the shares of his posterity; and so on until the asset is exhausted, simultaneously with which v_n will vanish.

In this case the cost to each speculator will be, the difference between the amounts paid by and to him, (*d*) *i.e.*,

(*d*) Writing i for the interest of 1 for one year, and f for $(1 + i)$ so that $f^n =$ the amount of 1 accumulated during n years, No. 1 will pay P but recover $(P - v_1)f$. That is to say, he will have expended v_1 but having also invested throughout his year, $(P - v_1)$ will have earned $(P - v_1)i$ interest on that capital.

Similarly No. 2 will pay $(P - v_1)f$ but recover $(P - v_1 - v_2)f^2$ and so for the general expression No. n will pay $\cdots$ $(P - \Sigma v_{n-1})f^{n-1} \cdots$ but recover $(P - \Sigma v_n)f^n \equiv \{(P - \Sigma v_{n-1} - v_n)f^{n-1}(1 + i)\}$ so that his cost will be $v_n f^{n-1} - i\,(P - \Sigma v_n)f^{n-1} \cdots$

each year the tenant for the year will expend during his year, the original present value of his year's enjoyment, with interest thereon to date of payment, but will earn from his posterity one year's interest upon the amount that he pays for them (*e*).

(*e*) Viz. upon the original present value of their shares accumulated to the commencement of his year.

Obviously the rates of interest and of discount here employed must be equal, but how are they to be determined?

I submit that since, in such a case, every prudent speculator must, and does, either consciously or otherwise, at the time of making his purchase, carefully estimate the value of the interest upon his money, over the period for which he is about to invest it, and include this estimate as a factor in determining the price he is willing to pay. It is this same estimate which supplies the answer to our present question—*i.e.*, the speculators must at the time of purchase jointly agree upon an estimate of the fair rate of interest to represent the value of their money during the life of the asset, and then base their calculations of discount and interest upon this rate, and adhere to it. It may be that this rate will prove to differ from those actually prevalent in future years, but if so the differences caused, will be, *not* profit or loss *of the years in which they occur*, but an original error of the speculators at the date of purchase, and must be dealt with in their accounts, not as normal depreciation, but as an unexpected variation in the market value of their property.

Similar remarks will apply to fixing the values of b_n. It may be uncertain what the real value of the enjoyment of the asset during future years will be, and it may be very difficult to estimate these values, but undoubtedly, it is upon his estimate of this value and of the interest on his money, that, consciously or otherwise, (*f*)

(*f*) And either for the one year, or for several, in which he may be interested, each prudent speculator fixes the price he is willing to pay, and makes his purchase.

A list, then, of these estimated values of the enjoyment of the asset during each year of its life, is obtainable; and given this, with the actual price paid for the asset, and the rate of interest, the values of b_n can be found by calculation (*g*).

(*g*) For representing this series of estimated values by the compound symbol ab_n where a is an arbitrary constant, and taking y as the life of the asset, we have:*

$$P = \Sigma\, v_y \equiv \Sigma\, \frac{b_y}{f^{y-1}}$$

$$b_n \equiv ab_n \times \frac{1}{n}$$

$$aP = \Sigma\, \frac{ab_y}{f^{y-1}}$$

$$b_n \equiv ab_n P\, \Sigma\, \frac{f^{y-1}}{ab_y}$$

$$a = \Sigma\, \frac{ab_y}{Pf^{y-1}}$$

whence, returning to the formula in note (*d*) for

$$v_n f^{n-1} - i(P - \Sigma v_n) f^{n-1}$$

we may now write $\qquad b_n - i(P - \Sigma v_n) f^{n-1}.$

and the general expression for the cost to each speculator, becomes a known quantity, payable during his year, and equivalent to the agreed value of his year's enjoyment of the asset, less his year's interest upon the amount paid by him for his posterity.

Here, then, we have the cost which each successive joint speculator should bear, and since it can make no difference whether these speculators be separate traders or be copartners in one firm (*h*)

(*h*) For in any case the amounts chargeable to the respective years will be unchanged.

it is clear that this is also, the true principle upon which we should distribute the cost of, *i.e.*, write off Depreciation from, any asset, of any individual, firm or company (*i*).

---

* Author's note. The equation $b_n \equiv ab_n P\Sigma \frac{f^{y-1}}{ab_y}$ originally appeared as " $\equiv ab_n P\Sigma \frac{f^{y-1}}{a_y}$. This was probably a typesetting error.

(*i*) In the case of a company we may carry the analogy even closer, by regarding the shareholders as changing from year to year, and the directors as acquiring assets as agents of, and in trust for, the various sets of shareholders whom they will represent in the respective years.

And now, putting this into bookkeeping form, we have the theory for each year working thus:

Bring forward the amount from the previous year (or in first year charge cost).

Deduct the agreed value of the current year's enjoyment (*i.e.*, b_n).

Add a years interest at the agreed rate upon the balance, and carry forward the sum thus shown.

Let us now compare this theory with the rules cited in my preface.

Suppose the asset to be part of the plant of a gasworks, costing £120, and having an estimated life of 20 years, when it will be worth £20 for old material; and that, after 10 years use, the electric light is adopted generally in the neighbourhood, so that the plant is now far too large for the company's use, and the market value of it greatly reduced.

By the first method cited, upon the re-valuation at the end of year 11 there would have to be a great reduction.

Is our 11th speculator to bear the whole of this loss? The idea is clearly preposterous. There is a reduction in the capital value of the joint venture, and the loss must be shared by all.

By the second method, each year would bear £5. But we may well conceive that this plant might be nearly as useful, and productive of revenue in the 10th year as in the first. Yet whilst each of our speculators would pay off £5, No. 1 would in addition, have to keep £115 of capital lying out through his year, and No. 10 £70 only, which is arbitrary and often unfair.

Trying the third method, we should find that approximately No. 1 would pay off £11.3 and invest £109 whilst No. 10 would pay off £4.6 only, and invest £49, thus increasing yet further the arbitrary advantage of No. 10.

If we turn to the fourth method, so often put forth as the true and scientific one, we find no improvement. For though our plant may be *nearly* as useful through the 10th year as the first, it clearly will not be *quite* so—there will be more flaws discovered, and more repairs needed to keep it up to its work. Surely, then, it is not fair that with these increasing expenses to pay, *i.e.*, with less net benefit to each successive speculator, the amounts to be contributed to the cost should be uniform. But if we apply the theory expanded above we shall find none of these objections.

Our estimates may be made on various bases—we may agree to estimate the benefit of each year under normal circumstances only; or we may agree that all chances shall be taken into account, and the values of b_n be reckoned accordingly. (*k*)

(*k*) And similarly any number of special circumstances may be dealt with, each having its appropriate bearing upon the original estimates of b_n .

In the first case we should, in the 11th year write off capital (*l*)

(*l*) Or our speculators would all subscribe to a fund, for the use of Nos. 11 to 20.

an amount equivalent to the extraordinary loss that had occurred—not as depreciation, but as a special loss of capital to be dealt with by itself. In the second case Nos. 11 to 20 could not complain. They have agreed to take their chance, and have already had a fair allowance for so doing. In fact, when this second method is adopted we may generally consider the charge born by each year as consisting of two parts, which may be stated either in one sum, or separately, one part being for the enjoyment of the asset under normal circumstances, and the other part, an insurance premium against casualties.

Here Nos. 11 to 20 have received this premium, to cover the risk which has now ripened into loss, and must stand to their bargain. Still not throwing it entirely on to No. 11, but sharing it between them (*m*) and in practice we may

(*m*) Either by adhering to their original estimates, or by paying at once to No. 11, such a proportion of the present values of their respective shares, as shall together, amount to the loss sustained. Or in our books—by writing off from the asset as a special item, the amount of the loss; and reducing the charge to each present and future year accordingly.

often prefer to adopt this plan; remembering, that it is safer for future years, to have these premiums in hand, than to have a right to contribution from years which are past and gone. But to proceed, the objections to the second, third, and fourth methods, are entirely met—as to the varying capital employed, by the fair interest allowed upon it; as to their arbitrary character, by our whole system being based upon *reasonable* estimates; and as to the decreasing revenue, by the yearly benefits having been fairly estimated in view of that circumstance.

Having now concluded our discussion of this theory—if it be desired to glance also at the practical application of it in detail we shall see that the main points of it, are, the fixing the rate of interest and the values of the series of b_n .

For the interest—we have simply to settle the rates which may fairly be expected from investments such as we are dealing with, during the life of our asset—being careful, generally, for the sake of safety, to keep the rate low enough. (*n*)

(*n*) For since a part of the charge to later years consists of interest earned from them by earlier years; if the rate of this interest be higher than the real value of money, the effect will be, to unduly tax these later years, in favour of the earlier ones. By increasing the rate of interest, the total charge is increased, but the vendor gets the same, and the difference, is profit to the early years, at the expense of the later ones.

Coming however to the values of b_n our task is sometimes much more intricate, for to arrive at a fair estimate of the net value of the future enjoyment of our asset we must consider alike, the chance of ever getting that enjoyment, the income to be derived from it when got, and the outgo to be spent in making that income.

And here we may require the advice of other experts intimately acquainted with the business concerned. (*o*)

(*o*) As for example, when our chance depends upon the survival of a life, the life of plant, machinery, or buildings; or the stability of various works, &c.; or where our income and outgo are not constant, but require time for development, have their prime and their decay, are likely to increase or decrease, to be depressed, or augmented, by new inventions; or depend upon the many other special circumstances which affect the revenues from different classes of property—we may have to seek the assistance of actuaries, engineers, architects, merchants, &c.—and frequently those concerned in managing our particular business.

We may frequently too find it desirable to deal with these points separately, and for the purposes alike of convenience in working, and of supplying useful information in our account, to state, as one item, the depreciation based on calculations as to the normal income alone; as another item, an amount based on calculations as to the normal outgo alone; and as a third, a reserve to meet contingencies. (*p*)

(*p*) As *e.g.* with our gas works, we may write off depreciation on the assumption that the plant is kept in constant repair free of expense to us, and then state separately the amount payable to a repairs fund, from which to pay this expense, and those carried to a reserve to provide for casualties.

And when this is done we may conveniently arrange the bookkeeping thus:—

In a ledger ruled with two money columns on each side, open an account from the particular class of asset—say gasometers—a second for depreciation of gasometers, a third for repairs of gasometers, and a fourth for reserve on gasometers. To gasometers' account debit in the inner column the cost of gasometers, extend yearly the total (or balance) of the year's expenditure, and cast the outer column after each extension. To the depreciation account credit each year (by P. & L.) the agreed amount of depreciation, irrespective of repairs.

To the repairs account debit the cost of repairs, extending yearly as before, and credit each year (by P. & L.) the agreed charge for that year's repairs.

To the reserve account credit each year (by P. & L.) the agreed amount of reserve for that year.

In drawing the accounts it may be well to show the balance remaining on gasometers, after adding or deducting the balance of these other accounts, but in the books themselves I prefer to keep them distinct, showing upon the gasometers account the total cost to date, on the depreciation and reserve accounts, the total sums charged or reserved to date, and on repairs account the yearly balance, for I find that this gives a ready view of the position, and is very convenient in working.

If gasometers be realized (or thrown aside) we should credit to gasometers account, the original cost, debit to depreciation account the depreciation that has been charged in respect of them, and then carry to the reserve account the difference between the balance of these two items and the price realized (or value of residue). And in books thus kept this is easily done, for, having each part of the account by itself, we can readily ascertain the cost, and the depreciation charged against it to any given date, and so cease charging at the proper time, whereas when the depreciation is credited yearly to the plant account, and the balance only carried forward, these are not so readily seen, and it is easy to charge depreciation of assets, either in excess of their original cost, or after they have ceased to exist.

The repairs account should balance, or nearly so, at intervals, and if it fail to do so, it may be necessary to assist it by a transfer to the reserve account.

The reserve account will, of course, be a continually increasing credit, subject to such debits as may be occasioned by the casual losses charged against it, but it clearly cannot survive the particular assets to which it is related, so that when they disappear this account too should be carried to a general reserve, or dealt with in other suitable way.

In doing thus, however, we must bear in mind that we are really dealing with different parts only of one subject, and that though we may state them separately, we should consider them together—(*q*)

(*q*) In determining our quantities the same arguments and the same formulae will apply. Our symbols may be sometimes positive, and sometimes negative, but we shall be using the sȧme principle, and subject to the same considerations.

and we should be careful, too, to keep our yearly estimates as regular as circumstances will allow. (*r*)

(*r*) As *e.g.* Find some regular progression, applicable to our particular case and then deviate from it as little as possible, for this generally adds greatly not only to our convenience in making our calculations, but also to the readiness with which others can grasp their business import when made, whilst accounts in which such items fluctuate from year to year are generally open to suspicion.

We may frequently find results thus obtained agree with those given by the methods cited in my preface, and particularly with the second of them, and some might thereby be led to think that all these investigations were useless, as we might have adopted at once the simpler method.

But this is fallacious—The results will agree, not invariably, but under certain conditions only. (*s*)

(*s*) Where the yearly prǿfit happens, as it so often does, to decrease throughout by constant sums, our results will agree with those of this second method. Where it decreases in a constant ratio, we shall agree with the third method; and where it is stationary, through a given time, and then lapses entirely, we shall agree with the fourth, and sometimes, too, correct results may be obtained from a combination of these rules, for in these particular cases, our formulae happen to be identical with those giving these rules.

We may often see what the conditions are, and apply at once a suitable rule, but except where these particular conditions occur, these particular rules, which are attached to them, are useless, and we must revert to the general principle.

[Editor's Note: This concludes the Ladelle essay. We are indebted to *The Accountant* for permission to reproduce it.]

A Biographical Note

In 1890 Ladelle, 28, had taken first prize in the Final Chartered Accountant Examination in June and had accepted a position with Messrs.

Price, Waterhouse & Co. His paper was to have been presented at a regular meeting of The Chartered Accountants Students' Society of London on October 22, 1890, and it had been circulated among the members for discussion at this meeting; shortly before this date, Ladelle became ill with typhoid fever while on an audit engagement and died on October 31, 1890. According to a headnote in *The Accountant,* "the consideration of the paper was adjourned *sine die.*" Aside from an obituary notice and a comment in the January 3, 1891 issue of *The Accountant* where his unexpected death was noted with regret in a "Retrospect" of 1890, there appears to be no further mention of this paper or its author.

One can only speculate why this noteworthy contribution to the theory of depreciation was overlooked. Perhaps Ladelle's contemporaries did not understand his concepts and he did not live long enough to explain them. Later writers, like Hatfield, who made frequent use of *The Accountant,* probably overlooked this paper which was awkwardly placed in the two issues in which it appeared; since each annual volume contained approximately 1000 pages, this article could easily have been missed.

Historical Perspective

Although Ladelle made no specific references to previous work, a number of articles and several books on the subject of depreciation had been published prior to 1890.[5] These laid the foundation for contemporary depreciation methods, and the stock of knowledge about both depreciation principles and practices has not increased substantially since.

One paper of 1883 contains one of the first expositions of the concept that underlies modern depreciation practice—the going-concern principle.

> Manufacturers and traders do not construct business premises or lay down special plant in the intent of a short period.... A large, irrecoverable outlay is generally expended in preparation of a factory, and unless speedy destruction overtakes any certain business, the method of treatment for annual accounting is one of "going concern." Otherwise, since all machinery may be said to be secondhand when once it has turned round, and perhaps unsaleable then at half its cost..., a depreciation of 50 per cent would probably not be sufficient to represent the realisable value at the end of the first year. Manifestly, the career of the business contemplated must have an assumed term, and the cost of the consumption of machinery and other erections must be attributed to the whole term.[6]

Other concepts can be traced to the period prior to 1890. The practice

[5] Numerous articles on depreciation appeared in *The Accountant* during the last quarter of the nineteenth century. Papers written on other topics, e.g., auditing and balance sheets, also were relevant to the depreciation problem. The first book relating to this subject was apparently written in 1870: E. Price Williams, *Maintenance and Renewal of Railway Rolling Stock* (William Clowes & Son, 1870). Fourteen years later the well-known book, Ewing Matheson, *Depreciation of Factories* (London: E. & F. N. Spon, 1884) appeared.

[6] Edwin Guthrie, "Depreciation and Sinking Funds," *The Accountant,* April 21, 1883.

of valuing an asset at original cost less depreciation and the calculation of (systematic and rational) annual provisions for depreciation were intensively discussed by some of the leading accountants of the day. There were, of course, exceptions taken to these views, both in principle and certainly in practice,[7] but depreciation accounting, as it is currently practiced, was soon structured. However, a *theory* of depreciation had not developed; that is, there were no concepts to be used in evaluating specific depreciation practices.

Ladelle saw the question of depreciation as an allocation problem, and he may have been the first to associate the problem of depreciation with the more general problem of allocating joint costs. His theory of depreciation is consistent with the so-called "accounting approach" to depreciation. This approach has been condemned because it abandons the attempt to value assets and accepts many methods of arriving at book values which are considered "systematic and rational." Consequently, it has been argued that this approach is "sterile" because "without a theory of valuation we cannot have a theory of depreciation." [8]

Ladelle, however, argued that depreciation accounting *is* a system of cost allocation not asset valuation. He arrived at this conclusion using scientific rather than pragmatic reasoning, and this is his major contribution to depreciation theory. According to Ladelle, the cost of an asset is joint to the periods during which it is in use, and the allocation of depreciation to each period must be based on the expected net enjoyment to be derived during the period, after adjusting for the *agreed* interest on the unallocated portion of cost. The interest that is earned during the period is equivalent to the "normal" rate of profit.

Gains or losses arising from unexpected changes in market values, interest rates, etc., cannot be allocated to the period in which the unanticipated event occurs. The *capital* gain or loss is joint to all periods and is not assignable to any one period. The gain or loss must be "shared by all."

In effect, Ladelle reasoned that *ex post* asset valuations affect only the capital account. Thus, if all expected flows, both negative and positive, were agreed on at the time of purchase, all differences between *ex ante* and *ex post* flows must be viewed as aberrations, i.e., capital gains or losses, caused by an "original error of the speculators." These *ex post* changes, i.e., unanticipated changes in the value of an asset are capital gains or losses and, in principle, cannot be assigned to the profit of a particular period because they are joint to all periods. Ladelle's theory of depreciation therefore has relevance to profit theory. Some 30 years after Ladelle, Frank Knight explicitly introduced the notion of risk and uncertainty, i.e., error,

[7] Richard P. Brief, "Nineteenth Century Accounting Error," *Journal of Accounting Research*, 3 (Spring, 1965); "The Origin and Evolution of Nineteenth-Century Asset-Accounting," *Business History Review*, XL (Spring, 1966).

[8] F. K. Wright, "Towards a General Theory of Depreciation," *Journal of Accounting Research*, 2 (Spring, 1964).

into the economic theory of profit.[9] A number of articles by Knight and others were written on the subject, culminating in a series of papers that appeared in the early 1950's.[10] Many of Ladelle's views can be found in these writings.

---

[9] Frank H. Knight, *Risk, Uncertainty and Profit*, Harper Torchbook ed. (New York: Harper & Row, 1965). First published in 1921.

[10] J. Fred Weston, "A Generalized Uncertainty Theory of Profit," *American Economic Review*, Vol. XL (March, 1950). See also comments on this article and the rejoinder by Weston in *op. cit.*, Vol. XLI (March, 1951). More recently, some of the ideas expressed by Ladelle have been introduced in accounting literature. See, for example, Hector R. Anton, "Depreciation, Cost Allocation and Investment Decisions," *Accounting Research*, April, 1956.

A Solution to the Allocation Problem

Errata
"A Least Squares Allocation Model"

Two typographical errors appeared in the original. The expression in the brackets in the numerator of the second term on the right hand side of equation (2) originally appeared with with a **W**, not **X**. Also, the sign of the second term on the right hand side of equation (8A) was positive, not negative. These errors have been correction in the reprint of this article.

A Least Squares Allocation Model

RICHARD P. BRIEF* and JOEL OWEN†

This paper presents a general mathematical model for allocation. The model offers one approach to the unification of a broad class of allocation (amortization) problems and provides a basis for summarizing, comparing, and evaluating diverse allocation schemes. It does not, however, justify the use of any particular scheme.[1] The model is introduced in the first part of this paper and its application to the allocation problem is discussed next.

The Least Squares Allocation Model

The generalized least squares allocation model[2] can be defined as follows:

* Associate Professor of Business Statistics, New York University. †Assistant Professor of Quantitative Analysis, New York University.

[1] The objective of this paper is somewhat similar to that of Arthur L. Thomas in "The Amortization Problem: A Simplified Model and Some Unanswered Questions," *Journal of Accounting Research*, 3 (Spring, 1965), pp. 103–13.

[2] The reader may wish to consider first a more familiar model as a motivation for the discussion that follows. Define the model for selecting a number, M, to describe a set of observations, X_i, as follows:

Minimize, with respect to M,

$$\sum_{i=1}^{n} \frac{(X_i - M)^2}{W_i},$$

where

X_i = Numerical characteristic of ith unit

M = Number chosen to describe the set of X_i

W_i = Numerical characteristic chosen to standardize differences, $(X_i - M)^2$.

The model for determining M implies a method of computation that minimizes the sum of the standardized differences. Alternatively, we could state that M is made as close as possible to X_i, where "closeness" is measured in terms of the W_i. By differentiating the above expression with respect to M and solving for the value of M which makes the derivative zero, we have:

Minimize with respect to p_i,

$$Q(p_1, p_2 \cdots p_n) = \sum_{i=1}^{n} \frac{(X_i - p_i C)^2}{W_i}, \tag{1}$$

subject to $\sum_{i=1}^{n} p_i = 1$, where

C = Joint cost, amortizable asset, etc.

p_i = Proportion of C allocated to the ith joint product, activity, segment, period, etc.

X_i = A numerical characteristic describing or assigned to the ith product, etc.

W_i = A numerical characteristic chosen to standardize the differences, $(X_i - p_i C)^2$.

In the Appendix, we show that the set of allocation schemes, p_i, consistent with the general model is:

$$p_i = \frac{X_i}{C} - \frac{W_i}{\Sigma W_i}\left[\frac{\Sigma X_i - C}{C}\right], \tag{2}$$

and the actual cost assigned to the ith product, etc. is:

$$p_i C = X_i - \frac{W_i}{\Sigma W_i}[\Sigma X_i - C]. \tag{3}$$

The fraction,

$$\frac{X_i - p_i C}{W_i},$$

is constant. That is,

$$\frac{X_i - p_i C}{W_i} = \frac{X_i - \left[X_i - \frac{W_i}{\Sigma W_i}(\Sigma X_i - C)\right]}{W_i} = \frac{\Sigma X_i - C}{\Sigma W_i}. \tag{4}$$

The constant equality (4) among the products, segments, periods, etc., is the unifying property of all schemes derived from the general model.

$$M = \frac{\Sigma W_i^{-1} X_i}{\Sigma W_i^{-1}}.$$

This is the general solution for all methods derived from the model.

This model offers one approach to the generalization of the problem of selecting a number, M. It is, of course, not the only one that might be made, but it is, in fact, a generalization of some commonly used methods. For example, when $W_i = 1$, M is the simple arithmetic mean; when $W_i = X_i$, M is the harmonic mean. The model therefore provides a unified view of various methods of computing M and gives insight into their comparative nature. It does not, however, justify the use of a particular method. The model also has important stochastic properties which are well known. The cost allocation model also has these properties, although we do not discuss them in this paper.

Allocation Schemes Used in Practice

The allocation schemes considered in this section should be regarded as a sample of those that are actually used in practice; a complete codification is beyond the scope of this paper.

Schemes with $W_i = X_i$. Equation (2) may be viewed as the universal set of schemes, p_i, derived from the general model. One subset of these schemes is defined by substituting $W_i = X_i$ in (2). Simplifying the expression, we have

$$p_i = \frac{X_i}{\Sigma X_i}. \tag{5}$$

Many commonly used allocation schemes are therefore in this class.

Consider various methods used to allocate joint product costs. Some of the characteristics chosen in the specification of $W_i = X_i$ are: sales price of product; sales price of product before split-off; physical weight; and other characteristics.[3]

Notice that it is difficult to interpret the equality (4) unless the characteristic chosen is a measure of value or is assumed to be highly correlated with such a measure. For example, if the characteristic chosen is a weight variable, the method insures that the difference between the weight of the ith product and the cost assigned to it is proportional to its weight. Without additional information about the relationship between weight and value, this equality has no intuitive appeal; in fact, it makes no sense at all. However, when measures of value are selected as the X_i (and W_i), "profits" assigned are proportional to value. One rather obvious conclusion to be drawn from this discussion is that methods that establish a "value equality" among products, segments, etc., seem more reasonable than those that do not. Of course, alternative definitions of "value" are possible but this is a separate problem.

Some methods of depreciation accounting are essentially the same as those used to apportion joint product costs, i.e., they result from specifying $W_i = X_i$. For example, the characteristic chosen may be a physical measure of planned output or it may be expected annual services. Assuming that these variables are correlated with the "value" *produced* by an asset in a particular period, such methods are simply variants of the "relative sales" method of allocating joint product costs and insure (loosely-speaking) that profits are proportional to value produced in each period. Thus, justification of the straight-line method on *this* basis would be tantamount to arguing that all periods should be assigned equal profits.

Depreciation methods are, however, frequently discussed without ref-

[3] No useful purpose would be served either by providing references to these methods or elaborating on them. Most standard accounting texts contain a complete examination of these methods and many more. This comment also applies to the other allocation schemes discussed in this paper.

erence to the equality of "profit" to value in each period. Such discussions imply that the selection of the characteristics, W_i and X_i, are made without reference to future expectations, i.e., the X_i and W_i are *arbitrarily* selected. For example, the straight-line method may be derived from the general model by specifying $W_i = X_i = K$, where K is an arbitrary constant; the sum-of-the-digits method by specifying $W_i = X_i = n - (i - 1)$. The equality (4) has no obvious interpretation for methods derived in arbitrary manner.

In accounting for installment sales, the characteristic chosen is the planned cash payments, and the cost of the installment sale is allocated in proportion to cash payments received. Each period therefore earns profits proportional to cash payments. To apportion the cost of a composite investment, $X_i = W_i =$ market value of ith security. Unrealized profits are thus proportional to the value of the security. There is a large class of allocation methods in accounting that result from specifying $W_i = X_i$. Such schemes may be evaluated by exposing the specification of these variables and the particular form of equality that results.

Schemes with $W_i \neq X_i$. Many of these schemes are concerned with the problem of allocating cost over time; some of them have been referred to as "interest methods."

Consider the depreciation problem. Let X_i equal net revenues at the end of the ith period; C, the cost of the asset; and W_i, the present value of net revenues at the beginning of the ith period. Assuming $W_1 = C$ and a constant rate of interest and discount, equation (3) shows the depreciation (cost of the asset) allocated to the ith period. The equality (4) insures that ex ante income is a constant proportion of the present value of the asset in each period. Thus, the excess of revenues over cost, $\sum X_i - C$, is divided among years in proportion to the W_i. This division insures a constant return on W_i, $(X_i - p_iC)/W_i$, in each year.

Two classes of methods for allocating the premium, C, on term bonds and serial bonds may be distinguished with respect to the specification of W_i. In the first class, both the straight-line method (for term bonds) and the bonds outstanding method (for serial bonds) are derived by letting W_i equal the par value of bonds outstanding and X_i equal the stated interest payment which is assumed to be a constant proportion of bonds outstanding. For term bonds, $W_i =$ a constant and the premium allocated to the ith period is

$$p_iC = X_i - \frac{1}{n}[\Sigma X_i - C].$$

For serial bonds,

$$p_iC = X_i - \frac{W_i}{\Sigma W_i}[\Sigma X_i - C].$$

The other class of methods result from setting W_i equal to the present value of bonds outstanding, the value being based on the "true" rate of interest.

Problems of accounting for payments on long-term purchase contracts are similar. When no interest is explicitly provided in such a contract, we can calculate it by letting C equal the present value of the contract; X_i, the payment on the contract; and W_i, the present value of the remaining payments.

As a last example, we note that the problem of allocating capital gains among years would have been brought into clearer focus by considering it in terms of the general model.[4]

Conclusion

None of the allocation methods that we have discussed (and there are many more) are new. Furthermore, many of the comments about these methods have already been made. What, then, does the general model add to our present knowledge?

First, the model formally unifies a number of accounting problems. Thus, methods that have been proposed to account for joint product costs, depreciation, installments sales, etc., share a common allocation model. This unification of different accounting problems gives insight into their comparative nature. Stated differently, the fact that methods to allocate costs in a wide range of problems share a common model implies that the problems themselves are similar or at least regarded as being similar. Second, the model provides a convenient way of summarizing, classifying, and comparing diverse allocation methods. Third, all methods consistent with the general model result in an underlying equality. Exposure of this equality facilitates the evaluation of these methods.

We can provide no ultimate justification for the model and therefore for schemes derived from the model. It does, however, give us additional insight into certain allocation problems and the methods that have been proposed to deal with them.

APPENDIX

The Allocation Model

We wish to determine p_i, the set of allocation schemes, which minimizes

$$Q(p_1, p_2, \cdots, p_N) = \sum_{i=1}^{n} W_i^{-1}(X_i - p_iC)^2 \qquad (1A)$$

subject to $\sum_{i=1}^{n} p_i = 1$,
where

X_i = Characteristic of ith product, segment, etc.
C = Joint cost
W_i = Characteristic chosen to standardize differences, $(X_i - p_iC)^2$.

[4] Richard P. Brief and Joel Owen, "Depreciation and Capital Gains: A New Approach," *Accounting Review*, XLIII (April, 1968), 367–72.

The Minimization

Since $\sum_{i=1}^{n} p_i = 1$, then $p_n = 1 - \sum_{i=1}^{n-1} p_i$. We rewrite (1A) as

$$Q(p_1, \cdots, p_n) = \sum_{i=1}^{n-1} \frac{(X_i - p_i C)^2}{W_i} + \frac{\left[X_n - \left(1 - \sum_{i=1}^{n-1} p_i\right) C\right]^2}{W_n}. \tag{2A}$$

Then minimizing $Q(p_1, \cdots, p_n)$ with respect to p_i,

$$\begin{aligned} \frac{\partial Q}{\partial p_i} = 0 &= \frac{-2C(X_i - p_i C)}{W_i} + \frac{2C\left(X_n - C + \sum_{i=1}^{n-1} p_i\right)}{W_n} \\ &= -\frac{X_i}{W_i} + \frac{C}{W_i} p_i + \frac{X_n}{W_n} - \frac{C}{W_n} + \frac{C}{W_n} \sum_{i=1}^{n-1} p_i. \end{aligned} \tag{3A}$$

Since $\sum_{i=1}^{n-1} p_i = 1 - p_n$, equation (3A) becomes

$$\begin{aligned} 0 &= -\frac{X_i}{W_i} + \frac{C}{W_i} p_i + \frac{X_n}{W_n} - \frac{C}{W_n} + \frac{C}{W_n} - \frac{C}{W_n} p_n \\ &= -\frac{X_i}{W_i} + \frac{C}{W_i} p_i + \frac{X_n}{W_n} - \frac{C}{W_n} p_n. \end{aligned} \tag{4A}$$

Solving for p_i, we have

$$\begin{aligned} p_i &= \frac{\dfrac{X_i}{W_i} + \dfrac{C}{W_n} p_n - \dfrac{X_n}{W_n}}{\dfrac{C}{W_i}} \\ &= \frac{X_i}{C} - \frac{W_i}{W_n} p_n - \frac{W_i X_n}{C W_n}. \end{aligned} \tag{5A}$$

To get the value of p_n, we must sum up both sides of equation (5A), and since $\sum p_i = 1$ we have

$$1 = \frac{\sum_{i=1}^{n} X_i}{C} + \frac{\sum_{i=1}^{n} W_i}{W_n} p_n - \frac{\left(\sum_{i=1}^{n} W_i\right) X_n}{C W_n}. \tag{6A}$$

Solving equation (6A) for p_n, we have

$$p_n = \frac{1 + \dfrac{\left(\sum_{i=1}^{n} W_i\right) X_n}{C W_n} - \dfrac{\sum_{i=1}^{n} X_i}{C}}{\dfrac{\left(\sum_{i=1}^{n} W_i\right)}{W_n}} \tag{7A}$$

$$= \frac{W_n}{\sum_{i=1}^{n} W_i} + \frac{X_n}{C} - \frac{W_n}{\sum_{i=1}^{n} W_i}\left[\frac{\sum_{i=1}^{n} X_i}{C}\right].$$

Substituting the results of (7A) into equation (5A) obtains the required expression for p_i. Thus,

$$\begin{aligned} p_i &= \frac{X_i}{C} - \frac{W_i}{W_n}\left[\frac{W_n}{\sum_{i=1}^{n} W_i} + \frac{X_n}{C} - \frac{W_n}{\sum_{i=1}^{n} W_i}\left(\frac{\sum_{i=1}^{n} X_i}{C}\right)\right] - \frac{W_i X_n}{C W_n} \\ &= \frac{X_i}{C} - \frac{W_i}{\sum_{i=1}^{n} W_i}\left[1 - \frac{\sum_{i=1}^{n} X_i}{C}\right] \\ &= \frac{X_i}{C} - \frac{W_i}{\sum_{i=1}^{n} W_i}\left[\frac{C - \sum_{i=1}^{n} X_i}{C}\right] \\ &= \frac{X_i}{C} - \frac{W_i}{\sum_{i=1}^{n} W_i}\left[\frac{\sum_{i=1}^{n} X_i - C}{C}\right]. \end{aligned} \tag{8A}$$

Reprinted from JOURNAL OF ACCOUNTING RESEARCH
Vol. 8, No. 2, Autumn, 1970
Printed in U.S.A.

The Estimation Problem in Financial Accounting

RICHARD P. BRIEF and JOEL OWEN*

In this paper we begin to develop a theory of estimation in financial accounting. This theory will be discussed within the context of the joint cost problem, although it has implications for other accounting problems as well.

The problem of allocating costs to different periods of time has been debated for nearly a century. A general agreement exists that it has no completely logical solution.[1] Of course, without such a solution, there is no completely satisfactory way to measure periodic performance.

Presently, accounting methods are evaluated through the use of certainty models. In structuring subjects like depreciation, accounting for leases, deferred taxes, etc., numbers associated with future outcomes are usually given as part of the problem, even though the future is uncertain and these numbers are not actually known. What is not realized is that this common procedure of assuming certainty about the future completely obscures the information content of period earnings reports. That is, accounting measurements are necessarily irrelevant to the period-by-period evaluation of decisions when the outcomes of all decisions are assumed to be known in advance. Thus, the crucial economic distinction between anticipations and realizations is not associated with accounting methods.[2]

* Associate Professors, New York University.

[1] See Arthur L. Thomas, *The Allocation Problem in Financial Accounting Theory* (American Accounting Association, 1969), p. 104.

[2] Recently the concept has been advanced that accounting measurements should contain predictive information [American Accounting Association, *A Statement of Basic Accounting Theory* (1966)]. However, the relationship between accounting measurements and predictive information has no operational content because earnings concepts in accounting may be interpreted only in terms of accounting methods and these methods are essentially arbitrary. There also has been research attempting to

It is uncertainty about the future that gives rise to the problem of measuring period earnings. Therefore, the explicit recognition of uncertainty is essential to the development of a theory of measurement in financial accounting.

A Definition of the Estimation Problem

In a previous paper we observed that most allocation methods in practice produce an "equality" among periods and we stated the nature of this equality mathematically.[3] For example, if cost is allocated over time in proportion to sales (assuming certainty and no variable costs), each period's rate of return on sales is equal. That most allocation schemes have this general property is hardly an original finding. The only contribution in that paper was to make a more generalized and formal statement of this property and to show that different allocation methods can be compared on this basis. Other writers have also classified accounting methods in this way.[4]

We have also discussed the problem of insuring an equality of period rates of return under conditions of uncertainty.[5] However, it is not the equality among period rates of return that is the important property of an allocation scheme; it is the relationship between each period's rate of return and the overall return that is the crucial conceptual construct.[6]

The estimation problem in financial accounting is formulated by focusing on the relationship between each period's rate of return and the overall rate of return. Under conditions of uncertainty, the period rate of return can be used to form an estimate of the overall rate of return.

Although we generalize the problem later, for ease of exposition let k be the overall rate of return on sales for the period, $(0, N)$, x_i sales in the ith period, C fixed costs, and p_i, $i = 1, 2, \cdots, N$, the allocation scheme. Assume for simplicity that fixed costs are incurred in the base period and that there are no variable costs. The return on sales in period i, r_i, is

---

relate ex post accounting measurements to future events, not future measurements (see William Beaver, "Financial Ratios as Predictors of Failure," *Empirical Research in Accounting: Selected Studies, 1966,* Supplement to Vol. 4, *Journal of Accounting Research*). But this empirical approach to questions about the predictive content of accounting information has not dealt with accounting methods, and the various models on which it is based cannot be deduced from accounting theory. Similar comments can be made about aspects of other empirical research, e.g., David Green, Jr. and Joel Segall, "The Predictive Power of First-Quarter Earnings Reports," *Journal of Business,* 40 (January, 1967).

[3] Richard P. Brief and Joel Owen, "A Least Squares Allocation Model," *Journal of Accounting Research,* 6 (Autumn, 1968).

[4] For example, Orace Johnson, "Two Concepts of Depreciation," *Journal of Accounting Research, ibid.*

[5] Richard P. Brief and Joel Owen, "On the Bias in Accounting Allocations under Uncertainty," *Journal of Accounting Research,* 7 (Spring, 1969).

[6] Thomas *almost* argues along similar lines (*op. cit.,* p. 86), but his earlier views are inconsistent with this argument (p. 71).

$$r_i = \frac{x_i - p_i C}{x_i}, \tag{1}$$

and the overall return on sales for the period, (0, N), is

$$k = \frac{\sum x_i - C}{\sum x_i}. \tag{2}$$

The estimation problem is defined as follows: A rule or formula must be determined for translating the rate of return in each period r_i into an estimate of k. This rule or formula is called an estimator.[7]

By viewing the allocation problem as part of an estimation problem, the concept of period earnings is radically transformed. Instead of focusing on the question of what the true earnings of a period are—a measure which conceptually cannot be solved—the emphasis now shifts to a measure of performance in any arbitrarily defined time period, t, which provides an efficient estimate of overall performance k.

Thus, a theory of estimation in financial accounting may provide a resolution to the problem usually associated with allocating costs over time. A joint time stream of costs and revenues need not be severed. Rather, time itself is divided up into periods in order to calculate estimates of a number associated with the joint stream. The periods are "samples" from an overall stream.

To obtain an estimator of the overall rate of return, we must consider a number of statistical questions as well as the issues associated with defining k. Some of these statistical problems are formulated in the next section and we then address ourselves to the specification of k.

An Allocation Criterion

The first problem is to determine the allocation scheme, p_i, which is used to derive the period returns r_i. Again, assuming that x_i are period sales, which are random variables, and k is the overall rate of return on sales, we want to formulate a criterion which relates the r_i and k.

Let $r_i - k$ be the difference between the return reported in the ith period and the overall rate of return. Since $x_i k$ is period profit based on the overall rate of return on sales and $x_i r_i$ is period profit based on the period rate of return on sales, $x_i(r_i - k)$ is the difference between these quantities. The expression, $x_i(r_i - k)$, is a measurement error. It depends on two factors: the variability of the x_i and the choice of the estimator.

In order to measure the error without regard to sign, we redefine the measurement error in the ith period as $x_i(r_i - k)^2$. The use of the squared

[7] Therefore, the estimation problem in financial accounting is a special class of statistical estimation problems [see Ernest Kurnow, Gerald Glasser and Frederick Ottman, *Statistics for Business Decisions* (Homewood, Ill.: Richard D. Irwin, Inc., 1959), ch. 7].

error in defining the measurement error is somewhat arbitrary. However, similar problems in defining an error term are encountered in statistics, and a least-squares error is frequently employed.

The quantity,

$$Q(p_1, p_2, \cdots, p_N) = E \sum_{i=1}^{N} x_i(r_i - k)^2, \tag{3}$$

measures the total expected measurement error, where E is the expected value operator.

If equation (3) is expanded we have

$$\begin{aligned} Q = E \sum_{i=1}^{N} x_i(r_i - k)^2 &= E\,[\sum x_i r_i^2 - 2 \sum x_i r_i k + \sum x_i k^2] \\ &= E\,[\sum x_i r_i^2 - 2\,\frac{\sum x_i \sum x_i r_i k}{\sum x_i} + \sum x_i k^2]\,. \end{aligned}$$

Since $\dfrac{\sum x_i r_i}{\sum x_i} = k,$[8]

$$\begin{aligned} Q &= E\,[\sum x_i r_i^2 - 2 \sum x_i k^2 + \sum x_i k^2] \\ &= E\,[\sum x_i r_i^2 - \sum x_i k^2] \\ &= E \sum x_i \left(\frac{x_i - p_i C}{x_i}\right)^2 - E \sum x_i k^2. \end{aligned} \tag{4}$$

The second term on the right hand side of (4) does not depend on p_i. Therefore, the criterion for determining the allocation scheme is to minimize, with respect to p_i, and subject to the constraint that $\sum p_i = 1$ and $p_i \geq 0$, the quantity:

$$E \sum_{i=1}^{N} x_i r_i^2 = E \sum_{i=1}^{N} x_i \left(\frac{x_i - p_i C}{x_i}\right)^2 = E \sum_{i=1}^{N} \frac{(x_i - p_i C)^2}{x_i}. \tag{5}$$

In introducing this allocation criterion we initially assumed that the relevant ratio to measure performance was the rate of return on sales. We now present a more general criterion for determining p_i.

Let $r_i = (x_i - p_i C)/w_i$ and $k = (\sum x_i - C)/\sum w_i$, where x_i and w_i are random variables. For example, if, as in the previous example, x_i is sales less variable costs and w_i sales, r_i is the net profit on sales in period i and k is the overall net profit on sales. The specification of x_i and w_i therefore determines r_i, k, and p_i (we assume C is given). We have shown elsewhere that other specifications of x_i and w_i have been associated with

[8] It is assumed that $\Sigma p_i = 1$. Thus, k is a weighted average of period returns r with the weights being $x_i/\Sigma x_i$. Note also that k does not depend on the allocation scheme.

different allocation schemes.[9] Implicit in the use of most accounting allocation methods is a definition of r_i and k.

Generalizing the criterion (3), we have

$$q(p_1, p_2, \cdots p_N) = E\sum_{i=1}^{N} w_i(r_i - k)^2 = E\sum_{i=1}^{N} \frac{(x_i - p_iC)^2}{w_i} - E\sum_{i=1}^{N} w_ik^2. \quad (6)$$

Equation (6) is the generalized criterion, and the exact solution to the minimization of (6) with respect to p_i is given in the Appendix, equation (1A). An approximate solution to (6) is given in (6A). When $w_i = x_i$, (6) reduces to (3) and an approximate solution for this special class of schemes is given in equation (8A).

Measures of Performance

In the previous section, we presented a criterion for determining p_i and a derivation of an exact and an approximate method for calculating the resulting allocation scheme. We now discuss some of the problems relating to the specification of x_i and w_i. As will be demonstrated, their specifications depend on the particular decision model employed.

Recall that a specification of x_i and w_i will determine r_i, k, and p_i. Actually, this statement is misleading because it inverts the problem. The first step in formulating an estimation problem involves a choice of the object of measurement. The performance measure k implies a particular x_i and w_i. It should be immediately apparent that the determination of k is a crucial part of the estimation problem. Unfortunately, it is too complex to solve here. Our discussion below is intended only to clarify, by use of an example, the general nature of the problem.

We will consider the specification of the overall rate of return k associated with an investment decision. The financial accounting problem is to obtain period-by-period estimates of the parameter k[10] in the appropriate decision model. Of course, it is not the accountant's responsibility to determine the "appropriate" decision model, and therefore k, but he must know the relationship between k and x_i and w_i.

It is well-known that there are many vexing and unsettled issues associated with the investment decision. In order to steer clear of them we confine our attention to four basic investment decision models that are frequently given as alternative ways of evaluating the investment decision.[11] It turns out that the parameter k associated with at least one of them is ill-defined.

---

[9] Brief and Owen, "A Least Squares Allocation Model," *op. cit.*

[10] Technically, k is a random variable in this context, but the decision-maker might chose to describe the distribution of k with a parameter.

[11] See Ezra Solomon, *The Theory of Financial Management* (New York, Columbia University Press, 1963), pp. 122–31.

Payback Method. We define the parameter k associated with the payback method as the number of times a project will be paid in N periods, where N is the life of the project. Strictly speaking, the definition of the parameter in this model is incorrect, but it is close enough for illustrative purposes.

The parameter k is explicitly defined as $\sum x_i/C$. If we specify $x_i = w_i =$ cash flows in the ith period, then

$$k' = \frac{\sum x - C}{\sum x_i},$$

and k is defined in terms of k'. That is,

$$k = \frac{1}{1 - k'} = \frac{\sum x_i}{C}.$$

Book Return on Book Investment. The parameter k, book return, cannot be specified directly since it is derived from the resulting allocation scheme.

Internal Rate of Return. For this model, k is the internal rate of return r. Specify w_i as the present discounted value in the ith period of all remaining cash flows, discounted at the internal rate of return, and x_i as cash flows. Since $w_1 = C$

$$\begin{aligned} k &= \frac{\sum x_i - C}{\sum w_i} \\ &= \frac{\sum x_i - w_1}{\frac{1}{r}\sum x_i[1 - (1+r)^{-i}]} \\ &= \frac{\sum x_i[1 - (1+r)^{-i}]}{\frac{1}{r}\sum x_i[1 - (1+r)^{-i}]} \\ &= r. \end{aligned}$$

Contribution to Net Present Worth. When the discount rate d is less than the internal rate of return the present value of cash flows at the beginning of period 1, w_1, exceeds the cost of the project A parameter which could be associated with the excess present value model is $k = (w_1 - C)/w_1$. This definition of k implies that x_i and w_i are both specified as the cash flows in the ith period, discounted at $(1 + d)^i$. Then

$$\begin{aligned} k &= \frac{\sum x_i - C}{\sum w_i} \\ &= \frac{w_1 - C}{w_1} = \textit{Excess Present Value Index}. \end{aligned}$$

Conclusion

This paper has restructured the allocation problem in financial accounting as part of a more general estimation problem. This new perspective of the allocation problem resolves the traditional dilemma relating to the jointness of costs and revenues over any time horizon, and this is probably the most obvious and important implication of developing a theory of estimation in accounting. However, there are other implications which are also important.

First, although accounting is a "statistical" discipline, its relationship to statistical theory has never been made clear. Our approach formally links financial accounting with statistical estimation theory. Thus concepts in financial accounting like "bias" and "accuracy" can be redefined in terms of this theory. Presently, these are ill-defined concepts which lack operational content.

Second the definition of measurement error (6) is a first attempt to define the idea of an "accounting error" in operational terms. Our earlier argument that measurement error depends on the variability of x_i, w_i, and the allocation scheme suggests that an ex post measure of risk, e.g., variability of the return on book value, really consists of two components: pure risk, which is a result of uncertainty, and the choice of the allocation scheme. Thus, a theory of estimation in accounting also has implications for empirical research.

Third, we have integrated the measurement problem in financial accounting with financial decision theory. Although the idea that the parameter of a decision model should enter into the accounting process is not new, previous discussions of the subject have been rather vague about this relationship. Much more work needs to be done in this area.

Two important and complex problems which we have not considered in this paper are (1) how to operationally translate the period returns r_i into an estimate of k and (2) how to update the allocation scheme as new information is obtained. In addition, the entire question relating to the specification of performance measures needs more attention. At best, we have merely outlined the first stages of a theory of estimation in financial accounting. Its complete development is yet to be achieved.

APPENDIX

The General Solution

We assume that x_i, w_i, and C are random variables. If $p_1, \cdots, p_N$ are any allocation scheme, we assume that the measurement error from using this scheme prior to observing the variables x_i and w_i is given by

$$Q(p_1, \cdots, p_N) = E \sum_{i=1}^{N} \frac{(x_i - p_i C)^2}{w_i} - \sum_{i=1}^{N} w_i k^2$$

the expectation taken with respect to the joint distribution of x_i, w_i, and C. We wish to minimize the function with respect to the parameters p_1, $\cdots, p_N$.

Theorem

If (i) $\min_i EC(x_i/w_i) + \min_i E[(C^2/N)(1/w_i)] \geq \max_i E(x_iC/w_i)$

(ii) $E(C^2/w_i) \geq 0$

then the allocation scheme that minimizes the measurement error is

$$p_i = E^{-1}(C^2/w_i)\, E\left(\frac{x_iC}{w_i}\right) - \frac{E^{-1}(C^2/w_i)}{\sum_{i=1}^{N} E^{-1}(C^2/w_i)} \cdot \left[\sum_{i=1}^{N} E^{-1}(C^2/w_i) E\left(\frac{x_iC}{w_i}\right) - 1\right] \tag{1A}$$

where $p_i \geq 0$ and $\sum_{i=1}^{N} p_i = 1$.

Proof

Taking the derivative of $Q(p_1, \cdots, p_N)$ with respect to p_i and setting it equal to zero yields

$$\frac{\partial Q}{\partial p_i} = -2E\left(\frac{x_iC}{w_i}\right) + 2\, p_iE(C^2/w_i) + 2E\left(\frac{x_NC}{w_N}\right) - 2p_NE(C^2/w_N) = 0.$$

Then

$$p_i = E^{-1}(C^2/w_i)E\left(\frac{x_iC}{w_i}\right) + p_NE^{-1}(C^2/w_i)E(C^2/w_N) - E^{-1}(C^2/w_i)E(x_NC/w_N).$$

Imposing the condition that $\sum p_i = 1$, it follows that

$$p_N = E^{-1}(C^2/w_N)E(x_NC/w_N) + \frac{1 - \sum E^{-1}(C^2/w_i)E(x_iC/w_i)}{E(C^2/w_N)/\sum E^{-1}(C^2/w_i)}.$$

Substituting this value into p_i gives

$$p_i = E^{-1}(C^2/w_i)E(x_iC/w_i) - \frac{E^{-1}(C^2/w_i)}{\sum E^{-1}(C^2/w_i)} [\sum E^{-1}(C^2/w_i)E(x_iC/w_i) - 1].$$

The p_i are positive if

$$E\,\frac{x_iC}{w_i} - \frac{\sum E^{-1}(C^2/w_i)E(x_iC/w_i)}{\sum E^{-1}(C^2/w_i)} \geq -\frac{1}{\sum E^{-1}(C^2/w_i)}. \tag{a}$$

(We have divided by $E^{-1}(C^2/w_i)$ which is assumed to be positive.) We have

$$\begin{aligned} E(x_iC/w_i) - \frac{\sum E^{-1}(C^2/w_i)E(x_iC/w_i)}{\sum E^{-1}(C^2/w_i)} &\geq \min_i E(x_iC/w_i) - \max_i E(x_iC/w_i) \\ &\geq -\min E(C^2/N\ 1/w_i) \text{ [by assumption } (i)] \\ &\geq -\frac{1}{\sum E^{-1}(C^2/w_i)}. \end{aligned}$$

Therefore (a) is satisfied and the theorem is proved.

We next show that when C is assumed to be known, the allocation scheme of the theorem produces constant expected return, r_i, in all periods.

Corollary

Let p_i be computed as above. Assume C is a known constant. Then $E[(x_i - p_iC)/w_i]$ does not depend on i, i.e., is a constant.

Proof

$$\begin{aligned} E\,\frac{x_i - p_iC}{w_i} &= E\left(\frac{x_i}{w_i}\right) - p_iC\,E\left(\frac{1}{w_i}\right) \\ &= E(x_i/w_i) - E\left(\frac{1}{w_i}\right)\left[E^{-1}\left(\frac{1}{w_i}\right)E\left(\frac{x_i}{w_i}\right)\right. \\ &\quad \left. - \frac{E^{-1}(1/w_i)}{\sum E^{-1}(1/w_i)}\left[\sum E^{-1}\left(\frac{1}{w_i}\right)E\left(\frac{x_i}{w_i}\right) - C\right]\right] \\ &= \frac{\sum_{i=1}^{N} E^{-1}(1/w_i)E(x_i/w_i) - C}{\sum^{N} E^{-1}(1/w_i)}. \end{aligned} \tag{2A}$$

This completes the proof.

1. Special Case: x_i random, w_i, and C known

Under these conditions

$$\begin{aligned} p_i &= \left(\frac{C^2}{w_i}\right)^{-1}\left(\frac{C}{w_i}\right)E(x_i) - \frac{(C^2/w_i)^{-1}}{\sum(C^2/w_i)^{-1}}\left[\sum\left(\frac{C^2}{w_i}\right)^{-1}\left(\frac{C}{w_i}\right)Ex_i - 1\right] \\ &= \frac{\mu_i}{C} - \frac{w_i}{\sum w_i}\left[\frac{\sum\mu_i}{C} - 1\right]. \end{aligned} \tag{3A}$$

2. Special Case: x_i, w_i, and C known

$$p_i = \frac{x_i}{C} - \frac{w_i}{\sum w_i}\left[\frac{\sum x_i}{C} - 1\right]. \tag{4A}$$

3. Special Case: x_i and w_i independent and C known

$$\begin{aligned} p_i &= \frac{Ex_i}{C} - \frac{E^{-1}(1/w_i)}{\sum E^{-1}(1/w_i)}\left[\sum\frac{Ex_i}{C} - 1\right] \\ &= \frac{\mu_i}{C} - \frac{E^{-1}(1/w_i)}{\sum E^{-1}(1/w_i)}\left[\sum\frac{\mu_i}{C} - 1\right]. \end{aligned} \tag{5A}$$

Approximation of Results

The results of the theorem and corollary require that we compute the expectation of the reciprocal of random variables. In this section we approximate the results derived above by more easily available statistics. Let $E(x_i) = \mu_i$, $E(w_i) = \theta_i$, $V(w_i) = \sigma_i^2$, $C_i = \mathrm{Cov}(x_i, w_i)$, $b_i^2 = \sigma_i^2/\theta_i^2$,

and
$$B_i = \frac{C_i}{\mu_i\theta_i(1 + b_i^2)}.$$

By Taylor expansion to quadratic terms we have

$$\frac{1}{w_i} = \frac{1}{\theta_i} - \frac{1}{\theta_i^2}(w_i - \theta_i) + \frac{1}{\theta_i^3}(w_i - \theta_i)^2.$$

Then
$$E\left(\frac{1}{w_i}\right) \doteq \frac{1}{\theta_i}\left[1 + \frac{\sigma_i^2}{\theta_i^2}\right] = \frac{1}{\theta_i}[1 + b_i^2].$$

To second order terms we have

$$\begin{aligned}\frac{x_i}{w_i} &= \frac{\mu_i}{\theta_i}\frac{1 + x_i - \mu_i/\mu_i}{1 + w_i - \theta_i/\theta_i}\\ &\doteq \frac{\mu_i}{\theta_i}\left[1 + \frac{x_i - \mu_i}{\mu_i} - \frac{w_i - \theta_i}{\theta_i} - \frac{x_i - \mu_i}{\mu_i}\frac{w_i - \theta_i}{\theta_i} + \frac{(w_i - \theta_i)^2}{\theta_i^2}\right].\end{aligned}$$

Then

$$E\left(\frac{x_i}{w_i}\right) = \frac{\mu_i}{\theta_i}\left[1 + b_i^2 - \frac{C_i}{\mu_i\theta_i}\right].$$

Evaluating the p_i with these approximate values (and assuming C = constant) we have

$$\begin{aligned}p_i &= \frac{1}{C}\frac{\theta_i}{1 + b_i^2}\frac{\mu_i}{\theta_i}\left[1 + b_i^2 - \frac{C_i}{\mu_i\theta_i}\right]\\ &\quad - \frac{\theta_i/1 + b_i^2}{\sum\theta_i/1 + b_i^2}\left[\frac{1}{C}\sum\frac{\theta_i}{1 + b_i^2}\frac{\mu_i}{\theta_i}\left(1 + b_i^2 - \frac{C_i}{\theta_i\mu_i}\right) - 1\right] \qquad (6A)\\ &= \frac{\mu_i}{C}[1 - B_i] - \frac{\theta_i/1 + b_i^2}{\sum\theta_i/1 + b_i^2}\left[\frac{1}{C}\sum\mu_i(1 - B_i) - 1\right].\end{aligned}$$

Special Case $w_i = x_i$

We now illustrate all of the results for the case $w_i = x_i$, still assuming C = constant.

When $w_i = x_i$ and C = constant, conditions (i) and (ii) of the theorem reduce to the single condition $E(1/x_i) \geq 0$ for all i. Then

$$\begin{aligned}p_i &= \frac{1}{C}E^{-1}\left(\frac{1}{x_i}\right) - \frac{E^{-1}(1/x_i)}{\sum E^{-1}(1/x_i)}\left[\frac{1}{C}\sum E^{-1}\left(\frac{1}{x_i}\right) - 1\right]\\ &= \frac{E^{-1}(1/x_i)}{\sum E^{-1}(1/x_i)}.\end{aligned} \qquad (7A)$$

This can be approximated by

$$p_i \doteq \frac{\mu_i/1 + b_i^2}{\sum \mu_i/1 + b_i^2}. \tag{8A}$$

Also

$$E\,\frac{x_i - p_i C}{x_i} = \frac{\sum E^{-1}(1/x_i) - C}{\sum E^{-1}(1/x_i)},$$

which can be approximated by

$$1 - \frac{C}{\sum \mu_i/1 + b_i^2}. \tag{9A}$$

Reprinted from JOURNAL OF ACCOUNTING RESEARCH
Vol. 11, No. 1, Spring, 1973
Printed in U.S.A.

A Reformulation of the Estimation Problem

RICHARD P. BRIEF AND JOEL OWEN*

In an earlier paper [5] we outlined the first stage of a theory of estimation in financial accounting. In this paper we extend the development of estimation theory and offer further implications of the theory for accounting.

The first section is restricted to the single-asset situation which dominates the exposition of modern theory. After illustrating the use of alternative estimation methods under conditions of certainty and uncertainty, we argue that estimation theory provides an extremely flexible model for reinterpreting a wide range of subjects. However, we then point out that the single-asset approach to accounting theory has major conceptual limitations. These are partially removed by extending estimation theory to the multi-asset (firm) situation. In structuring the multi-asset estimation problem, a distinction between the ex ante and updating problems is made, and the choice of an estimating horizon and allocation scheme is formally introduced in a decision-theory framework.

The Single-Asset Approach

The particular problem on which estimation theory was developed can be stated as follows: The accountant wishes to select a method for allocating the known cost of an asset over its useful life, which also is assumed to be known. The purpose of the cost assignment is to obtain a number called "period income," which can be translated into an estimate of a financial parameter associated with the asset.

The theory was developed on the following assumptions which are now made explicit.

---

* Professor and Associate Professor, New York University. The authors wish to thank Professors J. Kennelly and A. L. Thomas for their helpful comments on earlier drafts of this paper.

1. A single asset is purchased at the beginning of time period 1.
2. The cost of the asset, C, is known and deterministic.
3. The life of the asset, N, is known and deterministic.
4. Cash flows received at the end of the period, x_i, $i = 1, 2, \cdots, N$, are uncertain, but the probability density function, $f(x_i/N)$, is known and summarizes subjective opinion about future cash flows, assuming N is given.
5. The selection of the allocation scheme, p_i, $i = 1, 2, \cdots, N$, is made at the beginning of period 1.

To illustrate how estimation may be applied to this single-asset situation, we consider the problem of estimating two parameters—future cash flows and internal rate of return. For simplicity and clarity of exposition, we first develop the estimation procedure by assuming certainty about the future.

ESTIMATING FUTURE CASH FLOWS

Define

$$k^1 = \frac{\sum_{i=1}^{N} X_i - C}{\sum_{i=1}^{N} X_i} \tag{1}$$

where X_i represents cash flows in period i (known with certainty, as is N), and C is the initial investment cost. The superscript on k is used to distinguish this specification of the parameter from others that are used.

The quantity we wish to obtain from the information in period reports is $\sum_{i=1}^{N} X_i$, which can be derived from k^1 and C. That is,

$$\sum_{i=1}^{N} X_i = \frac{C}{1 - k^1}. \tag{2}$$

The accountant reports income, defined as

$$X_i - p_i C. \tag{3}$$

Now the ratio,

$$r_i^1 = \frac{X_i - p_i C}{X_i}, \tag{4}$$

also can be calculated from the information furnished in periodic reports. Therefore, if p_i is chosen so that $r_i^1 = k^1$, equation (2) can be used to obtain future cash flows. It is easy to show that when

$$p_i = \frac{X_i}{\sum_{i=1}^{N} X_i}, \tag{5}$$

$r_i^1 = k^1$. Therefore, if (5) is used to allocate the investment cost, C, future cash flows can be obtained from periodic reports from the relationship in (2).

When the distinction is made between x_i as a random variable and X_i as the realization of that variable, the method must be modified. Since future cash flows are now random variables (we continue to assume that C and N are known), k^1 (equation (1)) also becomes a random variable. One solution is to take the expected value of the numerator and denominator of (1) and to assume that the user of accounting reports wants to estimate $E(\sum_{i=1}^{N} x_i)$, where E is the expectation operator.

Define

$$k^1 = \frac{E\left(\sum_{i=1}^{N} x_i - C\right)}{E\left(\sum_{i=1}^{N} x_i\right)}. \tag{1'}$$

Therefore

$$E\left(\sum_{i=1}^{N} x_i\right) = \frac{C}{1 - k^1}. \tag{2'}$$

Consider the problem of choosing the allocation scheme at the end of period 1. The user can calculate r_1^1 directly from the statement in period 1. If r_1^1 can be used to estimate k^1, i.e.,

$$r_1^1 = \hat{k}^1 \tag{6}$$

(where the symbol $\wedge$ means "an estimate of"), then an estimator of $E(\sum_{i=1}^{N} x_i)$ is

$$\frac{C}{1 - \hat{k}^1} = \frac{C}{1 - r_1^1}. \tag{2'}$$

Therefore, the question becomes how to choose p_1 so that r_1^1 is a good estimate of k^1.

Elsewhere [5], we have argued that p_i should be chosen to make r_i^1 close to k^1, where the overall criterion was of the quadratic form:

Minimize, with respect to $(p_1, p_2, \cdots, p_N)$, subject to $\sum_{i=1}^{N} p_i = 1$ and $p_i \geq 0$,

$$Q(p_1, p_2, \cdots, p_N) = E \sum_{i=1}^{N} x_i (r_i^1 - k^1)^2. \tag{7}$$

The allocation scheme that satisfies this criterion is

$$p_i = \frac{E\left(\frac{1}{x_i}\right)}{\sum_{i=1}^{N} E\left(\frac{1}{x_i}\right)} \doteq \frac{E(x_i)/1 + b_i^2}{\sum_{i=1}^{N} E(x_i)/1 + b_i^2}, \tag{5'}$$

where b_i is the coefficient of variation of the distribution of x_i. (Under certainty (5′) becomes (5)). As further justification of this procedure, note that the minimization of (7) with respect to k^1 yields (1′).

ESTIMATING THE INTERNAL RATE OF RETURN

Define

$$V_i = \sum_{t=i}^{N} X_t(1+d)^{-(t-i+1)}, \tag{8}$$

where d is the internal rate of return or the discount rate which equates V_1 and C. Thus, V_i is the present discounted value of cash flows in period i. Certainty is assumed.

Now let

$$k^2 = \frac{\sum_{i=1}^{N} X_i - C}{\sum_{i=1}^{N} V_i}. \tag{9}$$

It can be shown that k^2 is equal to d.

The book value of the asset at the beginning of period 1 is C. At the end of period 1, information to compute

$$r_1^2 = \frac{X_1 - p_1 C}{C} \tag{10}$$

will be reported by the accountant. If

$$p_1 = \frac{X_1}{C} - \frac{V_1}{\sum_{i=1}^{N} V_i}\left[\frac{\sum_{i=1}^{N} X_i - C}{C}\right] = \frac{X_1 - dV_1}{C}, \tag{11}$$

then

$$r_1^2 = k^2 = d. \tag{12}$$

Under uncertainty cash flows and the internal rate of return are random variables and a discount rate to equate C and the discounted cash flows cannot be calculated. However, if d is redefined as the discount rate which equates the expected value of discounted cash flows, $E(v_1)$, and C, the ratio

$$k^2 = \frac{E\left(\sum_{i=1}^{N} x_i - C\right)}{\sum_{i=1}^{N} E(v_i)} = d. \tag{13}$$

The estimation problem is to choose p_1 so that r_1^2 is an estimate of $k^2 = d$. Since $C = E(v_1)$, one way to achieve this objective is to modify the criterion (7) by replacing $x_i(r_i^1 - k^1)^2$ with $E(v_i)(r_i^2 - k^2)^2$.

Other parameters also could be estimated from period reports, but we have chosen to discuss two in detail in order to illustrate the nature of the estimation methods.

A CRITIQUE OF THE SINGLE-ASSET PROBLEM

In so far as single-asset problems are concerned, estimation methods are quite flexible. All present value methods, whether applied to lease accounting, depreciation, bond discount, etc., as well as other procedures such as percentage completion methods, can be recast as estimation methods [4]. Thus, estimation theory provides a new way to interpret both the matching principle and the realization postulate, two of the most basic ideas in financial accounting [12].

Other theoretical issues in accounting also can be developed as estimation problems. For example, using a deterministic model Bierman [3] showed that when future cash flows are stated in current dollars, book values based on present value depreciation methods equal the present discounted value of the asset. Alternatively, as Shwayder [14] showed, methods that estimate the internal rate of return (money return) under inflation yield identical results. On the other hand, Dyckman [10] was concerned with estimating the real internal rate of return. In all of these cases, the idea of estimation has important implications for the price level problem. As another example, Dyckman [9] implicitly argued that the question of deferred taxes becomes an artificial problem when it is initially structured as part of an estimation problem.[1]

When estimation theory is applied to the single-asset situation, the problem of allocating joint costs over time is also resolved because the question of separating time periods will be circumvented. Estimation focuses on performance during a multi-period time span and the income statement of an individual time period is viewed as a "sample" or *interim report* from this longer time segment.[2]

However, most firms are multi-asset firms and the question arises as to how accountants should develop allocation schemes for more than one asset. One approach is to assign revenues to each individual asset of the firm. But, as Thomas has argued [16, p. 33], "Revenues are a joint product of *all* the inputs of a firm, and the attempt at simultaneous allocation of total revenues to all individual inputs leads to much the same difficulties as . . . attempts to allocate joint costs [over time]."

---

[1] Other writers such as Drake and Dopuch [8] also have recognized the implications of building expectations into accounting models. Expectation models are closely related to estimation models.

[2] This interpretation of the income concept is not really new. For example, the AICPA stated several decades ago: "income is used to describe a general concept, not a specific and precise thing, and . . . the income statement . . . is at best an interim report" [1, p. 59]. A similar concept of income is expressed in the *Accountant's Handbook*. "The periodic matching of costs and income may be characterized as a 'test reading' of the results of the efforts and accomplishments of the continuing business activity" [2, p. 1–17]. Estimation theory formally structures the income concept as an interim report and thus gives empirical meaning to income numbers. Such meaning cannot be extracted from existing methodology. See, for example, Sterling [15, p. 277].

The logical answer to this difficulty is to treat all assets—all inputs—as a single economic good. Indeed, this alternative is considered by Thomas, but he concludes (p. 87) that "It is hard to see how such compression could stop short of having almost all unexpired nonmonetary economic goods reflected in a single figure on the balance sheet, and almost all expirations of such goods reflected in a single expense figure on the income statement." Thomas then rejects the approach because, as Devine [7] puts it,[3] "businessmen probably feel a need to examine the individual agents that contribute to future events in some way that appeals to their intuitive feeling for cause and effect and responsibility."

This intuitive feeling is probably the chief factor responsible for a continuation of a single-asset approach in accounting, even for the multi-asset firm. It is undoubtedly related to the cameralistic origin of accounting as well as the influence of legal institutions. However, on a theoretical level, cause and effect and responsibility cannot be assigned to the individual assets of a firm, as cause and effect and responsibility cannot attach to arbitrarily defined time periods. Jointness exists for the firm in both a time and space dimension.[4] Consequently, allocation schemes are either arbitrary (e.g., straight-line depreciation) or they are chosen on the basis of assumed cash flows attributable to individual assets. Notice that an individual asset's cash flows are, in general, never observed but merely imputed.

In the following section, we extend estimation theory to the multi-asset case. This should provide a more systematic approach to allocation than presently exists.

The Multi-Asset (Firm) Approach

The new assumptions that are required to meet these objections and to extend the estimation problem to the multi-asset situation are:

1. The life of the firm is h periods, which is uncertain, and the probability density function, $g(h)$, is known and summarizes subjective opinion about the life of the firm.

2. Cash flows received at the end of the period, x_i, $i = 1, 2, \cdots, h$, are uncertain and the joint probability density function, $f(x_i/h)g(h)$, summarizes subjective opinion about future cash flows. These assumptions represent a modification of assumptions 3 and 4 in the single-asset case.

Given these new assumptions, there are now two parts to the estimation problem: (1) despite the fact that the life of a firm is uncertain, a definite time horizon must be chosen for estimating purposes. We shall call this time period the *estimating horizon*; and (2) the allocation scheme must be determined for this estimating horizon.

At the outset, the two parts of the problem must be solved *ex ante*. As time passes, the estimating horizon and allocation scheme must be updated.

[3] Quoted by Thomas [16, p. 87].

[4] Thomas [16] deals extensively with this issue. See, especially, p. 78.

The ex ante and updating solutions are dealt with below in a decision-theory framework, and the concept of a loss function is introduced.

THE EX ANTE SOLUTION

There are four parts to a formal statistical decision problem: (1) set of acts, (2) states of nature, (3) probability function over the states of nature, and (4) the loss function.

1. *Set of Acts.* The accountant must select an estimating horizon and allocation scheme for this reporting period. These represent the acts available to him. Let the closed interval $(0, n) = n$ be the estimating horizon and $p = (p_1, p_2, \cdots, p_n)$ the allocation scheme. Then the set of acts is

$$a = (p, n). \tag{14}$$

2. *States of Nature.* The choice of acts depends on expected future cash flows and the life of the firm. Let $x = (x_1, x_2, \cdots, x_h)$. Then the states of nature are

$$\alpha = (x, h), \tag{15}$$

i.e., the actual but unknown cash flows, x_i, over the life of the firm, and h, the life of the firm which is also unknown.

3. *Probability Density.* The probability density over the states of nature is assumed known and is given by

$$f(\alpha) = f(x/h)g(h). \tag{16}$$

4. *Loss Function.* The loss function, in its most general form, is

$$L(a, \alpha), \tag{17}$$

the loss incurred by the accountant in choosing an allocation scheme for the estimating horizon n when, in fact, the life of the firm is h with cash flows, x. Thus, the loss function evaluates the loss incurred in making a mistake, i.e., in choosing a nonoptimal act.

It is an understatement to assert that the problems of defining the accountant's loss function raise difficult questions. What is a nonoptimal act? How is the loss associated with this act to be measured? How do legal constraints, the economics of the profession, etc., affect the specification of (17)?

Some of these questions are considered by Demski and Feltham [6]. They use a loss function to compare various techniques of prediction, and the loss function in their work serves as a device to measure the quality of these techniques. Their work is very general. For example, if information about future cash flows were needed, they could evaluate various techniques to forecast future cash flows. Our use of the loss function is to measure the quality of different allocation methods. Our approach takes as given the statistical properties of the predictions that might be forthcoming from their work.

Our initial solution to the estimation problem [5] was based on the minimization of the following function with respect to p:

$$Q(p) = E \sum_{i=1}^{n} w_i (r_i - k)^2, \tag{18}$$

where

$$w_i = \text{an unspecified characteristic of period } i$$

$$r_i = \frac{x_i - p_i C}{w_i}$$

$$k = \frac{E\left(\sum_{i=1}^{n} x_i - C\right)}{E\left(\sum_{i=1}^{n} w_i\right)}.$$

The choice of w_i determines the financial parameter to be estimated by the period return, r_i [see 4 and 5].[5] (The symbol n in (18) was the life of the asset in [5]; in this paper n is the estimating horizon.)

In [5], it was also shown that the minimization of (18) was equivalent to the minimization, with respect to p, of

$$Q(p) = E \sum_{i=1}^{n} \frac{(x_i - p_i C)^2}{w_i}. \tag{19}$$

Equation (18) was discussed in the context of measurement error and the criterion for determining p was to minimize that error, a type of least-squares solution. However, the minimization of equation (19), first mentioned in [4], was shown to reproduce under conditions of certainty most of the allocation schemes that are actually used in practice by the appropriate specification of x_i, w_i and C. Neither argument gives substantial justification for reinterpreting either (18) or (19) as a loss function, but these arguments do lend some credence to their use as a component of the loss function in the revised estimation problem. On that basis, we will use (19) in specifying (17).

We can simplify the problem by assuming the loss function (17) can be divided additively into two parts. Thus, we have

$$L(a, \alpha) = L_1(p, x) + L_2(n, h), \tag{20}$$

where the vector x is a $n \times 1$ vector, i.e., we consider the cash flows in keeping with the assumed estimating horizon.

Let

$$w = \begin{pmatrix} 1/w_1 & & 0 \\ & \ddots & \\ 0 & & 1/w_n \end{pmatrix},$$

[5] More accurately, the choice of k determines w_i. For example, k^1 implies w_i is period cash flows, x_i; k^2 implies w_i is the present discounted value of cash flows, v_i.

an $n \times n$ matrix that could depend on x but not p.
Then,

$$L_1(p, x) = (x - pC)w(x - pC)'. \tag{21}$$

The new component of the estimation problem dealt with in this paper concerns the selection of n which has been redefined as the estimating horizon. Since the set of acts (14) include the selection of n, $L_2(n, h)$ must be specified.
Let

$$L_2(n, h) = t(n - h)^2, \quad \text{where } t \text{ is a constant.} \tag{22}$$

Again, we cannot give substantial justification for (22) but work done by Ijiri and Kaplan [11] on the choice of service life under uncertainty for determining depreciation methods lends some support for its use here.

Now, if we assume that the decision maker is rational as defined by the von Neumann and Morgenstern axioms of utility theory, then there is a best act and it is determined by a minimization problem. The vector a^* which attains the smallest expected loss is consistent with the preferences of the decision maker, i.e., a^* must satisfy

$$E[L(a^*, \alpha)] = \min_a E[L(a, \alpha)]. \tag{23.1}$$

In integral form, we wish to minimize

$$\int L(a, \alpha)f(\alpha)d\alpha = \int L(a, \alpha)f(x \mid h)g(h)dxdh \tag{23.2}$$

with respect to a.

To this minimization problem there may be added constraints that the P_i might have to satisfy. The constraint, $\sum_{i=1}^{n} p_i = 1$, added to the problem above, will be called the Lagrangian Problem. It states that all the cost must be allocated but allows for a negative assignment of cost to a period. If we further constrain the p_i to be in some interval $L_i \leq p_i \leq U_i$, then the problem will be called the Programming Problem. For example, if all the p_i are to be nonnegative, $L_i = 0$ and $U_i = 1$. This implies that negative costs are not permitted.

In a decision-theory framework, the specific estimation problem becomes: Minimize, with respect to a,

$$E[L(a, \alpha)] = E(x - pC)w(x - pC)' + Et(n - h)^2. \tag{24.1}$$

The constraint on P_i is $\sum_{i=1}^{n} p_i = 1$ and we therefore wish to minimize the Lagrangian function,

$$F(p, n, \lambda) = E[(x - pC)'w(x - pC) + t(n - h)^2] + \lambda\,(l'p - 1) \tag{24.2}$$

with respect of p, n, λ (and where l is the $n \times 1$ vector all of whose elements are one).

The necessary conditions for the solution are:

$$\frac{\partial F}{\partial p} = -2CEw(x - pC) + \lambda l = 0$$

$$\frac{\partial F}{\partial n} = 2tE(n - h) = 0$$

$$\frac{\partial F}{\partial \lambda} = l'p = 1.$$

The solution is given by

$$n^* = E(h) = \mu_h \tag{25}$$

and

$$p^* = \frac{[E(w)]^{-1}E(wx)}{C} + \frac{C - l'[E(w)]^{-1}E(wx)}{Cl'[E(w)]^{-1}l}[E(w)]^{-1}l. \tag{26}$$

The expression in (26) is identical to the result in [5] except that (26) is in matrix form and n is interpreted here as the time horizon.

When n^* and p^* are determined, the ex ante problem is solved. The solution is given at the moment the firm begins operations. At the end of period 1 all information must be updated and the allocation scheme and the time horizon are revised.

UPDATING WITH ADDITIONAL INFORMATION

We now assume that a single period of time which is less than n has passed and that additional information about the states, α, may be available. If the additional information is based only on observed cash flows, we may proceed by computing the conditional probability of the future cash flows conditioned on the observed values.[6] Generalizing the problem of updating at the end of any period j, let

$$x_k^{j\prime} = (x_1, x_2, \cdots, x_j),$$

the vector of observed cash flows;

$$x_f^{j\prime} = (x_{j+1}, x_{j+2}, \cdots, x_h)$$

[6] If the additional information is exogenous, i.e., the results of exterior events not included in the ex ante probabilistic considerations, then a total reassessment of the problem must be initiated. Thus, the chief conceptual difference between the problem of updating with exogenous information and updating with endogenous information is that in the latter case the expectations are taken with respect to the conditional distribution of $\alpha^j{}_f$ and these expectations can be determined formally by rules of probability, whereas in the exogenous case, there is no formal method of updating and therefore the distribution of future cash flows must be determined anew resulting in a situation similar to the ex ante case. However, in either case, the observed cash flows do not provide sufficient information with respect to the problem of estimating k.

the vector of remaining future cash flows;

$$p^j = (P_j, p_{j+1}, \cdots, P_n),$$

the possible selection of an allocation scheme;

$$\alpha_f^j = (x_f^j, h),$$

the future states of nature;

$$a^j = (p^j, n),$$

the acts;

$$f(a_f^j/x_k^j) = f(x_f^j/x_k^j)\ r\ (h/x_k^j),$$

the conditional density function of α_f^j, given x_k^j; and

$$L(a^j, \alpha_f^j),$$

the loss function.

Thus, the updating problem is solved by invoking the von Neumann-Morgenstern criterion: Find a^j which minimizes

$$\int L(a^j, \alpha_f^j)\, f(\alpha_f^j/x_k^j)\, d\alpha_f^j, \tag{27.1}$$

or

$$E_{\alpha_f{}^j/x_k{}^j}\,[L(a^j, \alpha_f^j)] \tag{27.2}$$

subject to

1. $\sum_{i=j}^{n} P_i = 1$ (Lagrangian Problem)

or

2. $L_i \leq P_i \leq U_i$ (Programming Problem).

UPDATING AND CAPITALIZATION POLICY

Modern accounting tends to confound attempts to unify methodology by defining classes of single-asset problems and dealing with each individually. While interpretations of the Hicksian view of wealth and income have been offered as a substitute concept for more conventional models, this work bears only a slight relationship and yields little insight into what accountants actually have been doing for the past century. One of the major implications of estimation theory is that it offers a way to begin unifying theory within a traditional framework.

Estimation theory in the multi-asset situation has interesting implications for the age-old capital versus revenue expenditures problem. Because of the importance of this subject, it merits comment here.

Future cash flows consist of all cash receipts and disbursements. Some of these disbursements are capital expenditures; some are revenue expenditures. The criterion used to distinguish between them has been, and continues to be, one of the major classes of controversies in accounting. Under estimation theory, this controversy becomes an "empty box."

As we pass from the beginning of time period 1 (the ex ante situation) to the end of time period 1 (the updating situation), the accountant may wish to capitalize certain expenditures, e.g., inventory. What effect does capitalization policy have on the estimation procedure?

For the purpose of illustrating the effect of capitalization policy, assume that at the beginning of year 1, an asset is purchased for $160 with expected net cash flows of $50, $50 and $100 in years 1, 2 and 3, respectively. For simplicity, we also assume that the future is deterministic and the life of the firm is three years. We further assume, for convenience, that the parameter to be estimated in the period reports is (expected) future cash flows.

The allocation scheme for the three years to achieve this objective at the beginning of period 1 (5) is $p = (\frac{1}{4}, \frac{1}{4}, \frac{1}{2})$. The estimation procedure was described earlier but capitalization policy was ignored.

Now consider the estimation procedure at the end of period 1. Suppose the net cash flows of $50 are the result of subtracting $50 in expenditures on inventory from gross cash flows of $100. The asset account, before allocation, is $160 plus $50 equals $210 in inventoried expenditures. The procedure to allocate total assets of $210 at the end of period 1 must be changed to reflect capitalization policy.

Let $I_1 = X_1 + c_1$, where X_1 is observed cash flows and c_1 is capitalized expenditures, both known quantities at the end of the first period. Thus $I_1 = \$50 + \$50 = \$100$. Let us call I_1 "accounting income" before the allocation of total assets at the end of period 1. Net income in period 1 is $I_1 - p_1C_1$. Thus the rate of return on net cash flows in period 1 is

$$r_1^{\,1} = \frac{I_1 - p_1C_1}{X_1},$$

and

$$r_i^{\,1} = \frac{x_i - p_iC_1}{X_i} \qquad \{i = 2, 3\}.$$

Capitalization policy affects only the definition of the rate of return in period 1. All other $r_i^{\,1}$ are unchanged. The value of k^1 is unchanged since capitalized expenditures in period 1 were a deduction from cash flows of $100 in the ex ante situation; when c_1 becomes known, it is added to C to obtain $C_1 = \$210$. But c_1 also is added to X_1 to obtain accounting income. Thus, in the ex ante situation,

$$k^1 = \frac{\sum_{i=1}^{N} X_i - C}{\sum_{i=1}^{N} X_i}.$$

At the end of period 1

$$k^1 = \frac{I_1 + \sum_{i=2}^{N} X_i - C_1}{\sum_{i=1}^{N} X_i}.$$

These two values of k^1 are equal.

A revised estimation procedure[7] is required to determine $p = (p_1, p_2, p_3)$ at the end of period 1. (N is assumed known.)

Let the vector $x = (x_1, x_2, x_3,)$ and the matrix

$$w = \begin{pmatrix} 1/X_1 & & 0 \\ 0 & 1/X_2 & \\ & & 1/X_3 \end{pmatrix}.$$

Then, substituting in (24.1) and minimizing, we have (assuming $n = h = N$)

$$p_1 = \frac{I_1}{C_1} - \frac{X_1}{\sum_{i=1}^{N} X_1}\left[\frac{I_1 + \sum_{i=2}^{N} X_i - C_1}{C_1}\right] = 3/7\,,$$

$$p_2 = \frac{X_2}{C_1} - \frac{X_2}{\sum_{i=1}^{N} X_i}\left[\frac{\sum X_i - C_1}{C_1}\right] = 4/21\,,$$

and similarly, $p_3 = 8/21$.

Thus, the capitalization of expenditures in the updating situation requires a modification of the estimation procedure. Capitalization policy has no effect on the parameter, k^1, assuming that all estimates made in the ex ante situation are unchanged at the end of period 1. Nor does capitalization policy have any effect on net income which is the identical quantity in both the ex ante and updating situations. If, in the uncertainty case, the estimates of future cash flows were modified at the end of period 1, the procedures would have to reflect the new information, in addition to the effect of capitalization.

Estimation Theory and Accounting Practice: A Concluding Comment

One of our major purposes in developing the estimation problem in financial accounting was to build a theory that does not depart significantly from traditional practice. In order to achieve this objective, we have made an assumption which also is the foundation of modern accounting: In any

[7] The mechanics of choosing an allocation scheme to achieve the objective of estimating k^1 under these conditions is described in [4].

period the accountant is constrained from directly reporting to the user of financial statements information about the future. This assumption is essential to the model because in the absence of such a reporting constraint, the accountant could report to the user of annual statements an estimate of future cash flows. Or perhaps the probability distribution of future cash flows would be given because it represents the most complete information that could be given to the user of financial statements. But if the accountant were to report this kind of information instead of the more traditional data, accounting practices would necessarily undergo a drastic change.

Therefore, our theory implies a less radical departure from existing practices than, for example, the recent proposals of Ronen and Sorter [13]. Estimation methods are essentially cost-based allocation schemes and therefore have much in common with the allocation procedures used today.

Conclusion

This paper has reviewed the application of estimation theory to a single-asset problem and also has extended the theory to the multi-asset (firm) situation.

The single-asset approach dominates modern accounting, and estimation theory provides a new way to reinterpret such subjects as the allocation problem, the matching principle and the realization postulate. In addition, substantive issues such as the price-level problem also can be restructured in terms of estimation. The model addresses these issues more directly and less ambiguously than traditional theory because its assumptions and objectives are stated in more explicit, operational terms.

However, single-asset analysis has major conceptual limitations. In an attempt to avoid these, estimation theory has been extended to the multi-asset or firm situation. This framework allows for a more systematic approach to the allocation problem than presently exists because it circumvents the joint cost problem, both in the time and in the space dimension.

The multi-asset estimation problem was developed in a decision-theory framework and the concept of an *estimating* horizon for reporting purposes was introduced in the context of the accountant's loss function. In addition, the updating problem was formalized and discussed in terms of the capital versus revenue expenditures problem. We argued that this classic issue in accounting is an empty box when structured as part of the multi-asset estimation problem.

Finally, we pointed out that estimation theory has been developed on the assumption that the accountant cannot directly report estimates of future events in financial statements, and the implications of this assumption were mentioned.

Future research on estimation theory can proceed in several directions. First, the theory has focused on the problem of estimating a single, overall parameter. It might be broadened so as to provide additional information about the firm's activities. Second, the implications of estimation theory for empirical work in accounting may be a fruitful area of research. Because estimation theory gives meaning to the statistical concepts of error and bias in financial accounting, the theory might be useful in evaluating accounting data. Third, many conventional single-asset problems could be recast as estimation problems. For example, the subject of lease accounting could be analyzed more systematically under an estimation approach.

Lastly, there are a number of specific issues that require more attention. These include a further examination of (1) problems related to the accountant's loss function, (2) questions concerning the prediction of cash flows, and (3) behavioral issues associated with the accounting profession's acceptance of a theory where responsibility for the preparation of financial reports is extended far beyond historical areas. In short, much more work needs to be done in extending estimation theory in general and its application to specific areas.

REFERENCES

1. AMERICAN INSTITUTE OF CERTIFIED PUBLIC ACCOUNTANTS. "Restatement and Revision of Accounting Research Bulletins," *Accounting Research and Terminology Bulletins*. Final ed. New York: AICPA, 1961.
2. *Accountants' Handbook*. 4th edition. New York: Ronald Press, 1956.
3. BIERMAN, HAROLD, JR. "Discounted Cash Flows, Price Level Adjustments and Expectations," *Accounting Review*, XLVI (October, 1971).
4. BRIEF, RICHARD P., AND JOEL OWEN. "A Least Squares Allocation Model," *Journal of Accounting Research*, 6 (Autumn, 1968).
5. ——, AND ——. "The Estimation Problem in Financial Accounting," *Journal of Accounting Research*, 8 (Autumn, 1970).
6. DEMSKI, JOEL S., AND GERALD A. FELTHAM, "Forecast Evaluation," *Accounting Review*, XLVII (July, 1972).
7. DEVINE, CARL THOMAS. *Essays in Accounting Theory*. Privately printed, 1962.
8. DRAKE, DAVID F., AND NICHOLAS DOPUCH. "On the Case for Dichotomizing Income," *Journal of Accounting Research*, 3 (Autumn, 1965).
9. DYCKMAN, THOMAS R. "Discussion of Accelerated Depreciation and Deferred Taxes: An Empirical Study of Fluctuating Asset Expenditures," *Empirical Research in Accounting: Selected Studies, 1967*, Supplement to vol. 5, *Journal of Accounting Research*.
10. —— "Discounted Cash Flows, Price-Level Adjustments and Expectations: A Comment," *Accounting Review*, XLVII (October, 1972).
11. IJIRI, YUJI, AND ROBERT S. KAPLAN. "Probabilistic Depreciation and Its Implication for Group Depreciation," *Accounting Review*, XLIV (October, 1969).
12. JARRETT, JEFFREY E. "The Principles of Matching and Realization as Estimation Problems," *Journal of Accounting Research*, 9 (Autumn, 1971).
13. RONEN, JOSHUA, AND GEORGE H. SORTER. "Relevant Accounting," *Journal of Business*, 45 (April, 1972).
14. SHWAYDER, KEITH. "Expected and Unexpected Price Level Changes," *Accounting Review*, XLVI (April, 1971).
15. STERLING, ROBERT R. *Theory of the Measurement of Enterprise Income*. Lawrence, Kansas: University Press of Kansas, 1970.
16. THOMAS, ARTHUR L. *The Allocation Problem in Financial Accounting*. Studies in Accounting Research #3. Evanston, Illinois: AAA, 1969.

Interest Rate Approximations

THE JOURNAL OF FINANCE • VOL. XXXVIII, NO. 3 • JUNE 1983

Yield Approximations: A Historical Perspective: A Correction

RICHARD P. BRIEF*

THE ORIGINAL SOURCE OF the 1670 yield approximation formula given in Hawawini and Vora [2] on page 149 and referred to on page 148 is a letter written by Isaac Newton to John Collins (Turnbull [3, pp. 24–25]). Hawawini and Vora incorrectly attribute the formula to John Newton. Also, the analytical solution to the implicit yield problem (Hawawini and Vora [2, p. 147]) can be traced to a letter written by Michael Dary to Isaac Newton, not John Newton (Turnbull [3, p. 326]). These errors were probably a consequence of the fact that de Morgan [1], who Hawawini and Vora use as a basic reference for the early history of yield approximations, did not clearly distinguish between the work of the two Newtons. John Newton was a minor scientist of the period.

* Professor of Business Statistics and Accounting, New York University.

REFERENCES

1. Augustus de Morgan. "On the Determination of the Rate of Interest of an Annuity." *The Assurance Magazine and the Journal of the Institute of Actuaries* 8 (1859), 61–67. In Gabriel Hawawini and Ashok Vora, eds., *The History of Interest Approximations*. New York: Arno Press, 1980.
2. Gabriel Hawawini and Ashok Vora. "Yield Approximations: A Historical Perspective." *Journal of Finance* 37 (March 1982), 145–56.
3. H. W. Turnbull, ed. *The Correspondence of Isaac Newton*, 1661–1675. Cambridge: University Press, 1959.

INTEREST APPROXIMATIONS

In 1972 Ijiri[1] published a note which gave simple approximations for some common interest formulas. He and other researchers may not be aware of the fact that mathematicians and actuaries have been studying interest approximations for over three centuries.[2]

Several of Ijiri's approximations were derived a long time ago. In 1851 a short note published in the Journal of the Institute of Actuaries gave an approximation for the interest rate, i, given the future value, a, of an annuity of 1 for n periods.[3] This result is equivalent to Ijiri's equation (16), solved for i. That is,

$$i \cong \frac{2(a - n)}{(n - 1)a} . \tag{1}$$

Equation (1) was originally obtained by directly expanding $\log(ai + 1) = n\log(1 + i)$ and neglecting all terms except the first in the expansions.

Another simple approximation for i was published in 1857.[4]

$$i \cong \frac{4(a - n)}{(n - 1)(a + n)} . \tag{2}$$

This note also contained an approximation for i, given the present value, p, of an annuity of 1.

$$i \cong \frac{8(n - p)}{(n + 1)(3p + n)} . \tag{3}$$

Ijiri got a slightly different approximation for i, given p.[5]

The British actuaries' text did not discuss these approximations because they were considered unreliable.[6] However, one result did survive.[7] In 1897 Todhunter derived the rate of interest yielded by a bond bought at a discount or premium.[8] It was modified several times and all standard texts mention it.[9] This approximation involved the direct expansion of $1/p$.[10] The direct expansion of $1/p$ also yields Ijiri's equations (15) and (18).

In 1967 more accurate approximations of this nature were found.[11]

Many other articles and notes on the general subject appeared in the actuarial literature in the nineteenth and twentieth centuries. One article i particular is worth mentioning because it is related to a current topic in finance.

Lidstone developed an approximation to find the rate of interest for an increasing annuity.[12] If B is the present value of an annuity, Lidstone showed that an increasing annuity, IB, equals

$$IB = -(1 + i)\,\frac{dB}{di}\,. \qquad (4$$

In 1975 Hopewell and Kaufman[13] proved a theorem about duration,[14] which is equal to IB/B. The proof can be obtained by dividing both sides of equation (4) by B and rearranging terms, i.e.,

$$\frac{dB}{B} = -\,\frac{IBdi}{B(1 + i)}\,. \qquad ($$

Fisher's[15] use of duration in formulating an algorithm for finding exact rates of return is more closely related to Lidstone's paper. Also, Hicks' discussion of "average period" and "interest elasticity" could have been motivated by Lidstone since one might suppose that Hicks noted the possible economic implications of equation (4) in Todhunter's chapter on applications of calculus.[16]

Students of finance should take a closer look at the work done by actuaries. Even if topics in the the theory of interest and annuities-certain are not exactly avant garde, research in the area will probably continue for some time.[17]

Footnotes

[1] Y. Ijiri, "Approximations to Interest Formulas," Journal of Business 45, no. 3 (July 1972): 398-402.

[2] For a brief history of the subject from the late seventeenth century until the middle of the nineteenth century, see A. De Morgan, "On the Determination of the Rate of Interest of an Annuity," Journal of the Institute of Actuaries VIII (1860): 61-67.

[3] I (1851), p. 332.

[4] Journal of the Institute of Actuaries VI (1857), p. 56.

[5] Ijiri, p. 401, equation (18).

[6] R. Todhunter, Institute of Actuaries' Text-Book, Part I (London: Charles & Edwin Layton, 1915). The first edition of this text was published in 1882. The 1901 edition (p. 105) did contain other approximations for i, but they were not published in later editions.

[7] Ijiri, p. 401, equation (20).

[8] R. Todhunter, "On the Approximation to the Rate of Interest Yielded by a Bond Bought at a Premium," Journal of the Institute of Actuaries XXXIII (1898): 356-359. Todhunter pointed out that this approximation equals the average ratio of interest to a bond's book value using straight-line amortization of premium. The idea that accounting numbers can be used to estimate financial parameters has never really caught on.

[9] R. Henderson, "On the Determination of the Rate of Interest Yielded By on Investment," Transactions, Actuarial Society of America 10 (1907-08): 659-661; G. J. Lidstone and R. Todhunter, "On the Determination by Means of Bond Value Tables of the Rate Yielded By a Redeemable Bond when Income Tax is Taken into Account," Journal of the Institute of Actuaries XLIX (1915): 366-369. J. I. Craig, "The Yield on a Debenture Bought at a Premium," Journal of the Institute of Actuaries LX (1929): 341-344. D. W. A. Donald, Compound Interest and Annuities-Certain (Cambridge: University Press, 1963), pp. 248-254.

[10] Donald, pp. 247-248.

[11] H. Karpin, "Simple Algebraic Formulas for Estimating the Rate of Interest," Journal of the Institute of Actuaries LXLIII (1967): 297-309.

[12] G. J. Lidstone, "On the Approximate Calculation of the Values of Increasing Annuities and Assurances," Journal of the Institute of Actuaries XXXI (1895): 68-72.

13 M. H. Hopewell and G. G. Kaufman, "Bond Price Volatility and Term to Maturity," American Economic Review LXIII (September 1973): 749-753.

14 R. L. Weil, "Macaulay's Duration: An Appreciation," Journal of Business 46, no. 4 (October 1973): 589-592.

15 L. Fisher, "An Algorithm for Finding Exact Rates of Return," Journal of Business 39, no. 1, pt. 2 (January 1966): 111-118.

16 J. R. Hicks, Value and Capital (Oxford: Clarendon Press, 1939), p. 186. Todhunter, Text-Book (1915), Ch. X.

17 For example, two articles on the same subject were recently published. J. H. Hunt, "An Analysis of the 'Rule of 78' -- Actuarial Note," Transactions, Society of Actuaries, XXVI, pt. 1 (1974): 225-240, and D. Bonker, "The Rule of 78," Journal of Finance XXXI (June 1976): 877-888. Bonker did not cite Hunt's article.

Richard P. Brief
NEW YORK UNIVERSITY

BAILY'S PARADOX

The following question appeared in Francis Baily's celebrated 1808 text on interest and annuities: "If a *penny* had been put out at 5 percent *compound* interest at the birth of Christ; to what sum would it amount at the end of the year 1810?" . Baily gave this solution :

> By the first theorem . . . it will be seen that its amount in that time would be .004166666 × $(1.05)^{1810}$ = 938469 000000 000000 000000 000000 000000 pounds. Now the diameter of the earth is about 8000 miles; consequently its solid contents* will be 68 188963 498145 531559 936000 cubic inches: and if it were made of standard gold, each cubic inch being worth 38 *l.* 10 *s.***, the total value of such a globe would be 2625 275094 678602 965057 536000 pounds. But the amount of a penny in 1810 years as above stated, is more than 357 474 600 times the value of such a globe: consequently if one penny had been put out at 5 percent compound interest at the time above mentioned, it would, at this period, have amounted to more money than could be expressed by THREE HUNDRED AND FIFTY-SEVEN MILLIONS of globes, each equal to the Earth in magnitude, and all solid gold!!! Whereas if it had been put out at the same rate of *simple* interest, the amount in the same time would have been only *seven shillings and seven-pence half-penny.*

Baily's calculation is "slightly" different than the 357,426,300 globes determined by my own calculation. Even allowing for a possible error, perhaps someone might want to consider planning for

*To find the solid contents of a sphere, multiply the decimal .785398 163397 448309 615&c, by the cube of the diameter, and take two-thirds of the product.

**Since a cubic inch of distilled water weighs about 254 grains, and the specific gravities of standard gold and water are to each other as 18.888 to one, it follows that a cubic inch of gold, at the mint price of 3 *l.* 17 *s.* 10½ *d.* per ounce, will amount to 38 *l.* 10 *s.* 1½ *d.*

Utopia by putting a dollar in trust in 1979 for some needy cause in the year 4000!

REFERENCE

Baily, Francis. *The Doctrine of Interest and Annuities* London: John Richardson, 1808.

from
The Accounting Review, Vol. LII No. 4
(October 1977), 810–12

THE ACCOUNTING REVIEW
Vol. LII, No. 4
October 1977

A Note on "Rediscovery" and the Rule of 69

Richard P. Brief

ABSTRACT: The Rule of 69, an approximation for determining the number of periods in which a sum will double at a given interest rate, was "rediscovered" in 1974. However, the rule actually was derived by an accountant in 1900. This note briefly summarizes the recent "controversy" about the Rule of 69 and mentions some of the historical implications of the 1900 paper on the subject.

In 1974 Gould and Weil "discovered" a rule for approximating the number of periods it takes for a sum to double at a given interest rate. They called the approximation the "Rule of 69." However, Thornton recently noted that the Rule "has been well known for a great many years," and he gave a *1960 reference* to it [1976, p. 515].

This Rule has been known since at least 1900. On 14 March 1900, at a meeting of the Incorporated Accountants' Students' Society of London, T. Tinner, who was a member of that society, presented a paper, "Some Actuarial Calculations for Accountants." In the paper he derived the Rule of 69 for determining the number of periods required to depreciate an asset to one-half its original value without reference to tables. The paper was reprinted in the *Lectures and Transactions of the Incorporated Accountant's Students' Society of London for the Year 1900* [1901, pp. 27–39]. Tinner's derivation[1] was identical to Thornton's.

The Rule also was mentioned in an article by W. A. Robertson, which appeared in the *Encyclopaedia of Accounting* "Interest and Annuities-Certain." [Lisle, 1903, p. 368]. Robertson derived

[1] "Starting with $(1-d)^n = \frac{1}{2}$, and taking Napierian logarithms, we get [d is the percentage (in decimals) of book value written off each period]—

$$n \log_e(1-d) = \log_e \tfrac{1}{2} = -.69$$

$$n = \frac{-.69}{\log_e(1-d)} = \frac{-.69}{-\left(d + \frac{d^2}{2} + \frac{d^3}{3} + \text{etc.}\right)}$$

$$= \frac{.69}{d\left(1 + \frac{d}{2}\right)},$$

neglecting the third and higher powers

$$= \frac{.69}{d}\left[1 - \frac{d}{2} + \left(\frac{d}{2}\right)^2 - \left(\frac{d}{2}\right)^3 + \text{etc.}\right]$$

$$= \frac{.69}{d} - \frac{.69}{2},$$

neglecting the square and higher powers of d within the brackets

$$= \frac{.69}{d} - .35.$$

This formula is fairly accurate when d is not greater than .1, that is, when the rate of depreciation does not exceed 10 percent" [1901, p. 38]. (The expansion of $\log_e(1-d)$ has been corrected. Thanks are due to my colleague, Professor S. Chatterjee, for catching the error.)

Richard P. Brief is Professor of Business Statistics and Accounting at New York University.

the rule for doubling a sum and cited G. F. Hardy in connection with its derivation; but he did not give a reference to Hardy's work. Hardy wrote a number of papers on actuarial problems in the last two decades of the nineteenth century [*Catalogue of Scientific Papers*, 1916, XV, p. 638].

The 1900 paper and the 1903 article have at least three implications. First, it is certainly of historical interest that the Rule of 69 was derived more than 75 years ago in connection with depreciation calculations and that the rule for doubling a sum also can be found in the early literature.

Second, and more important, both the Tinner and Robertson papers, like Ladelle's [Brief, 1967], suggest that accounting thought during the profession's first quarter century of development (1875–1900) was more advanced than most people realize. When many accountants think about the history of the field, only 15th century double entry bookkeeping comes into mind. But historical thought, that is, late 19th and early 20th century, was of exceptionally high quality. A few hours, minimumly, with early issues of publications such as *The Accountant*, *The Accountants' Magazine*, *The Journal of Accountancy*, as well as other materials, should be a mandatory requirement for all accountants.

Third, it is clear than many basic problems in accounting are perennial and that many basic ideas were repeated again and again, as if they were new ideas. The British (1875–1900) and the American (1900–1925) accountants were quite thoughtful and very conscientious in their attempt to develop theory and to understand the nature of broader issues.

As an example, consider the concluding remarks about Tinner's paper that were made by the Chairman of the session.

> This subject shows very clearly how the scope of an accountant's work is enlarging and extending. Some few years ago it would have been thought entirely outside the duties of an accountant to deal with calculations such as these. An accountant was only expected to concern himself about the result of trading. Time, however, changes all things, and at the present day not only is it useful to an accountant to have some actuarial knowledge, but it is almost necessary that he should know something about these matters [1901, p. 38].

These comments have a remarkably modern tone and this lesson can be learned from them: A greater attention to the historical development of accounting thought undoubtedly would have a beneficial influence on progress. Just as the Rule of 69 was "rediscovered" in 1974, other aspects of accounting problems continually are being rediscovered. These early papers, debates, lectures and articles are not only of historical interest, but also in many cases, they have relevance to contemporary problems and their solutions.

Thus it would be useful, generally, for researchers to devote more time to the past. Describing the current situation with less-than-scientific precision, those engaged in accounting research are divided into two camps: searchers and discoverers. Discoverers would benefit by changing their production functions (or is it investment strategies?) so as to increase the proportion of time spent searching. More literature search would benefit the individual and the community at large insofar as the subject of accounting is concerned.[2]

[2] The final paragraph of this paper was written in response to one reviewer's question concerning the optimal tradeoff between literature search and discovery. In this writer's (perhaps not unbiased) view, the "decision" can be made on a priori grounds. However, the question obviously merits further consideration. The author is grateful to Roman L. Weil for his thoughtful comments.

REFERENCES

Brief, R. P., "A Late Nineteenth Century Contribution to the Theory of Depreciation," *Journal of Accounting Research* (Spring 1967), pp. 27–38.

Catalogue of Scientific Papers, Fourth Series (1884–1900), Compiled by the Royal Society of London (At the University Press 1916).

Gould, J. R. and R. L. Weil, "The Rule of 69," *The Journal of Business* (July 1974), pp. 397–398.

Lectures and Transactions of the Incorporated Accountants' Students' Society of London for the Year 1900 (1901).

Lisle, George, ed., *The Encyclopaedia of Accounting* (William Green & Sons, 1903).

Thornton, D. B., "The Rule of 69 in Perspective: A Note on the Force of Interest," *The Journal of Business* (October 1976), pp. 515–516.

Weighted Averages and Earnings Per Share

A recent article by Coughlan [1988] states that "Little discussion can be found of why the weighted average [in earnings per share (EPS) calculations] is a useful denominator" (p. 81). Coughlan comments that APB 15's justification for the use of weighted average shares outstanding in calculating earnings per share is "more dogma than defense" (p. 81) and that the nearest the APB come to justifying the use of the weighted average is in paragraph 47 of APB 15 [1969]:

> Use of a weighted average is necesary so that the effect of increases and decreases in outstanding shares on earnings per share data is related to the portion of the period during which the related consideration affected operations.

The stated purpose of Coughlan's article is to show that the use of a weighted average in calculating EPS can produce anomolous situations and to recommend a new method for calculating EPS.

The object of this paper is to question Coughlan's argument and to explain the justification for using a weighted average in EPS calculations. The anomoly in using weighted averages is more apparent than real; the use of weighted averages in this and other accounting calculations has an economic rationale. Time weighted averages also have a long history in mercantile calculations.

Weighted Averages and EPS Calculations

To support the argument the use of weighted averages in EPS calculations produce anomolous results, the section, "The Investment Anomoly" [Coughlan, 1988, pp. 82-84], presents an example in which two companies are presumed to be alike in all respects except that B "is larger and more profitable than A." The example is based on the following data.

Period 1:	A	B
Income	0	1000
Shares Outstanding	200	$1000
EPS	0	$1

Period 2:		
Income	$6000	$7000
Shares Outstanding	1000	1000
EPS	$6	$7

Coughlan assumes that "income translates into dividends shortly after it is earned and ... the above information may reasonably be predicted by the market" (p. 81). He also concludes that "Lacking other relevant information not given here and basing the appraisal of management on the above information only, one would infer that the management of B must be superior to that of A. B earns more per share in both years" (p. 81). Further on (p. 81), he states that

> Surely such a market would place a higher price on the stock of company B; it earns more per share and pays a higher dividend in both years.... surely an efficient market would have to value a share of stock in company B more highly that [sic] a share in company A.

But given the assumption of certainty and efficient markets, the rate of return required by investors would be the same for these companies, i.e., although absolute earnings of these companies might differ, their rates of return would not to differ if markets were efficient. Therefore, the market would be expected to price a share of stock in company A higher than a share in company B, and this conclusion is the opposite of Coughlan's.[1]

To see why the prices of A and B would differ, assume that the two period situation in the above example is one in which investments are made at the beginning of each period and dividends are paid at the end of the period. Assume also that at the end of period 2, equity capital is maintained intact in the sense that assets at the end of period 2 are equal to equity investment.[2] Since dividends equal income, this will be the case providing that income is all-inclusive. Further, let the rate of return be .10 and P_A and P_B be the price of a share of company A and company B, respectively.

Given these assumptions, the values of P_A and P_B can be found by solving the following present value equations:

----

1. The formal proposition in the Appendix (p. 87) raises other questions. The proposition is that "<u>other things being equal</u>, given a choice between two courses of action, a choice which results in a higher EPS for at least one subperiod and does not result in a lower EPS for any subperiod is superior from the point of view of the company and its stockholders. An anomaly results if that choice leads to a lower earnings per share for the year than the alternative." The problem that arises with this proposition is even in the absence of risk considerations, two companies cannot be compared on the basis of EPS alone. Share prices must be taken into account.

2. Note that assuming that capital is maintained implies that equity book value of these companies at the end of period 2 equals the number of shares outstanding times the share price.

$$200P_A = -800P_A/1.10 + 6,000/1.21 + 1,000P_A/1.21$$

$$1000P_B = 1,000/1.10 + 7,000/1.21 + 1,000P_B/1.21.$$

Solving these equations, $P_A = \$49.18$ and $P_B = \$38.57$.

Assume that each period is 6 months. Basing EPS on the weighted average outstanding shares, EPS for company A is $10 and EPS for company B is $8. Therefore, the earnings/price ratio for company A is .203 and the earnings/price ratio for company B is .207.

It is no coincidence that these P/E ratios are approximately equal to the simple interest equivalent of the 12-month rate of return. All time weighted averages in calculations of this kind can be viewed as simple interest approximations of compound interst formulas. The use of the weighted average in the EPS calculation is similar, for example, to the computation made to divide the income of a partnership according to the ratio of the partners' capital.

This connection between weighted averages and interest calculations was recognized long ago. Hatton [1982, p. 135], first published in 1695, discussed the problem as follows.

Case 2.

> When several Merchants make a Common Stock for a certain Time, and at the End thereof make a Dividend, to find each Man's share of the Gain or Loss according to his stock and time.

Rule.

> Multiply each Man's share in the Common stock, by the Time continued therein, and proceed with the Products, as with the shares in the last Case.

The same problem was discussed in an early American text [Lee, 1982], which was first published in 1797. Significantly, both Hatton and Lee discussed the question of dividing the profits of a partnerships in sections that were in close proximity to the discussion of interest.

The early "arithmetics" called this problem "compound partnership" and "double fellowship" and many current texts also deal with the subject. The calculation of EPS using the weighted average shares outstanding is similar to the partnership problem and it has essentially the same solution.

References

Accounting Principles Board, Opinion No. 15, "Earnings Per Share," (New York: AICPA, May 1969).

John W. Coughlan, "Anomolies in Calculating Earnings Per Share," Accounting Horizons (December 1988), pp. 80-88.

Edward Hatton, The Merchant's Magazine; or, Trades-man's Treasury (New York and London: Garland Publishing, Inc., 1982). First published in 1696.

Chauncey Lee, The American Accomptant (New York and London: Garland Publishing, Inc., 1982). First published in 1797.

Financial Reporting and Analysis

CPA SERVICES

CORPORATE FINANCIAL REPORTING AT THE TURN OF THE CENTURY

BY RICHARD P. BRIEF

THE 1890S-1900S WAS A PERIOD IN WHICH ACcounting thought and practice were in the takeoff stage of development in the United States. The first CPA law was passed by New York State in 1896, and almost all states followed suit in the next two decades.[1] Arthur Young & Company, F. W. Lafrentz, Haskins & Sells and Lybrand, Ross Bros. & Montgomery were founded before the turn of the century. Touche, Niven & Co. was formed in 1900, Price Waterhouse & Co. in 1901, Ernst & Ernst in 1903, and Arthur Andersen & Co. and Marwick, Mitchell & Co. were established about a decade later.[2] Several of these firms had much earlier British origins. Names now connected with major U.S. accounting firms, such as Cooper, Deloitte and Whinney, can be traced back to as early as 1845. Indeed, Parker recently observed that of the 16 men whose surnames are associated with the largest eight accounting firms of today, 10 began to practice in Great Britain during the 19th century.[3]

In 1923, A. C. Ernst protested council's restrictions on advertising.

The turn of the century also was an era of the "Big Trust," which was the subject of an investigation by the U.S. Industrial Commission. Companies already in business included such familiar names as American Telephone & Telegraph, American Can, DuPont, General Electric, International Paper, U.S. Steel and Westinghouse. The growth of capital markets paralleled economic growth as did the establishment of governmental bodies, for example, the Federal Reserve Board in 1913 and the Federal Trade Commission in 1915. Of special interest to accountants was the enactment of the corporation excise tax in 1909 and, a few years later, the personal income tax. Although government's role had grown significantly in the 19th century, the economic environment was predominantly *laissez-faire*.

Even though railroads had been disclosing financial data for a half-century or so, the records for most companies were spotty. However, by 1900, the debate over the costs and benefits of financial reporting for industrials in the United States had begun.

The purpose of this article is to give readers a glimpse into the nature of this debate and to survey briefly and selectively financial reporting practices at the turn of the century.

RICHARD P. BRIEF, *PhD, is professor of business statistics and accounting at New York University. A past president of the Academy of Accounting Historians, he was the American Accounting Association representative to the First International Symposium of Accounting Historians in Brussels in 1970. He is also the author and editor of numerous articles and books on accounting history, accounting theory, finance and economics, and has held several visiting professorships.*

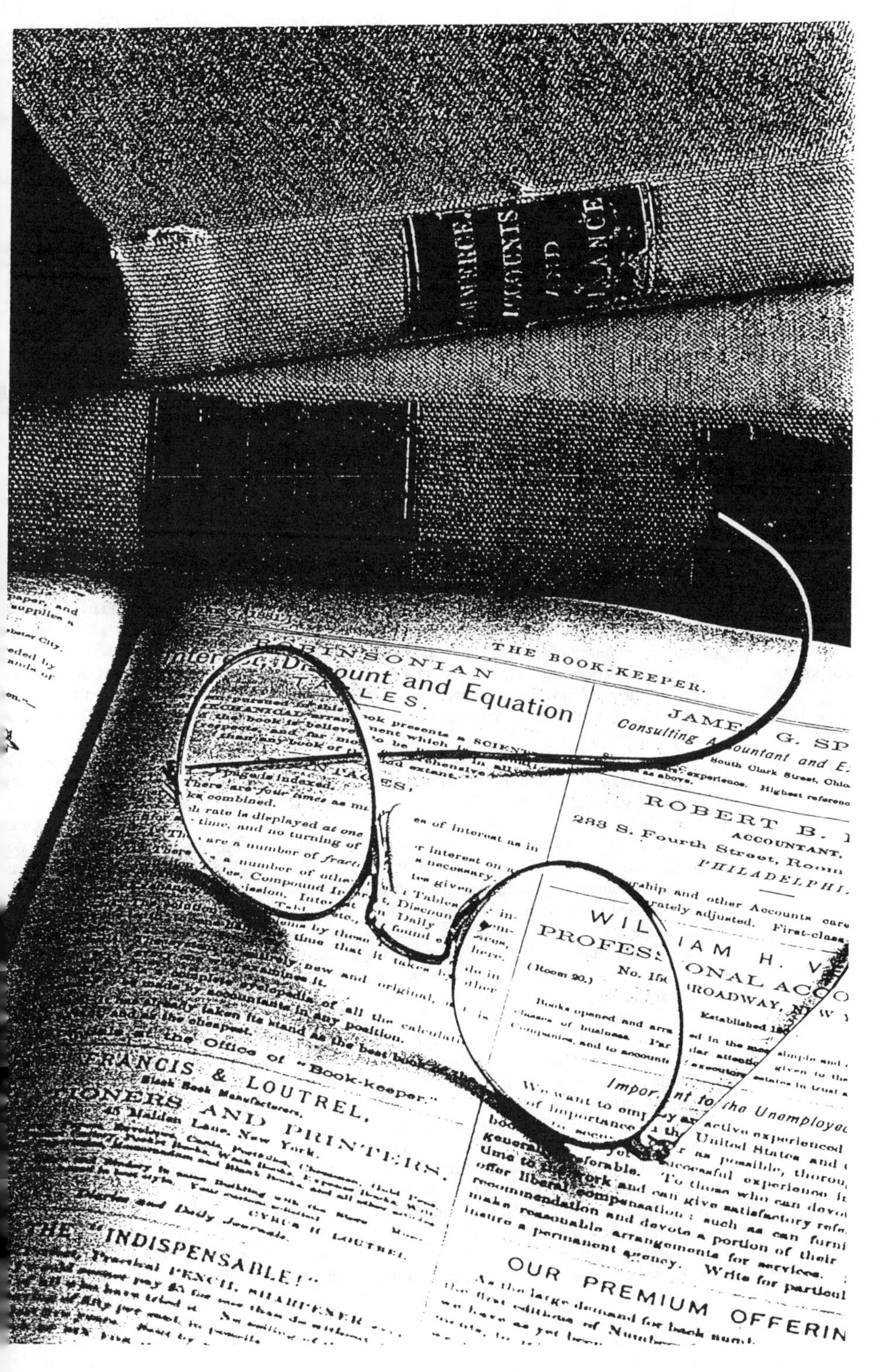
THE BOOK-KEEPER.
and Equation
ROBERT B.
ACCOUNTANT,
283 S. Fourth Street, Room
(Room 20.)
FRANCIS & LOUTREL,
INDISPENSABLE!
OUR PREMIUM

The Debate Over Financial Reporting

The big corporations had many critics who called for improved reporting. Accountants also advocated better disclosure of financial records and emphasized the importance of an independent audit. The cover page of the January 12, 1901, issue of *Commerce, Accounts & Finance*, a publication of the School of Commerce, Accounts & Finance at New York University, illustrates prevailing sentiment. Quoting in bold print from the Bible, John 3:19, the headline read: "Men loved darkness rather than light, for their deeds were evil." The editorial, probably written by C. W. Haskins, who was dean and professor of both auditing and the history of accountancy as well as a founding partner of Haskins & Sells, elaborated on this theme as follows:

"... a public conscience...is shocked by corporate immorality."

"The conspicuous lack of definite information in the reports of industrial corporations has created a feeling of suspicion on the part of the public, from which feeling such corporations are themselves the chief sufferers. The public does not understand why industrial corporations should not give to their affairs the same detailed publicity as is given by moneyed institutions and transportation companies. In taking this position the public is entirely right. Suspicion has already developed into antagonism, which is shown in the sentiment of the legislatures of the various states. If industrial corporations persist in preferring darkness to light, they will soon be compelled to do that which they ought to do voluntarily. Free, fair and full reports of industrial organizations should be founded upon thorough, independent audit of accounts by disinterested certified public accountants, whose signed certificates, to be published with the report, are a more nearly perfect guarantee of reliability than any other yet to be discovered."

The same point was made several years later in the October 1906 issue of the *Journal of Accountancy*, which took the position that the demand for publicity "has proceeded from a public conscience which is shocked by corporate immorality. Publicity is asked for in order that the State may exercise the proper police control. Our sense of business immorality and justice would be protected. If, however, we are to have corporate control which looks toward efficiency and economy the intelligence necessary to such control must come to the administration through the accounts, and must be regularly produced to the investor in the form of authoritative reports."

This editorial introduced a series in the *Journal*, written by Thomas Warner Mitchell, on corporation reports. The series was published until September 1907.

Others advocated more government intervention via a system of public auditing[4]:

"First, each corporation should be required to make periodical reports of its business, supplemented by other reports upon official demand, all verified by the oaths of certain of its officers. Second, official examiners should also be maintained, who should, at irregular periods and without notice, appear at the offices of each corporation and make rigid examinations of its affairs, using its books in the first instance but verifying the correctness thereof by every practicable method."

On the other hand, some said that disclosure would have adverse economic consequences.[5] "I cannot but regard corporate publicity of the kind and to the extent advocated by many as a certain and serious hindrance to effective competition. So far from accomplishing the purpose expected in this regard, its practical tendency, in my judgment, would be in the contrary direction. Just as the Sherman Anti-Trust law, which is based upon an economic fallacy, has indirectly aided the very results it was designed to prevent, so the compulsory disclosure of all corporate transactions would, as I believe, undermine the competition it was intended to support.... The enforcement of corporate publicity would be an added incentive to industrial combination."

The argument against disclosure was put more bluntly in testimony before the Industrial Commission in 1899 by Henry O. Havemeyer, president of the American Sugar Refining Company, in response to a question by Thomas Phillips, a commission member who was previously cited[6]:

"*Phillips*: You think, then, that when a corporation is chartered by the State, offers stock to the public, and is one in which the public is interested, that the public has no right to know what its earning power is or to subject them to any inspection whatever, that the people may not buy stock blindly?

"*Havemeyer*: Yes; that is my theory. Let the buyer beware; that covers the whole business. You cannot wet-nurse people from the time they are born until the day they die. They hav

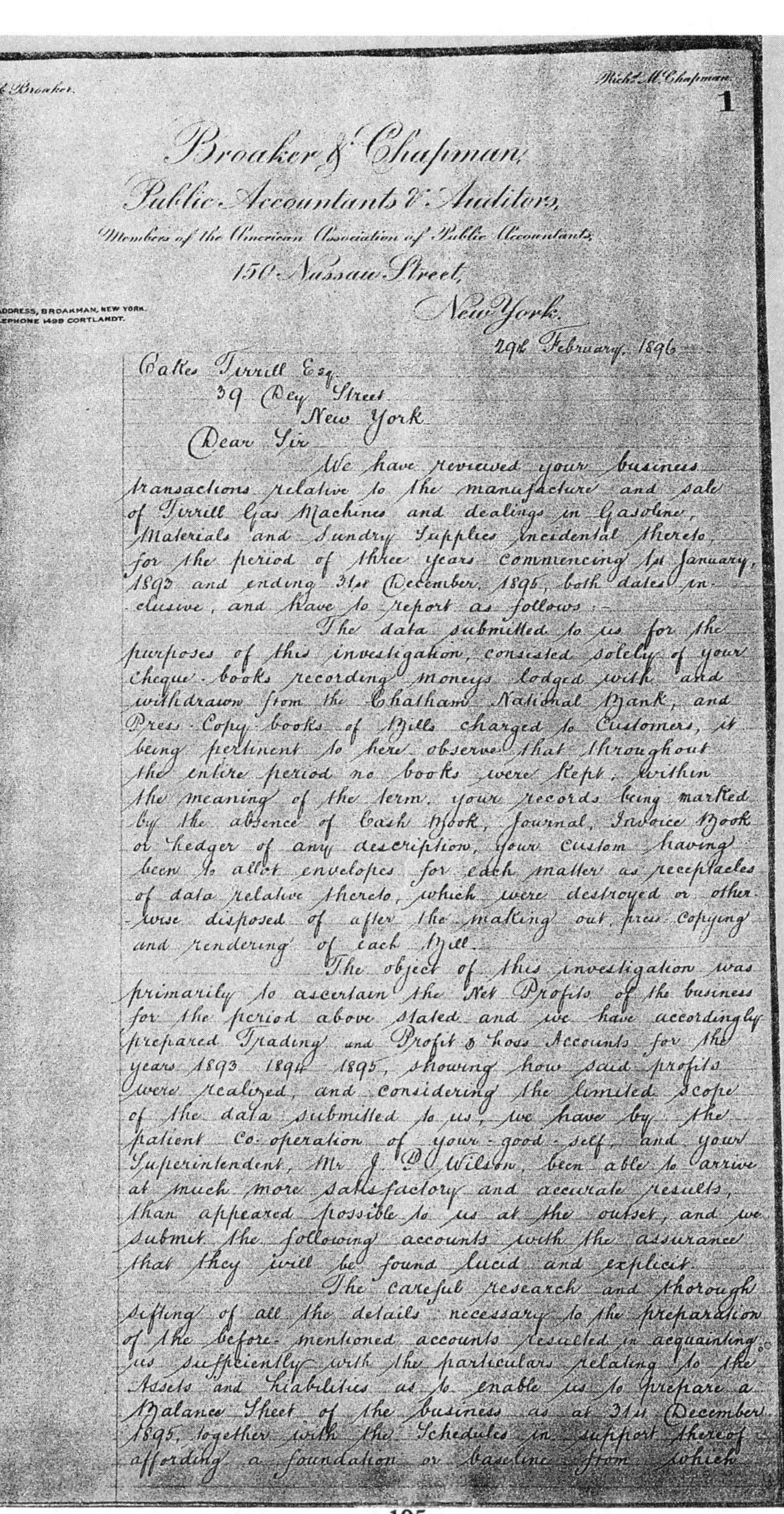

k. Broaker. Richd. M. Chapman. 1

Broaker & Chapman,
Public Accountants & Auditors,
Members of the American Association of Public Accountants,
150 Nassau Street,
New York.

ADDRESS, BROAKMAN, NEW YORK.
TELEPHONE 1499 CORTLANDT.

29th February, 1896

Oakes Tirrill Esq.
39 Dey Street
New York

Dear Sir

We have reviewed your business transactions relative to the manufacture and sale of Tirrill Gas Machines and dealings in Gasoline, Materials and Sundry Supplies incidental thereto, for the period of three years commencing 1st January, 1893 and ending 31st December, 1895, both dates inclusive, and have to report as follows:–

The data submitted to us for the purposes of this investigation, consisted solely of your Cheque books recording moneys lodged with and withdrawn from the Chatham National Bank, and Press Copy books of Bills charged to Customers, it being pertinent to here observe that throughout the entire period no books were kept, within the meaning of the term, your records being marked by the absence of Cash Book, Journal, Invoice Book or Ledger of any description, your custom having been to allot envelopes for each matter as receptacles of data relative thereto, which were destroyed or otherwise disposed of after the making out, press copying and rendering of each Bill.

The object of this investigation was primarily to ascertain the Net Profits of the business for the period above stated and we have accordingly prepared Trading and Profit & Loss Accounts for the years 1893 1894 1895, showing how said profits were realized, and considering the limited scope of the data submitted to us, we have by the patient co-operation of your good self, and your Superintendent, Mr J. D. Wilson, been able to arrive at much more satisfactory and accurate results, than appeared possible to us at the outset, and we submit the following accounts with the assurance that they will be found lucid and explicit.

The careful research and thorough sifting of all the details necessary to the preparation of the before-mentioned accounts resulted in acquainting us sufficiently with the particulars relating to the Assets and Liabilities as to enable us to prepare a Balance Sheet of the business as at 31st December 1895, together with the Schedules in support thereof affording a foundation or baseline from which proper Books of Accounts could be opened and continued from that time on.

The amounts due from Customers at 31st December 1895, and constituting one of the supporting Schedules to the Balance Sheet at that date, heretofore scattered indiscriminately throughout the press copy books will be found alphabetically arranged, and where several separate charges appear against the same party they are grouped together for ready reference as to the whole account, and the Bills Receivable appear in separate Schedule in like arrangement.

All bad and doubtful amounts due from Customers, or dishonored Notes, have been written off against the profits of the year in which the original transactions appear, but we, nevertheless, have furnished you with complete schedules thereof, so that in the event of an opportunity occurring to realize upon the same in part or whole. A record of the same is herein presented for reference.

We would refer you to the index preceding this Report showing the pages on which the several business and financial statements, schedules and inventory contained in this Accounting are to be found.

Without else, We are dear Sir

Faithfully yours

Broaker & Chapman

;ot to wade in and get stuck and that is the way nen are educated and cultivated."

Hawkins[7] has suggested several reasons why companies began voluntarily to disclose inancial information: (1) recognition by man-gement of public responsibility; (2) criticism f reform groups; (3) federal government reg-lations such as the securities acts (which, of ourse, were not enacted until 1933 and 1934); nd (4) the growing influence of the accounting rofession. Hawkins also cites heavy depen-ence on outside sources of capital as another notivation for issuing more detailed reports.

A different reason for more detailed report-ng is given by Merino and Neimark, who tress that firms improving their quality of re-orting did so to avoid the political costs of reater government regulation.[8]

A good example of what Merino and Neimark were talking about is the case of Equitable Life Assurance Society, which an-ounced on December 14, 1905, that "it will be he policy of the new administration of the So-iety to insist on an independent audit of its ac-ounts as to its fiscal condition once each year, he result of which will be published."

According to an editorial in the *Journal of Accountancy*, which applauded the action,[9] he decision by Equitable to disclose was an ef-ort to restore public confidence and to avoid estrictive legislation.

There was a variety of reasons for corpora-ions to disclose financial information, but the ommon impression today is that financial re-orting in the late 19th and early 20th centu-ies was at best rudimentary and at worst non-xistent. These impressions of accounting are ue to many factors, one of which is the work f William Z. Ripley, a Harvard professor who as a critic of early disclosure practices. His ook, *Main Street and Wall Street*, was first ublished in 1927 and was reprinted by cholars Book Co. in 1972. One of the chapters ; based on an article, "Stop, Look, Listen!—he Shareholders' Right to Adequate Infor-nation," which appeared in the September 926 issue of a literary magazine, the *Atlantic Monthly*. It's interesting to note that George . May, who was at this time the senior part-er of Price Waterhouse, quickly responded to Ripley's criticisms of financial reporting by riting a letter that was printed in the August), 1926, edition of the *New York Times*. While May agreed "that stockholders are entitled to receive reasonably full information regarding the affairs of a company in which they are in-terested," he also said the article by Ripley was "unfair both in detail and in the large."

Shortly thereafter, May delivered a paper entitled "Corporate Publicity and the Audi-tor" at a meeting of the American Institute of Accountants (which later became the Ameri-can Institute of CPAs) in Atlantic City on Sep-tember 22, 1926. This address also was pub-lished in the November 1926 issue of the *Journal of Accountancy*. Again, May dis-agreed with some of Ripley's facts, but he also expressed satisfaction "at the success with which he [Ripley] has attracted the attention of the public to the subject," and he urged ac-countants to "consider what we ... can do to bring about that improvement in the informa-tion furnished to stockholders and potential stockholders of corporations for which his ar-ticle is a plea." The next day the *New York Times* reported in one of its columns that "Ac-countants Back More Publicity" and men-tioned May's comment that the "attribution of income to particular periods of time is largely arbitrary" and that "too much significance" is attached to the income statements. This view has been reiterated many times in the years that have followed.

Some of Ripley's examples were more than 20 years old when his book was published. Ripley[10] cites Westinghouse Electric and Man-ufacturing Co. as a striking example of a "sealed" situation because it held no annual meeting during the years 1897-1906. The July 26, 1906, issue of the *New York Times* also pointed out that the 1906 stockholders' meet-ing at Westinghouse "was called an annual meeting, though it was the first of the kind held since July 28, 1897." The *Times* said:

"Minority stockholders, who assert that they have been long ignored, made heated re-marks, and finally brought about a test vote. Finding themselves outnumbered, they did not try to beat the slate of officers which had been prepared and went through.... One com-plaint was that the company had bought $6,300,000 in bonds of Lackawanna & Wyo-ming Valley Company at double its value.... The Westinghouse officials say that all the trouble at the meeting was started by small brokers who own one or two shares of stock and who seek to hammer down the stock in or-der that they may buy on the fall."

The Equitable building was at 120 Broadway in New York City.

Hawkins also used the example of Westinghouse to illustrate that "most managements did not seem to care about public opinion."[11] He then quotes from *Report of the Board of Directors of the Westinghouse Electric and Manufacturing Co. to the Stockholders, Special Meeting* (February 20, 1901): "... if some should be surprised that more complete statements have not been previously submitted to them, it can only be said that the Directors as well as the Stockholders who own the largest amounts of stock, have believed that in view of the existing keen competition and the general attitude towards industrial enterprises, the interests of all would be served by avoiding, to as great an extent as possible, giving undue publicity to the affairs of the Company." The Westinghouse example actually is misleading because, by 1911, the company's disclosure policy had become exemplary. In sharp contrast to others, Arthur Stone Dewing, also a Harvard professor who was a leading authority on the financial policy of corporations at this time, had this to say about Westinghouse's 1911 annual report[12]:

This is the seal that first appears in the 1927 annual report of Westinghouse.

"This annual report of March 31, 1911, is worthy of permanent preservation for its fulness, frankness, and the willingness of Mr. Mather to express opinions of the 'worth' of the inventoried investments. It was his last report and shows clearly the foundation of a policy, the good results of which were just beginning to bear fruit. In its detailed completeness, the present writer knows not its equal among corporation reports. He has used it in his classes in 'Corporation Finance' and 'Accounting' as a model of this kind."

While the quality of practices at this time was mixed and the motives were varied, many companies such as Equitable and Westinghouse did begin to publish financial reports and to employ independent auditors who were asked to "certify" to a company's financial condition. The examples of early financial reporting practices shown in the following section are a not-so-random sample of the kinds of conditions that existed nearly a century ago.

Early Financial Reporting Practices

Most of the studies of financial reports in the United States deal with the situation in the 1920s and thereafter.[13] Here, however, samples are given of reporting information from earlier times. The first item discussed is an 1896 "audit report" for a small business. Then after briefly describing the nature of som early audit certificates, several extracts fron annual reports are provided.

A pre-1900 investigation. Although de scribed as an "audit report" of the Tirrill Ga Machine Co. in the pre-1950 card file of th AICPA library, the purpose of this investiga tion by the firm of Broaker & Chapman was t determine the financial condition of the com pany, evidently in preparation for incorpora tion. Although not much is known about th company, there is a listing in *Holbrook's Neu ark City and Business Directory for the Yea Ending April 1, 1882* for "Tirrill Oakes, under ground gasmachines." In 1896, the listing wa "Tirrill's Gas Machine Co." The 1912 director lists "Tirrill Gas Machine Lighting Co.," whic name appears until 1929. After this, there is n listing. Part of the historical significance o this "audit" lies in the fact that Frank Broake was the first CPA in the United States whil Richard M. Chapman was the second.[14]

The cover letter of this report to Oakes Ti rill, written in elegant script, is reproduced o pages 145 and 146.

In preparing the financial statements, infor mation about inventories was needed. The fo lowing letter, written to Tirrill by his compan superintendent in response to Broaker Chapman's request, would hardly constitut sufficient evidence under today's standards:

"I am in receipt of the letter of Broaker an Chapman calling for inventory for the years c 1892 & 1893. It seems entirely useless to me t attempt an approximation because I kno positively within a very small margin what i is, and for the following reason. When I too the inventory in 1890 you gave me explicit o ders to keep that inventory good both as t manufactured goods and also as to all kinds c materials. On that order I have acted an hence you will find that from 1890 to th present date the inventories will vary *very* lit tle. If I take an inventory for 1895 ending Jar uary 1, 1896, you will find scarcly any varia tion. The manufactured stock this year may b even a little less than that of last year, as yo have been lately selling a little faster than could replace. Thus far I am safe in saying tha if I had taken an actual inventory in the year named it would hardly have varied enough t have paid the cost. Under my system of keep ing an account of what went out of the factor and replenishing as ordered, which I have substantially done."

Other documents provide evidence on the amount of personal expenses to be deducted from salaries and "pocket expenses," as well as to the appraised value of land and buildings. References to these documents were made in notes that appeared directly on the financial statements. For example:

"The amounts deducted from Wages and Salaries and Pocket Expenditures are authorized in a letter addressed to us by Mr. Tirrill bearing date 29th February, 1896 a copy of which is shown on page 10 of this report. This Trading and Profit & Loss Account is based upon the supposition that the Inventory at the commencement of the year was identical in value with the Inventory at the close of the year as stated in a letter of Mr. J. P. Wilson, Supt. addressed to Mr. Oakes Tirrill and bearing date 24th December, 1895, a copy of which appears on page 9 of this report."

The overdraft, which was shown as a liability, had this explanation:

"This overdraft is explained by Mr. Tirrill as being occasioned by cheques drawn by him in 1892, and which were never presented for payment but held in reserve with the intention of either cancelling or redepositing same—the object being to make the actual Bank Balance a matter of private information apart from the apparent balance shown in the Cheque Book."

While this early "small business" audit has some humorous aspects, it is nevertheless characterized by a full disclosure of the evidence on which it is based.

Accountants at this time didn't have any guidance in preparing reports and certificates because there simply wasn't much literature on the subject pertaining to the U.S. environment. The first major American publication aimed at practitioners was, interestingly, Broaker and Chapman's *American Accountant's Manual.*[15] Montgomery's authorized edition of Dicksee's *Auditing* appeared in 1905,[16] followed by Montgomery's classic work on auditing, which was published in 1912 and is still in print in a revised form.[17] The 1912 edition signaled a departure from the earlier emphasis of auditors on the detection of fraud and errors to the modern focus on the "financial condition and earnings of an enterprise...."[18] With the inception of the *Journal of Accountancy* in late 1905 and work by Cole[19] and Hatfield,[20] the foundation of an American accounting literature was in place. However, until 1917 nothing was published in the United States resembling "authoritative standards." The first publication that can be considered to contain financial reporting standards was the Federal Reserve Board's "Uniform Accounts," which appeared in the *Federal Reserve Bulletin* in April 1917.

Financial statements contained in the stockholders' report and the audit certificate that often accompanied them ranged from sketchy to detailed. Some examples of early audit certificates and extracts from financial reports illustrate the diversity that characterized reporting practices at the beginning of the century. Yet, in spite of this diversity, there is clear evidence of an awareness of accounting and reporting problems which continues to be debated to this day.

Audit certificates circa 1900. A complete history of audit reports hasn't been written, but some early examples found in the literature on this subject suggest that most contained only a few words. For example, the first audit report of the Imperial and Continental Gas Association in 1827 consisted of one word: "Examined."[21] From 1838-1862 the certificate read: "We have examined the above account on the books of the Association and certify that it is correct."

British 19th-century audit reports were brief, but there were exceptions.[22]

The wording of U.S. audit reports was influenced by various British statutes enacted in the 19th century.[23] For example, the 1856 act[24] required that "The Auditors shall make a Report to the Shareholders upon the Balance Sheet and Accounts, and in every such Report they shall state whether, in their Opinion, the Balance Sheet is a full and fair Balance Sheet, containing the Particulars required by these Regulations, and properly drawn up so as to exhibit a true and correct View of the State of the Company's Affairs...."

The Acts of 1862, 1879 and 1900 had similar provisions.

It has been suggested by Cochrane[25] that, from 1900 until well after World War I, the wording of the audit certificate was as follows: "We have audited the books and accounts of the ABC company for the year ended December 31, 1915, and we certify that, in our opinion, the above balance sheet correctly sets

Author Lawrence R. Dicksee was a professor of accounting in England.

Robert H. Montgomery's book is a classic in accounting literature.

forth its position as at the termination of that year, and that the accompanying profit and loss account is correct."

This form of audit report was often used, but there were many variations. Accounting firms often had different reports, and the reports of a particular firm might differ not only among its clients but also for a particular client over a period of time.

For example, in 1898, Bragg & Marin certified the United States Rubber Company's financial statements as follows: "We have examined the books of accounts of the United States Rubber Company from which the Treasurer's Report contained in the foregoing statements was made up, and we hereby certify that said report and statements correctly show the condition of the United States Rubber Company, April 1st, 1898."

George Wilkinson was president of the Illinois Society of Public Accountants in 1902.

Similar statements were made by the new auditors, Haskins & Sells, in the 1903 "Certificate of Net Quick Assets," with paragraphs about quick assets and depreciation policy added. For example:

"That on that date the Quick Assets of the United States Rubber Company and its Subsidiary Companies, including Inventories of Raw Materials and Manufactured Goods on hand exceeded all the Liabilities, other than Capital Stock, Reserves, Surplus Accounts and the $12,000,000 collateral funding gold notes, to the extent of $20,411,479.27.

"It is the custom of the Company, in lieu of a general charge to depreciation, to charge to expense all betterments and improvements to plants and property."

In 1909 it was shortened and, although modified in later years, the 1933 certificate was almost identical to the 1898 version.

In contrast, the 1906 Haskins & Sells report to Westinghouse was more extensive and covered a six-year period:

"We have made an audit of the books and accounts of the Westinghouse Electric and Manufacturing Company and its subsidiary manufacturing companies....

"We have verified the Cash and the Stock and Bonds owned, by actual count or by proper certificates from depositaries. We have also verified the Bills and Accounts Receivable.

"The inventories of Raw Materials and Supplies, Work in Progress and Finished Parts and Completed Apparatus were properly taken and have been carefully and accurately calculated at cost, and

"We Hereby Certify that the accompanying General Balance Sheet of March 31, 1906, correctly sets forth the Company's true financial condition on that date, that the accompanying statement of Income and Profit and Loss for the six years ended March 31, 1906, correctly states the results of the Company's operations for that period and that the books of the Company are in agreement with these statements."

Length and wording of audit certificates varied as well as their content and focus. Price Waterhouse stated the following in its 1909 report to the Lackawanna Steel Company: "As a result of revaluation of properties mentioned in the President's report, the asset of 'Discount and Commission on Bonds, Expenses during Organization Period and Improvements to Leased Properties' as it appeared in the Balance Sheet of December 31, 1907, has been merged in the book values of the Company's Ore Properties and its Investments in Ore Companies, and in view of the increase in value as stated therein, we approve of this action."

This followed a statement in 1908, which said: "In accordance with the policy which is outlined in the President's report, no part of Organization Expenses has been charged off in the accounts for the year."

Other certificates focused on problems such as the valuation of receivables. Presented below is the 1914 audit report of the Audit Company of New York for the Goodyear Tire & Rubber Company. For an early discussion of the desirability of audit companies, see the *Official Record of the Proceedings of the Congress of Accountants*, published in New York by George Wilkinson in 1904, which was reprinted by Arno Press in 1978.

"The current assets have been carefully reviewed and there have been eliminated therefrom any which are doubtful of collection. These latter are included under the caption 'Suspended Assets' and full provision for non-collection is provided in the Reserve for Doubtful Accounts. This reserve covers not only the full amount of the present known doubtful accounts but also includes, in our opinion, ample provision for possible non-collection of any accounts now considered good. Owing to the large number of Accounts Receivable, confirmations were not obtained from the various debtors."

Special paragraphs of this kind typically concerned valuation problems, for instance, whether only expenditures on additions and betterments should be capitalized and whether depreciation was reasonable. They also addressed questions about inventory valuation and the verification of cash.

However, the audit reports of International Paper Co. seem to be more typical of the period, containing only a short paragraph or two consisting of phrases such as "correctly show the condition" (1904—Charles Hatch, Auditor); "are in accord with the books ... and, in our opinion, correctly exhibit the true financial condition" (1907—Loomis, Conant & Co.); and a "true and correct exhibit of financial condition" (1909—Loomis, Conant & Co. and Haskins & Sells).

This review suggests that there were basically only two kinds of early reports. The first type, which seems more common, was a short statement similar to that of Arthur Young in the 1912 annual report of Swift & Co:

"We have examined the accounts and records of the Company for the fiscal year ending 28 September, 1912, and hereby certify that the foregoing Balance Sheet is in accordance therewith, and is drawn up to exhibit the true condition of the Company's affairs at that date."

The second type, a more extended report, addressed particular accounting issues such as the valuation of fixed assets, receivables and inventories[26] and verification of cash. One can only suppose that these issues were, at the time, of immediate concern to the company and its auditor.

A glimpse into financial reports. Published financial reports in the 19th and early 20th centuries were usually addressed to stockholders and signed by the president. The reports almost always contained a balance sheet, but the quantity and quality of other information in these reports showed a considerable amount of variation.

U.S. Steel's reports were a milestone, as were those of International Harvester and Westinghouse.[27] The information provided by American Can and International Paper, for example, was far below these standards, whereas General Motors was somewhere in between. Some companies provided extensive historical information while others, for example, American Telephone & Telegraph Company, used their annual reports primarily as public relations documents. Indeed, the emphasis on growth in the 1883 report of Western Union Telegraph Company shows that not much has changed very much in 100 years:

"Attention is especially called to the last preceding table exhibiting the growth and increase of the property and business of the Company since July, 1866. During this period the lines have been increased fourfold, with nearly six times as much wire facilities and six times as many offices, handling seven times as many messages, earning three times as much gross revenue, and making threefold as much net profits in one year."

Company presidents often discussed accounting issues in their organizations' annual reports. For example, U.S. Steel's 1904 report deals with consolidation:

"Under the plan of accounting now in vogue these intermediate Inter-Company profits are, in effect, carried into the combined accounts for all companies, first, to the specific surplus account representing such profits, not being included or reported, however, in the statements of net earnings of all properties as from time to time published *except* when and as they are transferred from said specific surplus account as hereinafter stated. When materials carrying such Inter-Company profits are worked up into finished products and are shipped to customers outside of the organization, and thus converted from an inventory asset into cash or accounts receivable, the Inter-Company profits previously accrued on such materials and carried theretofore in the specific surplus account referred to, are transferred to and reported in the current earnings statements. Therefore, the net earnings reported under this plan for all companies represent practically cash earnings to the organization. This method of accounting is conservative and assures greater uniformity from month to month with reference to the net earnings reported in comparison with the cash income of the organization as a whole, and any possible adjustment at the close of the year in the inventory valuation of Inter-Company materials on hand will be made without affecting in any way the current year's earnings and income as previously reported. Any such adjustment would be made against the specific or

Cover page of an early annual report of International Paper Co.

suspended surplus account. The plan also permits the ascertainment of operating and production expense statistics on a more uniform basis from month to month."

The same report notes that inventory valuations are conservative and that the percentage-completion method recognizes only 50 percent of profit prior to completion of a project:

"They were taken on the basis of actual purchase or production cost of materials to the respective companies holding the same, unless (as happened in some instances) such cost was above the market value on December 31, 1903, in which cases the market price was used.... The estimated profits carried as an asset in inventories for gains on uncompleted bridge and structural contracts equal only about one-half of the profit which it is expected will be realized thereon when completed." International Harvester's 1908 report also detailed the principles on which inventories were valued, as well as other accounting policies:

Early annual report cover of one of America's largest companies.

"The annual deductions from earnings to provide for losses which may ultimately be sustained in the realization of Bills and Accounts Receivable taken on each season's sales are based on long experience in this business and are considered sufficient to cover such contingencies.... Furthermore, a systematic and careful investigation into the financial responsibility of prospective customers insures to the Company a high grade of notes and accounts. A recent compilation of bad debts incurred on the business of the seasons 1903 to 1906, inclusive, taking all accounts and notes already charged off in the books together with an estimate of the realization loss on balances still outstanding, the value of which can now be closely ascertained, proves that the reserves for contingent losses provided out of earnings in those seasons will cover all such contingencies.

"The annual appropriations from earnings for depreciation and extinguishment reserves constitute the necessary provision for the impairment and consumption of plant assets utilized in the output of the product and should prove sufficient to reproduce the properties as their replacement becomes necessary. Depreciation on plant property is based on rates established by recognized authorities. Amortization of ore is calculated at rates which will provide sinking funds sufficient to retire the whole of the Company's capital invested in mining properties before the extinguishment of the ore bodies. Timber depletion is figured at the market values of stumpage for the various kinds of timber cut. This stumpage provision will equal the original cost of timber properties when the present standing timber is exhausted, after allowing a fair residual value for the lands either for reforestry or for agricultural purposes."

And commenting on the retained earnings, the report states: "By this investment of surplus the Company should continue to refinance itself and the stockholders ultimately derive the full benefit of the increased earning power resulting from improved and additional manufacturing facilities, a greater variety of products, and better control of the raw material situation."

The 1911 Westinghouse report was, as mentioned earlier, a model for its time. Some of its interesting comments are excerpted below:

"Certain other conditions affect the estimate for the immediate future of the earning power of your Company. On March 31, 1896 your Company entered into an agreement with the General Electric Company whereby for a period of fifteen years thereafter each Company licensed the other under the patents controlled by it during the term of the agreement, with provision for the payment of royalties by each on the basis of its use of the patents of the other. For the past few years under the operation of this agreement your Company has received substantial sums by way of royalties. This agreement expired by limitation of time on April 30, 1911. No renewal of it is contemplated. This source of revenue, therefore, cannot now be counted on.

"Your Directors have in mind the purpose of strengthening your Company's position in every possible direction. To that end they have authorized considerable increase in expenditures of the selling organization, for increasing the number of salesmen in the field, for remuneration of its representatives adequate to secure the best effort on their part, for the extension of advertising, and to provide for proper warehouse facilities for carrying stocks at distributing points. This has added considerably to the aggregate selling expense, but the results, we believe, have been justified.... It is a matter of simple computation, on the basis of the operations of the past two years, to ascertain the point at which the volume of gross business fails to provide a surplus over operating expenses and fixed charges.

"...It must be borne in mind that your Company must keep pace in technical skill and inventive ingenuity with its competitors even though their combined capital and manufacturing facilities are greatly in excess of yours. The cost of all new development and redesigning is charged monthly as a part of the current costs....

"After a careful consideration of all of the circumstances, having due regard for the true condition of your balance sheet, hereinbefore minutely described to you, the elements of uncertainty as to the immediate future of your Company's business, the need for cash for new foundry facilities, for extension of the Newark plant and other factory improvements, and the necessity of making wise provision for shortly maturing obligations, your Directors have felt that it is not wise at the present time to weaken your Company's position by diverting its surplus earnings, even in part, to the payment of dividends on the assenting stock."

A focus on inventory valuation is seen in the 1912 annual report of General Motors:

"These companies have also subjected their inventories to a rigid re-examination and scrutiny, as a result of which your officers have directed that an additional $1,444,967.41 be written off, substantially all of which represents the diminished value of inventories and assets compared with book values as carried on the balance sheet of October 1, 1910. This sum is included in the total of $2,833,663.14 deducted from Profit and Loss Account above. These companies will produce probably close to 95 per cent of your output during the coming year, and they will thus enter the new season with their manufacturing and sales organizations wholly relieved of the expense and embarrassment of having to endeavor to salvage or utilize any semi-obsolete or undesirable models or materials or products of any sort."

Inventories were discussed in the next year.

"As explained in last year's report, the inventories of the subsidiary companies operated at a profit were subjected to a rigid reexamination and scrutiny, so that prior to August 1, 1912, a sufficient amount was written off to eliminate from the book value of those inventories all semi-obsolete or undesireable models or materials or products of any sort. At that time the reorganization of those companies whose operations were not yet on a satisfactory basis had not proceeded far enough to permit the same scrutiny to be extended to their inventories. During the year just ended the inventories of two of the companies of this last class have been liquidated, and the operations of the remainder thereof have been reorganized and their surplus stock of materials have either been worked up and sold or else disposed of as scrap....

"It is satisfactory to know that no further readjustments in respect to the period prior to October 1, 1910, will be required, and that the earnings of the past three years have been sufficient to permit inventories and receivables to be put on a conservative basis on which they are now carried...."

Illustrated in 1909 International Harvester Co. annual report.

Conclusion

These and other reports published around the turn of the century demonstrate that financial reporting practices were rich and varied. While there was considerable variability in the quality of financial reports and disclosure often was inadequate, it is clear that at this early date accounting and reporting issues started to become of great concern to companies, their shareholders and the public. Before there was anything that could be described as accounting standards, and 30 years or so before the establishment of the Securities and Exchange Commission, the great experiment in financial reporting had begun.

The financial reports in the early 1900s of companies like General Motors, International Harvester, U.S. Steel and Westinghouse had an important influence on later developments in accounting. It was a period of experimentation and innovation; many of the features of modern financial reporting are in evidence, such as the disclosure of accounting policy, comparative reports and the statement of sources and uses of funds. Of course, this does not mean that most companies produced financial statements that would be termed satisfactory by today's standards, but it does suggest that the path that corporations would follow had already been marked by this time.

We should know more than we do about the reporting practices of the 1890s and early 1900s and how these practices have evolved over time. The 100-year anniversary of the U.S. accounting profession should give us the opportunity to redirect our attention to this important episode in American accounting history and to reflect on how further progress in the field might be achieved. ◆

[1] James Don Edwards, *History of Public Accounting in the United States* (East Lansing, Mich: Bureau of Business and Economic Research, University of Michigan, 1960), p. 111.

[2] T.A. Wise, *Peat, Marwick, Mitchell & Co.—85 Years* (New York: Peat Marwick, 1982); Paul D. Montagna, *Certified Public Accounting* (Houston: Scholars Book Co., 1974).

[3] R. H. Parker, *The Development of the Accountancy Profession in Britain to the Early Twentieth Century* (Academy of Accounting Historians, 1986), p. 3.

[4] Thomas W. Phillips, "Recommendation as to Publicity," U.S. Industrial Commission, *Final Report*, vol. XIX (Washington, D.C.: U.S. Government Printing Office, 1902), pp. 669-72; reprinted in Richard P. Brief, ed., *Corporate Financial Reporting and Analysis in the Early 1900s* (New York: Garland Publishing, 1986).

[5] Martin A. Knapp, "Capitalization and Publicity," speech before the American Association for the Advancement of Science, December 30, 1902; printed in *Commerce, Accounts & Finance* (February 1903).

[6] *Preliminary Report of the Industrial Commission on Trusts and Industrial Combinations* (Washington, D.C.: Government Printing Office, 1900), p. 122; quoted in David F. Hawkins, "The Development of Modern Financial Reporting Practices among American Manufacturing Corporations," *Business History Review* (Autumn 1963), pp. 135-68; in J. R. Edwards, ed., *Studies of Company Records* (New York: Garland Publishing, 1984), pp. 261-94.

[7] Ibid., pp. 135-68.

[8] Barbara Dubis Merino and Marilyn Dale Neimark, "Disclosure Regulation and Public Policy: A Sociohistorical Reappraisal," *Journal of Accounting and Public Policy* (1982), pp. 33-57.

[9] JofA, Jan.06, pp. 233-34.

[10] William Z. Ripley, *Main Street and Wall Street* (Houston: Scholars Book Co., 1972), p. 159.

[11] Hawkins, p. 147.

[12] Arthur Stone Dewing, *Corporate Promotions and Reorganizations* (Cambridge, Mass.: Oxford University Press, 1914), p. 200.

[13] The books on the subject include William H. Bell, *Accountants' Reports* (New York: Ronald Press, 1921); 2d ed., 1925; 3d ed., 1934; 4th ed., 1949; David Himmelblau, *Auditors' Certificates* (New York: Ronald Press, 1927); James H. Wren, *Accountants' Certificates* (New York: Ronald Press, 1937); N. Loyall McLaren, *Annual Reports to Stockholders* (New York: Ronald Press, 1947). In 1947 the research department of the American Institute of Accountants began the publication of *Accounting Techniques Used in Published Corporate Annual Reports*.

[14] Norman E. Webster, *The American Association of Public Accountants—Its First Twenty Years 1898-1906* (New York: American Institute of Accountants, 1954). Reprint (New York: Arno Press, 1978).

[15] Frank Broaker and Richard M. Chapman, *American Accountant's Manual* (New York: Broaker & Chapman

1897). Volume I contains CPA examination questions "prepared by the State Board of Examiners of expert public accountants appointed by the Board of Regents of the University of the State of New York...." Actually, the book is more of a literature review than a series of questions and answers. According to Gary John Previts and Barbara Dubis Merino, *A History of Accounting in America: An Historical Interpretation of the Cultural Significance of Accounting* (New York: John Wiley, 1979), p. 101, the book sold for $3 and the revenue went to Broaker's private account. Broaker also was accused of forming a society of accountants with himself as president.

16 Robert Lawrence Dicksee, *Auditing: A Practical Manual for Auditors*. Authorized American edition, Robert H. Montgomery, ed. (New York: Robert H. Montgomery, 1905).

17 Robert H. Montgomery, *Auditing Theory and Practice* (New York: Ronald Press, 1912).

18 Ibid., p. 9.

19 William Morse Cole, *Accounts: Their Construction and Interpretation for Business Men and Students of Affairs* (Boston: Houghton Mifflin, 1908).

20 Henry Rand Hatfield, *Modern Accounting: Its Principles and Some of Its Problems* (New York: Appleton, 1909).

21 T. A. Lee and R. H. Parker, eds., *The Evolution of Corporate Financial Reporting* (Middlesex, England: Thomas Nelson and Sons, 1979), p. 11. Reprint (New York: Garland Publishing, 1984).

22 See, for example, Peter Boys and Brian Rutherford, "The Most Universal Quality: Some Nineteenth Century Audit Reports," *Accounting History* (September 1982), pp. 6-26, and Harold Pollins, "Railway Auditing—A Report of 1867," *Accounting Research* (January 1957), pp. 14-22. Reprinted in J. R. Edwards, *Studies of Company Records*.

23 J. R. Edwards, ed., *British Company Legislation and Company Accounts 1844-1976* (New York: Arno Press, 1980).

24 19 & 20 Vict., Cap. 47, S. 84.

25 George Cochrane, "The Auditor's Report: Its Evolution in the U.S.A." *The Accountant*, CXXIII (1950), pp. 448-60. Reprinted in Lee and Parker, pp. 164-92.

26 Three audit reports issued by Price Waterhouse & Co. are reprinted in their entirety in James Don Edwards, pp. 90-92.

27 U.S. Steel issued its first annual report in 1902. Its early reports have been the subject of many articles. These are discussed in Richard Vangermeersch, ed., *Financial Accounting Milestones in the Annual Reports of United States Steel Corporation—The First Seven Decades* (New York: Garland Publishing, 1986), which compiles the major accounting events of U.S. Steel as described in annual reports from 1902–1968. The 1902 annual report of U.S. Steel, along with the 1909 International Harvester report, the 1910 American Telephone & Telegraph Company report and the 1911 Westinghouse Electric & Manufacturing report, are reprinted in their entirety in Brief, *Corporate Financial Reporting*. In addition, the financial reports of 20 industrial companies since 1861 are described in Richard Vangermeersch, *Financial Reporting Techniques in 20 Industrial Companies Since 1861* (Gainesville, Fla.: University Presses of Florida, 1979).

THE ACCOUNTING REVIEW
Vol. LV, No. 3
July 1980

Notes

Cumulative Financial Statements

Richard P. Brief, Barbara Merino and Ira Weiss

ABSTRACT: This paper devises two graphical forms of cumulative financial statements using data from Chrysler Corporation over the period 1923–1975 as an example to display the nature of these reports. The first set of graphs shows the relationship between cumulative income and cumulative cash flows to suppliers of capital. The second set shows the relationship between annual accounting rates of return and a backward-moving cumulative average multi-period rate of return. Although Chrysler's 53-year average rate of return to stockholders' equity was .130, the time series of multi-period rates of return have shown a declining trend since the late 1930's. These graphs reflect the firm's activities as a cumulative process instead of a series of annual ventures. Consequently, they integrate annual reports within a longer time frame. The cumulative graph is an efficient and effective device for presenting a firm's financial history, and, like other methods of data analysis, also stimulates analytical thinking.

MANY years ago, Paton [1934, p. 131] predicted that more attention will be given to multi-period financial statements having cumulative aspects because "an occasional snapshot of a rather artifically conceived financial condition, accompanied by glimpses of severed segments of activity, are rather inadequate tools with which to limn the financial fabric of a business in a vital fashion." Paton argued, in effect, that a year's duration in a firm's life should not be viewed as an "annual venture" and that one annual report does not adequately present the financial condition of a firm.[1] Although this proposition is convincing, accountants continue to debate the issues of interim reporting only in the more narrow context of quarterly reports, even though periods of a quarter, a year, three years, *etc.* are essentially alike in that they are artifically-defined time segments.

The type of cumulative reports discussed by Paton [1934, p. 132] and Kester

[1] Paton discussed the subject of cumulative reports elsewhere [1938, pp. 199–200; 1941, pp. 103–105]. Cumulative reports also were mentioned by Kester [1946, pp. 546–547], and in the third, fourth, and fifth editions of the *Accountants' Handbook* [Daniels, 1943; Schindler, 1956; Schindler, 1970]. A decade earlier, Finney [1923, Ch. 4, p. 2] described three-year cumulative statements in his text. The idea of a three-year financial statement can be traced to the Federal Reserve Board publication, *Uniform Accounts* [1917]. The second edition of Karrenbrock and Simons [1953, p. 946] contains a reference to cumulative reports in the index, but there appears to be no discussion of the subject in the text. Apparently, the reference was carried over in error from the first edition. Notwithstanding this early support for the concept of cumulative reports, the idea never really caught on.

The authors are indebted to David O. Green and Joel Owen for their helpful comments. The authors also thank Tien-Shan Sih for computational assistance.

Richard P. Brief is Professor of Business Statistics and Accounting, New York University; Barbara Merino is Assistant Professor of Accounting, New York University; and Ira Weiss is Assistant Professor of Accounting, University of Houston.

Manuscript received July, 1979.
Revision received October, 1979.
Accepted October, 1979.

[1946, pp. 546–547] took the form of tabular summaries in highly aggregated form covering a time period since the firm's inception.[2] This kind of financial statement may be useful and informative, but it is a multi-period report in very abbreviated form. Therefore, while the general argument in support of cumulative statements is persuasive, more attention needs to be given to devising a cumulative report which (1) has a multi-period dimension, (2) retains the information provided in the annual report, and (3) presents these data in a clear and concise way. These objectives can be achieved using cumulative graphs [Brinton, 1914, Ch. IX].[3]

In a cumulative graph, each point on the graph represents the cumulative sum of the variable being measured up to the time for which the last point is plotted. Cumulative graphs are particularly useful to depict the history of the firm for several reasons. First, all balance sheet accounts are cumulative. Therefore, if the cumulative additions and subtractions in an account are plotted over time, the vertical difference between these two time series equals the book value of the account. Second, since the balance sheet and income statement articulate, a single graph can be used to present both statements in a multi-period framework. For example, the difference between cumulative income and cumulative net cash flows to equity interests at any point of time is the book value of equity.[4]

Third, a cumulative graph of annual data covering the history of a firm since its inception contains information about any historical period of activity that the financial analyst might define. The graph reports on one-year periods, two-year periods, *etc.* Whereas it is usual to make annual comparisons over time, a cumulative graph makes it possible to compare, for example, five-year periods over a 25-year period. Fourth, and at a more conceptual level, a cumulative graph helps to illuminate the nature and limitations of accounting because it underscores the fact that the interim characteristic dominates all other aspects of financial statements. Thus, viewing the activities of a going concern as a cumulative process instead of a series of annual ventures not only gives a clearer understanding of a firm's past efforts and accomplishments, but it also provides a framework for beginning to discuss the nature and magnitude of the transactions that remain to be completed before a firm liquidates. At any point of time, these incomplete transactions are the central issue in accounting theory and a cumulative perspective of the firm forces the user to notice the uncertainty inherent in financial reports.

The purpose of this paper is to devise two graphical forms of cumulative reports: cumulative graphs of income and cash flows and graphs which superimpose data on annual rates of return on a moving cumulative average multi-period rate of return. Data from Chrysler Corporation over the period 1923–1975 are used as an example to display the nature of cumulative reports in concrete terms. Before presenting the cumulative graphs, several issues related to the data collection process are dealt with.

[2] Páton also mentioned three-year cumulative statements that were actually in the form of three-year comparative statements with averages and totals for the three years. However, most of the references to cumulative reports alluded to long-run statements, usually covering a period of time since the firm's inception.

[3] Graphical analysis is an expanding area of research [Gnanadesikan, 1977; Tukey, 1977]. Although accountants have been aware of the value of graphical methods for some time [Saliers, 1923; Sec. 15; Briggs, 1932; Vance, 1956], there has been, with the exception of Moriarity's recent article [1979], almost no new work in this area since Brinton's early text which contained a chapter on corporation financial reports (Ch. XV).

[4] In this paper, the terms, equity and stockholders' equity, are interchangeable.

Cumulative Reports: A Graphical Presentation

Data Collection

The data used in this analysis were taken directly from the annual reports of Chrysler Corporation. Chrysler is used as an example because it has a long history, is in a cyclical industry, and has had financial problems in recent years.

Although Chrysler's history dates back to 1913, a reorganization occurred in 1921 and was not completed until 1922. Therefore, our study covers the period 1923–1975.[5]

Our methodology required that a clean surplus be maintained. Therefore, we began by preparing statements of changes in financial position during the time period being studied. This enabled us to isolate those procedures that violated a clean surplus. In the 1930s, losses were often written off directly to surplus, and "reserve accounting" was frequently used in the 1920s and 1940s. Typically, reserves for contingencies, future losses, employee benefits, and war-related reserves were expensed and charged to income in an orderly and systematic fashion. When the reserves were reversed in subsequent years, they were credited directly to surplus. The necessary adjustments were made to reported data to ensure that all gains and losses would be reflected in the income account.

Two sets of computations were made. First, after-tax income to stockholders, the book value of stockholders' equity, and net cash flows to stockholders were calculated for each year over the 53-year period. Cash flows to stockholders equal dividends and share repurchases, less proceeds from the sale of new equity securities. Second, after-tax income to bondholders and stockholders, the book value of bondholder and equity accounts, and net cash flows to bondholders and stockholders were calculated. Net income in this calculation was determined before all revenue and expense transactions involving bondholders, and cash flows included interest payments plus bond redemptions less amounts received from the floatation of new bonds. The first set of calculations views Chrysler from the perspective of equity interests (E). The second set views the firm in terms of the major suppliers of capital, *i.e.*, bondholders and stockholders (BE). The definitions corresponding to cash flows under each of these perspectives of the firm are identical to those used in the financial theory of the firm [Haley and Schall, 1973].

The basic assumptions needed to derive these data from the financial statements are that: (1) the income statement and balance sheet articulate; (2) there are no debits or credits made directly to equity accounts, *i.e.*, clean surplus; and (3) all changes in the equity or bondholder account reflect constructive cash flows [Ijiri, 1978, p. 343]. Constructive cash flows are cash flows that are deemed to have occurred even if they actually did not. For example, an exchange of common stock for bonds may not actually involve cash flows, but our methodology requires the assumption that transactions of this type involve cash.

[5] Maxwell Motor Corporation, the predecessor of Chrysler Corporation, was organized in 1913 and underwent a forced liquidation and reorganization in 1921 when the company failed. The first consolidated balance sheet of the new entity, a combination of Maxwell Motor Corporation with Chalmers Motor Corporation, was issued in 1921. The reorganized company was in effect a purchase of Chalmers by Maxwell Motor Corporation which owned 95 percent of the preferred and common stock of Chalmers. The Board of Directors of Chalmers Motor Corporation "is composed of the same persons as the Executive Committee of Maxwell Motor Corporation" (*Annual Report*, June 1, 1921). But the reorganization and takeover was not finalized until 1922, and, therefore, our analysis begins at the end of that year. The name Chrysler Corporation was adopted by the company in 1925 when Walter Chrysler replaced William Robert Wilson as President and became the major stockholder in the firm.

These assumptions and the adjustments enabled us to calculate cash flows in a period by subtracting from (adding to) income the increase (decrease) in the book value determined for each set of computations, *i.e.* for stockholders and for bondholders and stockholders. Preferred stockholders were classified as bondholders and minority stockholders were classified as stockholders.[6]

It must be pointed out explicitly that we have not dealt with the effect of changing prices in this paper. Although it is easy to index cash flows for the effect of inflation, the appropriate techniques for adjusting accounting numbers like income and book value remain a matter of dispute. Therefore, the data in this presentation have not been adjusted for the changing purchasing power of the monetary unit.

Cumulative Income and Cash Flows

In a graph of cumulative income and cumulative cash flows, each point represents total income (or total cash flows) up to the time for which the last point is plotted.

Cumulative graphs of income and cash flows have three important characteristics. First, the rate of change in income or cash flows over any short period of time can be approximated by the slope of the straight-line "fit" through the cumulative points on the graph over that time period. Second, at any point of time in a firm's history, the difference between cumulative income and cumulative cash flows equals the net asset book value of the firm. Thus, the graph integrates the income statement and balance sheet and shows the growth of book value. Third, since total income must equal total cash flows when a firm liquidates because the book value at the end of a firm's life is, by definition, zero, the cumulative graph indicates how cash flows will have to behave in the future to justify the level of investment (book value of firm) at any point of time. That is, unless a firm has an infinite life, either cumulative cash flows eventually must rise to the level of cumulative income or cumulative income eventually must fall to the level of cumulative cash flows. History cannot tell us the direction in which these time series will move, but it does add more concreteness to any discussion about the relationship between income and cash flows.

Figures 1 and 2 show cumulative income and cumulative cash flows in period t, $t = 1923, \ldots, 1975$, for stockholders (E) and bondholders and stockholders (BE).[7] In Figure 1, cumulative income and cash flows reached low points in 1935, and both series then rose until 1957, with income rising more rapidly than cash flows. Income then leveled off until 1961 and rose dramatically until 1973. During this 12-year period of income growth, cumulative cash flows to equity fell in 1963 and 1965 and then leveled off to about the 1958 level. Thus, despite the growth of income, stockholders as a group did not receive dividends in excess of their capital contributions for the 1957–1975 period.[8]

Figure 2 shows that when Chrysler is viewed in terms of the interests of bond-

[6] As a check on these calculations, we determined cash flows by calculating the change in book value in two ways. First, the book value of stockholders' equity (E) and bondholders and stockholders (BE) in each period was determined directly from bondholder and stockholder accounts. Second, these book values were calculated indirectly from all other accounts. For example, in the calculation for the book value of equity, we also computed the book value of equity by determining the net book value of all non-equity accounts. This check uncovered a number of errors.

[7] The dollar sign ($) means that $x = *$.

[8] It also might have been useful to plot cumulative dividends on the same graph. Then the vertical difference between cumulative income and cumulative dividends would show the cumulative amount of income reinvested. And the difference between cumulative dividends and cumulative cash flows would show the cumulative amount of new capital contributions.

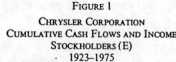

FIGURE 1
CHRYSLER CORPORATION
CUMULATIVE CASH FLOWS AND INCOME
STOCKHOLDERS (E)
1923–1975

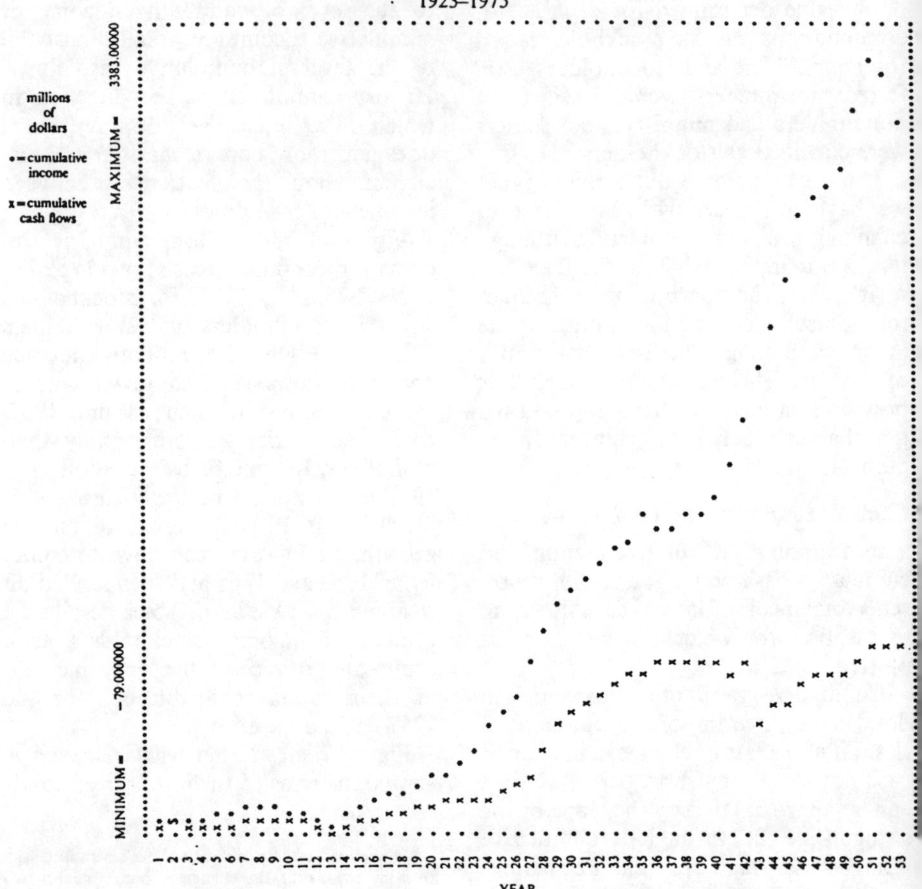

holders and stockholders, the graph of cumulative income closely corresponds to the time series in Figure 1. But cash flows show a markedly different pattern. After 1954, cumulative cash flows to bondholders and stockholders display a generally declining trend, falling to virtually zero in 1974.[9]

Over the 1923–1975 period, income to bondholders and stockholders amounted to approximately $3.8 billion. Stockholders received about $.7 billion in cash, and bondholders contributed, net, $.4 billion in cash, leaving a net book

[9] We also calculated cumulative cash flows from operations (net income plus non-cash expenses minus non-cash revenues) over the 53-year period. Significantly, the ratio of cumulative cash flows from operations to cumulative income to equity was approximately 1.7 at the end of 1939, 1.6 at the end of 1949, 2.3 at the end of 1959, 2.5 at the end of 1969, and 3.1 at the end of 1975. In view of the fact that suppliers of capital were required to provide significant amounts of funds in the post-World War II period to maintain productive capacity, it is clear Paton's argument [1963] that cash flows from operations is an "illusion" has considerable merit.

FIGURE 2

CHRYSLER CORPORATION
CUMULATIVE CASH FLOWS AND INCOME
BONDHOLDERS AND STOCKHOLDERS (BE)
1923–1975

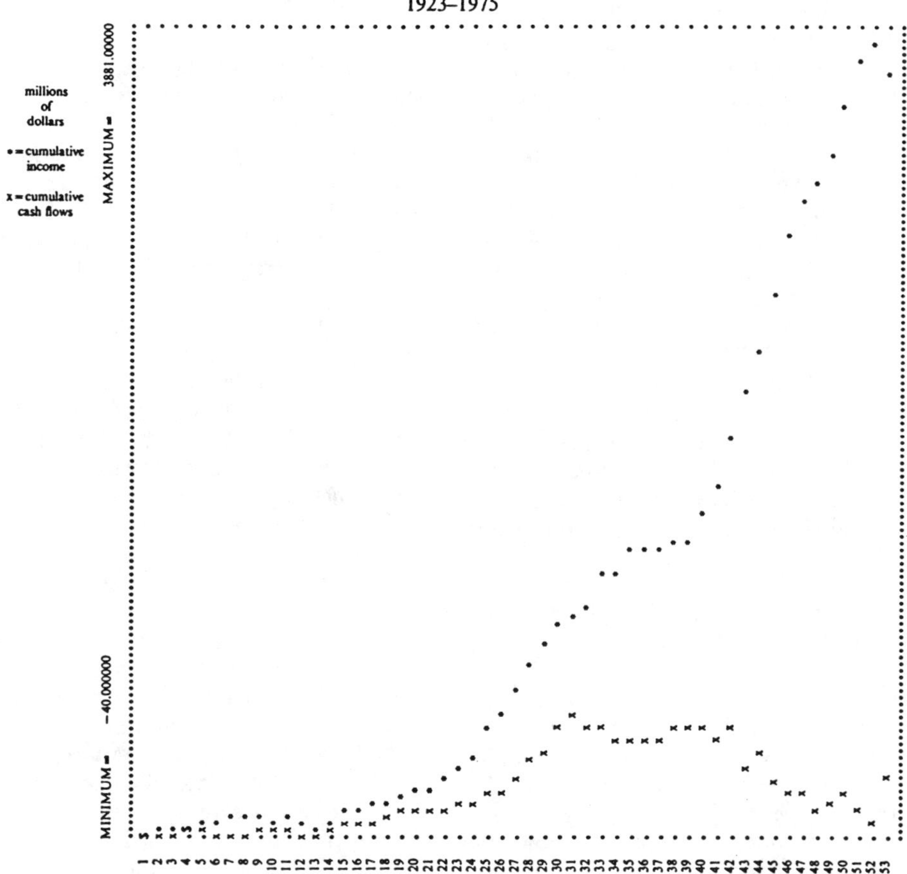

value of $3.5 billion. (In this period Chrysler paid $2.5 billion in income taxes.) This 53-year history is clearly too short a period in which to make an assessment of what the *ultimate* relationship between income and cash flows will be. Indeed, *any* period which is less than the life of a firm (which would not be known until its demise) is "too short" a period for making such an assessment.

The cumulative graphs show that the net book value of Chrysler rose rapidly since the late 1950s and early 1960s, especially when viewed from the perspective of bondholders and stockholders (BE) in Figure 2. For further insight into Chrysler's historical performance, information about the rate of return on investment is needed.

Analysis of Rate of Return on Investment

There are 53 single-period accounting rates of return over the 1923–1975 period. There are 1,431 possible multi-period rates of return that might be analyzed over this period, *i.e.*, 53 one-period returns, 52 two-period returns, 51 three-period returns, *etc.* Two questions arise in analyzing rates of return over long time periods. First, what kind of framework is needed to analyze multi-period returns? Second, how should this average rate of return be determined?

The historical perspective adopted here is that of an analyst in 1975 who is looking back in time and is interested in evaluating the rate of return on book value from any earlier period until 1975. This framework requires the calculation of rates of return from 1923–1975, 1924–1975, . . ., 1974–1975. The sequence of these 53 rates of return is a backward-moving cumulative average. A forward-moving cumulative average rate of return would anchor all calculations in 1923, and each successive cumulative average would show the effect on overall profitability since 1923 of adding another year's operation. Each successive cumulative average in the backward-moving average shows the effect on the cumulative average rate of return to 1975 of subtracting another year's operations. The backward-moving average moves to the present whereas the forward-moving average is anchored in the past. For this reason, the backward-moving average provides more information about the trend of the series of cumulative average rates of return.

The multi-period rate of return for any interim period (j, t), in a firm's life of n periods, $(0 \leq j < t \leq n)$, is defined as the rate of return, r, that solves.

$$C_j = \frac{X_j}{1+r} + \frac{X_{j+1}}{(1+r)^2} + \cdots \frac{X_t}{(1+r)^{t-j+1}} + \frac{C_{t+1}}{(1+r)^{t-j+1}}, \quad (1)$$

where

X_i = cash flows in period i, $i = j, \cdots, t$

C_j = book value at the beginning of period j

C_{t+1} = book value at the end of period t.

This multi-period return also can be calculated directly from single-period financial statements [Kay, 1976, p. 453]. Therefore, the definition of r is internally consistent with accounting data, and it has a more straightforward analytical interpretation than either a simple or weighted average of the single-period rates of return.[10]

In Figures 3 and 4 the single accounting rates of return for E and BE, respectively, are plotted over the 53-year period (asterisk). The rate of return, r, is calculated for 1923–1975, 1924–1975, *etc.*, and each of these rates of return is plotted (x) in the year which begins the period. For example, the rate of return for 1923–1975 is plotted in 1923.

All figures show extremely variable single-period accounting rates of return and a much smoother pattern in the backward-moving cumulative average rate of return. In analyzing these graphs, it should be borne in mind that the earlier cumulative average rates of return (1923–1975, 1924–1975, *etc.*), which are on the left, will be much more stable than the multi-period returns based on shorter periods. For example, when 1976 data are included in analysis, we would not

[10] The multi-period rate of return, r, may be calculated directly from information about income and book values by modifying Kay's Equations (8) and (9) [1976, p. 453] to reflect discrete time instead of continuous time. If income and book value were constant over time or grew at the same rate, then the single-period accounting rates of return would be constant and equal to r. Under other conditions, accounting rates of return cannot be interpreted this way. It should be pointed out that Kay's analysis assumes that the "depreciation" is a firm concept. For the firm, depreciation (appreciation) is the change in its book value. Also, Kay does not seem to realize that cash flows, as defined in this paper, *can* be obtained from financial statements (p. 452).

FIGURE 3
CHRYSLER CORPORATION
COMPARISON OF SINGLE AND MULTI-PERIOD RATES OF RETURN
STOCKHOLDERS (E)
1923–1975

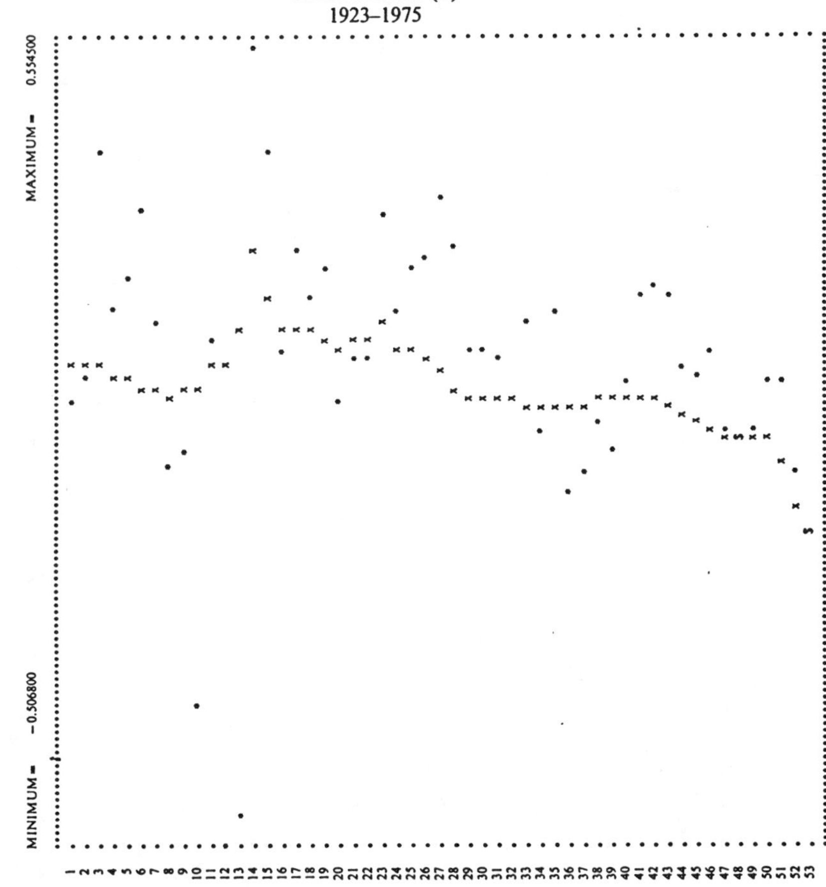

expect the average rate of return over the 54-year period to differ very much from the 53-year period. There are two reasons to expect this kind of stability. First, the multi-period return, r, is an average. An average based on 54 observations cannot be expected to differ very much from an average based on 53 observations. Second, if we begin a discounting process in 1923 we would not expect that cash flows 54 years later would have much impact on the calculation of r. On the other hand, the multi-period returns based on shorter periods will be unstable as we move into the future because these returns (right to left) are based on 1 period, 2 periods, 3 periods, *etc.* Therefore, the right-hand side of this time series can be expected to behave like a wagging tail. Thus, if the profitability of Chrysler were to improve, the right-hand side of the graph would rise.

FIGURE 4

CHRYSLER CORPORATION
COMPARISON OF SINGLE AND MULTI-PERIOD RATES OF RETURN
BONDHOLDERS AND STOCKHOLDERS (BE)
1923–1975

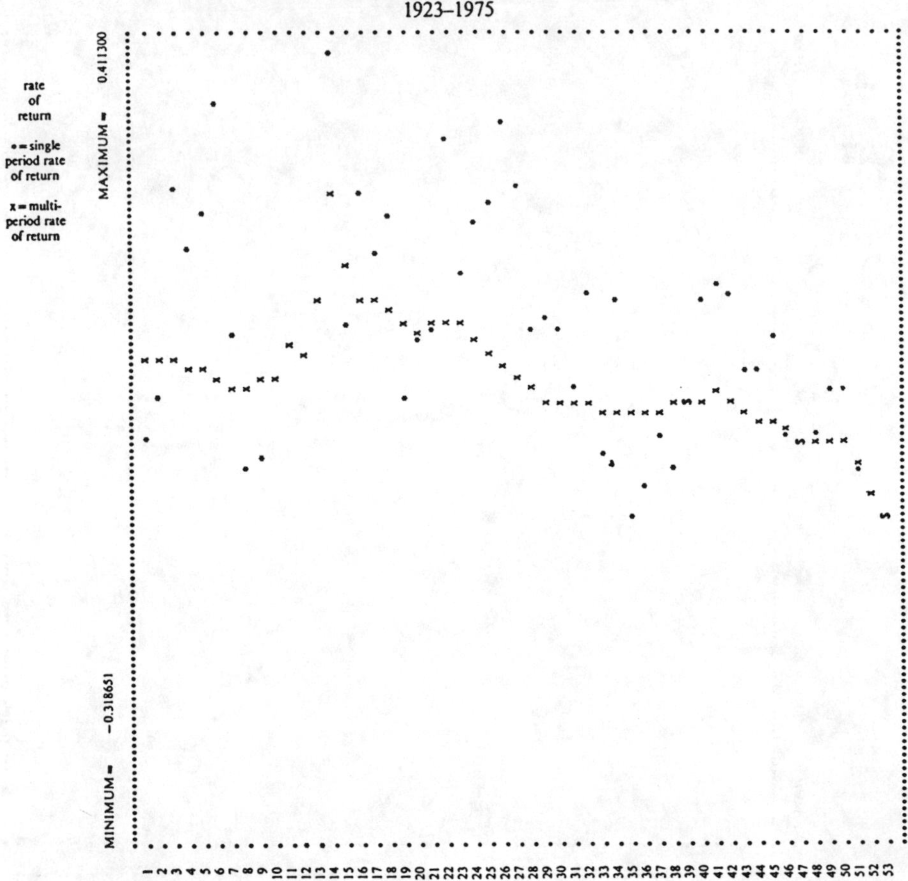

The backward-moving cumulative averages in both graphs show that Chrysler's rate of return was highest in the periods anchored in the late 1930s and experienced a decline since then. Rapid declines occurred in the mid 1940s, just after World War II, and in the early 1960s. These periods also were ones in which income grew at relatively high rates (Figures 1 and 2). However, although income was growing rapidly in these periods, cash flows to suppliers of capital was on the verge of a steady decline (BE, Figure 2) or beginning a long period of virtually no growth (E, Figure 1). Thus, the rapid increase in the book value of Chrysler was accompanied by a declining rate of return.

We also calculated, but did not graph, the forward-moving cumulative average which provides the analyst with information about long-term profitability. Thus, for cumulative average rates of return anchored in 1923, the return to bondholders and stockholders (BE) stabilized at .111 by 1923–1941 and varied by only .01 as the period 1923–1941 is stretched to 1923–1975. The return to equity (E) was .121 in the period 1923–1941, rose to .138 in the period 1923–1955, and fell to .130 in the 1923–1975 period. This kind of information was recently discussed in a study of the profitability of the Suez Canal over the period 1859–1956 [Hansen and Tourk, 1978].[11]

Conclusion

Using data from Chrysler Corporation as an example, this paper has devised two graphical forms of cumulative reports. The first shows the year-by-year relationship between cumulative income and cumulative net cash flows to suppliers of capital. The second shows the over-time relationship between annual rates of return on capital and a backward-moving cumulative average rate of return.

Figures 1 and 2 show that the connection between earnings and net cash flows to suppliers of capital is a very long-run concept since only a fraction of Chrysler's income has been translated into positive net cash flows to bondholders and stockholders. But if this is true, in what sense can one argue that financial statements for a short-time period should reflect the cash flows that suppliers of capital will ultimately receive and how can this objectives be achieved [cf. FASB, 1976]? While the emphasis in accounting today is on using financial statements to provide information about future earning power, might not some useful insights be obtained into these vexing conceptual issues by studying the actual long-term relationship between the past and the present? Thus, the cumulative report might be a foundation stone for bringing some critical issues in accounting into sharper focus. It could force us to notice what we never expected to see in the same way that any "exploratory data analysis" might aid in achieving this objective [Tukey, 1977, p. vi].

Figures 3 and 4 provide additional insight into the profitability of Chrysler. These graphs show that whereas the amount being invested by Chrysler have been rapidly growing since the late 1950s, the cumulative average rate of return on investment has been declining steadily. Whether Chrysler's rate of return will continue at present levels or rise in the future clearly cannot be determined from these cumulative statements. What can be obtained from these graphs is a clear description of the firm's historical performance and a greater appreciation of the interim characteristic of financial statements.

The availability of computers has reduced the cost of preparing cumulative reports and has made available a number of other data analytic techniques which were not practical tools of analysis in earlier times. The development of new kinds of financial statements is long overdue, and this intriguing area of research needs further exploration. Although this paper has only scratched the surface of the subject, it is plain to us that more effort should be expended in devising new ways to present financial data in accounting reports so that users of financial statements, not just accounting

[11] As previously noted, no adjustments to the data were made for the effect of changing prices. However, since the long-term forward-moving cumulative average rate of return becomes stable as the time horizon lengthens, it would have been possible to estimate the real rate of return over the 1923–1975 period by subtracting the average rate of inflation over the 53 years from the nominal rate of return, r [Kay, 1976, p. 460].

researchers, will be provided with more analysis, as well as an improved understanding, of the data that accountants produce.

REFERENCES

Briggs, R. P., "Graphic Presentation," in W. A. Paton, ed., *Accountants' Handbook* (Ronald Press, 1932), Sec. 3.

Brinton, W. C., *Graphic Methods for Presenting Facts* (The Engineering Magazine, 1914).

Daniels, M. B., "Financial Statements—Form and Content," in W. A. Paton, ed., *Accountants' Handbook* (Ronald Press, 1943), Sec. 1.

Federal Reserve Board, "Uniform Accounts," *Federal Reserve Bulletin* (April 1917), pp. 270–284, reprinted in M. Moonitz, *Three Contributions to the Development of Accounting Thought* (Arno Press, 1978).

Financial Accounting Standards Board (FASB), Discussion Memorandum, *Conceptual Framework for Financial Accounting and Reporting: Elements of Financial Statements and Their Measurement* (FASB, 1976).

Finney, H. A., *Principles of Accounting* (Prentice-Hall, 1923).

Gnanadesikan, R., *Methods of Statistical Data Analysis of Multivariate Observations* (John Wiley & Sons, 1977).

Haley, C. W. and L. D. Schall, *The Theory of Financial Decisions* (McGraw-Hill, Inc. 1973).

Hansen, B. and K. Tourk, "The Profitability of the Suez Canal as a Private Enterprise, 1859–1956," *The Journal of Economic History* (December 1978), pp. 938–958.

Ijiri, Y., "Cash Flow Accounting and Its Structure," *Journal of Accounting, Auditing and Finance* (Summer 1978), pp. 331–348.

Karrenbrock, W. E., and H. Simons, *Intermediate Accounting* (South-Western Publishing Co., 1953).

Kay, J. A., "Accountants, Too, Could be Happy in a Golden Age: The Accountant's Rate of Profit and the Internal Rate of Return," *Oxford Economic Papers* (November 1976), pp. 447–460.

Kester, Roy B., *Advanced Accounting* (Ronald Press, 1946).

Moriarity, S., "Communicating Financial Information Through Multi-Dimensional Graphics," *Journal of Accounting Research* (Spring 1979), pp. 205–224.

Paton, W. A., "Shortcomings of Present-Day Financial Statements," *Journal of Accountancy* (February 1934), pp. 108–132.

Paton, W. A., "Comments on 'A Statement of Accounting Principles'," *Journal of Accountancy* (March 1938), pp. 196–207.

Paton, W. A., *Advanced Accounting* (The Macmillian Co., 1941).

Paton, W. A., "The 'Cash Flow' Illusion," THE ACCOUNTING REVIEW (April 1963), pp. 243–251.

Saliers, E. A., ed., *Accountants' Handbook* (Ronald Press, 1923).

Schindler, J. S., "Financial Statements, Form and Content," in R. Wixon and W. G. Kell, eds., *Accountants' Handbook* (Ronald Press, 1956), Ch. 2.

Schindler, J. S., "Financial Statements, Form and Content," in R. Wixon, W. G. Kell, and N. M. Bedford, eds., *Accountants' Handbook* (Ronald Press, 1970), Ch. 2.

Tukey, J. W., *Exploratory Data Analysis* (Addison-Wesley, 1977).

Vance, L. L., "Mathematical and Statistical Methods and Tables," in R. Wixon and W. G. Kell, eds., *Accountants' Handbook* (Ronald Press, 1956), Ch. 29.

*INTRODUCTION**

The articles and notes reprinted in this book address the problem of using accounting data to estimate the economic rate of return. In all of these papers, which were written over the last twenty years, the economic rate of return is defined as the internal rate of return on a series of cash inflows and outflows. While the economic interpretation of the internal rate of return has been questioned, many economists seem to agree that "the economic rate of return on an investment is . . . that discount rate that equates the present value of its expected net revenue stream to its initial outlay."[1]

Most of this work has sought to determine the conditions under which the accounting rate of return would be a "good" estimate of the economic rate of return. While the detailed models differ, the general idea underlying several of the more influential articles is as follows. The firm is assumed to invest in a project or mix of projects depreciated by a standard method such as straight-line depreciation or sum-of-the-years digits depreciation. The project generates a series of cash flows. The firm is assumed either to reinvest a fixed percentage of its cash flows or to grow at a constant rate. Depending on the specific assumptions made about these variables, a steady-state situation is reached. A comparison is then made of the accounting rate of return with the economic rate of return.

In a sense, all of this research can be traced to the early efforts made by actuaries to find a simple approximation for the yield on an annuity or a bond.[2] However, there is a significant difference between the motivation for finding an approximation to the interest rate and the problem of estimating the economic rate of return from accounting data. In approximating the rate of interest on an annuity or bond, complete information about cash flows is given and the approximation of the interest rate is necessary because of the difficulty of finding a solution to a polynomial equation. Obviously, with modern computers the problem of approximating the interest rate has become obsolete.

On the other hand, most of the articles concerned with the problem of estimating the economic rate of return from accounting data have assumed

* The articles and papers that were reprinted in the book are listed at the end of the Introduction. In the actual book, the contents preceded the Introduction.

that information about the firm's cash flows is not available, at least directly. It is the absence of such information that provides the motivation for using accounting data to estimate the economic rate of return.

Ten articles and six notes and comments are reprinted in this volume. Seven of these papers were published in British journals and the rest appeared in U.S. publications. While these writings are available in most libraries, bringing them together in one book should facilitate research on this important subject.

The first article reprinted in this anthology is by Harcourt (1965), who compared the accounting and economic rates of return under a variety of assumed conditions. His final comment was that "any 'man of words' (or 'deeds' for that matter) who compares rates of profit of different industries, or of the same industry in different countries, and draws inferences from their magnitudes as to the relative profitability of investments in different uses or countries, does so at his own peril." Fisher, who overlooked this article in his 1983 study with McGowan, commented in his 1984 reply that "of all the literature, Harcourt's valuable article is perhaps the one most closely related to our own work."[3]

Solomon's 1966 paper is also a classic in the field. He studied the relationship between the accounting rate of return (book yield) and the economic rate of return (true yield) in the no-growth and growth situations under different assumed conditions about the life of a project, capitalization policy, depreciation policy, inflation, and lags in cash flows. The basic conclusion was simply that the accounting rate of return is "not a reliable measure" of the rate of return on investment.

Zeff's comment on Solomon's paper gives a short history of the subject and also sketches a proposed solution to the problem, which seems to suggest that some method of direct calculation of the economic rate of return might be feasible.

Vatter's article is also a comment on Solomon, and in private correspondence[4] Vatter said that he thought this article was "loves labor lost!" Basically, Vatter was critical of the idea that the purpose of calculating a period's accounting rate of return was to estimate the economic rate of return. He showed that the same answer would be obtained by discounting cash flows at the book rate or the internal rate of return: "The book yields for individual years, (which Solomon dismissed as misleading and capricious), will discount the cash receipts to exactly $1,000, just as the 10 per cent average rate did! . . . Evidently, the 'distorted' annual rates of return still have as much validity as the 10 per cent 'true' yield." Peasnell, in his 1982 article reprinted here, proved this result.

Solomon's second article on the subject is an elaboration of his earlier work where he once again points out the hazards of using the accounting rate of return to estimate the economic rate of return. Cautioning against the misuse of "rates of return," Solomon stresses that accounting and economic rates of return are different things, not estimates of the same thing.

The next item in this book is by Livingstone and Salamon. They review and synthesize the earlier work area and then, using examples that assume different cash-flow profiles, project lives, economic rates of return, and the proportion of cash flows reinvested, discuss the relationship between the accounting rate of return and the economic rate of return. Livingstone and Salamon conclude that these variables must be analyzed jointly. They also found that a constant reinvestment rate tends towards a constant rate of growth in gross investment.

The 1971 article by Stauffer extends and qualifies Solomon's results, but his conclusion is basically the same: ". . . the accounting rate of return is generally a very poor proxy for the economic . . . rate of return, which is relevant either for capital budgeting decisions within the firm or for external assessment of the firm/industry's market performance." Stauffer's analysis assumes that the firm invests in a project and reinvests a fixed proportion of cash flows in each period in identical projects. The investment process associated with this assumption is described by a Voltera integral equation of the second kind; the associated mathematics is not easy.[5] Within the framework of this model, Stauffer analyzes the impact of cash-flow time shapes, depreciation methods, capital structure, and income taxes on the relationship between two accounting-based rates of return and the economic rate of return.

Next is an article by Kay, followed by Wright's comment, Kay's reply, and a note on Kay's work by Stark.[6] Kay derived an algorithm that purports to estimate the economic rate of return from accounting data. However, as Wright points out, the algorithm assumes that the accountant's figure for the firm's book values at the beginning and end of the multiperiod time horizon over which the economic rate of return is estimated is equal to the value of the firm at these points of time. Stark then noted that if this assumption is correct, the economic rate of return could be calculated directly by finding the rate of return that equates the firm's initial value with its discounted future cash flows (counting the terminal point value as the final cash flow).

Thus, while Kay's method does not really bring us any closer to finding a solution, it does identify the "terminal value" problem as one of the central issues in attempting to estimate the economic rate of return from accounting data. In other words, the deficiency in Kay's method makes it quite apparent that the problem of estimating the economic rate of return boils down to one issue, namely, estimating the firm's cash flows over its uncertain future.

Whittington's paper takes a slightly different tack. He attempts to "define those uses in which the deficiencies of ARR [accounting rate of return] are relatively unimportant and to identify the specific sources of deficiencies in ARR, so that they can be corrected or allowed for in uses in which they are potentially important." While Whittington agrees that there are dangers inherent in using the accounting data to estimate the economic rate of return, he suggests that "the absence of better information will force him [the user of accounting information] to continue to use ARR, and it is better to define the nature of the peril and draw up safety rules, rather than to forbid the use of ARR." A point in this article is clarified by Whittington and Skerratt in the note that follows.

In the next paper Salamon tries to solve the problem of estimating the economic rate of return by proposing a method that is invariant to accounting methods, thereby avoiding some of the difficulties previous researchers have stressed. His method requires information about the firm's cash recovery rate and also depends on estimates of the time shape of cash flows, the growth rate in gross investment, the rate of inflation, and the life of the projects in which a firm invests. However, Salamon's method is based on a model that, as Brief points out in a note, in effect assumes that the firm's future cash flows grow at a constant rate. Obviously, the external validity of this assumption (which is in doubt) needs to be determined.[7] Nevertheless, Salamon's work is interesting and merits further study.

In many ways Peasnell's article is a synthesis of some of the earlier work, and its contribution is in its emphasis on the basic analytical aspects of accounting rates of return within the framework of the double-entry bookkeeping process. On the assumption of "clean surplus" and the articulation of the balance sheet and income statement, Peasnell presents a number of properties of accounting numbers. Since accounting is in part a statistical discipline, accountants should become better acquainted with these properties.

In addition to the writings reprinted in this volume, there have been a number of other articles, notes, and comments written on the subject, including:

L. A. Gordon, "Accounting Rate of Return vs Economic Rate of Return," *Journal of Business Finance & Accounting* (Autumn 1974), pp. 343–356.

F. K. Wright, "The Ex-Post Internal Rate of Return: Who Needs It?" *Accounting and Finance* (May 1979), pp. 71–79.

F. M. Fisher and J. J. McGowan, "On the Misuse of Accounting Rates of Return to Infer Monopoly Profits," *American Economic Review* (March 1983), pp. 82–97.

Ira Horowitz, "The Misuse of Accounting Rates of Return: Comment," *American Economic Review* (June 1984), pp. 492–493.

William F. Long and David J. Ravenscraft, "The Misuse of Accounting Rates of Return: Comment," *American Economic Review* (June 1984), pp. 494–500.

Stephen Martin, "The Misuse of Accounting Rates of Return: Comment," *American Economic Review* (June 1984), pp. 501–506.

Michael F. van Breda, "The Misuse of Accounting Rates of Return: Comment," *American Economic Review* (June 1984), pp. 507–508.

F. M. Fisher, "The Misuse of Accounting Rates of Return: Reply," *American Economic Review* (June 1984), pp. 509–517.

Peter F. Luckett, "ARR vs. IRR: A Review and Analysis," *Journal of Business Finance & Accounting* (Summer 1984), pp. 213–231.

Gerald L. Salamon, "Accounting Rates of Return," *American Economic Review* (June 1985), pp. 495–504.

Robert N. Anthony, "Accounting Rates of Return: Note," *American Economic Review* (March 1986), pp. 244–246.

Anthony's 1986 note, which is the latest paper written on the subject, claims that "a substantial part of the difference between the measurement of profitability by accountants and by economists can be eliminated by making two changes in accounting principles": (1) require companies to use annuity (economic) depreciation, and (2) recognize the cost of equity capital in financial reports.[8]

This latest proposal does not, of course, solve the problem, because it assumes a situation in which all relevant cash flows are known. As Zeff pointed out in his discussion of Solomon's 1966 paper, economic depreciation is a "weak reed for the very reason that the problem exists: uncertainty."

The search for a solution to the problem of using accounting data to estimate the economic rate of return has been an important episode in the history of accounting thought. The papers reprinted in this book are the foundation of this intellectual effort, which will, undoubtedly, continue in the future.

NOTES

1. F. M. Fisher and J. J. McGowan, "On the Misuse of Accounting Rates of Return to Infer Monopoly Profits," *American Economic Review* (March 1983), p. 83.

2. Gabriel Hawawini and Ashok Vora, eds., *The History of Interest Approximations* (New York: Arno Press, 1982).

3. F. M. Fisher, "The Misuse of Accounting Rates of Return: Reply," *American Economic Review* (June 1984), p. 510.

4. Letter of June 29, 1985.

5. Preinreich's much earlier work employs related methodology. See Gabriel A. D. Preinreich, "Annual Survey of Economic Theory: The Theory of Depreciation," *Econometrica* (July 1938), pp. 219–241; reprinted in R. P. Brief, ed., *Depreciation and Capital Maintenance* (New York: Garland Publishing, 1984). The model developed by Dorfman also has certain similarities to Stauffer's. See Robert Dorfman, "The Meaning of Internal Rates of Return," *Journal of Finance* (December 1981), pp. 1010–1022.

6. Stark's 1982 article actually appears after Whittington's, which is discussed below.

7. In addition, Stark, in a recent note that is forthcoming in the *Journal of Business Finance & Accounting*, has shown that the observed cash recovery rate, on which the estimate of the economic rate of return depends, is a biased estimate of the "true" cash recovery rate in Salamon's when current assets are factored into the analysis. Andrew W. Stark, "On the Observability of the Cash Recovery Rate."

8. The extensive literature on the subject of economic depreciation is directly related to the problem of using accounting data to estimate the economic rate of return. Many of the papers reprinted in this book or mentioned in this introduction cite these references.

CONTENTS

F. K. Wright, "Accounting Rate of Profit and Internal Rate of Return," *Oxford Economic Papers* (May 1978), pp. 464–468.

J. A. Kay, "Accounting Rate of Profit and Internal Rate of Return; A Reply," *Oxford Economic Papers* (May 1978), pp. 469–470.

Geoffrey Whittington, "On the Use of the Accounting Rate of Return in Empirical Research," *Accounting and Business Research* (Summer 1979), pp. 201–208.

L.C.L. Skerratt and G. Whittington, "On the Use of the Accounting Rate of Return in Empirical Research: A Correction," (Spring 1986).

A.W. Stark, "Estimating the Internal Rate of Return from Accounting Data–A Note," *Oxford Economic Papers* (November 1982), pp. 520–525.

Gerald L. Salamon, "Cash Recovery Rates and Measures of Firm Profitability," *The Accounting Review* (April 1982), pp. 292–302.

K.V. Peasnell, "Some Formal Connections Between Economic Values and Yields and Accounting Numbers," *Journal of Businesss Finance & Accounting* (Autumn 1982), pp. 361–381.

Richard P. Brief, "Limitations of Using the Cash Recovery Rate to Estimate the IRR: A Note," *Journal of Business Finance & Accounting* (Autumn 1985), pp. 473–475.

Journal of Business Finance & Accounting, 18(1), January 1991, 0306-686X $2.50

APPROXIMATE ERROR IN USING ACCOUNTING RATES OF RETURN TO ESTIMATE ECONOMIC RETURNS

RICHARD P. BRIEF AND RAEF A. LAWSON*

Research on the relationship between accounting and economic rates of return has gone down two paths. One group of articles on the subject, e.g., Harcourt (1965), Solomon (1966), Stauffer (1971) and Fisher and McGowan (1983), assumed that the firm invested in a project or mix of projects which was depreciated by a standard method like straight-line or sum-of-years digits. The firm also was assumed either to reinvest a percentage of its cash flows or to grow at a constant rate. After a steady-state is reached, a comparison is made of the accounting rate of return and the economic return. Unless the standard depreciation method happened to be equivalent to economic depreciation, the accounting rates of return would not equal the economic return. Conclusions like 'the accounting rate of return is generally a poor proxy for the DCF rate of return...' (Stauffer, 1971, p. 467) were not uncommon.

Another line of research is based on work by Kay (1976) who showed that if a firm's book values at the beginning and at the end of a multiperiod time horizon were equal to economic values, it would be possible to derive the economic return from the sequence of accounting rates of return. The error in using accounting rates of return to estimate the economic return was discussed by Kay (1978), Wright (1978), Stark (1982), Peasnell (1982) and Steele (1986). The error term was shown to depend on the ratios of book value to economic value at the beginning and end of the time period.

This paper follows the second line of inquiry into the relationship between the accounting rate of return and the economic rate of return. Extending the work of Peasnell (1982) and Steele (1986), the error term is simplified and an approximation of the error is derived. The approximation is then used to simulate the error. The simulations provide some support for the conclusion by Fisher and McGowan (1983, p. 90) that 'There is no way in which one can look at accounting rates of return and infer anything about relative economic profitability.' They also show how the critical variables in the error term, the initial and terminal book value/economic value ratios, affect the magnitude of the error.

*The authors are respectively, Professor of Business Statistics and Accounting, Leonard N. Stern School of Business, New York University; and Visiting Associate Professor of Accounting, State University of New York at Albany. (Paper received August 1988, revised March 1989)

APPROXIMATION OF THE ERROR TERM

Let

P_t = accounting profits in period t
A_t = accounting book value of equity at the end of period t
R_n = liquidating receipt (or economic value of assets) at the end of period n
C_t = cash flows in period t
C_0 = initial cash flow (or economic value of assets) at the beginning of period 1
a_t = accounting rate of return in period t, defined as P_t/A_{t-1}
r = economic rate of return (IRR)
a = average accounting rate of return (*pseudo* IRR)
E = error term.

Based on Peasnell (1982, p. 370), the economic rate of return, r, can be stated as a weighted average of single period accounting rates of return, a, plus an error term, E[1], i.e.,

$$r = a + E, \tag{1}$$

where

$$a = \sum_{t=1}^{n} w_t a_t,$$

$$w_t = \frac{A_{t-1}/(1+a)^t}{\sum_{j=1}^{n} A_{j-1}/(1+a)^j}$$

and

$$E = \frac{(R_n - A_n)/(1+r)^n - (C_0 - A_0)}{\sum_{j=1}^{n} A_{j-1}/(1+r)^j}. \tag{2}$$

Assume that the growth of book value is at a constant rate, g, i.e., $A_t = A_0(1+g)^t$ and let $d = (1+g)/(1+r)$, $q_o = C_0/A_0$ and $q_n = R_n/A_n$. Substituting in equation (2), summing up the geometric progression and simplifying,[2]

$$E = \frac{(1+g)(d-1)}{d(d^n-1)}\,[d^n(q_n-1)-(q_0-1)].$$

Since $d-1 = (g-r)/(1+r)$,

$$E = \frac{(g-r)}{(d^n-1)}\,[d^n(q_n-1)-(q_0-1)]$$

$$= -(r-g)(q_n-1) + \frac{(q_n-q_0)(r-g)}{1-d^n}. \tag{3}$$

Equation (3) decomposes the error term into two parts.[3] The first is due to the valuation error at the end of period n. The second is caused by the difference between the valuation errors at the beginning and at the end of the multi-period time horizon.

An approximation of equation (3) can be obtained in two steps. First, approximate $d = (1+g)/(1+r)$ by dividing $1+r$ into $1+g$ and ignoring higher order terms, i.e.,

$$d \cong 1 + g - r.$$

Second, substitute this result into d^n and approximate $(1+g-r)^n$.

A method to approximate $(1+g-r)^n$ was first derived (implicitly) in a note published in the first volume (1851) of *The Assurance Magazine and The Journal of the Insitute of Actuaries* (p. 333). More than a century later, Ijiri (1972, p. 13) showed that when i is the interest rate,

$$(1+i)^n \cong \frac{2+i(n+1)}{2-i(n-1)}.$$

Letting $i = g-r$ gives

$$d^n \cong \frac{2+(g-r)(n+1)}{2-(g-r)(n-1)}.$$

Substituting back into equation (3) and simplifying yields

$$E \cong -(q_n-1)(r-g)+(q_n-q_0)\left(\frac{1}{n}+\frac{(r-g)(n-1)}{2n}\right). \tag{4}$$

Comparing equation (4) to equation (3) shows that the accuracy of the approximation depends on how the second term in equation (4) relates to the second term in equation (3). As the difference between q_n and q_0 gets smaller, the accuracy increases.

Simulations were done to assess the accuracy of the approximation of E. They show that for values of $r-g<0.15$, the approximation was reasonably accurate. When the difference between $q_n$and q_0 is small, the approximation also is quite accurate, even when $r-g$ is as large as 0.25.

ANALYSIS OF THE APPROXIMATE ERROR

A clearer idea of how changes in these factors affect the error is shown in Tables 1, 2 and 3 which gives values for the approximate error for various values of q_0, q_n, $r-g$ and $n=5$, $n=10$ and $n=20$. The main conclusions are summarized below.

1. In general the error is positive for values of $q_0<q_n$ (above the diagonal) and negative for $q_0>q_n$ (below the diagonal). On the diagonal the error

is positive for small values of q_0 and q_n and negative otherwise. A positive error implies that $r>a$ and a negative error implies that $a>r$.

2. As q_0 increases, the error increases in absolute terms and the variability of the error with respect to variation in $r-g$ increases.
3. As q_n increases, the error increases but the increase is, in absolute terms, less than the increase due to changes in q_0. Variability of the error with respect to variation in $r-g$ is relatively constant.
4. As q_0 goes from 0.5 to 3, the relative effect of the increase in $r-g$ becomes greater. The same is true for q_n.
5. As n increases from 5 to 10, the error decreases about 50 percent for small values of $r-g$ and the reduction in the error is less for large values of $r-g$. Increasing n from 10 to 20 has roughly the same effect.
6. As the difference between q_n and q_0 increases, changes in n reduce the error at an increasing rate.
7. When $q_0 = q_n$, the error is independent of n.
8. The expressions, $q_0 - 1$ and $q_n - 1$, are valuation errors. Accordingly, it is clear that large initial valuation errors have a greater effect on E than equivalent terminal valuation errors.
9. Generally, when $q_0 > 2$, the absolute size of the error is extremely large. This is especially so if $n = 5$. Generalizing on the conditions when the error is small is difficult. When q_0 is in the vicinity of 1, q_n is between 0.5 and 2 and $n = 20$, the size of the error is small. Otherwise, the absolute magnitude of the error depends on $r-g$. For example, when $q_0 = 2$, and $q_n = 3$, the error is 0 when $r-g$ is about 0.025.

CONCLUDING COMMENT

This note has analyzed the error term in the equation, $r = a + E$. A linear approximation of E was obtained in terms of n, q_0, q_n and $r-g$. The approximation shows clearly how each of these variables affects E. For example, if the time period is set at $n = 10$, the error becomes

$$E \cong -(q_n - 1)(r-g) + (q_n - q_0)(0.1 + 0.45(r-g)).$$

This expression is easy to study.

The analysis of the error term has both good news and bad and some implications for future research. First, over short periods of time and without information about q_0, q_n, and $r-g$, the error in using accounting rates of return to estimate economic returns can be enormous. On the other hand, the error decreases over longer time periods and become relatively small when q_0 is close to 1 and q_n is 2 or less. Thus, if a is used to estimate r over a long time period that begins when a firm is first organized when it can be assumed that $A_0 = C_0$, i.e., $q_0 = 1$, E is small.

Second, it is clear that the critical factors in using accounting rates of return

Table 1

Approximate Error as a Function of q_0 and q_n
Evaluated for $r-g=0$, 0.05, 0.10 and 0.15 and $n=5$

	$q_n=0.5$	$q_n=1$	$q_n=2$	$q_n=3$
$q_0=0.5$				
$r-g=0$	0	0.10	0.30	0.50
$r-g=0.05$	0.03	0.11	0.28	0.45
$r-g=0.10$	0.05	0.12	0.26	0.40
$r-g=0.15$	0.08	0.13	0.24	0.35
$q_0=1$				
$r-g=0$	−0.10	0	0.20	0.40
$r-g=0.05$	−0.09	0	0.17	0.34
$r-g=0.10$	−0.07	0	0.14	0.28
$r-g=0.15$	−0.05	0	0.11	0.22
$q_0=2$				
$r-g=0$	−0.30	−0.20	0	0.20
$r-g=0.05$	−0.31	−0.22	−0.05	0.12
$r-g=0.10$	−0.31	−0.24	−0.10	0.04
$r-g=0.15$	−0.32	−0.26	−0.15	−0.04
$q_0=3$				
$r-g=0$	−0.50	−0.40	−0.20	0
$r-g=0.05$	−0.53	−0.44	−0.27	−0.10
$r-g=0.10$	−0.55	−0.48	−0.34	−0.20
$r-g=0.15$	−0.58	−0.52	−0.41	−0.30

Note: numbers are rounded to two decimal places

to estimate the IRR are the ratios, q_0 and q_n.[4] The question that needs to be addressed, therefore, is whether reliable point or interval estimates of these ratios can be obtained for individual firms, portfolios of firms, industries and the economy as a whole.

Another implication concerns the need for a greater understanding of the purely analytical character of the rate of return relationships. For example, Barlev and Levy (1979) found that accounting rates of return were generally higher than market rates of return and they comment that one of the reasons that may explain this phenomenon is that 'accountants use unadjusted equity numbers and historical assets figures in computing accounting returns' (p. 305). But accounting rates of return are higher than market returns when $E<0$ and Tables 1, 2 and 3 show that $E<0$ when $q_0<q_n$, which was the case over the 1959–1974 period, the time period which Barlev and Levy studied. But over other time periods in recent history the reverse is true and $E>0$.

Table 2

Approximate Error as a Function of q_0 and q_n
Evaluated for $r-g=0$, 0.05, 0.10 and 0.15 and $n=10$

	$q_n=0.5$	$q_n=1$	$q_n=2$	$q_n=3$
$q_0=0.5$				
$r-g=0$	0	0.05	0.15	0.25
$r-g=0.05$	0.03	0.06	0.13	0.21
$r-g=0.10$	0.05	0.07	0.12	0.16
$r-g=0.15$	0.08	0.08	0.10	0.12
$q_0=1$				
$r-g=0$	−0.05	0	0.10	0.20
$r-g=0.05$	−0.04	0	0.07	0.15
$r-g=0.10$	−0.02	0	0.05	0.09
$r-g=0.15$	0	0	0.02	0.04
$q_0=2$				
$r-g=0$	−0.15	−0.10	0	0.10
$r-g=0.05$	−0.16	−0.12	−0.05	0.02
$r-g=0.10$	−0.17	−0.15	−0.10	−0.06
$r-g=0.15$	−0.18	−0.17	−0.15	−0.13
$q_0=3$				
$r-g=0$	−0.25	−0.20	−0.10	0
$r-g=0.05$	−0.28	−0.25	−0.17	−0.10
$r-g=0.10$	−0.31	−0.29	−0.25	−0.20
$r-g=0.15$	−0.34	−0.34	−0.32	−0.30

Note: numbers are rounded to two decimal places

The results assume an all inclusive or comprehensive income concept. The specific characteristics of the accounting system needed to derive these rate of return relationships are discussed in more detail by Stark (1982). While accounting policy makers in the United States have not strictly adhered to the comprehensive income concept in *Statement of Financial Accounting Standards Nos. 12, 52 and 87*, there has been renewed attention given to it in *Statement of Financial Accounting Concepts No. 6* (paragraphs 70–77). The importance of the concept of comprehensive income in deriving the relationships between accounting and economic rates of return is a strong argument for its adoption.

Table 3

Approximate Error as a Function of q_0 and q_n
Evaluated for $r-g=0$, 0.05, 0.10 and 0.15 and $n=20$

	$q_n=0.5$	$q_n=1$	$q_n=2$	$q_n=3$
$q_0=0.5$				
$r-g=0$	0	0.03	0.08	0.13
$r-g=0.05$	0.03	0.04	0.06	0.08
$r-g=0.10$	0.05	0.05	0.05	0.04
$r-g=0.15$	0.08	0.06	0.03	0
$q_0=1$				
$r-g=0$	−0.03	0	0.05	0.10
$r-g=0.05$	−0.01	0	0.02	0.05
$r-g=0.10$	0	0	0	0
$r-g=0.15$	−0.01	0	−0.03	−0.06
$q_0=2$				
$r-g=0$	−0.08	−0.05	0	0.05
$r-g=0.05$	−0.09	−0.07	−0.05	−0.03
$r-g=0.10$	−0.10	−0.10	−0.10	−0.10
$r-g=0.15$	−0.11	−0.12	−0.15	−0.18
$q_0=3$				
$r-g=0$	−0.13	−0.10	−0.05	0
$r-g=0.05$	−0.16	−0.15	−0.12	−0.10
$r-g=0.10$	−0.19	−0.20	−0.20	−0.20
$r-g=0.15$	−0.23	−0.24	−0.27	−0.30

Note: numbers are rounded to two decimal places

NOTES

1 a can be derived directly from cash flows and the initial and terminal book value. For this reason, Archer and Peasnell (1982) called a the *pseudo* IRR. If the time series of accounting rates of return is random with no trend, a simple average of accounting rates of return equal a.

2 Note that Steele's equation (4) (1986, p. 6) is based on the identity, $A_n = A_0(1+g)^n$. Assuming a constant growth rate in each period takes the simplification of the error term a step further. The external validity of this assumption can, of course, be tested. However, as an empirical matter, the assumption probably does not introduce a significant bias for reasonably well-behaved data. For example, using a terminal points estimate of the growth rate for Steele's data for the 1968–1980 period, the exact value of E based on Steele's computations is −0.1283. Using the estimate of a constant growth rate and solving equation (3), $E = -0.1244$.

3 Almost all of the special cases of E considered by Peasnell (1982) can be derived with ease from equation (3).

4 The same point is made by Franks and Hodges (1983) who analyze the error term over a single time period.

REFERENCES

Archer, S. and K.V. Peasnell (1982), 'Cumulative Financial Statements: A Comment', unpublished (1982).

Barlev, B. and H. Levy (1979), 'On the Variability of Accounting Income Numbers', *Journal of Accounting Research* (Autumn 1979), pp. 305–315.

Fisher, F.M. (1984), 'The Misuse of Accounting Rates of Return: Reply', *American Economic Review* (June 1984), pp. 509–517.

_____ and J.J. McGowan (1983), 'On the Misuse of Accounting Rates of Return to Infer Monopoly Profits', *American Economic Review* (March 1983), pp. 82–97.

Franks, J.R. and S.D. Hodges (1983), 'The Meaning of Accounting Numbers in Target Setting and Performance Measurement: Implications for Managers and Regulators', unpublished (December 1983).

Harcourt, G.D. (1965), 'The Accountant in the Golden Age', *Oxford Economic Papers* (March 1965), pp. 66–80.

Ijiri, Y. (1972), 'Approximations to Interest Formulas', *Journal of Business* (July 1972), pp. 388–402.

Kay, J.A. (1976), 'Accountants, Too, Could be Happy in a Golden Age: The Accountants Rate of Profit and the Internal Rate of Return', *Oxford Economic Papers* (November 1976), pp. 447–460.

_____ (1978), 'Accounting Rate of Profit and Internal Rate of Return: A Reply', *Oxford Economic Papers* (May 1978), pp. 469–470.

Peasnell, K.V. (1982), 'Some Formal Connections Between Economic Values and Yields and Accounting Numbers', *Journal of Business Finance & Accounting* (Autumn 1982), pp. 361–381.

Solomon, E. (1966), 'Return on Investment: The Relation of Book-Yield to True Yield'; in R.K. Jaedicke, Y. Ijiri and O. Nielsen, eds., *Research in Accounting Measurement* (American Accounting Association, 1966).

Stark, A.W. (1982), 'Estimating the Internal Rate of Return from Accounting Data — A Note', *Oxford Economic Papers* (November 1982), pp. 292–302.

Stauffer, T.R. (1971), 'The Concept of Corporate Rates of Return: A Generalized Formulation', *The Bell Journal of Economics and Management Science* (Autumn 1971), pp. 434–469.

Steele, A. (1986), 'A Note on Estimating the Internal Rate of Return from Published Financial Statements', *Journal of Business Finance & Accounting* (Spring 1986), pp. 1–13.

Wright, F.K. (1978), 'Accounting Rate of Profit and Internal Rate of Return', *Oxford Economic Papers* (May 1978), pp. 464–468.

Journal of Business Finance & Accounting, 18(6), November 1991, 0306-686X $2.50

APPROXIMATE ERROR IN USING ACCOUNTING RATES OF RETURN TO ESTIMATE ECONOMIC RETURNS: A CORRECTION

RICHARD P. BRIEF AND RAEF A. LAWSON*

In Brief and Lawson (1991) there is an error involving one of the assumptions. The error does not, however, lead to basic changes in the analysis or the conclusions.

As before, define P_t as the accounting profits in period t; A_t as accounting book value at the end of period t; R_n as the liquidating receipt (or economic value of assets) at the end of period n; a_t as the accounting rate of return where $a_t = P_t/A_{t-1}$; a as the constant accounting rate of return; r as the internal rate of return; and E as the error term.

Brief and Lawson state that the relationships they derive are based on Peasnell (1982, p. 370–371) who shows that r can be expressed as a weighted average of the accounting rates of return plus an error term. That is,

$$r = \sum_{i=1}^{n} w_t a_t + E, \tag{1}$$

where

$$w_t = \frac{A_{t-1}/(1 + r)^t}{\Sigma_{j=1}^{n} A_{j-1}/(1 + r)^j}, \tag{2}$$

and

$$E = \frac{(R_N - A_N)/(1 + r)^n - (C_0 - A_0)}{\Sigma_{j=1}^{n} A_{j-1}/(1 + R)^j}. \tag{3}$$

These derivations, which assumed that a comprehensive income concept is adhered to, hold for *any* sequence of a_t and A_t, whereas Brief and Lawson actually deal with a special case where all $a_t = a$. Since $\Sigma_{i=1}^{n} w_t = 1$, it might appear that equation (1) can be rewritten as

$$r = a + E.$$

However, a constant rate of return, a, is not associated with *any* sequence of book values, A_t, and profits, P_t. Rather the constant return has the same properties as an internal rate of return and is associated with book values and

*The authors are respectively, Professor of Business Statistics and Accounting and Associate Dean of Academic Affairs, New York University; and Visiting Associate Professor of Accounting, State University of New York at Albany. (Paper received March 1991)

profits that must be imputed. These imputed values are analogous to the concepts of economic value and economic income. If these imputed quantities are designated A_t^* and P_t^*, then the accounting rate of return, a_t, which is P_t^*/A_{t-1}^* also equals a. Thus, when the a_t are replaced by a in equation (1), A_t^* must replace A_t because the error term is expressed in terms of A_t^*, not A_t, for this special case.

When Brief and Lawson (1991) simplified the error term by assuming a constant growth of book value, they were actually assuming that A_t^*(instead of A_t) grows at a constant rate. Since $P_t^* = aA_{t-1}^*$, profit and also must grow at the same rate and cash flows grow at the rate, $a - g$. The assumption that A_t^*grows at a constant rate is, therefore, more restrictive than the assumption that A_t grows at a constant rate.

The change in the assumption may, or may not, affect the estimate of the growth rate of book value, g, and, therefore, the estimate of the error, E. If g is estimated using the terminal points method of estimating growth, i.e.

$$g \approx \sqrt[n]{\frac{A_n}{A_0}} - 1,$$

then the estimate of growth would not change because $A_0 = A_0^*$ and $A_n = A_n^*$. However, if growth is estimated using the method of least squares, then the new assumption would affect the estimate of E.

REFERENCES

Brief, R.P. and R. Lawson (1991), 'Approximate Error in Using Accounting Rates of Return to Estimate Economic Returns, *Journal of Business Finance & Accounting*, Vol. 18, No. 1 (January 1991), pp. 13–20.

Peasnell, K.V. (1982), 'Some Formal Connections between Economic Values and Yields and Accounting Numbers', *Journal of Business Finance & Accounting*, Vol. 9, No. 3 (Autumn 1982), pp. 361–81.

THE ACCOUNTING REVIEW
Vol. 67, No. 2
April 1992
pp. 411–426

The Role of the Accounting Rate of Return in Financial Statement Analysis

Richard P. Brief
New York University
Raef A. Lawson
State University of New York at Albany

SYNOPSIS AND INTRODUCTION: The accounting rate of return (*ARR*) is "not only a central feature of any basic text on financial statement analysis but also figures commonly in the evaluation by investment analysts of the financial performance of firms" (Whittington 1988, 261). Notwithstanding the prominence given to this financial ratio (Foster 1986, 77-79), many writers have warned that the *ARR* lacks economic significance and can be a very misleading measure of profitability. Fisher and McGowan (1983, 90), for example, conclude that "there is no way in which one can look at accounting rates of return and infer anything about relative economic profitability." In the same vein, Rappaport (1986, 31) states flatly that the comparison of the *ARR* with the cost of capital is "clearly like comparing apples with oranges."

The limitations of using *ARR*s to estimate the economic rate of return have been discussed over the last 25 years; for example, Harcourt (1965), Solomon (1966), Kay (1976), Fisher and McGowan (1983), Salamon (1985), Edwards et al. (1987), and Brief and Lawson (1991). This research has focused mainly on the question of whether the *ARR* is a good proxy for the economic return and the literature contains virtually no discussion of other ways in which the *ARR* might be used in financial analysis. An important exception is Peasnell (1982b) who presents a common analytical framework connecting conventional economic concepts of value and yield and accounting models of profit and return. However, even here, the main emphasis is on the relationship between accounting and economic rates of return. This emphasis is quite evident in Peasnell's concluding comment

The authors thank Joshua Livnat, Andrew Stark, and the reviewers for their helpful comments and suggestions.

Submitted January 1991.
Revised September 1991.
Accepted November 1991.

that "it is difficult to assign economic significance to accounting yields except either (1) as surrogate measures of IRR or (2) when they are defined in terms of entry- or exit-market prices" (379–80).

A different slant on the economic significance of *ARR*s is presented here where the focus is on the use of the *ARR* in the valuation process, not in the determination of profitability. The purpose is to show that an expression for an accounting-based measure of discounted cash flows (DCF) can be derived in terms of the *ARR*. Thus, quite apart from the question of whether or not the *ARR* is an accurate estimate of the economic rate of return, this financial ratio has a key role to play in the valuation process.

The results have both analytical and practical significance. On an analytical level, the derivations can be viewed as basic "bookkeeping relationships" that are associated with a double-entry system. On the more practical side, while the DCF techniques currently used in practice "are largely *accounting*-based valuation approaches" (DeAngelo 1990, 100), the use of accounting data in DCF valuations is very indirect. Present practice is to "use historical accounting relationships to forecast future earnings, from which future cash flows are estimated" and, in addition, to estimate terminal values "from projections of future earnings" (p. 100). However, instead of basing DCF valuations on cash flows which are derived from accounting data, a more direct method of analysis is to base the DCF valuations directly on accounting data. Understanding how accounting data can be used in *DCF* analysis leads to a greater appreciation of the general nature of accounting and provides a compelling reason to give the *ARR* a more prominent place in financial statement analysis.

Key Words: *Accounting rate of return, Discounted cash flow analysis, Double-entry bookkeeping, Valuation.*

THE present value of a project (which could be a division of a firm or the firm itself) is the discounted value of free cash flows out to a *valuation horizon*, plus the forecasted value of the project at the horizon, discounted back to present value (Brealey and Myers 1988, 63). The first section of this paper derives a general accounting-based formula for the present value of a project. The second section simplifies the formula in two steps. First, and with no loss of generality, a constant *ARR*, called the *pseudo* internal rate of return (*IRR*), can be substituted for the variable, single-period rates of return. Second, a constant-growth model is assumed. Several other special cases also are derived. The third section considers the use and practical limitations of the DCF formula and deals with questions relating to the calculation of the constant *ARR* as well as the error introduced by the assumption of constant growth. An example illustrating the application of the accounting-based DCF model also is presented.

I. Derivation of Accounting-based DCF Formula

Let V_0 be the present value of the project at the end of period 0, C_t the net cash flows in period t, R_n the residual value of the project, and k the cost of capital.[1] The time horizon is any time segment during the life of the project where $t=0$ is the beginning of period 1 and $t=n$ is the last period in the time slice. If the project is initiated in $t=0$ and terminates in $t=n$, the time segment is the life of the project. The standard definition of V_0 is:

$$V_0=\sum_{t=1}^{n}\frac{C_t}{(1+k)^t}+\frac{R_n}{(1+k)^n}. \tag{1}$$

This section derives the accounting-based equivalent of V_0.

Define I_t as accounting income in period t and A_t as accounting book value at the end of period t and assume that accounting income is based on a comprehensive income concept. Also, define the ARR in period t, a_t, as:

$$a_t=I_t/A_{t-1}.$$

From the accounting identity:

$$I_t=C_t+(A_t-A_{t-1}),$$

it immediately follows that:

$$C_t=(1+a_t)A_{t-1}-A_t.$$

The accounting-based equivalent of:

$$\sum_{t=1}^{n}\frac{C_t}{(1+k)^t}$$

is derived by replacing C_t with $(1+a_t)A_{t-1}-A_t$. This substitution links traditional DCF analysis with accounting information. Thus:

$$\sum_{t=1}^{n}\frac{C_t}{(1+k)^t}=\sum_{t=1}^{n}\frac{(1+a_t)A_{t-1}}{(1+k)^t}-\sum_{t=1}^{n}\frac{A_t}{(1+k)^t}.$$

Since:

$$\sum_{t=1}^{n}\frac{A_t}{(1+k)^t}=(1+k)\sum_{t=0}^{n-1}\frac{A_t}{(1+k)^{t+1}}+\frac{A_n}{(1+k)^n}-A_0,$$

$$\sum_{t=1}^{n}\frac{C_t}{(1+k)^t}=\sum_{t=1}^{n}\frac{(1+a_t)A_{t-1}}{(1+k)^t}-(1+k)\sum_{t=0}^{n-1}\frac{A_t}{(1+k)^{t+1}}-\frac{A_n}{(1+k)^n}+A_0.$$

[1] A number of issues are sidestepped in this presentation. First, cash flows can be interpreted from different viewpoints, e.g., from the viewpoint of equity interests or all suppliers of capital, but these different meanings of cash flows are not discussed. Second, we do not dwell on the difficulties of defining R_n which can be thought of as "economic value" at the end of the valuation horizon. In finance textbooks, R_n is sometimes referred to as the "horizon" value at the end of period n (Brealey and Myers 1988, 64). Finally, we make the standard assumption that the cost of capital is constant. The analysis would hold for a variable cost of capital but the results would be more complex.

Equivalently:

$$\sum_{t=1}^{n}\frac{C_t}{(1+k)^t}=\sum_{t=1}^{n}\frac{(a_t-k)A_{t-1}}{(1+k)^t}-\frac{A_n}{(1+k)^n}+A_0. \tag{2}$$

Substituting back into equation (1):

$$V_0=A_0+\sum_{t=1}^{n}\frac{(a_t-k)A_{t-1}}{(1+k)^t}+\frac{R_n-A_n}{(1+k)^n}. \tag{3}$$

Equations (2) and (3) are accounting-based valuation models. These equations reflect basic bookkeeping relationships which assume only that the accounting procedures are based on a comprehensive income concept, i.e., clean surplus. Equation (3) shows that the present value of a project is the sum of: (1) initial book value, (2) present discounted value of the project's residual income in period t, $(a_t-k)A_{t-1}$, and (3) the present discounted value of the difference between the terminal economic value of the project and the terminal book value.

Equation (3) is almost identical to *Theorem 1* in Peasnell (1982b, 364) which can be derived by subtracting C_0, the initial cash outflow (when $t=0$ begins the life of the project) or "economic value" (when $t=0$ is an interim period in the life of the project), from both sides of equation (3). Equation (4) in Peasnell (1981, 52) can be derived from equation (3) by assuming that $A_0=C_0$ and $A_n=R_n$. Ohlson (1988, 33), who uses a general equilibrium framework, shows that the equity price of the firm is the sum of its book value plus discounted expected abnormal earnings. Ohlson points out (p. 31) that abnormal earnings can be viewed as residual income; therefore, his derivation can be viewed as a special case of equation (3) when $n=\infty$. Preinreich (1938, 240) derived the same result in continuous time and assumed $A_n=R_n$.

II. Simplification With Constant *ARR* and Constant Growth

Equations (2) and (3) can be simplified if the single-period *ARR*s are constant and a constant-growth rate is assumed. Further simplification is possible for other special cases.

Constant ARR

Several writers who have been concerned with the use of accounting data in the valuation process, e.g., Preinreich (1932, 1937), Fruhan (1979), Wilcox (1984), and Leibowitz and Kogelman (1990), have developed accounting-based DCF models by assuming a constant *ARR*. None of this work discusses the nature of this constant and how to compute it. The general properties of a constant *ARR* are discussed here and the final section of the paper deals with questions relating to its computation.

If a sequence of *ARR*s is constant, the constant must be equal to the value of a that solves:

$$A_0=\frac{C_1}{(1+a)}+\frac{C_2}{(1+a)^2}+\ldots+\frac{C_n}{(1+a)^n}+\frac{A_n}{(1+a)^n}. \tag{4}$$

The proof that a constant accounting rate of return must take the same form as the internal rate of return (*IRR*) is given by Kay (1976, 449).[2] Note that when A_0 equals C_0

[2] Throughout this analysis, it is assumed that a is unique. Since the terminal values (R_n) "typically constitute the majority of DCF-generated values" (DeAngelo 1990, 100), the terminal book value (A_n) would, in

(the initial cash outflow or "economic value") and A_n equals R_n (the *horizon* value), a is the same as the *IRR*, r. Unlike some other work related to *ARR*s that is concerned with issues related to profitability analysis, e.g., Edwards et al. (1987, 50–68), the analysis here does not assume that beginning and ending book values also are equal to economic values.

In an unpublished paper, Archer and Peasnell (1982, 2) questioned the significance of a except as a proxy for the *IRR*.[3]

> We cannot see how to assign conceptual significance to an internal rate of return derived from accounting data except as an attempt to operationalise economic IRR. It seems to us that the rate of return concept *per se* is meaningful only in relation to ventures and time periods such that the calculation of the rate of return is based upon a well-determined entry price and final exit price (either of which may be zero), not upon accountants' "pseudo-prices."...

Again, like other researchers in this area, Archer and Peasnell are concerned primarily with the use of the *ARR* to estimate the economic rate of return.

Even though a is based on *pseudo* prices and, therefore, might be described as a *pseudo IRR*, this performance measure has two important properties. First, if a sequence of *ARR*s is constant, the constant must be equal to a, i.e., all $a_t = a$. In other words, whenever an *ARR* is constant, or is assumed to be constant, over any time segment, the *ARR* must be equal to a, as defined in equation (4). This property of a constant *ARR* has not been discussed in the literature that assumes a constant *ARR*.

Second, the quantities, I_t and A_t, are reported in actual or *pro forma* financial statements. In contrast to these reported values, a series of I_t^* and A_t^* can be imputed so that the ratio of I_t^* to A_{t-1}^* is constant and equal to:

$$a = I_t^* / A_{t-1}^*.$$

where I_t^* and A_t^* are similar to the concepts of economic income and economic value, respectively, and these concepts have a long history in accounting.[4] They are most often discussed in connection with the theory of economic income and depreciation where a reference to Hicks (1939) usually can be found. It is shown here that these concepts have a more practical application in financial analysis.

Since any sequence of A_t, I_t, and a_t can be redefined as A_t^*, I_t^*, and a, equation (2) can be rewritten, without loss of generality, as:

$$\sum_{t=1}^{n} \frac{C_t}{(1+k)^t} = (a-k)\sum_{t=1}^{n} \frac{A_{t-1}^*}{(1+k)^t} - \frac{A_n}{(1+k)^n} + A_0. \tag{5}$$

Thus, V_0 becomes:

$$V_0 = A_0 + (a-k)\sum_{t=1}^{n} \frac{A_{t-1}^*}{(1+k)^t} + \frac{R_n - A_n}{(1+k)^n}. \tag{6}$$

Equation (6) is a simplification of equation (3) when the *ARR* is constant.

---

cases where equity valuation was concerned, generally be large enough to insure the uniqueness of a. This conjecture assumes that in cases where cash flows were negative, A_n and R_n would have the same order of magnitude and, therefore, dominate in the caculation of a. For a discussion of issues related to the uniqueness of an internal rate of return, see Teichroew et al. (1965).

[3] The paper is an unpublished comment on Brief et al. (1980).

[4] Note that $A_0 = A_0^*$ and $A_n = A_n^*$.

Further Simplification Based on Constant Growth

Equations (5) and (6) can be simplified by defining g as the growth rate per period of book value from $t=0$ to $t=n$, i.e.,

$$g=\sqrt[n]{\frac{A_n}{A_0}}-1.$$

Therefore:

$$A_n=A_0(1+g)^n$$

is an identity and present discounted cash flows can be rewritten as:

$$\sum_{t=1}^{n}\frac{C_t}{(1+k)^t}=(a-k)\sum_{t=1}^{n}\frac{A_{t-1}^*}{(1+k)^t}+A_0(1-d^n), \tag{7}$$

where:

$$d=\frac{1+g}{1+k}.$$

A further simplification is made possible by assuming that g is also the growth rate of book value in *each* period over the valuation horizon so that:

$$A_t^*=A_0(1+g)^t,$$

for $t=1,2,\ldots,n-1$. In effect, assuming that the A_{t-1}^* grow at a constant rate, g, is equivalent to assuming that income grows at the rate, g, and that cash flows grow at the rate, g. This means the underlying model is in effect, identical to the constant-growth dividend model except that it is expressed in terms of the initial book value, not price.[5]

Substituting $A_0(1+g)^t$ for A_t^*, summing the geometric progression and assuming that $k\neq g$:

$$\sum_{t=1}^{n}\frac{A_{t-1}^*}{(1+k)^t}=\sum_{t=1}^{n}\frac{A_0(1+g)^{t-1}}{(1+k)^t}=A_0\left(\frac{1-d^n}{k-g}\right).$$

Then replacing:

$$\sum_{t=1}^{n}\frac{A_{t-1}^*}{(1+k)^t},$$

by:

$$A_0\left(\frac{1-d^n}{k-g}\right),$$

equation (7) becomes:

$$\sum_{t=1}^{n}\frac{C_t}{(1+k)^t}=A_0\frac{a-k}{k-g}(1-d^n)+A_0(1-d^n). \tag{8}$$

[5] Even when the assumption of constant growth is violated, the next section shows that for reasonably "well-behaved" data, the estimate of V_0 based on the constant growth assumption seems to be quite accurate.

Equivalently,

$$\sum_{t=1}^{n} \frac{C_t}{(1+k)^t} = A_0 \frac{a-g}{k-g}(1-d^n), \tag{9}$$

and, adding:

$$\frac{R_n}{(1+k)^n},$$

to equation (9), V_0 becomes:

$$V_0 = A_0 \frac{a-g}{k-g}(1-d^n) + \frac{R_n}{(1+k)^n}. \tag{10}$$

Adding:

$$\frac{R_n}{(1+k)^n},$$

to equation (8), V_0 can be written as:

$$V_0 = A_0 + A_0 \frac{a-k}{k-g}(1-d^n) + \frac{R_n - A_n}{(1+k)^n}. \tag{11}$$

Other Simplifications

The use and limitations of equations (10) and (11) are discussed in the next section. Before dealing with these issues, some other special cases are noted. Some of these special cases have appeared in accounting, economics, and finance literature. One of these was derived almost 60 years ago by Preinreich (1932, 276) in an article in *The Accounting Review.*

$n \to \infty$ and $g < k$. When $n \to \infty$ and $g < k$, it immediately follows from equation (10) that:

$$V_0 = A_0 \frac{a-g}{k-g}. \tag{12}$$

Since $C_1 = A_0(a-g)$, it can be seen that equation (12) is similar to a constant-growth dividend model expressed in terms of accounting quantities.

When V_0 is defined as P_0, the price of a security, and E_1 is earnings in period 1, equation (12) can be redefined in terms of the price/earnings ratio. Since $E_1 = aA_0$:

$$\frac{P_0}{E_1} = \frac{1-g/a}{k-g}. \tag{13}$$

Defining q as the retention rate, g can be written as qa and:

$$\frac{P_0}{E_1} = \frac{1-q}{k-qa}. \tag{14}$$

Equation (14) appeared in Leibowitz and Kogelman (1990, 33).

$R_n/A_n = V_0/A_0$. By implication, $R_n = V_0(1+g)^n$. Substituting $V_0(1+g)^n$ for R_n in equation (10):

$$V_0 = A_0 \frac{a-g}{k-g}. \tag{15}$$

Equation (15) is the same as equation (12). A similar result also was obtained by Kay (1976, 455–56) who assumed a steady state situation with $k=r$.

$A_n = R_n$. Substituting $A_0(1+g)^n$ for R_n in equation (10) and dividing by A_0:

$$\frac{V_0}{A_0} = \frac{a-g}{k-g}(1-d^n)+d^n. \tag{16}$$

Equation (16) was derived by Preinreich (1932, 276) in a slightly different form. Similarly, substituting $A_0(1+g)^n$ for R_n in equation (11) and dividing by A_0:

$$\frac{V_0}{A_0} = \frac{a-k}{k-g}(1-d^n)+1. \tag{17}$$

Equation (17) appeared in Preinreich (1937, 135).

More recently, the expression:

$$\frac{V_0 - A_0}{A_0} = \frac{a-k}{k-g}(1-d^n), \tag{18}$$

appeared in Fruhan (1979) and Wilcox (1984) who were concerned with issues related to the determination of "shareholder value." Equation (18) can be derived from equation (17) by subtracting 1 from both sides of the equation. Fruhan and Wilcox did not consider the more general case when A_n does not equal R_n.

$k=r$. If the cost of capital, k, equals the *IRR*, r, $V_0 = C_0$. Then, from equation (11):

$$\frac{C_0 - A_0}{A_0} = \frac{(a-r)}{r-g}(1-d^n)+d^n \frac{R_n - A_n}{A_n}. \tag{19}$$

Solving for r:

$$r = a-(r-g)\left(\frac{C_0 - A_0}{A_0}\right) + \frac{(r-g)\left(\frac{R_n}{A_n} - \frac{C_0}{A_0}\right)}{1-d^n}. \tag{20}$$

The second and third terms on the right-hand side of equation (20) can be viewed as the error in using the *ARR* to estimate the internal rate of return. The error depends on the economic/book value ratios at the beginning and at the end of the time horizon. This expression was derived and analyzed in Brief and Lawson (1991a, 1991b).

Other Special Cases. When $a=k$, equation (11) becomes:

$$V_0 = A_0 + \frac{R_n - A_n}{(1+k)^n}.$$

In this case, the present value equals the initial book value plus an adjustment whose magnitude depends on the extent to which the terminal economic value and accounting book value differ.

When $a=g$, equation (10) can be written as:

$$V_0=\frac{R_n}{(1+k)^n}.$$

When earnings are entirely reinvested, there are no periodic cash flows and the present value of the project depends only on its residual value.

When $k=g$, equations (10) and (11) are not defined. However, $A_0(1+g)^t$ can be substituted for A_t^* in equation (5) which then becomes:

$$\sum_{t=1}^{n}\frac{C_t}{(1+k)^n}=A_0\frac{n(a-k)}{(1+k)}=A_0\frac{n(a-g)}{(1+k)},$$

and

$$V_0=A_0\frac{n(a-g)}{(1+k)}+\frac{R_n}{(1+k)^n}.$$

III. Use and Limitations of Equations (10) and (11) in Financial Analysis

There are two major issues concerning the use of equations (10) and (11) in financial analysis. First, if the single-period *ARR*s are not constant, how can a be computed? Second, suppose the growth of book value is not constant. How much error is introduced by assuming constant growth?

Calculation of a

One might argue that the use of equations (10) and (11) to estimate V_0 is, from a practical viewpoint, not really more direct than using the cash-based DCF model. This is because the calculation of a from equation (4) is based on cash flows. Therefore, if cash flows must be known to calculate a, using equation (1) to estimate V_0 would actually be more direct than using equations (10) and (11).[6] Thus, if equation (4) has to be used to determine a, the argument that the accounting-based valuation method is circular would have merit. However, a can be estimated directly from the sequence of single-period *ARR*s.

Insight into the nature of estimates of a from a sequence of *ARR*s can be obtained from the relationship between a and a weighted average of single-period *ARR*s. This relationship was first derived by Kay (1976, 452–53) and then elaborated on by Edwards et al. (1987, 37). Assuming the comprehensive income concept is employed, a can be defined for any time segment in the life of a project as the weighted average of actual single-period rates of return, a_t.[7] The definition of the constant, a, in equation (4) is the algebraic equivalent of the value of a that solves:

$$a=\sum_{t=1}^{n}w_t a_t, \tag{21}$$

[6] If the comprehensive income concept is employed, cash flows can, of course, be determined directly from accounting income, I_t, and book value, A_t, since by definition, $C_t=I_t-(A_t-A_{t-1})$.

[7] In their discussion, Edwards et al. were concerned with using a to estimate the *IRR* in both multi-period and single-period situations. Consequently, much of their discussion was devoted to issues related to how A_0 and A_n should be revalued so that the resulting rate of return had economic significance.

where the weights, w_t, are:

$$w_t = \frac{\dfrac{A_{t-1}}{(1+a)^t}}{\displaystyle\sum_{j=1}^{n} \frac{A_{j-1}}{(1+a)^j}},$$

and

$$\sum_{t=1}^{n} w_t = 1.$$

Thus, given A_t and a_t, a can be determined by solving equation (21) for a; but using this method also is equivalent to using equation (4) to calculate a. Therefore, once again, there seems to be circularity in the argument. However, the definition of a as a weighted average *ARR* is important because it provides insight into the nature of the bias in using more direct ways to transform a sequence of *ARR*s into an estimate of a.

Peasnell (1982a, 29) comments that "knowledge of the general weight function . . . is often informative" since, normally, there are restrictions on the w_t.[8] Under most circumstances, the book values, A_t, are positive. Therefore, since the weights sum to 1 and must be between 0 and 1, the analyst knows that in any sequence of accounting returns, the minimum and maximum values of a_t define the range of values that a might take.

Furthermore, when the *ARR*s are random with no time trend, a simple average of the *ARR*s will in expectation be equal to a. If the time trend of *ARR*s is positive, the simple average will overstate a if $g>a$ and understate a if $g<a$. If the time trend is negative, the opposite relationships will hold.[9]

The examples in table 1 show the relationship between a simple arithmetic average of the single-period *ARR*s and the *pseudo IRR* for different assumptions about the time series of a_t. All of the cases assume the same cash flows and opening and closing book values. Therefore, the *pseudo IRR* is the same in all cases and $a=0.12$. In the first case, which is taken directly from the example in Brealey and Myers (1988, 63), the *ARR* in each period equals 0.12. Case 2 illustrates "random" *ARR*s, varying from 0.09 to 0.15. The mean is 0.121 which is very close to a. In the next two cases the *ARR*s are upward and downward sloping time series with means of 0.117 and 0.125. Again, the means are close to a. Only in the last case, which displays a very unstable sequence of *ARR*s, is there a big difference between the arithmetic mean of the sequence of the a_t and the *pseudo IRR*.

These examples suggest that when the time series of a_t is reasonably stable, the bias in estimates of a based on a simple arithmetic mean of *ARR*s will not be large.[10] In practice, when dealing with the valuation of large units like a division of a firm or the

[8] Peasnell's concern here, as indicated earlier, was to estimate the *IRR*, not a, although much of his analysis is applicable to the questions being considered here.

[9] In Kay's (1976, 454) discussion of the relationship between the simple average and a over the life of a firm, he implicitly assumed that $g<a$ which is, of course, quite reasonable; however, over a limited time segment, g might be greater or less than a.

[10] Obviously, the bias in estimates of a using a simple average needs to be studied in more detail. The examples here are only suggestive of the amount of bias that might be expected.

Table 1
Effect of *ARR* Variability on Average *ARR*
(a=0.12)
(millions of dollars)

Year	*0*	1	2	3	4	5	6
Cash Flows		−0.80	−0.96	−1.15	−1.39	−0.20	−0.23
Book Value	10.00	—	—	—	—	—	26.47
Case 1: Constant ARRs			Average *ARR*=0.120				
ARR		0.120	0.120	0.120	0.120	0.120	0.120
Income		1.20	1.44	1.73	2.07	2.49	2.89
Book Value	10.00	12.00	14.40	17.28	20.74	23.43	26.47
Case 2: "Random" ARRs			Average *ARR*=0.121				
ARR		0.140	0.100	0.150	0.110	0.090	0.135
Income		1.40	1.22	2.16	1.95	1.89	3.12
Book Value	10.00	12.20	14.38	17.69	21.02	23.11	26.47
Case 3: Increasing ARRs			Average *ARR*=0.117				
ARR		0.070	0.080	0.100	0.130	0.140	0.181
Income		0.70	0.92	1.34	2.06	2.70	4.01
Book Value	10.00	11.50	13.38	15.87	19.32	22.23	26.47
Case 4: Decreasing ARRs			Average *ARR*=0.125				
ARR		0.200	0.165	0.130	0.100	0.085	0.072
Income		2.00	2.11	2.06	1.91	1.90	.175
Book Value	10.00	12.80	15.87	19.09	22.38	24.49	26.47
Case 5: Unstable ARRs			Average *ARR*=0.196				
ARR		1.174	0	0	0	0	0
Income		11.74	0	0	0	0	0
Book Value	10.00	22.54	23.50	24.65	26.04	26.24	26.47

The data on cash flows and opening and closing book values, and the data in case 1, are taken from Brealey and Myers (1988, 63).

firm itself over a short time horizon, the *ARR* would be expected to be reasonably stable. Indeed, if the *ARR*s displayed a great deal of instability, it would be doubtful if the analyst would, either directly or indirectly, base DCF analysis on such data.

Error in Assuming Constant Growth of Book Value

Another estimation error is introduced by assuming that book value grows at a constant rate. The error in assuming that $A_t^* = A_0(1+g)^t$ can be evaluated as follows. Define:

$$S = \sum_{t=1}^{n} \frac{A_{t-1}^*}{(1+k)^t},$$

and

$$s = A_0 \frac{(1-d^n)}{(k-g)},$$

where S is the exact value and *s* is the approximate value of:

$$\sum_{t=1}^{n} \frac{A^*_{t-1}}{(1+k)^t}.$$

Further, let:

$$x = \frac{s}{S}.$$

Thus, equation (5), which is the *exact* value of:

$$\sum_{t=1}^{n} \frac{C_t}{(1+k)^t},$$

can be written as:

$$EXACT = S(a-k) + xS(k-g),$$

and equation (8), which is the *approximate* value of:

$$\sum_{t=1}^{n} \frac{C_t}{(1+k)^t},$$

can be written as:

$$APPROXIMATE = xS(a-k) + xS(k-g).$$

Therefore,

$$\frac{APPROXIMATE}{EXACT} = \frac{x(a-k) + x(k-g)}{(a-k) + x(k-g)}.$$

If we now assume that $a \neq k$ and $k \neq g$ and let:

$$k - g = y(a-k),$$

then the accuracy of the approximation is:

$$\frac{APPROXIMATE}{EXACT} = \frac{x + xy}{1 + xy}. \tag{22}$$

In preliminary work, it was apparent that even if the A^*_t display substantial variability about a trend line of constant growth, the accuracy of the approximation will, nevertheless, be quite high. For example, if $n=10$, $A_0=10$, and $A_n=20$, the growth rate, g, will be equal to 0.0718. Let:

$$A^*_t = 10(1.0718)^t + e_t,$$

where $e_t = -8$ in periods $t=1$, 2, 5, 6, and 9 and $+8$ in periods $t=3$, 4, 7, and 8. If

Table 2
Accuracy of Approximation of Present Value of Cash Flows
(x=1.0911)

xy	$\frac{x+xy}{1+xy}$	xy	$\frac{x+xy}{1+xy}$
5	1.02	−5	.98
4	1.02	−4	.97
3	1.02	−3	.95
2	1.03	−2	.91
1.5	1.04	−1.5	.82
1	1.05	−1	Not Defined
.5	1.06	−.5	1.18
.2	1.08	−.2	1.11
.1	1.08	−.1	1.10
.05	1.09	−.05	1.10
.01	1.09	−.01	1.09

$\frac{x+xy}{1+xy}$ = ratio of approximation of the present discounted value of cash flows to the exact value of the present discounted values of cash flows.

$k=0.10$, then $S=74.3275$, and $s=81.0987$, and

$$x=\frac{81.0987}{74.3275}=1.0911.$$

Table 2 shows the accuracy of the approximation of the present discounted value of cash flows when $x=1.0911$, calculated from equation (22) for various values of xy. The error in the approximation is under 10 percent except for negative values of xy in the region between about $xy=-2$ and $xy=-0.1$. It should be borne in mind that since x is positive, xy is negative only when y is negative and this will occur when $g>k$ or $k>a$. Neither of these conditions is likely to occur with great frequency. Therefore, in most "normal" situations, y and xy are positive and x can be viewed as a lower bound on the accuracy of the approximation.

Example

The data on cash flows and opening and closing book values, and the data in case 1, in table 1 are taken from Brealey and Myers (1988, 63). The accounting rate of return in this example is constant and, therefore, equal to the *pseudo IRR*. Brealey and Myers calculate present value by computing the present value of free cash flows for years 1 to 6 and then add to this amount the present discounted value of the horizon value which is the present value of the stream of cash flows after year 6. In the example, free cash flow in period 7 equals 1.59 and is assumed to grow indefinitely at 6 percent per period. Also, the cost of capital is assumed to be $k=0.10$. The net present value of 18.8 million dollars is obtained using equation (1) by calculating:

$$\sum_{t=1}^{n}\frac{C_t}{(1+k)^t}=\frac{-0.80}{1.1}+\frac{-0.96}{(1.1)^2}+\frac{-1.15}{(1.1)^3}+\frac{-1.39}{(1.1)^4}+\frac{-0.20}{(1.1)^5}+\frac{-0.23}{(1.1)^6}=-3.6,$$

and

$$\frac{R_n}{(1+k)^n}=\frac{1}{(1.1)^6}\frac{1.59}{0.10-0.06}=22.4.$$

Therefore,

$$V_0=-3.6+22.4=18.8.$$

An approximation of the present discounted value of cash flows from periods 1 to 6 can be obtained directly from the accounting data by substituting $k=0.10$, $a=0.12$, $A_0=10$, and

$$g=\sqrt[6]{\frac{A_n}{A_0}}-1=\sqrt[6]{\frac{26.47}{10}}-1=0.176$$

into equation (10). Thus,

$$\sum_{t=1}^{n}\frac{C_t}{(1+k)^t}=10\frac{(0.12-0.176)}{(0.10-0.176)}\left[1-\left(\frac{1.176}{1.10}\right)^6\right],$$

which gives:

$$\sum_{t=1}^{n}\frac{C_t}{(1+k)^t}=-3.6.$$

Since the example assumes that after period 6, $g=0.06$, and an infinite time horizon is assumed, terminal value can be calculated in the same way that the present discounted value of cash flows is calculated, i.e.,

$$\frac{R_n}{(1+k)^n}=\frac{26.47}{(1.10)^6}\frac{(0.12-0.06)}{(0.10-0.06)}=\frac{39.71}{(1.10)^6}=22.4.$$

The accounting-based method to calculate V_0 yields the same results as the method based on cash flows.

IV. Conclusion

Research on *ARR*s has more than a 25-year history and most of it has focused on the limitations of using the *ARR* to make inferences about a firm's profitability. In this paper, the focus is on valuation, not profitability, and a general accounting-based DCF formula that assumes only that accounting policies are based on the comprehensive income concept is derived. The extant accounting system is taken as given and the main concern of this paper is on how to value a project over a limited time slice using accounting data.

Without loss of generality, the model is simplified by replacing the variable, single-period *ARR*s with a constant. Then a constant-growth assumption is made and several other special cases are also discussed.

The results can be viewed as basic relationships that are derived from a double-entry system. Students of accounting should be more familiar with these analytical properties. On a more practical side, financial analysts can base DCF valuations on accounting data instead of following the current practice of using historical accounting data to forecast future earnings and then to estimate cash flows from earnings. The analysis does not resolve all of the relevant issues—clearly, more work needs to be done in assessing the biases inherent in the estimation procedures suggested—but it does suggest that the *ARR* has a new role to play.

The *pseudo IRR* has a straightforward interpretation and useful properties. In previous work, the *pseudo IRR* has been discussed as a proxy for the *IRR*. In this paper, it is discussed as a parameter that enters into the valuation process. This parameter depends only on opening and closing book values and cash flows, not on accounting numbers in interim periods.

This has implications for conventional accounting theory which is, in effect, based on a one-period model. Conventional theory does not address questions about multi-period analysis where the determination of assets and liabilities at the beginning and at the end of the multi-period time horizon appears to be the overriding accounting issue.[11] Thus, when two or more periods are analyzed, only the cash flow series and the change in book value (which sum up to total income over the time horizon) are relevant, not the separate amounts of income reported in the individual periods. If cash flows and the change of book value are specified over any time segment, there are infinitely many *ARR* sequences consistent with that specification whereas there is only one value of the *pseudo IRR*.[12]

While accountants and financial analysts often talk about how accounting data are used in the decision making process, such discussions are characterized by generalities rather than specifics. Even though the DCF techniques used to value equity investments are often accounting-based valuation approaches, the link between accounting numbers and the calculation of present value is, in practice, indirect. Understanding how DCF analysis can be based directly on accounting data leads to a greater appreciation of the general nature of accounting and also provides a compelling reason to give the *pseudo IRR* a more prominent place in financial statement analysis.

[11] From this viewpoint, revenue and expense determination in the interim periods are relevant only insofar as revenues and expenses affect beginning and ending book values. Edwards et al. (1987, 32) make a similar point when they comment that "... focusing attention on the opening and closing valuations of capital employed ... serves to emphasize the issue that lies at the heart of the debate on the relevance of accounting profitability."

[12] See footnote 2.

References

Archer, S., and K. V. Peasnell. 1982. Cumulative financial statements. Unpublished paper. University of Lancaster. United Kingdom.

Brealey, R. A., and S. C. Myers. 1988. *Principles of Corporate Finance*. 3d ed. New York: McGraw-Hill.

Brief, R. P., and R. A. Lawson. 1991a. Approximate error in using accounting rates of return to estimate economic returns. *Journal of Business Finance & Accounting* 18 (January): 13–20.

——, and ——. 1991b. Approximate error in using accounting rates of return to estimate economic returns: A correction. *Journal of Business Finance & Accounting* 18 (November): 915–16.

——, B. D. Merino, and I. Weiss. 1980. Cumulative financial statements. *The Accounting Review* 55 (July): 480–90.

DeAngelo, L. E. 1990. Equity valuation and corporate control. *The Accounting Review* 65 (January): 93–112.

Edwards, J., J. Kay, and C. Mayer. 1987. *The Economic Analysis of Accounting Profitability*. Oxford, United Kingdom: Clarendon Press.

Fisher, F., and J. J. McGowan. 1983. On the misuse of accounting rates of return to infer monopoly profits. *American Economic Review* 73 (March): 82–97.

Foster, G. 1986. *Financial Statement Analysis*. 2d ed. Englewood Cliffs, NJ: Prentice-Hall.

Fruhan, W. E., Jr. 1979. *Financial Strategy*. Homewood, IL: Richard D. Irwin.

Harcourt, G. C. 1965. The accountant in a golden age. *Oxford Economic Papers* 5 (March): 66–80.

Hicks, J. R. 1939. *Value and Capital*. Oxford, United Kingdom: Clarendon Press.

Kay, J. A. 1976. Accountants, too, could be happy in the golden age: The accountants rate of profit and the internal rate of return. *Oxford Economic Papers* 17 (November): 66–80.

Leibowitz, M. L., and S. Kogelman. 1990. Inside the P/E ratio: The franchise factor. *Financial Analysts Journal* 46 (November/December): 17–35.

Ohlson, J. A. 1988. Accounting earnings, book value, and dividends: The theory of the clean surplus equation (part I). Unpublished manuscript. New York: Columbia University.

Peasnell, K. V. 1981. On capital budgeting and income measurement. *Abacus* 17 (June): 52–67.

——. 1982a. Estimating the internal rate of return from accounting profit rates. *The Investment Analyst* (April): 26–31.

——. 1982b. Some formal connections between economic values and yields and accounting numbers. *Journal of Business Finance & Accounting* 9 (Autumn): 361–81.

Preinreich, G. A. D. 1932. Stock yields, stock dividends and inflation. *The Accounting Review* 7 (December): 271–89.

——. 1937. Fair value and yield of common stock. *The Accounting Review* 12 (June): 130–40.

——. 1938. Annual survey of economic theory: The theory of depreciation. *Econometrica* 6 (July): 219–41.

Rappaport, A. 1986. *Creating Shareholder Value: The New Standard for Business Performance*. New York: The Free Press.

Salamon, G. L. 1985. Accounting rates of return. *American Economic Review* 75 (June): 495–504.

Solomon, E. 1966. Return on investment: The relationship of book-yield to true yield. In *Research in Accounting Measurement*, edited by R. K. Jaedicke, Y. Ijiri, and O. Nielsen. American Accounting Association.

Teichroew, D. A., A. A. Robichek, and M. Montalbano. 1965. An analysis of criteria for investing and financing decisions under certainty. *Management Science* 12 (November): 151–80.

Whittington, G. 1988. The usefulness of accounting data in measuring the economic performance of firms. *Journal of Accounting and Public Policy* 7 (Winter): 261–66.

Wilcox, J. W. 1984. The P/B-ROE valuation model. *Financial Analysts Journal* 40 (January–February): 58–66.

Accounting Error

from

Journal of Accounting Research

(Spring 1965)

Nineteenth Century Accounting Error*

RICHARD P. BRIEF†

I

Only fleeting attention has been given to the possibility of persistent error or bias in the calculations on which investment, output, and/or pricing decisions were based in the nineteenth century. This is an indirect tribute to the influence of Max Weber and other "rationalists" who stressed the concept of a rational capitalistic establishment that employs capital accounting, "that is, an establishment which determines its income yielding power by calculation according to methods of modern bookkeeping and the striking of a balance."[1] Schumpeter's views are even more exalting.

> ...capitalistic practice turns the unit of money into a tool of rational cost-profit calculations, of which the towering monument is double-entry bookkeeping.... primarily a product of the evolution of economic rationality, the cost-profit calculus in turn reacts upon that rationality.... subjugating-rationalizing-man's tools and philosophies....[2]

It is rather startling, therefore, to find that the subject of accounting did not require specific analysis, for neither Weber nor Schumpeter concerned themselves with this topic; indeed, economists rarely mentioned the subject. As late as 1924, Hatfield commented that "the contempt for accounting is not limited to university circles but is well-nigh universal. It is evidenced by ignorance of the subject, condescension towards

* This paper is based on my unpublished dissertation, "Nineteenth Century Capital Accounting and Business Investment" (1964). I am indebted to New York University for a research grant that permitted me to write this paper under conditions less distracting than the usual.

† Assistant Professor of Business Statistics, New York University.

[1] Max Weber, *General Economic History* (New York: Collier Books, 1961), p. 207.

[2] Joseph Schumpeter, *Capitalism, Socialism and Democracy*, 3rd ed., The University Library (New York: Harper & Row, 1962), pp. 123–24.

its devotees, by their exclusion from polite literature."[3] Thus, the importance of accounting as a rational cost-profit calculus was acknowledged, but accounting practices and conventions were ignored.

This is not to say that the possibility of profit miscalculation was overlooked. However, Schumpeter, for example, attributes significance to the forces *causing* the errors in businessmen's predictions, i.e., the "causes" of the business cycle, and does not regard miscalculation, whether due to fraud, speculation, *or* accounting conventions, as an important independent "cause" of economic events.[4] Keynes, although not dealing directly with this subject, implies that there may have been persistent nonrandom error or bias in profit calculations during the nineteenth century when he suggests that the results of investment decisions "would have disappointed the hopes which prompted them"; but Keynes refers to the "precariousness of the basis of knowledge" and "a sufficient supply of individuals of sanguine temperaments and constructive impulses" as factors which might explain the phenomenon of miscalculation. He does not assign a special role to accounting practices.[5] On the other hand, accounting error is fundamental to Habakkuk's thesis on American and British technology in the nineteenth century.[6] Sawyer also discusses miscalculation and praises this "folly." At the same time he asserts that "the general validity of the dominant proposition seems beyond question. Sombart, Weber and the rest surely were right in emphasizing rationality in the allocation of resources."[7]

---

[3] Henry Rand Hatfield, "An Historical Defense of Bookkeeping," *Journal of Accountancy*, Vol. 37 (April, 1924); reprinted in W. T. Baxter and S. Davidson, eds., *Studies in Accounting Theory* (Homewood: Richard D. Irwin, 1962), p. 1. Canning provides historical insight into this disdainful attitude towards accountants. "Unlike economists, who from the beginning followed a very learned profession, the early writers on accounting were mostly without academic training... their dicta were amazingly positive and their arguments as amazingly inconsequential." John B. Canning, *The Economics of Accountancy* (New York: Ronald Press, 1929), p. 8. Nevertheless, the accounting profession did become competitive with the older, more influential, legal profession! "From the first, what we fear must be recognized as the bulk of the legal profession has looked upon accountants with ill-concealed dislike and jealousy." *The Accountant*, July 28, 1877, p. 2.

[4] Schumpeter does state that "the practical importance of the element of error is not denied, nor that of the elements which are usually designated by speculative fever, fraud, etc.—in which category overproduction also belongs. We assert only that all these things are in part consequential and that even insofar as this is not the case the nature of the phenomenon cannot be understood from them." *The Theory of Economic Development*, (New York: Oxford University Press, 1961), p. 228, n. 1.

[5] John M. Keynes, *The General Theory of Employment, Interest and Money* (New York: Harcourt Brace, 1936), pp. 149–50.

[6] H. J. Habakkuk, *American and British Technology in the Nineteenth Century* (Cambridge: Cambridge University Press, 1962).

[7] John Sawyer, "Entrepreneurial Error and Economic Growth," *Explorations in Entrepreneurial History*, No. 4 (May, 1952), p. 199.

Clark, however, seems far less impressed with the postulate of rational calculation.[8]

In the pages that follow we discuss the subject of accounting error as it relates to nineteenth-century, asset-accounting procedures and practices. Since the concept of "accounting error" has no unique meaning,[9] a description of its use here seems in order. Usually, three components of error—sampling, procedural, and conceptual—enter into any discussion of statistical data. To classify accounting error into these components is a formidable task; for example, to determine conceptual error one must first determine an "ideal" set of accounting procedures. To avoid this, accounting error is defined here as *the failure to systematically distinguish between capital and revenue expenditures* and *the failure to periodically allocate the original cost of fixed assets to expense.*

Some authorities believe that during the nineteenth century accounts were maintained on a conservative basis with all doubt resolved on the side of understatement of assets and profits. Others hold to an opposite view. This paper attempts to shed some light on the direction of the accounting error in this period.

II

In general, railroads, utilities, and other quasi-public companies practiced some form of replacement accounting in the nineteenth century. Other firms followed what might be called "valuation" accounting procedures. Within each set of procedures there was a great deal of diversity, and there was overlapping between the sets; but this generalization is necessary to structure the analysis. This section of the paper deals with replacement accounting; "valuation" accounting is examined in the next section.

The oldest assumption on which accounting practices were based implies that the value of fixed tangible assets remains constant if they are maintained in working order; this is implicit in the cash-receipts-less-disbursements concept of profit which was "in general use at least up to 1650 and probably much later."[10] Under this method, fixed assets purchased from the proceeds of stock and bond issues were considered permanent and valued at original cost. Replacement accounting is a by-

---

[8] J. M. Clark, *Economics of Overhead Costs* (Chicago: University of Chicago Press, 1923), p. 44.

[9] See, for example, Oskar Morgenstern, *On the Accuracy of Economic Observations*, 2nd ed. (Princeton: Princeton University Press, 1963), Chapter IV.

[10] Donald Kehl, *Corporate Dividends* (New York: Ronald Press, 1941), p. 55. This concept of profit persisted throughout the nineteenth century. It was confirmed in legal decisions in Britain and the United States (*ibid.*, p. 58, n. 181 and p. 63, n. 203) and expressed in United States income tax law. Floyd W. Windal, *The Accounting Concept of Realization, Occasional Paper No. 5* (Bureau of Business and Economic Research, Michigan State University), 1961, p. 23; George Terborgh, *Realistic Depreciation Policy* (Chicago: Machinery and Allied Products Institute, 1954), pp. 2–3.

product of strict cash accounting and was employed by most railroads and utilities in the United States and Great Britain during the nineteenth century.[11] Under replacement accounting, all expenditures on maintenance, repairs, and renewals (replacements) were charged directly to expense. Expenditures on additions and betterments, i.e., capital expenditures, made with funds provided from the proceeds of stock and bond issues *or* revenue were capitalized.[12]

Two major problems are connected with the application of replacement accounting. First, the recognition of depreciation associated with the original plant is delayed until those assets are replaced. Second, the distinction made between replacements and additions has a profound influence on profits. These two problems are not mutually exclusive because if an asset is considered an addition (rather than a replacement),

---

[11] Replacement accounting procedures were embodied in the accounting provisions of the British *Railway Act* of 1868 in the so-called "double-account system." Dicksee comments on the origin of the system: "The Double-Account System is probably the creation of lawyers rather than of accountants, and its object would appear to be to direct special attention to the importance of keeping a strict account of the expenditures of moneys received by the creation of Fixed Liabilities...." Later, Dicksee commented that "this idea, ingenious as it undoubtedly is, would appear to have emanated from a lawyer rather than an accountant. One seems to trace in it the well known affection of the Chancery for a cash statement as well as its rooted distrust of all accounts framed upon any other basis." L. R. Dicksee, *Advanced Accounting*, 2nd ed. (London: Gee & Co., 1905), p. 130. Hatfield's misgivings about the British double-account system are also applicable to the system of accounts used in the United States. It "...seems to encourage the idea that the Capital account, or at least plant purchased with receipts from capital [stocks and bonds] have little or nothing to do with the profits exhibited in the Balance Sheet." Henry Rand Hatfield, *Modern Accounting* (New York: D. Appleton & Co., 1909), p. 202. He also stated that the double-account system had more far-reaching effects. "In discussing the subject of the shrinkage in value of plant in reference to profits it will be shown that the double account form of balance sheet has had a considerable and perhaps baleful influence on the legal interpretation of accounts. It has indeed been argued that the placing of the capital in a separate account involves the principle that changes therein cannot affect the Profit and Loss appearing in the balance sheet." *Accounting* (New York: D. Appleton & Co., 1927), p. 8.

[12] The ambiguous way in which the word "capital" is used in combination with other terms is often responsible for various errors of interpretation. We will attempt to avoid using such phrases in uncertain contexts. However, it might be useful to provide a short list of some of these terms: 1) capital—assets; 2) capital costs—capital consumption charges; 3) charges to capital—expenditures which are capitalized, i.e., asset expenditures as distinguished from expenditures which are expensed, i.e., revenue expenditures; 4) capital—the difference between assets and liabilities. This residual is often called net worth and is equal to owners' contribution plus retained earnings (less deficit). Changes in capital measure profits after making certain adjustments such as dividend payments. 5) capital—contributions of partners or par value (stated value) of stocks and bonds; 6) pay dividends out of capital—dividends are paid out of capital if they are not paid out of earnings. Hence, there is a deficit. Whether or not the deficit is actually recorded is another issue. (We have ignored the problem of stock discounts, etc.)

the depreciation of worn-out equipment is ignored until the "official" replacement of the original assets.[13]

Critics of nineteenth-century accounting practices recognized these deficiencies. In 1841, the *Railway Times* (Britain) warned that "some companies, we fear, are running out their perishable stock, therefore exhibiting an appearance of a low scale expenditure, and a rate of dividend not warranted by the profit really made, and thus leaving a succeeding set of proprietors to make up from their income the replacing of the exhausted stock." [14] In 1843, a journal in the United States voiced an identical complaint. "Great errors have been committed by overlooking the fact that the progress of the wear is rarely ascertained or at least appreciated until the rail is destroyed.... There is not now to be found in the country a single road which has renewed its iron out of the proceeds of transportation." [15] Other writers also disapproved the financial policies of railroads. Evans, referring to the practices in England before 1850, states that "questionable tactics on the part of management, unchecked by the courts which were reluctant to interfere in the internal affairs of a company, are to be suspected in some instances." [16] He went on to say that "whether legal or not, both preferred and ordinary shareholders often received dividends out of capital." [17, 18]

Another writer described the practices of American railroads in 1852.

---

[13] The entire distinction between "capital" and "revenue" expenditures raises certain fundamental questions which go beyond the scope of this study. In theory, expenditures should be capitalized if they represent future discounted services. In practice the value of these services is almost impossible to compute; therefore, rules of thumb are employed to distinguish between capital and revenue expenditures. This subject obviously will arise in connection with our discussion of "valuation" accounting in the next section.

[14] Harold Pollins, "Aspects of Railway Accounting Before 1868," *Studies in the History of Accounting*, eds. A. C. Littleton and B. S. Yamey (Homewood, Illinois: Richard D. Irwin, 1956), p. 344; quoting from *Railway Times*, October 30, 1841, p. 1142.

[15] Perry Mason, "Illustrations of Early Depreciation Practices," *Accounting Review*, VIII (Sept., 1933), p. 209; quoting from *Railroad Journal*, December, 1843.

[16] George Herberton Evans, *British Corporation Finance: 1775–1850* (Baltimore: Johns Hopkins Press, 1936), p. 103.

[17] *Ibid.*, p. 119. *The Accountant* confirmed the opinion that many early English railroads neglected capital consumption, paid dividends out of capital, and went bankrupt. *The Accountant*, June 27, 1885, p. 8.

[18] Although depreciation was recognized as an expense in some early rate cases (*R* v. *Grand Junction Railway* [1844] 4QB 18; *The Accountant*, February 12, 1910, p. 232), depreciation did not become an issue in dividend litigation until the later part of the nineteenth century (*Davison* v. *Gillies* [1879] 50 LJ [CH] 193). The issue here actually concerned the company's articles and not depreciation, per se. When the British courts finally deliberated on the validity of the depreciation (depletion) charge, they ruled that it was a capital loss not chargeable to profit (*Lee* v. *Neuchatel* [1889] 41 LR Ch 1). The United States Supreme Court did not pass judgment on depreciation until 1909, but that was a rate case (*Knoxville* v. *Knoxville Water Company*, 212 US 1).

> In a majority of cases the [financial] policy pursued is to extract a dividend at the earliest possible moment; to pay that dividend to the last farthing of surplus over working expenses; and to trust to the increase of traffic for providing, when the emergency may arrive, for the deterioration of the permanent way, and the rebuilding or replacement of worn-out stock. Very few companies, indeed, systematically provided for the renewal of perishable parts of their property....[19]

Utilities in England also pursued similar financial policies.

> In accordance with the generally accepted practice among public utility companies operating in this country, the Association made no provision for depreciation in its accounts. Expenditure for renewals was charged against revenue as it was incurred and since substantial sums were involved when the periodic renewal of major items of gas-works equipment took place, there were quite serious fluctuations of profits for particular half years and ... down to 1850 the Association used to distribute in dividend almost all its profits and had no fund of retained profits with which to finance capital expenditure.[20]

In the 1840's (and even earlier) some railroads, both in Britain and the United States, began to practice some form of depreciation accounting;[21] but the regular practice of providing for "unrealized" capital consumption apparently did not persist over time. Perhaps the task was too difficult or possibly railroad management did not wish to be committed to recording a "deferrable" expense. Pollins offers another explanation.

> Clearly the adoption of depreciation accounts from the late forties was a reaction to the scandals of the mid-forties, as well as a desire to keep dividends stable. That they did not last long was due to the increase in traffic in the fifties and sixties, when companies found their past allocations to depreciation were inadequate. Increasingly companies turned to the practice of not providing for depreciation as such but of debiting the actual expenditures on maintenance and renewals to the periodic revenue accounts.[22]

[19] Habakkuk, *op. cit.*, p. 89; quoting from E. W. Watkin, *A Trip to the United States and Canada*, 1852, p. 133. Compare this statement with the following comment. "Let it only be seen by six months working of that line [Grand Junction] that a profit will accrue to the owners of 8 or 10 per cent per annum and there is little hazard in predicting that other lines of great intercourse will be amply supported." *Railway Magazine*, July, 1837, p. 27. A year later the Grand Junction was evidently "short of profits" and charged £14,625, expended on rebuilding engines, to capital. The editor commented, "a more puny and meagre document we have never witnessed." *Railway Magazine*, July, 1838, p. 190. Pollins discusses this entry and refers to it as a "betterment" (*op. cit.*, p. 352). This may be an accurate description; however, in the reference previously cited, accidents during the winter and the need to replace deficient parts were among the reasons cited for the expenditure on engines.

[20] N. K. Hill, "Accounting Developments in a Public Utility Company in the Nineteenth Century," *Accounting Research*, VI (1955), p. 384.

[21] Pollins, *op. cit.*, pp. 343–349; S. Pollard, "Capital Accounting in the Industrial Revolution," *Yorkshire Bulletin of Economic and Social Research*, XV (Nov., 1963), p. 87; Mason, *op. cit.*, pp. 216–218.

[22] Pollins, *op. cit.*, p. 349. The scandals of the mid-forties occurred after the railroad mania. The following statistics provide some measure of the magnitude of the mania when "accounting for depreciation seems to have been dropped by some com-

Replacement accounting delayed the recognition of capital consumption until expenditures were made for renewals. Furthermore, since periodic renewals would require substantial sums, there would be a bias against recording renewals as costs because reserves for replacement were not generally maintained. On the one hand, a firm might not have been able to charge substantial renewals to expense without creating a deficit. On the other hand, without sufficient internal funds available, it would be necessary to finance replacement expenditures with sources external to the firm; and the proceeds of bond and stock issues were capitalized. Even bond discount was capitalized in the United States. This discussion suggests that the application of replacement accounting tends to create serious liquidity problems and that renewals and repairs might have been deferred or treated as additions in many cases. The protests and criticisms of nineteenth-century accountants give further insight into these issues.[23]

In 1877, the accounts of the Grand Junction Water Company, audited and certified "correct," were sarcastically reported on: "Everyone knows what this [an audit certificate] means ... it appeared that nearly fifty thousand pounds had been charged to capital instead of revenue, and that other irregularities ... had for years been certified correct." [24] Several weeks later the ordinary shareholder is again warned of excessive charges to capital. "They [the statistics of British railways] prove to demonstration that the excessive expenditure on capital account may be fraught with serious consequences in the not distant future to the ordinary shareholder." [25] The point was expanded. "Every little addition to stock, every extra rail, a change from iron to steel, and extra waggon, any little improvement to station and sidings, any change in signal apparatus, and much of the modern refittings necessary to the safety of the trains, all these things we find set down to capital." [26]

In 1878, an article on the "Audit of Railway Accounts" contributes to our understanding of the causes of imperfections in railway accounting.

> Nothing is more unsubstantial or delusive or could be made more unsatisfactory than the present system. Gentlemen are elected as auditors who are merchants, or shipowners, soldiers, sailors, or lawyers, anything in fact rather than professional auditors—these amateur critics ... are virtual nominees of the board whose doings they are to criticize and are supposed to control.[27]

---

panies" (*ibid.*, p. 347). "In November, 1845, there were no fewer than 1428 lines projected with an estimated capital of £701,243,208!! To the end of 1844 there had been 47 lines completed at a cost of £70,680,877." *The Accountant*, June 27, 1885, p. 9.

[23] Pollins, *op. cit.*, pp. 339–342, provides a number of examples showing improperly capitalized expenditures prior to 1868.

[24] *The Accountant*, June 23, 1877, p. 4.

[25] *The Accountant*, August 25, 1877, p. 8.

[26] *Ibid.*

[27] *The Accountant*, October 5, 1878, p. 4.

Several years later, in response to a suggestion that ordinary trading companies adopt the accounting methods used by railroads, railroad accounting is vehemently condemned. "It is not the practice of ordinary trading companies which is bad . . . but the practice of railway companies . . . a practice as vicious and as full of temptation to managers and directors to manipulate accounts for their own ends and purposes as can well be imagined. It is, in fact, little short of an inducement to fraud."[28] The criticism of railroad accounting persits over time but the tone is somewhat milder. "Although railway companies usually deal liberally [sic] in charging extraordinary outlays against profits, the extent of the expenditures to which they have been put in recent years could with difficulty have been foreshadowed when larger dividends were being earned."[29] Dicksee formulated the "principle" used to distinguish between capital and revenue expenditures. "The principle in railway accounts seems to be to maintain an even balance between Capital and Revenue accounts but under any circumstances the dividend is not allowed to suffer."[30]

The critics of American railroad accounting imply that the conditions in the United States were similar. Was Montgomery being sardonic when he said: "railway accounting in the United States has reached such a high state of perfection that the auditing department has at its head a thoroughly competent official. With a few noteworthy exceptions the accounts are not audited by professional accountants."[31] He continued, "it is not customary for any allowance to be made for depreciation and there is remarkable lack of uniformity in writing off so called betterments."[32]

George O. May addressed himself to the economic effects of replacement accounting; he concluded an examination of American railroad accounting by asserting: "To my mind, it is incontestable that the application of such depreciation accounting [as distinguished from replacement accounting] would have been that the construction of a large part of our railway mileage would at least have been greatly delayed if, indeed, some part would have been constructed at all."[33] May then noted that "since the development of other public utilities and commercial enterprises followed naturally on the development of railroads this portion of the growth of our capital equipment would have been greatly re-

[28] *The Accountant*, November 14, 1885, p. 3.

[29] *The Accountant*, August 8, 1903, p. 1015. The statement contradicts itself. Evidently the expenditures on extraordinary outlays were not liberal.

[30] L. R. Dicksee, *Auditing*, 10th ed. (London: Gee & Co., 1915), p. 123.

[31] L. R. Dicksee, *Auditing*, Auth. American ed., ed. R. H. Montgomery (New York: 1905), p. 137.

[32] *Ibid.*, p. 137.

[33] George O. May, *Twenty Five Years of Accounting Responsibility, 1911–1936*, ed. B. S. Hunt (New York: American Institute Publishing Company, 1936), Vol. II, p. 340.

tarded."[34] Parenthetically, May also stated that "it is no doubt true that as a result of accounting methods followed, large amounts of capital have been lost by investors."[35] Also of great significance is May's contention that the Interstate Commerce Commission's rule requiring depreciation of equipment was prompted by the failure of railroads to record the retirement of old, worn-out equipment.[36]

The error did not always result in the understatement of capital consumption charges; some railroads evidently made errors in the opposite direction. Instead of failing to amortize the cost of assets, additions were written off in the period in which the outlays were made. Creamer, although not referring explicitly to railroad accounting, believed that "it is also conceivable that before the use of formal depreciation accounting, many capital expenditures were treated as current operating expenditures and so were fully depreciated in a year or two."[37] It is, of course, difficult to determine whether the capital expenditures mentioned by Creamer were (1) bona fide additions which were depreciated in advance of the expiration of the services provided by these assets; (2) replacement expenditures which, in effect, provided for the depreciation on the replaced assets; or (3) expensed capital expenditures which compensated for past failure to expense renewals and record depreciation.

Matheson, in one of the first books on depreciation, also asserted that betterments were expensed in the United States although he warned that the "opposite extreme" is to be guarded against in Britain.[38] Another accountant commented: "Recent studies of railroad valuations give good evidence that the over-capitalization often complained of is not to be found there. Many roads have charged millions of dollars to maintenance that might have been properly charged to construction and used as a basis for new stocks and bonds."[39] It is difficult to reconcile this view with the fact that about fifty percent of the track mileage constructed in the United States before 1900 (assuming no double counting) was placed in receivership.[40] In this connection, an accountant

[34] *Ibid.*, pp. 340–41.

[35] *Ibid.*, p. 341. This statement confirms *The Accountant's* position that Mr. F. Skinner of the Bankers Institute was incorrect in maintaining that investors in United States' roads generally did not lose their stake. January 21, 1888, p. 34.

[36] *Ibid.*, p. 336. This view is in accord with the point made earlier. Not only does replacement accounting ignore depreciation during the life of an asset, but it also creates a climate in which there would be a natural tendency to ignore capital costs altogether, insofar as it is expedient to do so.

[37] D. Creamer, *et al., Capital in Manufacturing and Mining* (Princeton: Princeton University Press, 1960), p. 14.

[38] Ewing Matheson, *Depreciation of Factories*, 4th ed., (London: E. & F. N. Spon, 1910), p. 17.

[39] William Morse Cole, *Accounts, Their Construction and Interpretation*, rev. ed., (Boston: Houghton Mifflin, 1915), p. 211, n. 1.

[40] *Poor's Manual of Railroads*, 1900, p. lxxii.

studied the hypothesis that maintenance charges were *excessive* and said that the "same sort of idea prevailed" before the compulsory reorganization of a great number of railroads.[41] He concluded that it is really very difficult to distinguish between maintenance expenditures and outlays for additions. After the turn of the century some railroads did follow "ultra-conservative" practices,[42] but there is little evidence that these practices existed prior to 1900.

Many accountants, both in the past and the present, regard replacement accounting as a method that is inherently unstable.[43] The accounting error produced by replacement accounting may take any one of several forms. First, assuming that replacements were expensed and only bona fide additions were capitalized and also assuming that railroads and utilities in the nineteenth century were expanding their plant and equipment over time, the cumulative capital consumption charges recorded at any point of time would have been less than the costs that might have been computed under a formal system of depreciation accounting. This is true no matter what rate of depreciation had been assumed. Second, if replacements and other revenue expenditures were capitalized, the magnitude of the understatement would have been larger. Third, if bona fide capital expenditures were expensed, the accounting error for a particular period would have been in the opposite direction. Fourth, in years when replacement occurred, the reported capital consumption charges might have been higher when compared to costs that had been periodically written off. One must, therefore, distinguish between cumulative net error and the error in a particular fiscal period. Over time, replacement accounting understates capital consumption; in any particular period, there is no basis for determining the nature of the error. Clearly, certain decision makers would have been confused by these procedures, and the interests of some classes of investors might have been adversely affected while others might have benefited.

III

The system of accounts used by railroads and utilities did not deal *directly* with the problem of asset valuation. By assuming that an asset had constant value equal to original cost, the question of periodic depreciation or appreciation was thereby avoided. The distinction between capital and revenue expenditures was, however, considered in the cost-profit calculus of these companies, and the procedures used to record

[41] Francis How, "Maintenance of Way and Structures," *Journal of Accountancy*, I (1906), p. 372.

[42] Hatfield, *Accounting, op. cit.*, p. 321.

[43] Cf. Dicksee, *Advanced Accounting, op. cit.*, pp. 130–132. Arthur Andersen & Co., *Accounting and Reporting Problems of the Accounting Profession*, 2nd ed., 1962, pp. 123–133.

repairs, replacements, betterments, and additions actually determined the capital consumption charges.

Other firms dealt *directly* with the problem of asset valuation. It is difficult to restructure their methods because the procedures used to determine which expenditures should be added to the recorded value of an asset and the method of determining the value of an asset are not mutually exclusive. That is, if the value of an asset is arrived at by some method of direct appraisal, e.g., market value, the procedures used to distinguish between capital and revenue expenditures become irrelevant. The valuation would, in theory, adjust for depreciation or appreciation.

Early bookkeeping texts reveal little about the nature of capital accounting practices; there is a form of asset accounting but it is vague and imprecise. Assets were to be "valued" before reckoning profit which was defined as the change in the value of capital, i.e., net assets. Yamey, in a review of accounting practices in England before 1800, concluded that the "typical profit and loss measured the changes, from virtually all causes, in the recorded value of capital in the business between opening and closing dates."[44] Pollard, in his study of accounting records, commented that the method "most commonly found in our sample consisted of valuing the whole firm *de novo* at the data of striking the balance."[45]

To say that capital accounting practices called for the valuation of assets is a meaningless statement unless value is defined precisely. Assets might have been valued "at your discretion,"[46] with reference to "present value,"[47] at "cost or value,"[48] "as might be desired,"[49] or at "market value."[50] The extent to which these terms imply consideration of depreciation, appreciation, goodwill, and a distinction between capital

[44] B. S. Yamey, "Some Topics in the History of Financial Accounting in England, 1500–1900," *Studies in Accounting Theory, op. cit.*, p. 32. This view is similar to the following comment made about practices in the United States. "As increments other than earnings—such as capital gains, premium on stock, and unrealized appreciation—made their appearances, accountants at first were content to overlook their divergent natures, and the concept of one general surplus carried over into the twentieth century." Billy Lee Barnes, "The Development and Present Status of the Accounting Concept of Surplus," *Accounting Review*, XXXV [April, 1960], p. 302.

[45] Pollard, *op. cit.*, p. 82.

[46] A. C. Littleton, *Accounting Evolution to 1900* (New York: American Institute Publishing Co., 1933), p. 75; quoting from J. B. Geijsbeek, *Ancient Double Entry Bookkeeping* (Denver, 1914).

[47] "Bookkeeping," *Encyclopedia Britannica*, 4th ed., (Edinburgh, 1810), IV.

[48] B. F. Foster, *The Merchants Manual. The Principles of Trade, Commerce, and Banking* (Boston: Perkins & Marvin, 1838), p. 164.

[49] George Soulé, *Soulé's New Science and Practice of Accounts*, 6th ed. rev. (New Orleans: Published by the Author, 1901), p. 91. Soulé is referring to the bookkeeping procedures that *might* be employed to record asset appreciation.

[50] Pollins, *op. cit.*, p. 345; quoting from Grand Junction Railway, "Reports and Accounts," June 30, 1838.

and revenue expenditures depends on the underlying assumptions made about the nature of "value." For example, if all outlays on an asset are assumed to increase its value, all expenditures should be capitalized. Conversely, if assets are assumed to have a permanent value equal to original cost, all expenditures on those assets should be expensed. On the other hand, if value is related to earning capacity, an element of goodwill should be recognized.[51, 52] The modern accounting concept of "cost value," when viewed in this historical perspective, might be seen as a pragmatic reaction to the fact that value is a word of many meanings.[53] However, the accounting principle which based asset valuations on original cost and charged periodic depreciation based on historical cost developed only slowly in business practice.[54]

One does not need much insight into the subject of accounting to realize that, in the absence of an institutional compulsion for consistent behavior and during a period of businessman-determined business practices diversity is inevitable. That the accounting profession had little authority in this period meant that the presentation of financial data rested solely on the judgment of management.[55] Furthermore, since the

---

[51] Dicksee's argument against valuing assets on the basis of earning capacity constitutes a certain amount of evidence that this method was employed in some cases. He argues that "if increases in value be taken into account when the profits are good the effect will be to create the impression that the proprietors are doing from two to four times as well as is actually the case, and thus encourage them . . . on a scale of expenditure which they could not possibly maintain . . . which amounts to the same thing as 'killing the goose which lays the golden egg.'" *Goodwill and its Treatment in the Accounts*, 2nd ed., (London: Gee & Co., 1900), p. 17.

[52] In a lengthy footnote, Marshall discusses critically a number of accounting problems relating to the valuation of assets. *Principles of Economics*, 8th ed. (New York: Macmillan, 1948), pp. 354–55, n. 2.

[53] In the nineteenth century, accountants warned that "it is not safe to take value as a basis," *The Accountant*, November 5, 1887, p. 611; and Dicksee, referring to the computation of depreciation by appraisal, called it "theoretically perfect" but "defective in practice." *Advanced Accounting, op. cit.*, p. 349. In one case a company capitalized repairs and provided insufficient depreciation. When the auditor balked an *expert* appraiser was engaged. He appraised the assets at a high value. The auditor then certified the higher "value" and was subsequently fired! *The Accountant*, March 23, 1895, p. 265. The intensity of the reaction by accountants against appraisal valuations is suggested by Bonbright's comment on this subject. "One is almost tempted to say, with the hope that the remark will not be taken literally, that depreciation as an appraisal concept can be understood only by persons who know nothing about accounting." James C. Bonbright, *Valuation of Property* (New York: McGraw-Hill, 1937), Vol. I, p. 214.

[54] Although some nineteenth century accountants advocated the "cost principle" and the related "realization postulate," no consensus was reached until the twentieth century. Chapters III and IV of my unpublished dissertation, "Nineteenth Century Capital Accounting and Business Investment" (1964) deal with this subject.

[55] It is interesting to note that the detection of fraud was the primary purpose of an audit in the nineteenth century. Dicksee, *Auditing* (1915), *op. cit.*, pp. 7–8. The primary purpose of an audit in the present day is to detect "errors of principle."

standards of financial disclosure were ill-defined, financial reports from this period are at best ambiguous and at worst unreliable.[56] Accordingly, one method of determining the nature of accounting practices of this period is by examining the opinions of nineteenth-century accountants.

Warnings about American accounting practices appear in *The Book Keeper*.[57] "If a sufficient allowance is not made for the deterioration of property values ... the results shown are to be erroneous." [58] We are told that it is a "practice too frequently adopted to carry on from year to year assets which are practically valueless." [59] Yet, the "question of setting aside a sum annually for depreciation must depend upon the fact whether it has depreciated or not" and "it is impossible to lay down any fixed principles ... although ... the safest plan is to assume a depreciation." [60]

The "safest plan" evidently was not adopted by the average manufacturer. "One prominent fault with manufacturers is their neglect to make

---

The shift in emphasis became noticeable in the United States after the turn of the century. R. H. Montgomery, *Auditing, Theory and Practice* (New York: Ronald Press, 1912), p. v; A. C. Littleton, *Essays on Accountancy* (Urbana: University of Illinois, 1961), pp. 100–104. The various examples of accounting error presented in this section fall into the category of either errors due to fraud or near-fraud or "errors of principle." The latter category is somewhat ambiguous because it is difficult to distinguish between errors due solely to accounting conventions and errors due to incorrect forecasting of the lives of assets, etc. We do not, however, intend to settle this matter here, and we have attempted to avoid the complex problem of causation by defining accounting error without reference to cause.

[56] Throughout the last quarter of the nineteenth century, accountants in England tried, to no avail, to secure passage of disclosure laws. *The Accountant*, June 4, 1881, p. 5; Matheson, *op. cit.*, p. 167; H. C. Edey and Prot Panitpakdi, "British Company Accounting and the Law," *Studies in the History of Accounting, op. cit.*, p. 375. The editor of *The Accountant* called one proposal, that limited companies be compelled to state in their articles the rate of depreciation to be charged, "chimerical." November 12, 1887, p. 618. According to one authority, "it was not until 1908 that the first major step was taken on a path that was to lead to regulation far more detailed and effective than would have been dreamed of by nineteenth century businessmen." H. C. Edey, "Company Accounts in Britain: The Jenkins Report," *Accounting Review*, XXXVIII [April, 1963], p. 262. See also David F. Hawkins, "The Development of Modern Financial Reporting Practices Among American Manufacturing Corporations," *Business History Review*, XXXVII (Autumn, 1963).

[57] *The Book Keeper* is said to be the "only paper of its kind published in this or any other country." *The Book Keeper* (New York), February 15, 1881, p. 56. *The Accountant*, first published five years earlier, called it "a valuable little periodical." August 27, 1881, p. 4.

[58] *The Book Keeper*, September 14, 1880, p. 65.

[59] *The Book Keeper* (New York), July 5, 1881, p. 146. Habakkuk suggests that this was one of the reasons why a high proportion of early arms manufacturers went bankrupt. "The true rate of profit on the manufacture of arms, when capital costs were accurately accounted was low; and many concerns remained in business only because their primitive accounting concealed the fact that they were, in effect, treating capital as income and failing to provide for depreciation." *Op. cit.*, p. 45.

[60] *The Book Keeper* (New York), July 5, 1881, p. 147.

proper allowances for depreciation or deterioration of their manufacturing property."[61] Fifteen years later the criticism is more condemning.

> The natural depreciation of all kinds of machinery, or plant or fixtures does not so far seem to appeal to the average American manufacturer.... Even where we find depreciation is charged off, it is done arbitrarily and eccentrically, scarcely ever consistently and intelligently.... Cases where not only is depreciation not charged off, but repairs are added to first value of the asset, have been several times alluded to.[62]

It would appear that the census takers of 1890 were either somewhat confused or overly optimistic. They requested information on depreciation allowances since 1880 and also instructed the respondents to report the value of plant "at what the works would cost in 1890 if then to be erected, with such allowance for depreciation as may be suitable in the individual case."[63] These questions would involve complex considerations and it is small wonder that "the data furnished in the individual reports relating to depreciation of manufacturing plants were not sufficient to form a basis for correct computation."[64] It is not surprising to find that the *Census of Manufactures, 1900,* simplified the instructions and requested that capital be valued at "the amounts carried on the books."[65]

Depreciation involves no specific outlay of funds and can be ignored in the short run; even when recorded, many accountants apparently regarded depreciation as a segregation of profits rather than expense. This means that depreciation reserves, a subject that occasioned considerable confusion in the nineteenth century, were viewed as a kind of surplus account.

> May remarked that some accountants regard a provision for depreciation as a reserve coming literally within the terms of the definition of a reserve as a segregation of profits. Such a reserve is often loosely spoken of as being provided out of profits...and the reserve is sometimes regarded as remaining a part of the undivided profits or surplus. This view was frequently expressed twenty-five years ago [about 1897] when I first started practice, but so far as my experience qualifies me to express an opinion the vast majority of bankers, businessmen and accountants, both practical and theoretical, have by now completely disregarded it.[66]

---

[61] *American Counting Room,* Vol. 8 (1884), No. 1, p. 96.

[62] *The Book Keeper* (Detroit), XII (July, 1899), p. 82.

[63] *Census of Manufactures, 1890,* Part I, p. 10.

[64] *Ibid.*

[65] *Census of Manufactures, 1900,* Part I, p. xcvii; quoted in Creamer, *et al., op. cit.,* p. 12.

[66] George O. May, "On a proposed definition of depreciation," letter written in 1922; reprinted in May, *op. cit.,* p. 164. Dicksee made a similar comment. "In the absence of special provision in the articles of association, there is nothing to prevent directors from transferring the whole or any portion of the amount standing to the credit of the reserve fund to the credit of the Appropriation Account for the purpose of increasing the amount of profits available for dividends. Where such a course is

Hatfield made substantially the same point[67] and criticized accounting practices in the United States just after the turn of the century.

> At that time any recognition of depreciation was relatively uncommon in the accounts of American corporations and the relatively few companies which showed depreciation in prosperous years grew faint-hearted when business was poor.... Corporations are still apt to look upon the charge for depreciation as being an act of grace rather than of necessity and the allowance is frequently less in the lean than in the prosperous years.[68]

He also believed that "the earliest writers on accounting did not provide for regular depreciation charges, and the recognition that they were necessary has been a matter of slow growth. This is particularly true in the United States." [69]

The growth of depreciation accounting was also slow in Britain. Leake, an early British authority on depreciation, maintained that "the present neglect to account systematically year by year for expiring capital outlay [depreciation] ... is a matter of long established custom ... [that] continues in spite of, and not in consequence of, their [the accounting profession's] attitude." [70] British accountants did preach reform, but their efforts to influence the business community do not appear to have met with great success.[71] The warnings and incantations of British accountants shed further light on this subject.

Depreciation practices were denounced in several early issues of *The Accountant*. "In much more numerous cases, losses have been concealed or minimized, and capital values have been impaired without writing off due provision for replacement and repairs of plant...." [72] "It is greatly to be feared that in many cases which machinery (from the speed at which it is run) is subject to a high rate of wear and tear, sufficient allowance is not being made and dividends are paid out of capital." [73] On the other hand, it is argued that "it is no sin to raise its valuation (a building) to a reasonable point, crediting back to profit and loss

---

pursued, the auditor should ... acquaint the shareholders with the facts." *Auditing* (1915), *op. cit.*, p. 233.

[67] Hatfield, *Accounting, op. cit.*, p. 375. The "cash-flow illusion" seems to be a modern manifestation of this view. See, for example, William A. Paton, "The 'Cash-Flow' Illusion," *Accounting Review*, XXXVIII (April, 1960).

[68] Hatfield, *Accounting, op. cit.*, p. 140. Similar views are held by Terborgh (*op. cit.*, p. 2) and Saliers (*Depreciation, Its Principles and Applications*, 3rd ed., [New York: Ronald Press, 1939], p. 17).

[69] Hatfield, *Accounting, op. cit.*, p. 135.

[70] P. D. Leake, *Depreciation and Wasting Assets* (London: Henry Good & Son, 1912), pp. 5–6.

[71] The British income tax law of 1878 did permit (for the first time) a deduction for "diminished value by wear and tear." Matheson noted, however, that "surveyors of taxes did not always draw the attention of manufacturers and others to the relief and allowances provided by the Act of 1878." (Matheson, *op. cit.*, p. 28).

[72] *The Accountant*, June 4, 1881, p. 5.

[73] *The Accountant*, November 5, 1887, p. 12.

what has unnecessarily been taken therefrom." [74] However, the practice of crediting unrealized appreciation to profits was condemned.[75] Thus, accounting practices in the period appear to provide for maximum flexibility. Depreciation provisions may or may not be made; past provisions for depreciation may be restored to profit; and assets may be revalued to provide "profit" out of which dividends are paid.

When Matheson's book on depreciation was first published in 1883, the editor of *The Accountant* unhappily reported that "numerous letters have appeared from manufacturers and others, many of whom take exception to the sound principles laid down, and endeavor to show that depreciation of plant is often rendered difficult by lack of profit, and that in such cases it may be postponed." [76] In the Preface to the Second Edition, the same problem is elaborated on: "Auditors, and especially those who have to deal with joint stock or other concerns, where the remuneration of the management is made wholly or partly dependent upon declared profits, know in what varied forms resistance to an adequate charge against profits for depreciation is present." [77] The text is recommended to those who are "confronted with unfamiliar and specious arguments for avoiding the unwelcome charge against profits." [78] One such argument was that depreciation, if made compulsory in the law, "would stop all such enterprise, because it would be impossible for companies to pay dividends in the early years of their existence." [79]

"The unwelcome charge" evidently was avoided in many cases. "In comparatively few establishments . . . is the endeavor made to systematically approximate the amount charged to revenue for depreciation to actual deterioration which has taken place . . . or . . . and more rarely . . . to allocate it to various departments." [80] Consequently, "in the history of the great number of businesses which have disappeared, . . . insufficient depreciation was a more potent factor in their downfall than either prices or markets. Prices and markets are dependent on new machinery, and the obtaining of new machinery depends on the sufficiency of depreciation." [81]

---

[74] *The Accountant*, December 12, 1881, p. 5.

[75] *The Accountant*, October 15, 1881, p. 5. Montgomery also complains of this procedure. "The law on the subject of profits is not well settled and will not be, so long as the majority of lawyers retain their profound ignorance of the accounts, but it is quite likely that no legal obstacle would prevent a corporation from revaluing part of its assets and applying the excess so raised to surplus available for dividends." (Montgomery, *op. cit.*, p. 194).

[76] *The Accountant*, December 29, 1883, p. 15.

[77] Matheson, *op. cit.*, pp. ix–x.

[78] *Ibid.*, p. x.

[79] *The Accountant*, March 18, 1893, p. 254.

[80] E. Garcke and J. M. Fells, *Factory Accounts*, 4th ed. (London: Crosby Lockwood & Sons, 1893), p. 98.

[81] *The Accountants' Magazine*, XII (June, 1908), p. 313.

There is also some discussion about the tendency to capitalize repairs and other revenue expenditures.

> Unless a company is in a flourishing condition, there is a great tendency to add to the amount standing in the books, as representing the value of these assets, those sums which have actually been expended in repairing or replacing part of them, and which ought, therefore, to be included in the expenditure side of the Revenue account under repairs and renewals, or some similar heading.[82]

Another accountant cautioned that "much confusion and uncertainty exists in property and machinery accounts by reason of the way in which wear and tear and renewals are treated."[83] The problem is dealt with by other writers.

> In many instances a fixed deduction is made for wear and tear and the whole of the expenditure both for additions, renewals and repairs added to the property account, but it is submitted that the practice is very apt to lead to the plant and other accounts appearing in the books at a figure much above their real value.[84]

> In many manufacturing businesses the rough-and-ready method is adopted of charging to capital, in addition to original cost, the cost of all renewals, alterations and extension of building and machinery; and of debiting profit and loss account in respect of depreciation with a percentage of the total amount in the ledger under those heads. In some cases even the current repairs are charged to capital, in which case a proportionately larger percentage should be written off annually for depreciation.[85]

Finally in this connection, Dicksee states that "most of the errors of principle that are perpetrated in practice arise from the lack of ability or lack of desire to strictly discriminate between Capital and Revenue items."[86] These comments suggest that many firms did not charge all expenditures on, or related to, assets directly to expense.

Several other comments that refer to the general nature of capital accounting practices are pertinent to this discussion.

The Accountant reported on an early lecture that specifically discussed the probability of intentional *under*statement of assets.

> It would be interesting to know how many members of the Manchester Institute of Accountants had met with a tendency on the part of directors or managers of businesses to undervalue their plant. He [John Mather] had himself only found one instance of such a tendency and it was so rare that accountants might well be excused for being a little off their guard when they met with it.[87]

Dicksee shared this opinion almost forty years later. "Sometimes, for the purpose of providing a Secret Reserve, assets are intentionally under-

[82] Francis W. Pixley, *Auditors, Their Duties and Responsibilities*, 4th ed. (London: Henry Good & Son, 1887), p. 126.

[83] *The Accountant*, November 5, 1887, p. 611.

[84] *The Accountant*, December 21, 1889, p. 692.

[85] Garcke and Fells, *op. cit.*, p. 95.

[86] Dicksee, *Advanced Accounting*, *op. cit.*, p. 3.

[87] January 8, 1876, p. 6.

stated; except when done so advisedly, however, there is but little fear of the Auditor finding the assets understated."[88] Hatfield provided further insight on this issue.

> In the anxiety to escape the prevalent temptation to exaggerate the value of the assets, which in many cases has led to such disgraceful results, conservative financiers applaud an equally erroneous, but perhaps less dangerous tendency to understatement. But the creation of a secret reserve ... may be used as a means of refusing to pay dividends.... [or] it may lead ignorant stockholders ... to dispose of their stock....[89]

One authority on British accounting history holds to an entirely different view than the evidence which we have presented implies. Unfortunately, no evidence, except a statement by a company chairman in the 1930's, supports Yamey's assertion about the nature of the accounting error.

> In practice the exercise of accounting discretion or judgment was conditioned in general by an approved bias towards "conservatism." This means that it was better to err on the side of understatement rather than overstatement. Thus asset values in the balance sheets were to be understated rather than overstated; and possible losses were to be anticipated rather than deferred in the accounts, while the recording of gains was to be deferred until they had been realized.[90]

The only statement that we have found which might be offered in support of this belief is Matheson's assertion that monopolies sometimes overstate depreciation and repairs.[91]

Nineteenth-century accountants discussed the possibility of an accounting error but their views conflict with the idea that the accounting practices in this period were conservative. The evidence suggests that capital consumption costs were neglected in many cases. This means that assets and profits were overstated. It is possible that these early accountants directed their attention to the worst rather than average practices; however, there is a striking consistency in the views of both American and British accountants. Certainly, if "conservative" financial policies had been the rule as Yamey concludes, one would have expected to find *some* discussion of this subject in the literature dealing with asset accounting.

A comment by an accounting authority made to me in private correspondence illustrates the tenacious hold of the belief that accounting practices in the nineteenth century were "conservative." He wrote: "I might also comment that my general impression is that most authorities today would agree that assets were systematically *understated* in the 19th c." The point is that one can find very little evidence to support this view. DR Scott discussed the subject of conservatism and, in re-

[88] Dicksee, *Auditing* (1915), *op. cit.*, p. 203.
[89] Hatfield, *Accounting*, *op. cit.*, pp. 321–22.
[90] Yamey, *op. cit.*, p. 42.
[91] Matheson, *op. cit.* (2nd ed., 1893), p. 7.

ferring to the rules of business conduct, he stated that "these rules, or principles, have to do chiefly with industry, thrift and businesslike conservatism. They are the sort of thing for which Poor Richard was noted." [92] Then Scott elaborated on this point.

> With the change from individualistic to corporate management it was inevitable that much of the attitude of managers should be carried over from the old situation to the new. The emphasis of the old situation upon individualistic self-interest led logically to mismanagement, that is management in the interest of one or a few stockholders at the expense of the rest. Similarly the rules of conservatism and thrift of the earlier period were carried over into corporate management where their application sometimes has resulted in unintentional mismanagement. At other times it has been a cloak to fraud.[93]

Perhaps "conservatism" did exist during a particular period or was the policy of particular firms in the nineteenth century, but certainly the word is a misnomer. Errors of either direction are capable of misleading some decision makers. Furthermore, the acceptance of the doctrine of conservatism might condition some decison makers to assume that "things are better than they look."

IV

We have been discussing a vast subject and make no pretense about settling the issues. There is evidence that capital consumption charges were neglected or at least delayed by the accounting methods employed. On the other hand, the views of those authorities who suggest that all accounting matters with regard to the statement of assets and profits were resolved on the side of understatement cannot be dismissed. Thus, all those who have studied the subject agree that an accounting error did exist. The major unresolved question relates to the direction of the error.

The only conclusion that is consistent with the evidence is that the accounting practices and the nature of the accounting error in the nineteenth century were not stable. For permanent firms following replacement accounting procedures, the error in any given year might have been in either direction; but the cumulative net error would have resulted in the understatement of capital consumption charges when compared to costs recorded under a more formal system of depreciation accounting.[94]

---

[92] DR Scott, *Cultural Significance of Accounts* (New York: Henry Holt & Co., 1931), p. 151.

[93] *Ibid.*

[94] One argument that was often advanced to defend replacement accounting procedures is that the lives of assets employed in "permanent" enterprise were extremely unpredictable. It is interesting to find students of public enterprise economics advocating what might seem to be relatively short lives for public enterprise projects. Kuhn states, "As a general rule, unless compelling reasons dictate otherwise, the life of a public enterprise project should not be assumed to exceed 40 years." Tilo E. Kuhn, *Public Enterprise Economics and Transport Problems* (Berkeley: University of California Press, 1962), p. 64.

Since replacement does not usually occur until some years after an enterprise commences operations, the unrecorded capital consumption charges would have been greatest prior to the period in which replacement was required. For other firms, i.e., manufacturers, trading companies, etc., the evidence suggests a similar conclusion with respect to the error in any given period. The "long-run" error is more difficult to determine because there were a number of different sets of procedures employed by this class of enterprise. However, the accounting literature does not support the contention that accounts were maintained on a "conservative" basis.

A bookkeeping error and a decision-maker's error are not the same. In order to attach economic significance to the idea of an accounting error one would have to show that some decision makers acted as if the erroneous information has been correct. This is clearly beyond the scope of this study.[95] However, a persistent or short-run accounting error in either direction is capable of influencing the allocation of resources, the business cycle, prices and output, and therefore economic growth. May recognized this relationship when he said that "once it is recognized that accounting is largely a matter of convention, it is easy to perceive that the nature of the conventions adopted may greatly influence the development of an economy."[96] It would appear that accountants as well as economists have generally neglected this subject as it relates to the economic growth of the United States and Britain in the nineteenth century.

---

[95] Tucker's remarks on this subject are pertinent. "In the first half of the nineteenth century . . . the rate of profit became the dominant concept," and "it was the rate of return per annum generally available on invested capital. As such, it was based in practice on the calculations of business men and bookkeepers." G. S. L. Tucker, *Progress and Profits in British Economic Thought, 1650–1850* (Cambridge: Cambridge University Press, 1960), p. 75.

[96] May, *op. cit.*, Vol. II, p. 307.

Accounting error as a factor in business history

Richard P. Brief

Abstract

The questions and issues that arise in thinking about the role played by accounting in business history are complex. While accounting policies and practices have economic consequences, they also are a product of decisions made by individuals and organizations in their own self-interest. Cause and effect relationships in accounting are, therefore, difficult to identify.

Paradoxically, business and economic historians have not paid much attention to the details of accounting which is often seen as a technical craft. While it is not customary to regard accounting data as information in the sense that data can be translated into estimates of parameters of interest, a formal error concept is a useful one because it makes the case against viewing accounting as neutral and mechanistic quite compelling. Even if accounting is neutral and accounting choices do not reflect self-interest, accounting errors can influence behavior.

The purpose of this paper is to reflect on the nature of error in accounting by using standard statistical concepts as a frame of reference. A statistical framework is a useful starting point for thinking about the meaning of 'accounting error' and how errors might affect behavior.

The Crédit Mobilier was an important but short-lived nineteenth-century French investment bank with an innovative financial structure. The company's accounting policy was to carry forward the balance of a period's profits as a surplus item which was then added to the profits of the next period. The bank also was highly leveraged and paid dividends out of profits which included the unrealized appreciation of its portfolio.[1] After a period of rising stock prices, market values fell and failure was inevitable. While it has been argued that the antagonism of banking groups and the government's refusal to permit the flotation of a bond issue caused the Crédit Mobilier's demise, Newmarch (1858: 444) offers a more persuasive contemporary view: 'there were so many fundamental and grave errors connected with the whole of the system upon which the Society was

Accounting, Business and Financial History, Volume 1, Number 1, 1990

founded, that no long time could elapse before serious mischief might be apprehended'.[2] Newmarch's prediction was accurate.

Accounting policies also help to explain bank failures in another era. In the 1980s, the practice of valuing loan portfolios at historical cost, not market value, was a major cause of the massive bankruptcies in American banking institutions (White, 1989). In this case, the method of accounting delayed the recognition of a deteriorating financial condition, permitting unsound financial practices to continue.

In both of these situations, it can be argued that 'accounting error' had an important impact on historical events. If different accounting practices had been used, history might need to be rewritten.

The purpose of this paper is to reflect on the nature of error in accounting by using standard statistical concepts as a frame of reference. A statistical viewpoint requires a logical model, even if it exists only implicitly. While operational models in accounting are not always available, a statistical framework is, nevertheless, a useful starting point for business historians, and accountants as well, to think about the meaning of an 'accounting error' and how such errors might affect behavior.[3]

It will become evident that business historians who are not trained in accounting, and perhaps even those who are, should be aware of the dangers of drawing conclusions from accounting figures. The next section of this paper examines the dual role of accounting information both as a factor that affects behavior and as factor that is a consequence of behavior. In the second section, the concept of accounting error is discussed.

Accounting information: cause or effect?

Weber described accounting as 'quantitative reckoning' that became dominant 'over the whole extent of economic life' (1961: 170). The importance of accounting is also underscored by Schumpeter (1962: 123–4) who states that 'capitalist practice turns the unit of money into a tool of rational cost-profit calculations, of which the towering monument is double-entry bookkeeping'. Schumpeter sees double-entry as 'a product of the evolution of economic rationality', but he also observed that the 'cost-profit calculus . . . reacts upon that rationality . . . subjugating – rationalizing – man's tools and philosophies, his medical practice, his picture of the cosmos, his outlook on life, everything in fact including his concepts of beauty and justice and his spiritual ambitions'.

The connection made between accounting and mathematics is not a coincidence. Paciolo's treatise on bookkeeping also contained sections on arithmetic, algebra and geometry and, for more than three centuries, chapters on bookkeeping appeared in texts on arithmetic. Indeed, Cayley, a Cambridge mathematician, compared double-entry bookkeeping to Euclid's theory of ratios:

> The Principles of Book-keeping by Double Entry constitute a theory which is mathematically by no means uninteresting: it is in fact like Euclid's theory of ratios an absolutely perfect one, and it is only its extreme simplicity which prevents it from being as interesting as it would otherwise be. (Cayley, 1894: 5)

Even today, it is common to relate accounting to mathematics and, consequently, to assume that financial statements and other accounting information are factual. Business historians, economists and others often view the 'language of business' as a neutral technical craft which produces objective data on income and wealth.[4]

At the same time, 'no rigorous and undisputed standards of accuracy and reliability have been established' for accounting data (Morgenstern, 1963: 70). Nevertheless, the data have an impact on behavior because 'figures cause people to act one way or the other. Sometimes their acts are based on careful, lengthy computations, carried on with great attention to detail and precision. Yet the underlying information is such that the meaning of these calculations is in grave doubt' (Morgenstern, 1963: 79).

But the independent role of accounting in decision making is an open question because the accounting numbers may be the effect of decisions, not the cause.

> Costs thus arrived at do not necessarily determine how much profit or loss will be shown or how many dividends will be paid! These decisions often *antedate* the making of the corresponding balances. . . . Considerations such as the behavior of other firms, tradition, expectations of the future, prestige, etc., all play an important role. . . . The idea that 'profits' are an automatic consequence of costs of production and sales on the one hand and receipts from sales on the other is naive and has nothing to do with business reality. (Morgenstern, 1963: 79–80)

The 'dependent' nature of the accounting variable is explicitly emphasized when accounting is studied in an 'agency cost' framework. Instead of focusing on the notion that accounting choices are based on the independent effort by accountants to improve communication of financial performance, agency theorists are concerned with explaining 'why management and others reveal strong preferences for one accounting method over another' (Whittred and Zimmer, 1988: xiv). Looked at in this light, the accounting choice problem is like any other investment decision.

> the set of practices actually selected by a firm should be consistent with its goals; and given a choice, the one chosen would be that expected to yield maximum economic benefits. The nature of competition, the financial condition of the firm and its future capital requirements, the relationship between the decision-maker and other interested parties such as creditors, labor, investors, and a variety of other conditions

> would influence the selection of those practices that are to serve as the foundation for published financial data. (Brief, 1966: 1)

In a similar vein, Zeff (1980: 658) argued that the 'evidence has been abundant and well-publicized that considerations other than "the accounting model" have figured importantly in the setting of accounting standards – and are frequently invoked as powerful reasons why extant standards should be changed'. Watts and Zimmerman (1979: 300–1) take the argument a step further, dismissing the 'accounting model' of matching costs with revenues and claiming that 'the only accounting theory that will provide a set of predictions that are consistent with observed phenomena is one based on self-interest'. Accounting theories and accounting standards are the 'excuses' of vested interest groups.

Both Zeff and Watts and Zimmerman are, in effect, asserting that accounting theory and practice is a dependent variable in the sense that the choice among alternative accounting methods is an economic decision. For Zeff, the choice is to some extent constrained by the conventional accounting model. However, for Watts and Zimmerman, there is no such constraint because political and economic self-interest dictate the choice of accounting methods. This general framework now seems to be widely accepted. As Deakin (1989: 137) observes, 'Recent work suggests that accounting policy choices may be viewed as economic decisions made by managers coincident with investment and production decisions'.

May (1936: 13) recognized much earlier that, in a dynamic world, accounting data could be both cause and effect: 'Now, once it is recognized that accounting is largely a matter of convention, it is easy to perceive that the nature of the conventions adopted may greatly influence the development of an economy'. But May also commented that 'it is easy to see how considerations of policy may influence accounting' or, the opposite, 'how the form of accounting may influence the course of events' (1936: 14). Using the treatment of depreciation in the accounts of nineteenth-century railway companies as an example, May then elaborated on the question of whether accounting is an effect rather than a cause:

> I should perhaps anticipate here an objection that the methods of accounting adopted may have been an effect rather than a cause: the objection that this may be a case in which methods of accounting have been influenced by other than accounting considerations, rather than one in which accounting judgment has influenced the economic development. True, the methods followed here and in Great Britain might represent the giving of effect to an opinion deliberately reached as to what was economically desirable, or they might be the reflection of the views (born, perhaps, of the wishes) of those who were interested in the creation of such enterprises. There is, however, nothing to suggest that the depreciation method was regarded by those responsible for the enabling legislation, either here or in England, as sounder but was

> deliberately ignored because it was believed that the development and welfare of the country would be aided by ignoring it. . . . I believe that in dealing, or omitting to deal, with depreciation the railroads merely followed the general accounting practice of the times. (May, 1936: 175–6)

May was convinced, however, that accounting practices influenced nineteenth-century development and said that 'it is incontestable that the effect of the application of such depreciation accounting would have been that the construction of a large part of our railway mileage would at least have been greatly delayed – if, indeed, some part would ever have been constructed at all' (1936: 174–5). He then commented that if there had been 'proper' accounting, the results would have been 'exactly the opposite of that sought at the time by legislatures and the public'. Brief has similarly concluded that the result of this overstatement of profits and dividends was that 'economic growth was accelerated by the accounting conventions adopted' (1964: 189).

Attention continues to focus on 'possible motives for and effects of accounting choices as well as the effects of choices among alternative accounting methods' (Biddle, 1980: 235). A good illustration of the nature of the ongoing debate is found in the discussion by Ball (1980) of Dukes, Dyckman and Elliott's (1980) study of the economic effect of expensing instead of capitalizing research and development expenditures. Ball criticized the study for assuming that 'accounting policy changes are exogenous, as if they were acts of Nature or as if they were induced by the experimenter in a controlled laboratory environment' (1980: 37).

Whether or not accounting is viewed in terms of self-interest or as a neutral technology, an accounting error can have an independent effect. In either case, a statistical point of view helps to clarify the meaning of error in accounting.

Nature of accounting error

There are two distinct concepts of accounting error that are not mutually exclusive. First, accounting error can be defined in statistical terms as the difference between the estimate of a parameter based on accounting data and the true value of the parameter. One difficulty in making a statistical concept of accounting error operational is that financial accountants do not think of accounting data as sample information that can be translated into estimates of parameters of interest. Hicks's comment about 'estimates' of depreciation expense illustrates the nature of the problem.

> These are estimates in a different sense. . . . They are not statistician's estimates of a true figure, which happens to be unavailable; there is no sure figure to which they correspond. They are estimates that are

relative to a purpose; for different purposes they may be made in different ways. (Hicks, 1973: 155)

Second, there is the concept of accounting error arising from the use of an accounting procedure which is inconsistent with 'generally accepted accounting principles'. This kind of error is sometimes called an 'error of principle'. Thus, Brief defined accounting error as '*the failure to systematically distinguish between capital and revenue expenditures* and *the failure to periodically allocate the original cost of fixed assets to expense*' (1965: 14). In effect, Brief postulates that 'modern' accounting methods produce 'correct' numbers: 'In order to attach economic significance to the idea of an accounting error one would have to show that some decision makers acted as if the erroneous information has been correct' (1965: 31).

In the pages that follow, these concepts of accounting error are discussed in two settings. The first concerns Johnson and Kaplan's thesis (1987) about the failure of product-costing systems to reflect 'true' product costs. The second deals with arguments by May (1936) and Brief (1964, 1965) that the methods of accounting for fixed assets in the nineteenth century produced an error that stimulated investment. In the case of product-costing decisions, the basic decision/information models can be assumed known so that parameters of interest may be identified. In contrast, financial accounting models are not known so that the concept of accounting error is more tenuous. However, in both cases, focusing on the notion of 'parameters of interest' is useful because this framework contributes to an understanding of the concept of accounting error.

Failure of product-costing systems

Johnson and Kaplan argue that

> By 1925 virtually all management accounting practices used today had been developed. . . . These practices had evolved to serve the informational and control needs of the managers of increasingly complex and diverse organizations. At that point the pace of innovation seemed to stop. (Johnson and Kaplan, 1987: 12)

Johnson and Kaplan give two reasons for this failure of costing systems. First, the need to value inventory in external reports led to the use of simplistic methods to cost products. Second, academic accountants were 'led astray' (1987: 15) by the economist's simplified model of the single product firm. Questions about the accuracy of costing systems have been raised in the past and the technical problems in calculating product costs have been recognized for many years.

- Clark criticized 'inaccurate rules-of-thumb' that are used in practice.

> One source of confusion lies in the fact that the economist, being a scientist with accurate observation as his dominant purpose and

> omniscience as his will-o'-the-wisp, tends to give terms the meaning they would have to an omniscient observer, forgetting that if such beings exist they have no need of his analysis. And the businessman, wanting to know how much his costs will increase as the result of a given amount of business, but compelled to use inaccurate rules-of-thumb and rough-and-ready indexes, tends to describe these indexes in terms of what he wants them to tell him either forgetting their limitations or forgetting that others will not be so familiar with their limitations as he is himself. (Clark, 1923: 44)

- Dean criticized the influences of 'orthodox accountancy' on product costing.

> These incremental and opportunity costs that are needed for decision-making have no necessary relation to the product costs obtained by conventional cost accounting. (Dean, 1951: 314)

> When an executive asks the cost of a product, the answer he gets is a historical, fully-allocated, average unit cost. There are comparatively few executive decisions for which this kind of cost is relevant, although it occasionally approximates the relevant concept. There are problems of public relations for which full unit costs obtained by orthodox accountancy are precisely relevant because of their authoritarian ring. Hence, allocations of full costs should not be abandoned altogether, but they need less emphasis than they get in cost analysis and in management decisions. Serious economic errors may result if these full unit costs are used for decisions for which they are inappropriate. (Dean, 1951: 315)

- Solomons recognized the need to determine cost drivers and to model 'complexity'.

> In essence, it calls for the choice of some product characteristic which can be said to control the incidence of some one expense or more. For each expense, a different product characteristic might be chosen, though some, like weight or volume, might control the incidence of a number of expenses. In the case of some expenses, some combination of characteristics might have to be used, e.g., size-and-complexity. (Solomons, 1954: 224)

- Johnston lamented that the assumption of a single-product firm is as realistic as defining an octopus with one tentacle.

> The real world preponderance of multiple-product as against single-product firms is probably the inverse of the space their respective analyses occupy in economic theory. The theorist, in this context, is like a zoologist, whose task is to study the octopus. He reacts to the complexity of the beast by defining an octopus with only a single tentacle

and proceeding to study that hypothetical creature very thoroughly, but unfortunately the real octopus with many tentacles may behave very differently from an imaginary octopus with only one. (Johnston, 1960: 185)

The forces at work here which led to uneconomic decisions may have been unintended and due either to the ignorance of those responsible for product costing or to the inherent difficulty of estimating product costs.[5] On the other hand, the errors produced by orthodox accountancy may have been intended and the methods chosen may simply have reflected the interests of those responsible for the choices.

Putting aside questions of cause and effect, the current view is that accounting systems have failed to keep pace with changing product and process technology and a major consequence has been inaccurate product costs. To tackle this problem, Cooper and Kaplan (1987: 225) recommend that 'the allocation of costs from the cost pools to the products should be achieved using bases that reflect cost drivers'. What this means is that costing methods need to be explained in terms of the statistical relationships between product cost and cost drivers, i.e. by statistical cost models. By emphasizing methods instead of models, the purpose and limitations of most costing methods have often been obscured in the literature on the subject.[6]

For multi-product firms, the problem of dividing costs among products is very complex. A cost assignment can be arbitrary when producing a product does not increase costs, i.e. the method reflects a cause-effect relationship when none actually exists. For example, an overhead cost may be assigned to a product in proportion to direct labor hours spent producing the product. This method will reflect a cause-effect relationship when the model of cost behavior is $y = bx$, where y is overhead cost, x is the 'cost driver', e.g. direct labor hours, and b is the change in cost for each unit change in direct labor. However, if the model is not correct, estimates of product costs will contain errors. This is the point made by Noreen in connection with the idea advanced by Johnson and Kaplan of 'fully tracing' all product costs:

> it is far from obvious that the 'fully traced' costs which J & K advocate provide that information. Since in their system all overhead costs are fully allocated using average rates, it must be assumed that all overhead costs are directly proportional to cost-drivers (i.e., there are no fixed or joint costs relative to the cost-drivers) and that the cost-drivers associated with a particular product line are directly proportional to capacity in that product line. (Noreen, 1987: 115)

In other words, Noreen is suggesting that the 'true' model may be $y = a + bx$, where a is fixed overhead cost; therefore, fixed overhead costs are not causally related to the cost driver and, if they are included in product costs, cost estimates will be biased. While statistical models may be difficult to estimate due to lack of data, an unstable environment, etc., they are essential to understanding an error concept in product costing.

Error in accounting for fixed assets

Zeff (1980: 661) commented that teachers might choose not to encourage the belief that the choice of standards is shaped by political and economic consequences. Instead, they might prefer the point of view that the traditional accounting model 'brings more closure to debates over accounting alternatives – one can dismiss certain practices as not appropriately matching costs with revenues'. Zeff recognized that these economic consequences might 'frustrate students who prefer the security of a definitive answer'. By the same token, teachers have not done a very good job explaining the limitations of the traditional financial accounting model.

Dicksee was an exception. He used the single venture model, and the example of a ship voyage, to explicate the nature and limitations of financial statements. First, Dicksee explained that 'If a venture has been undertaken and carried to a conclusion before the accounts in relation thereto are balanced, and the ultimate result then reduced to a cash basis, the . . . statement will be a statement of *fact*' (1903: 470). However, he proceeded to observe that for most firms it would be inconvenient to wait until liquidation, and that interim reports are required which must necessarily be based on estimates.

> The division into years (or half years) is an entirely arbitrary one . . . it is absolutely impossible to draw a line at any particular date without its intersecting or 'cutting into' a large number of transactions which at the moment remain uncompleted. The precise effect and money value of these uncompleted transactions can only be estimated, and consequently a large number of the transactions . . . must also be, in greater or lesser degree, dependent upon estimates. (Dicksee, 1903: 472)

In spite of this early recognition of the need for estimates in accounting, a statistical viewpoint has not been developed. In statistics, the accuracy of an estimate is a function of the difference between the estimate of a parameter and its 'true' value, i.e. accuracy equals sampling error plus bias. Statistical error concepts are difficult to apply in financial accounts because parameters of interest have not been identified. Nevertheless, it is often the case that accounting data are analyzed as if the data do provide estimates of parameters of interest.

For example, May (1936) implicitly adopts a framework in which accounting data are used by investors to estimate the economic rate of return. He then concludes that the error in using the reported rate of return to estimate the economic rate of return stimulated investment. May developed this argument by using the following line of reasoning. First, he said that if depreciation had been included in the operating cost of railroads, 'only a small proportion of the enterprises proposed could have been claimed to present the prospect of being able to earn their fixed charges' and 'the published results of the ventures of those who had been bold enough to proceed would have discouraged others from attempting similar enterprises' (1936: 174). May then explained that, even without depreciation, railroads as a whole were not earning more than 5 per cent on the actual capital invested; therefore, 'the effect of the application of such depreciation accounting would have been that the construction of a large part of our railway mileage would at least have been greatly delayed' (1936: 174). The implication here is that accounting data were used by investors to estimate the economic rate of return.

The notion of an accounting error is also discussed without reference to parameter estimates. If there are alternative methods to account for a transaction, the one that produces 'more' income is often viewed as producing an error having economic consequences.

> It should be clear, at the outset, that to speak of an accounting bias implies that some standard set of accounting procedures does exist. That is, one could not say that a particular set of accounting practices produces an overstatement of profits unless a set of accounting procedures that 'correctly' states profits does, in fact, exist . . . the standard by which we will measure nineteenth century accounting practices is present-day accounting theory and procedures. This does not mean that twentieth century accounting is regarded as ideal. It is used as a standard of comparison because such a 'base' is conceptually necessary. (Brief, 1964: 9)

This argument focuses on a 'base' method as a standard of comparison, not a method that produces estimates of 'true' values. The framework is not statistical; the 'base' method is assumed to produce 'correct' numbers and, in comparison, other methods produce biased numbers. The standard of comparison is typically the 'conservative' method, i.e. the method that produces lower reported profits for some specified time period. Usually, but not always, the conservative method also is 'generally accepted'. Although this error concept is *ad hoc*, it is more widespread than the statistical concept of accounting error, as recent discussions about methods to account for corporate takeovers demonstrate.

Present-day British accounting rules permit companies to write off directly to retained earnings the excess of the purchase price of a company over its book value, i.e. goodwill, whereas US rules require the goodwill to be amortized and charged to future profits. Therefore, the British rules produce an accounting error in the sense that consolidated profits of a British company acquiring an American company would be, other things equal, higher than the consolidated profits of an American company making the same acquisition. The accounting error in this case has been used to explain why British companies take over American companies.[7] 'Behind the wave of British acquisitions of American companies, particularly in advertising and other service industries are tax and accounting rules that give British bidders a significant competitive edge.' When the Accounting Standards Committee proposed to force British companies to adopt US standards, it was argued that this new policy would be a 'body blow' to the US takeover market.[8]

The effect of an accounting error of this type is difficult to explain. Since 'true' profitability is not affected by accounting methods,[9] one would expect financial analysts to adjust for the differences reported by these methods. Yet, it is apparent that, in this case and in many others, accounting figures seem to affect human behavior.

Conclusion

The questions and issues that arise in thinking about the role played by accounting in business history are complex. While accounting policies and practices have economic consequences, they also are a product of decisions made by individuals and organizations in their own self-interest. Cause and effect relationships in accounting are, therefore, difficult to identify.

Business and economic historians have not paid much attention to the details of accounting.[10] Thus, while notable scholars like Schumpeter and Weber saw the fundamental role of accounting in economic affairs, others like Hatfield recognized that 'The contempt for accounting is not limited to university circles, but is well-nigh universal. It is evidenced by ignorance of the subject, by condescension towards its devotees, by their exclusion from polite literature' (1924: 241).

This disdain for accounting can be attributed, at least in part, to the common view that accounting is simply a set of mechanical techniques. Day's comments many years ago reflect this belief:

> If the design of studying the mathematics were merely to obtain such a knowledge of the *practical* parts, as is required for transacting business; it might be sufficient to commit to memory some of the principal rules, and to make the operations familiar, by attending to the examples. In this mechanical way, the accountant, the navigator, and the land surveyor, may be qualified for their respective employments, with very little knowledge of the *principles* that lie at the foundation of the calculations which they are to make. (Day, 1843: iii)

Paradoxically, even Day understood that, while the rules of accounting might be simple, the underlying problems were not: 'It may be thought, by some, to be unwise to form our general habits of arguing, on the model of a science in which the inquiries are accompanied by *absolute certainty*; while the common business of life must be conducted upon *probable* evidence, and not upon principles which admit of complete demonstration' (Day, 1843: iv).

Thus, accounting is often seen as a technical craft and it is common to assume that the technology produces objective, verifiable information that is free from bias. Similarly, accountants are regarded as disinterested, independent scorekeepers. Yet, economists like Morgenstern have also claimed that 'business is transacted in the illusion of dealing with "accuracy" where there is none in an ordinary or scientific sense' (1963: 86).

The statistical notion of 'accuracy' is an error concept and making it operational requires a model specifying the object of measurement. Since it is not customary to regard accounting data as information in the statistical sense that data can be translated into estimates of parameters of interest, a formal concept of error has not been developed. Even so, the framework is a useful one because it makes the case against viewing accounting as neutral and mechanistic quite compelling. Even if accounting is neutral and accounting choices do not reflect self-interest, accounting errors can influence behavior.

Hopwood recently remarked that

> Accounting is not . . . a mere reflection of unproblematic essences or imperatives. A detailed understanding of the specific contexts in which accounting change occurs demonstrates the diversity of influences that can impinge on accounting and its consequences, the often quite complex and shifting circumstances, issues, and practices with which accounting can be associated, and, of equal significance, the roles played by the unintentional and the unanticipated consequences of accounting change. (Hopwood, 1988: xxxi)

The concept of accounting error adds another dimension to the complex role that accounting plays.

Leonard N. Stern School of Business
New York University

Notes

This article is a revised version of a paper given at the conference, 'Accounting and Decision Making in Companies 1844–1938', held at the Cardiff Business School on 20–21 September 1989. The author is indebted to Eamonn J. Walsh for extremely helpful comments. The author also thanks the referees for their suggestions.

1 The financial practices of the Crédit Mobilier are detailed in Aycard (1867).
2 I am deeply indebted to Goran Ohlin for motivating my interest in the financial practices of the Crédit Mobilier in a course in European economic history at

Columbia University during the fall of 1960. This research led to further study of 'accounting error' (Brief, 1964, 1965).

3 One of the first papers to use a statistical framework to structure error concepts in accounting was written by Ijiri and Jaedicke (1966). Later work by Brief and Owen (1973) applied the basic idea of statistical estimation in the area of financial accounting. Their work inverts the traditional perspective but is, none the less, consistent with it. Instead of emphasizing the performance *of a period*, financial reports for three months, a year and longer periods are viewed as interim reports of the firm's continuing activities. A by-product of estimation theory is a statistical concept of accounting error, i.e. accounting error is the difference between the estimate of a parameter of interest derived from accounting numbers and the true value of the parameter. For more recent research in this area, see Demski and Sappington (1990).

4 The author thanks Eamonn J. Walsh for helping to make this point explicit.

5 For example, Habbakuk (1962: 59) argued that the difficulty of estimating capital costs relative to labor costs led nineteenth-century manufacturers to underestimate capital costs and, therefore, to overinvest in plant and equipment.

6 Business historians need to recognize that the terminology in product costing is very confusing. A cost is a sacrifice and is measured by comparing the economic effect of taking one course of action compared to another. While there is one basic cost dichotomy – fixed vs. variable – costing terms proliferate. Phrases like direct cost, separable cost, differential cost and avoidable cost are used to describe the variable costs in particular situations. Fixed costs are sunk costs, common costs, constant costs and joint costs. In a sense, all cost terms are redundant because 'from the short-run point of view, expenditures that do not fall under the heading of variable costs are best considered, not as "fixed", but as not being costs at all' (Kirzner, 1963: 192).

7 Jan M. Rosen, 'Accounting rules that aid mergers', *New York Times*, 10 July 1989.

8 *Wall Street Journal* article, 'Merger scene strafed by UK accountants', 6 February 1990.

9 Unless the accounting methods affect cash flows.

10 A notable exception is J. R. Hicks whom Klamer (1989) called 'an accountant among economists'. See also Brief (1982).

References

Aycard (1867) *Histoire du Crédit Mobilier*, Bruxelles: Libraire Internationale.

Ball, Ray (1980) 'Discussion of accounting for research and development costs: the impact on research and development expenditures', *Studies on Economic Consequences of Financial and Managerial Accounting: Effects on Corporate Incentives and Decisions*. Supplement to *Journal of Accounting Research*, 27–37.

Biddle, Gary C. (1980) 'Accounting methods and management decisions: the case of inventory costing and inventory policy', *Studies on Economic Consequences of Financial and Managerial Accounting: Effects on Corporate Incentives and Decisions*. Supplement to *Journal of Accounting Research*, 235–80.

Brief, Richard P. (1964) *Nineteenth Century Capital Accounting and Business Investment*. Ph.D. thesis, Columbia University. Revised and published (1976) New York: Arno Press.

Brief, Richard P. (1965) 'Nineteenth century accounting error', *Journal of Accounting Research*, Spring: 12–31.

Brief, Richard P. (1966) 'The origin and evolution of nineteenth-century asset accounting', *Business History Review*, Spring: 1–23.
Brief, Richard P. (1982) 'Hicks on accounting', *The Accounting Historians Journal*, Spring: 91–101.
Brief, Richard P. and **Joel Owen** (1973) 'A reformulation of the estimation problem', *Journal of Accounting Research*, Spring: 1–15.
Cayley, Arthur (1894) *The Principles of Book-Keeping by Double Entry*, Cambridge: Cambridge University Press.
Clark, J. M. (1923) *Studies in the Economics of Overhead Costs*, Chicago: University of Chicago Press.
Cooper, Robin and **Robert S. Kaplan** (1987) 'How cost accounting systematically distorts product costs', in William J. Bruns, Jr. and Robert S. Kaplan (eds) *Accounting and Management*, Boston, Mass.: Harvard Business School Press: 204–28.
Day, Jeremiah (1843) *Algebra*, 48th edition, New Haven: Durrie & Peck.
Deakin, Edward B. (1989) 'Rational economic behavior and lobbying on accounting issues: evidence from the oil and gas industry', *The Accounting Review*, January: 137–51.
Dean, Joel (1951) *Managerial Economics*, Englewood Cliffs, NJ: Prentice-Hall.
Demski, Joel S. and **David E. M. Sappington** (1990) 'Fully revealing income measurement', *The Accounting Review*, April: 363–83.
Dicksee, L. R. (1903) 'The nature and limitations of accounts', *The Accountant*, 4 April: 469–74.
Dukes, Roland E., Thomas R. Dyckman and **John A. Elliott** (1980) 'Accounting for research and development costs: the impact on research and development expenditures', *Studies on Economic Consequences of Financial and Managerial Accounting: Effects on Corporate Incentives and Decisions*. Supplement to *Journal of Accounting Research*, 1–26.
Habakkuk, H. J. (1962) *American and British Technology in the Nineteenth Century*, Cambridge: Cambridge University Press.
Hatfield, Henry Rand (1924) 'An historical defense of bookkeeping', *Journal of Accountancy*, April: 241–53. Reprinted in W. T. Baxter (ed.) (1950) *Studies in Accounting Theory*, London: Sweet & Maxwell.
Hicks, J. R. (1973) *Capital and Time*. Oxford: Clarendon Press.
Hopwood, Anthony G. (ed.) (1988) *Accounting from the Outside*, New York: Garland Publishing.
Ijiri, Yuji and **Robert K. Jaedicke** (1966) 'Reliability and objectivity in accounting measurements', *The Accounting Review*, July: 474–83.
Johnson, H. Thomas and **Robert S. Kaplan** (1987) *Relevance Lost: The Rise and Fall of Management Accounting*, Boston, Mass.: Harvard Business School Press.
Johnston, J. (1960) *Statistical Cost Analysis*, New York: McGraw-Hill.
Kirzner, Israel (1963) *Market Theory and the Price System*, Princeton, NJ: D. Van Nostrand.
Klamer, Arjo (1989) 'An accountant among economists: conversations with Sir J. R. Hicks', *The Journal of Economic Perspectives*, Fall: 167–80.
May, George O. (1936) 'The influence of accounting on the development of an economy', *Journal of Accountancy*, January, February and March.
Morgenstern, Oskar (1963) *On the Accuracy of Economic Observations*, 2nd edition, Princeton, NJ: Princeton University Press.
Newmarch, William (1858) 'On the recent history of the Crédit Mobilier', *Journal of the Statistical Society of London*, December.
Noreen, Eric (1987) 'Commentary on H. Thomas Johnson and Robert S. Kaplan, *Relevance Lost: The Rise and Fall of Management Accounting* (Boston: Harvard Business School Press, 1987), *Accounting Horizons*, December: 110–16.

Schumpeter, Joseph (1962) *Capitalism, Socialism and Democracy*, 3rd edition, New York: Harper & Row.

Solomons, David (1954) 'Cost, plans and prices', *Practice Note* #31, London: Society of Incorporated Accountants and Auditors. Reprinted in David Solomons (1984) *Collected Papers on Accounting and Accounting Education*, Volume 2, New York and London: Garland Publishing 217–26.

Watts, Ross L. and **Jerold L. Zimmerman** (1979) 'The demand for and supply of accounting theories: the market for excuses', *The Accounting Review*, April: 273–305.

Weber, Max (1961) *General Economic History*, New York: Collier Books.

White, Lawrence J. (1989) 'The reform of federal deposit insurance', *The Journal of Economic Perspectives*, Fall: 11–29.

Whittred, Greg and **Ian Zimmer** (1988) *Financial Accounting*, Sydney: Holt, Rinehart & Winston.

Zeff, Stephen A. (1980) ' "Intermediate" and "advanced" accounting: the role of "economic consequences" ', *The Accounting Review*, October: 658–63.